MAN
WITH
WINGS

ALSO BY EDWARD JABLONSKI

The Gershwin Years, with Lawrence D. Stewart

Harold Arlen: Happy with the Blues

George Gershwin

The Knighted Skies

The Great War

Flying Fortress

Warriors with Wings: The Story of the Lafayette Escadrille

Ladybirds: Women in Aviation

Atlantic Fever: The Great Transatlantic Aerial Adventure

Seawings

Double Strike

Airwar:
    1. *Terror from the Sky*
    2. *Tragic Victories*
    3. *Outraged Skies*
    4. *Wings of Fire*

Doolittle, a Biography, with Lowell Thomas

Pictorial History of World War II Years

Pictorial History of World War I Years

MAN
WITH
WINGS

A Pictorial History
of Aviation

EDWARD JABLONSKI

DOUBLEDAY & COMPANY, INC.

Garden City, New York

1980

For Ken and Bill Kuebler

Library of Congress Cataloging in Publication Data

Jablonski, Edward.
    Man with wings.

    Bibliography: p.
    Includes index.
    1. Aeronautics—History. 2. Astronautics—History.
I. Title.
TL515.J18   629.1'09

ISBN: 0-385-14107-6
Library of Congress Catalog Card Number 77-25596
   9 8 7 6 5 4 3

The one who has most carefully watched the soaring birds of prey sees man with wings and the faculty of using them.

James Means
The Aeronautical Annual, 1895

Contents

MAN
WITH
WINGS

1 FLIGHT AND FANTASY

Man, unlike bird, was not born to fly. This is a fact of which he has been reminded rather forcibly over the centuries. But certain men—dreamers, adventurers and some crackpots—were unable to accept that fact and aspired to "slip the surly bonds of Earth."

The dream of imitating the birds goes back a long time, perhaps to the dawn of history. Still, cave man did not leave us any of his observations on flight. He did scratch drawings on the walls of dwellings revealing a realistic preoccupation with food-gathering. These fine old drawings depict such creatures as the early deer, antelope, and buffalo, but no birds. It may have been because they were beyond the reach of the cave man. Earthbound as he was, early man must have peered into the skies and envied, say, the *Teratornis* and pondered, however dimly, why the winged creature could fly and he could not.

The myths of antiquity are rich in tales of flying beings and animals. From man's earliest records we learn, too, that the ability to fly was associated with either magic or religion. An early legend goes back more than two thousand years before Christ in the tales of the Chinese Emperor *Shun*, who flew by putting on "the work-clothes of a bird." He is also supposed to have saved himself from a fire by leaping from a tower using two large round hats as parachutes. Another legend has the Persian King Kai Kawus, around 1500 B.C., being borne aloft in his throne by four great eagles. From Arabia comes the story of the flying carpet. Any number of gods were winged: Ashur of Assyria, Khensu and Isis of

Egypt. The earliest biblical reference to flight occurs in the second Book of Kings, describing Elijah's ascent into heaven in "a chariot of fire."

The Greeks created the story of Pegasus, the flying horse, as well as the classic tale of Daedalus and Icarus. Daedalus, a great Athenian craftsman, had gone with his son to the island of Crete where the King, Minos, ordered him to construct a great labyrinth around the castle. Daedalus did such a fine job that when he and Icarus were imprisoned by King Minos, not even he could lead them out. But the ingenious Daedalus, observing the gulls, said to his son. "Escape may be checked by water and by land, but the air and the sky are free." Like the Emperor Shun, Daedalus fashioned wings of the "work-clothes of a bird," which he fastened to their arms with wax. Then he and Icarus flew away from Crete, over the labyrinth, and out to sea. Young Icarus, however, was carried away with the thrill of flight and could not resist the urge to stretch his wings. He soared higher and higher, despite the warnings of his father, until he came too close to the sun. The wax melted, and Icarus plunged to his death in the sea just to the west of the little island of Samos (now called the Icarian Sea). Saddened, Daedalus continued flying and escaped to Sicily.

As venerable as the legends of flying is the first successful flying device—if we except the arrow and boomerang—the kite. The first kites originated in China probably a thousand years before the birth of Christ. As they are today, the first kites may have been regarded as toys. Eventually, as

Daedalus and Icarus. (National Air and Space Museum, Smithsonian Institution)

they evolved into more sophisticated forms, kites were put to more practical use. Kites were used for signaling, for example, and very large kites were employed by the Chinese and Japanese to carry a man into the air for reconnaissance in battle. One Chinese general supposedly put an enemy army to rout by sending up flute- and whistle-bearing kites at night. Hearing the eerie sounds overhead, and assuming that their guardian angels had come to warn them of impending doom, the soldiers took to the hills.

Although Chinese kites were elaborate and often put to ingenious use, the Chinese did not conceive of the box kite, a more efficient "aircraft" than the single lifting surface kites of tradition. Nor, for that matter, did any European come up with the idea, although kites were known in Europe from about the fifteenth century. An Australian, Lawrence Hargrave, devised a box kite in 1893; about ninety years before that an Englishman, Sir George Cayley, recognized in the kite the germ of a real flying machine.

Rockets, too, were a Chinese invention. One now-forgotten pioneer, Wan-Hu, who flourished around 1500, devised a remarkable hybrid: He crossed two kites with forty-seven rockets, thereby producing a powered flying machine, at least on paper. Seated in this contraption, Wan-Hu instructed forty-seven servants to light each of the rockets at the very same instant. Accordingly, this

Fanciful Chinese kites. (Smithsonian Institution)

was done, and the imaginative Wan-Hu, a bit before his time, joined his ancestors in a spectacular display of sparks, smoke, and din.

Inspired by the myth of Daedalus and Icarus or by merely observing birds, a curious breed of aspiring birdmen have gone down—literally, alas—in the history of flight as "tower jumpers." One of the earliest such dreamers was the legendary King Bladud of Britain, who assumed the throne in 863 B.C. Bladud took exceptional pride in his magical powers; he used these powers to create the health-

Twelfth-century tower jumper. (U. S. Air Force)

A PIONEER OF THE 12TH CENTURY

giving warm springs in the city of Bath. He also believed that he was endowed with the ability to fly. Taking the precaution of applying feathers to himself, Bladud launched himself from the Temple of Apollo in Trinaventum (now London) in 852 B.C. Bladud succeeded only in breaking his neck and leaving his crown to his son, Lear. The latter chose not to follow his father in the art of flight and made a deeper impression on history as the hero in a play by Shakespeare.

Tower jumping seems not to have caught on immediately, for nearly a dozen centuries passed before the art is mentioned again. A Saracen of Constantinople in the eleventh century devised a kind of wearable glider of his cloak, and jumped from a tower. His improvised wings did not work too well, and "he broke his bones and his evil plight was such that he did not long survive."

Although he survived, English monk Oliver of Malmesbury was hardly more successful than his contemporary, the Saracen. Oliver, according to an account written in 1670, "made and fitted Wings to his Hands and Feet; with these on top of a Tower, spread out to gather air, he flew more than a Furlong; but the wind being too high, came fluttering down, to the maiming of all his Limbs; yet so conceited of his Art, that he attributed the cause of his fall to the want of a Tail, as Birds have, which he forgot to make to his hinder parts."

One tower jumper—an Italian, John Damian—blamed his failure on the fact that he had used chicken feathers instead of those of a more airworthy bird. They were a hard-dying breed. One, a Turk, Hezarfen Celebi, is supposed to have succeeded in the early seventeenth century. One of the last failures, that of Albrecht Berblinger, an air-minded tailor of Ulm, Württemberg, was reported as late as 1811. Flapping his homemade wings, Berblinger leaped from a scaffold specially constructed for his flight, and seconds later splashed into the Danube River. As a group, the tower jumpers had imagination, (though they were deluded by the envy of birds) and courage but little practical knowledge.

"A bird is an instrument working according to mathematical law, which instrument is within the capacity of man to reproduce in all its movements." These words were written in 1505 by one of the great geniuses of history, Leonardo da Vinci, artist and inventor. Like the tower jumpers, Leonardo was misled by the birds. Believing that man had the power to imitate the flapping of wings, Leonardo made drawings of various devices called ornithopters which he based upon the wing structure of birds and bats.

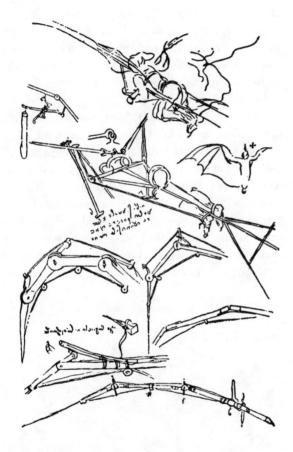

Da Vinci ornithopter sketches, ca. 1487. (Smithsonian Institution)

Da Vinci's inventive genius was not confined to dreams of flight and art; for a time he even served as a military engineer and devised the ancestors of the machine gun, tank, and submarine. His notebooks, which he kept "secret" by writing backward, are filled with remarkable observations on

hydraulics, mechanics, anatomy, geology, and botany.

Despite his knowledge and intuition, Leonardo did not realize that there was a great difference in the strength-weight ratio between man and birds. Otherwise it is unlikely that he would have given so much thought to the flapping wing ornithopters, which were incapable of flight. At the same time, however, Leonardo's drawings and notes reveal highly advanced ideas on finned projectiles, the parachute, and the helicopter. The irony of Leonardo da Vinci's thoughts on flight is that they contributed nothing to the advancement of aviation. His notebooks, left to a friend, were not made public until about three hundred years after his death. By that time man had given up trying to "imitate the birds" and had already devised working helicopters and actually made parachute jumps from balloons—a device Leonardo never seems to have considered. However, had his work on flight been made public sooner, the impact of Leonardo upon the history of aviation would have been great indeed, and it is likely that man would have flown earlier than he did.

The idea that the secret of flight for man lay locked in the wings of birds persisted for a long time. Among the earliest science-fiction tales, published in 1638, was *The Man in the Moone, or a Discourse of a Voyage thither by Domingo Gonsales the Speedy Messenger*. The author was the bishop of Hereford, Francis Godwin, who sent his hero, Domingo Gonsales, to the moon in a curious flying machine powered by geese. It was an ingenious conception, for the geese were tethered to the "aircraft" by means of a pulley and counterweight device, enabling them, supposedly, to fly with a certain degree of freedom. Domingo, apparently, steered the craft with a small sail. According to the story, Domingo reached the "moone" in an advanced design using twenty-five or so geese and with a small crew assisting him on the flight.

Godwin's story captivated the imagination of other writers and inspired further tales of such flights of fancy. He directly influenced another bishop, John Wilkins, who also speculated upon the probability of flight. Wilkins believed that man

Illustration from Godwin's *The Man in the Moone*, 1638.
(National Air and Space Museum, Smithsonian
Institution)

would thus be lighter than air and would naturally
rise. De Lana-Terzi obviously had an understanding of the vacuum, although he did not realize that
atmospheric pressure would have crushed the copper spheres. Despite this flaw, De Lana-Terzi was
the first man to visualize a feasible lighter-than-air
device. It was man's first glimpse of a balloonlike
object, a hundred years before the invention of the
balloon. De Lana-Terzi even thought of carrying
ballast in his aerial ship to assist in its ascent; he
also devised a means of refilling the copper spheres
(which, incidentally, were to have been twenty feet
in diameter) causing the ship to descend. These
two means of control, like the idea of the ship itself,
would be employed a hundred years later.

Francesco de Lana-Terzi, however, had no intentions of testing his idea. "For God would surely
never allow such a machine to be successful, since
it would cause much disturbance among the civil
and political governments of mankind." De Lana-
Terzi's vision also took in the probability of aerial
warfare. "Who can fail to see that no city would be
proof against surprise," he warned, "as the ship
could at any time be brought above its squares, or
even the courtyards of its dwellings, and come to
earth so that its crew could land. In the case of

would eventually travel "beyond the sphere of the
earth's magnetical vigour" by means of artificial
wings or by harnessing birds, as Godwin had visualized, or, finally, by "a flying chariot." He did not
suggest how this chariot might be lifted off the
ground or what kind of engine might be used to
power it. Later, Wilkins came up with the idea of
some kind of device that might float in the air, such
as a ship floats in water, but again he did not
supply any useful details.

Wilkins' vague conception was given actual form
in 1670 by a Jesuit priest, Francesco de Lana-
Terzi. De Lana-Terzi's design, which he called an
"aerial ship," took the form of a ship but truly
remarkable was his idea of four spheres of very thin
copper to lift it. It was De Lanna-Terzi's idea that
if these spheres were pumped free of air, they

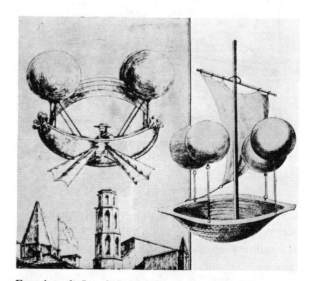

Francisco de Lana's "aerial ship." (National Air and
Space Museum, Smithsonian Institution)

ships that sail the sea, the aerial ship could be made to descend from the upper air to the level of their sails so that the rigging could be cut. Or even without descending so low, iron weights could be hurled down to wreck the ships and kill their crews; or the ships could be set on fire by fireballs and bombs. Not only ships, but houses, fortresses and cities could thus be destroyed. . . ." If Francesco de Lana-Terzi's "aerial ship" was more than a hundred years ahead of its time, his prophecy of a war in the air reached into the twentieth century.

That it was possible to fly with a flapping-wing device was claimed by a French locksmith by the name of P. Besnier in 1678. Using two long thin rods balancing on his shoulders, Besnier paddled these rods with his hands and feet (the rods were attached to his ankles by a short cord). At the end of the rods were fastened pieces of fabric, which

were hinged to fold on the upstroke and to open on the down. With this gadget, Besnier reported, he had jumped from a window and had flown over a barn like a bird. But not even his contemporaries believed him. Two years later, Italian mathematician and physiologist Giovanni Alfonso Borelli published his *De Motu Animalium* (Concerning Animal Motion), in which he proved that man simply did not have the muscle power to emulate birds; while his logic was absolutely correct, he also commented that he had "no faith in any invention designed to lift man from the earth."

The truth of this observation may have been demonstrated to all who agreed with Borelli when a curious flying machine was given a test flight in Portugal. It was the *Passarola* (Great Bird), the invention of a Brazilian-born Jesuit priest, Bartolomeo de Gusmão, who, in 1709, had been granted

Gusmão's *Passarola*, as depicted in an early drawing. (National Air and Space Museum, Smithsonian Institution)

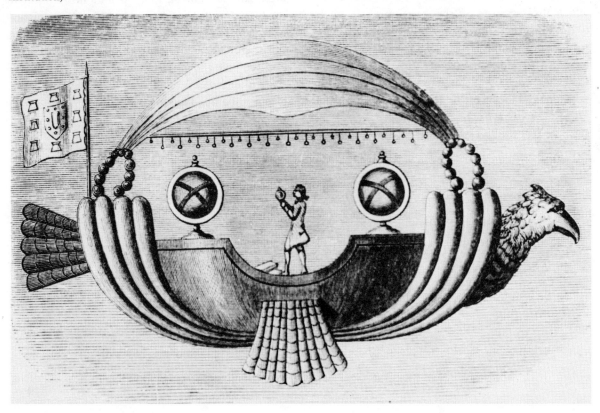

a patent by the King of Portugal for the strange vehicle of the air. From the inaccurate drawings of the *Passarola* that have come down to us, the craft appears to have been another vain attempt at a wing-flapping ornitopter; the very design of the *Passarola* is birdlike in the extreme, complete even to head as well as tail and wings. Early artists, however, took no chances and supplied the *Passarola* with lodestones (magnets) in two globes inside the "aircraft." It was believed that the power of magnetism was capable of lifting objects (as was done with the flying island in *Gullivers's Travels*).

Needless to say, when a full-sized *Passarola* was test-flown in June 1709, it was merely tested and not flown. It flapped helplessly on the ground like a giant wounded bird. But there is evidence that the disappointed Gusmão built a small model of the *Passarola*, perhaps in the form of a glider, and that he may have succeeded in flying it. Despite his error in attempting to duplicate bird flight, Gusmão was correct in understanding the need for tail and wings, as well as a canopylike overhead sail, which also served to lift the craft.

But Gusmão made an even more substantial contribution, although it was all but lost to history, later in the same summer of 1709. Having failed with the *Passarola*, he exhibited yet another invention for the benefit of the King. This was a small boatlike device (a "bark" according to an old manuscript) suspended from a "cloth of canvas." And then with "various spirits, quintessences and other ingredients he put a light beneath it, and let the said bark fly in the Salla das Embaixadas before His Majesty and many other persons. It rose to a small height against the wall and then came to earth and caught fire when the materials became jumbled together. In descending and falling downwards, it set fire to some hangings and everything against which it knocked. His Majesty was good enough not to take it ill."

Bartolomeo de Gusmão had, in fact, demonstrated the first successfully flown hot-air balloon in history. But if His Majesty did not "take it ill," Gusmão's experiments in flight seem to have ended with this rather fiery display. The superstitious may have regarded the priest as being in league with the devil, and talk of sorcery and witchcraft discouraged Gusmão as well as any others who may have been influenced by him. Gusmão himself eventually left Portugal for Spain, a misty figure in the history of flight (until rediscovered by aviation historian Charles H. Gibbs-Smith). When his "great Bird" had failed, Gusmão had possibly modeled the first glider and discovered the principle of the hot-air balloon more than seventy years before it had to be discovered again.

2 QUEST FOR WINGS

Hot air, as every hypothetical schoolboy is now supposed to know, rises. But it took man—also hypothetical—a long time before he realized this and grasped its significance in his dream of flight. De Gusmão's "small bark" stirred up little excitement outside the scorched walls of the King of Portugal's palace. Man flying remained a fallow issue for several decades, except in the imaginations of such writers as Jonathan Swift *(Gulliver's Travels)*, Robert Patlock *(The Life and Adventures of Peter Wilkins, a Cornish Man)*, and Ralph Morris *(The Adventures of John Daniel)* among others.

During these same decades certain truly scientific writings came to light also. If the early science-fiction tales stirred the blood and fancies of the younger generation, the scientific discoveries began to lay the groundwork for the realization of those fancies.

In 1766, for example, English chemist Henry Cavendish read a paper before the Royal Society describing his discovery of something he called "phlogiston" or "inflammable air." (Some years later French scientist Antoine Lavoisier renamed it hydrogen.) That this new substance was lighter than air was duly noted by Cavendish, but he gave no consideration to its application to aviation. Eight years later another English scientist, Dr. Joseph Priestley, isolated what he called "dephlogisticated air" (and which Lavoisier subsequently called oxygen). Priestley published his findings as *Experiments and Observations on Different Kinds of Air*, which appeared in a French translation in 1776.

Joseph Montgolfier, the older of two inventive brothers, French papermakers, read Priestley's book along with other publications on the subject. Legend has it that Montgolfier was also struck by the lifting properties of heated air while he sat near a fireplace watching bits of burned wood and paper rising up the chimney. A brilliant and inquisitive amateur scientist, a true child of his time, the so-called Age of Reason, Joseph Montgolfier was inspired to experiment by what he read and by what he had seen. He did not realize, however, that what he witnessed was nothing more than the expansion of heated air (the weight of which decreases as volume increases) and not yet another gas like hydrogen and oxygen.

What really concerned Joseph was that the mysterious "gas" rose and was capable of lifting objects—not its proper scientific name. It occurred to him that if that gas could be enclosed in some kind of envelope or bag, it should carry the bag skyward. In November 1782, he fashioned a small balloonlike bag of silk with an opening at the bottom. He placed burning paper under this opening. The bag was inflated with the "gas" and rose to the ceiling of Montgolfier's room. Obviously he had been correct in his speculations about what would be called for some time "Mr. Montgolfier's Gas."

The following summer, both Joseph and Étienne Montgolfier worked together in constructing a larger balloon, which they sent up about seventy feet in the air. Other, more ambitious balloons followed until the Montgolfiers felt they were

Joseph Montgolfier. (National Air and Space Museum, Smithsonian Institution)

Étienne Montgolfier. (National Air and Space Museum, Smithsonian Institution)

ready to demonstrate their invention in public. "The aerostatic machine," in the words of Étienne Montgolfier, "was constructed of cloth lined with paper, fastened together on a network of strings fixed to the cloth." The cloth sections, more correctly called gores, were shaped somewhat like the segments of an orange and buttoned together along the seams. The paper lining made the balloon more airtight. The crowd that gathered in the square at Annonay was skeptical. But then, under the direction of the Montgolfiers, the flabby-looking object was filled with "gas"—hot air, of course—bloomed into a graceful sphere, and, while the crowd watched in "silent astonishment," silently lifted some six thousand feet into the air. Swaying gently and carried by a northerly wind, the "aerostatic machine" drifted for about ten minutes and came to earth about a mile and a half away. The once-silent crowd broke into cheers. They had witnessed on that Thursday, June 5, 1783, the first ascent of a manmade object.

Word of the success of Montgolfier's experiments reached the Academy of Sciences in Paris. There was skepticism there also and some unscientific envy. It was assumed the "Montgolfier gas" could only be hydrogen, which was, after all, no mystery, although no one had been able to devise an envelope that could hold it. The scientists in the capital were rather put out because this supposedly first successful flight had been carried off by a couple of papermakers and not one of their own. So besides inviting the Montgolfiers to Paris to demonstrate ("To prove" might be the more precise phrase) their "aerostatic machine," the members of the Academy also encouraged one of their members, physicist Jacques Alexandre César Charles, to make studies into the possibility of producing a similar machine. Charles had an idea concerning the use of "inflammable air," for he knew of two mechanics, Jean and Nicolas Robert, who claimed that they had found a method of rubberizing silk. This, they were certain, would contain the hydrogen. A public subscription was taken up to raise funds for the balloon—a contribution entitled the donor and two friends to view its ascent from a special grandstand.

J. A. C. Charles, who devised the first hydrogen balloon. (Library of Congress)

The Roberts fashioned a rather small balloon (it was twelve feet in diameter); even so, it took several days to generate enough hydrogen to inflate the little globe. Then, on August 27, 1873, Charles released the balloon from the Champ-de-Mars (now the site of the Eiffel Tower) in Paris. It quickly rose to an altitude of three thousand feet and drifted for fifteen miles before settling to earth in the village of Gonesse. The astonished villagers, seeing their first balloon, which had probably sprung a leak and lay writhing and hissing on the ground, thought they had been invaded by some hideous flying monster.

The villagers of Gonesse attack Charles' "flying monster." (U. S. Air Force)

They attacked this creature from outer space with rocks, pitchforks, muskets, and finally tore it to shreds by tying it to a horse, which ran wild over the countryside. Thus concluded the first more or less successful flight of a hydrogen balloon.

Meanwhile, the Montgolfiers had come to Paris to demonstrate their balloon before an audience that would number among its members the King himself, Louis XVI, Marie Antoinette, and their Court. On September 19, 1783, the Montgolfiers released their hot-air balloon from the Ministers' Court at the Palace at Versailles. It might be noted that after a single whiff of the inflation process— for to produce their gas the brothers burned a mixture of straw and wool beneath the neck of the vessel—the King and Marie Antoinette kept a respectable distance. It was noted by those who had also observed the ascent of Charles' balloon, that "Mr. Montgolfier's gas" took only a fraction of the time to fill a much larger balloon. No one realized that the production of hot air was a good deal simpler than that of hydrogen. Nor did they realize that, as a lifting agent, hydrogen was much more efficient (though because of its combustibility, it was also more dangerous).

The Montgolfiers' balloon was a beautiful object, decorated in blue and gold and carrying the royal insignia in honor of the King. It was about fifty-seven feet high and forty feet in diameter; it also carried history's first passengers dangling beneath the neck of the balloon in a large wicker basket. Since the King would not hear of humans being carried aloft in the untried vehicle, the first passengers were a sheep, a rooster, and a duck. They were lifted some seventeen hundred feet in the air, drifted for about two miles, and after only about eight minutes came down in the forest of Vaucresson. Although the flight had not come up to the expectations of the Montgolfiers, the King and his entourage, as well as the great mass of people gathered at Versailles, were thoroughly impressed. The first person to reach the balloon was a young scientist, Jean-François Pilâtre de Rozier, who immediately became air-minded. Others, however, were apprehensive, for although the animals were generally unharmed and in good condition, the

First flight demonstration of the Montgolfier balloon, Versailles, 1783, with a sheep, rooster, and duck as passengers. (National Air and Space Museum, Smithsonian Institution)

rooster had an injured wing. This was attributed to the dangers of high flying, but witnesses were found who swore that the sheep had kicked the rooster before the balloon had taken off. There were still a number of skeptics, but not Pilâtre de Rozier, who became fired with the idea of flying.

King Louis was not easily convinced that in the next Montgolfier flight men should be substituted for livestock. Reluctantly the King consented, suggesting, however, that two criminals be selected to be the first air passengers. If they made it, the royal thinking went, they would be pardoned; if not, it would be no loss to France. But Pilâtre de Rozier, who was determined to be the first man to fly, was shocked. "Why," he is reported to have exploded, "should the honor of being the first to fly be given to criminals?" He enlisted as an ally (at the price of sharing the glory) one Marquis François d'Arlandes, who had influence in Court. Soon the determined would-be aeronauts brought pressure upon Louis via Marie Antoinette, and after some persuasion, royal sanction was granted.

Less than a month after the successful flight of the animal passengers, the Montgolfiers completed their man-carrying balloon. In size it was larger than its predecessor: about seventy-five feet tall from neck to the "north pole" (that is, the top of the bag). It was forty-nine feet in diameter, with a sixteen-foot neck. Around this was the passenger gallery, a wickerwork platform three feet wide and three and a half feet high. This gallery was sewn to

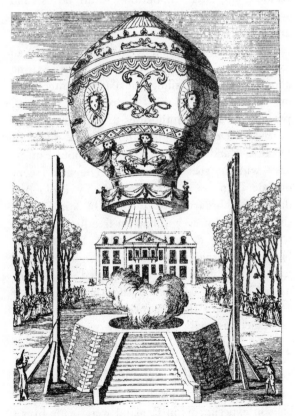

The start of the first voyage, Paris 1783, with passengers: De Rozier and the Marquis d'Arlandes. (National Air and Space Museum, Smithsonian Institution)

the fabric of the balloon. The balloon was filled with the foul-smelling "Montgolfier gas" (burned straw and wool) on a specially built launching platform. There was an ingenious added feature: provision for prolonging the flight. A wrought-iron brazier was hung below the balloon's neck and additional supplies of fuel were carried, which enabled the passengers to add fuel after the balloon was airborne. It was possible then to remain aloft longer and, winds willing, to travel farther. While not exactly the forerunner of the auxiliary fuel tank, the idea was a step in the right direction.

Before attempting a free flight, the Montgolfiers tested their balloon with Pilâtre de Rozier aboard in tethered flight. With the balloon tied by a rope eighty feet long, and with ballast added to compensate for the absence of a second passenger, De Rozier remained aloft for more than four minutes. Further tests followed, and De Rozier learned some of the techniques of manning a balloon as more rope was let out (well over three hundred feet). Even passengers were treated to the thrill of being airborne.

Finally, on November 21, 1783, from the garden of the Château La Muette in the Bois de Boulogne (near Paris), the "Montgolfière" lifted off the earth carrying the first air passengers in history, Pilâtre de Rozier and the Marquis de'Arlandes. "The aerostat left the ground at fifty-four minutes past one o'clock," an early report ran, "passed safely over some high trees, and ascended calmly and majestically into the atmosphere. The aeronauts having reached the altitude of 280 feet, took off their hats and saluted the surprised multitude." The two airmen floated across the Seine, over Paris, and after twenty-five minutes, during which they covered a distance of five and a half miles, De Rozier and the Marquis came safely and gently to earth. This first air journey was not without its hazards.

Because they were stationed opposite one other in the gallery, to balance the balloon, neither man saw the other during the flight. De Rozier, obviously the "pilot," shouted orders to the marquis, who apparently did all the work, throwing fuel into the brazier to raise the balloon in order not to hit trees and rooftops or sponging out the small fires that sparks had caused. From time to time the marquis took time out from his "copiloting" to be impressed with the magnificent aerial vistas of Paris, only to be put back to work by De Rozier shouting something like, "If you look at the river in that fashion you will be likely to bathe in it soon. Some fire, my dear friend, some fire!" What with the many dangerous possibilities, particularly of fire, the epochal flight of De Rozier and the Marquis d'Arlandes was a miracle in more ways than one. Their exploit was widely witnessed by thousands of people. One of them was the American representative to the French Court, Benjamin Franklin. When asked by one doubting member of the Court "Of what use is the balloon?" Franklin replied: "Of what use is a newborn baby?"

Ten days after the flight of the Montgolfière" (to distinguish the hydrogen-filled balloon from the hot-air balloon) made an ascent with humans. On December 1, Charles accompanied by Nicolas Robert made a much more spectacular flight than De Rozier and the Marquis d'Arlandes. More scientifically conceived by Charles than the Montgolfière flight (even to the degree of carrying a thermometer and barometer as well as sandbag ballast), the first man-carrying hydrogen balloon remained aloft for two hours and covered a distance of nearly twenty-five miles. Unlike the hot-air balloon, which had to be constantly tended, the hydrogen balloon remained more or less bouyant, its lifting force being quite constant because of the nature of the gas and not dependent on the heat of a fire. Charles could control ascent and descent by the use of ballast or the release of hydrogen: To rise he could toss out the ballast or return to earth by releasing the correct amount of hydrogen. Of course, the direction the balloon took was dependent upon the wind. Charles brought their "aerostatic machine," as it was called at the time, down to a perfect landing after a two-hour flight; proper documents were witnessed and signed. Robert stepped out of the car of the balloon, for Charles had decided he would make a lone ascent. He did not wait for a new supply of ballast, there being no

shovels to dig the earth, nor a supply of rocks about—and he did not wish to attempt an ascent too late in the day. Charles signaled to a group of "30 peasants" who held the balloon down to release it and—without the weight of Robert and very little ballast—shot up to a height of nine thousand feet in ten minutes. The rapid change in pressure caused Charles severe ear pain, although he continued to make meticulous scientific observations. Charles released hydrogen until he once again returned to earth on the Nesles plain. He had triumphed, but he never flew again after the painful experience of his solo flight. But he had proved that as a lifting agent hydrogen was superior to the Montgolfiers' hot air and that the use of ballast could, to some degree, control the aerostatic machine.

The triumphs of the Montgolfière and the Charlière ushered in an era of balloonomania. Miniature balloons appeared on buttons, snuff boxes, and were adapted as jewelry. Toy balloons were sold and soon filled the air over Paris. These toys, ranging in size from a tiny eight-inch balloon to an expensive silk one twelve feet in diameter, floating about Paris either trailing smoke (the Montgolfière) or filled with volatile hydrogen (Charlière), prompted Parisian authorities to ban them as fire hazards. At the same time, news of the flights of De Rozier and Charles spread throughout Europe and, with it, the desire to fly. The first ascent outside France was made in Italy by Paolo Andreani in February 1784. In June, back in France, the first woman ever to make a free flight (earlier, women had made tethered flights), Elisabeth Tible, rose to a height of more than eight thousand feet above Lyons and, accompanied by a pilot named Fleurant, floated about for three-quarters of an hour. Across the Channel in Britain there was excitement as well as controversy over ballooning. Late in December 1783, the *Morning Herald* reflected a no-doubt popular view when it directed "all men to laugh this new folly out of practice as soon as possible." Curiously, the first successful balloon experiments in England were made by an Italian adventurer, Count Francesco Zambeccari,

The first manned hydrogen balloon flight by Charles and Robert, 1783. (Library of Congress)

who had been inspired by the Montgolfières. Zambeccari released a number of small, and, of course, unmanned balloons late in 1783. The first Briton to fly, although without any great success, was James Tytler, a Scot, who managed to raise a Montgolfière about five hundred feet at Edinburgh in August 1784. Tytler's experiments were singularly afflicted with bad luck, injuries, and wrecked balloons, but he persevered for a time before giving up completely.

Another Italian, Vincent Lunardi, succeeded where Zambeccari had failed. The count ran out of money—and consequently also out of England—before he ever left the earth in one of his balloons. Lunardi was a dashing, handsome assistant to the Neapolitan Ambassador to the Court of St. James's. As volatile as hydrogen itself, Lunardi saw in the balloon an opportunity to make himself famous if not wealthy. According to Lunardi's original announcement, he intended to build a Charlière "on a plan entirely novel," the brainchild of an anonymous "gentleman" (most probably his friend and patron George Biggins). Lunardi's hopes of being the first aeronaut in England was nearly dashed when others simultaneously announced similar intentions. One such rival, a "learned Chevalier de Moret," appeared with a strange device that looked more like a Chinese pagoda than a balloon. An obvious charlatan, De Moret so infuriated the spectators who had come to see him fly that a riot ensued, the balloon burned to bits, and De Moret fled for his life. The riot frightened off Lunardi's original backer, Chelsea Hospital, from whose grounds the ascent was to have taken place. Meanwhile, another unsuccessful try was made by Dr. John Sheldon, whose bad luck it was to set his own balloon aflame before he got off the ground. By the time Lunardi was ready for his ascent, the London public was quite leery of aeronauts and their claims. But encouraged by the attentions of the ladies who flocked to see the handsome Lunardi—or rather his balloon, when it was placed on exhibit—the intrepid fledgling birdman was determined to fly despite all adversity. He acquired another takeoff site—the Artillery Ground of the

Honourable Artillery Company at Moorfields, London. It was part of the plan that the Company would be on hand to prevent Lunardi's balloon from falling into the hands of angry spectators should anything go wrong.

Despite the amateurishness of Lunardi, his balloon, in general, was an excellently designed one. A new system of filling it with hydrogen was devised by a Dr. George Fordyce. Although it was claimed to be an improved hydrogen generator, the system was very slow. A mixture of sulphuric acid and water was pumped into casks containing iron filings and zinc. The gas thus generated passed

Hydrogen generator of the Lunardi balloon, 1784, in preparation for the first aerial voyage in England. (National Air and Space Museum, Smithsonian Institution)

through an alkaline solution (to correct its acidity) and then through the neck of the balloon into the gas bag. After the balloon was properly filled, the gallery, which was to carry the passengers and which was attached to a hoop, could in turn be fastened to the netting of the balloon. This system was an improvement over Charles' balloon, which had a large hoop around the middle that wore away the fabric eventually. Also, Lunardi's gallery was less elaborate—a simple basket that became the standard eventually-and more practical. The hoop was fastened to the balloon netting by forty-five cords. After what must have seemed an eternity (during which the crowd muttered, nearly rioted— because of the rumor of a mad bull supposedly running amok among them—and the breakage of a wooden scaffold, stone throwing when carriages interfered with the view of some spectators, and the dunking of a hapless pickpocket), Lunardi finally decided to take off. The balloon was not completely inflated, which meant that George Biggins, Lunardi's patron, had to be left behind when the balloon rose into the air carrying Lunardi, a cat, a dog, a caged pigeon, and provisions, including sandwiches and a bottle of wine. The balloon was also equipped with wings (useless) and two movable oars (even more useless), with which Lunardi intended to "row" himself about the sky. When the cat appeared to be unhappy in the colder air, Lunardi did indeed row himself (he thought) to a cornfield, where he descended to release the cat; then, tossing out some ballast, he rose again. After more than two hours and a distance of twenty-four miles—plus a couple of slight mishaps; such as the pigeon's escaping and Lunardi's lunch being spoiled when it became mixed with ballast sand— he "rowed" himself down into a field at Standon, near Ware, Hertfordshire. A monument to Lunardi stands on the spot to this day. Lunardi's great dream had come true: He had been the first man to fly in England, and, more importantly perhaps, he had become the most famous man in Britain, the hero of the hour. Nineteen days later, on October 4, 1784, the first native-born English aeronaut, James Sadler, made an ascent at Oxford and, al-

Lunardi, airborne, September 1784; the adventurous aeronaut beleived he could achieve some control by using oars. (Musée de l'Air, Paris)

though he "received the approbation of the whole University, to whom he gave the utmost satisfaction," it was Lunardi who had captured the hearts of Englishmen—and women. In fact, Lunardi made several subsequent flights and was even responsible for the first balloon flight of an English-with his sponsor, an ex-American, Dr. John Jeffries, Blanchard made the first aerial crossing of the English Channel on January 7, 1785.

Dissatisfied with the lack of attention he had received in his native country (balloonists by late 1784 were rather common in France), Blanchard decided to try his luck in England where aeronauts, thanks to Lunardi, had begun to be properly appreciated. Blanchard made a couple of flights in England with passengers who paid for the privilege of going aloft in Blanchard's curiously designed

"The first Aerial Mariner, Citizen of Calais & Pensioner of the French King," Jean Pierre Blanchard. (Library of Congress)

Blanchard's English Channel crossing balloon, 1785. His passenger on the uncomfortable voyage was an American, Dr. Jeffries. (National Air and Space Museum, Smithsonian Institution)

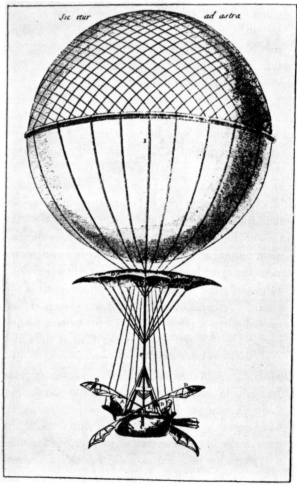

woman, Mrs. Letitia Sage. In a characteristic bit of gallantry, Lunardi stepped down from the gallery of his balloon, making it possible for George Biggins and Mrs. Sage to make the historic ascent (on June 29, 1785). Mrs. Sage, it seems, weighed some two hundred pounds, so that the balloon could not rise carrying all three passengers.

France, despite Lunardi's English triumphs, remained the home of the greater aeronauts, the first professional aviators. This may have been encouraged by the balloonomania as well as the fact that it was possible to get backing from wealthy French enthusiasts and to sell tickets to spectators. In the vanguard of these professionals was Jean Pierre Blanchard, "a petulant little fellow, not many inches over five feet," a devious, scheming egotist of great courage. This mean-spirited little man made one of history's epochal flights. In company balloon. One of the features of Blanchard's balloon was an umbrellalike device just below the balloon itself. This was a safety feature in the event that the balloon burst in the air. In fact, it is unlikely that it would have worked (in later years two pioneers were killed demonstrating such a "safety" device). Blanchard's balloon also came equipped with flapping wings which, he claimed, he used to steer the balloon—another unlikely story. For his cross-Channel flight Blanchard retained the flapping wings, added a gadget he called a *moulinet* (a large rotating fan; though as useless as the wings, it *was* a crude propeller), but removed the parachute. He also attempted to remove Jeffries, who had contributed money generously to the venture. When the two attempted to take off at Dover Castle, on the English side of the Channel, it was found that the reason they did not rise was the weights Blanchard had secretly added around his waist. He had hoped that he could have left Jeffries behind to his own greater glory. But the trick was discovered and after arguments and a reconciliation, Blanchard and Jeffries rather sluggishly lifted off Dover in the afternoon of January 7, 1785.

Either because of a leak in the envelope of the balloon, or because of the effect of cooler air upon the hydrogen, the balloon began descending rapidly about two thirds of the way across the Channel. The rest of the flight was anything but uneventful. First, the ballast was thrown overboard, then the various instruments, including the wings and *moulinet*. But too much gas had been lost, and more desperate ballasting was required: Out went their clothing, including their "trowsers." After all this frantic activity, the aeronauts were rewarded by an ascent and at about three o'clock crossed the coast of France at Calais. As the balloon rose higher, the air grew colder, and the airmen greatly missed their "trowsers," it being January. Twelve miles inland, after being dragged through treetops, to which they managed finally to cling until more gas could be released, the aeronauts came down to earth. They had made the first over-water flight over sea in history.

After this experience, Dr. Jeffries appears to

have confined his practice to medicine, but Blanchard went on giving exhibition flights, during which he introduced the balloon to Germany, Holland, Belgium (1785), Switzerland (1788), Poland, Czechoslovakia (1789), and in 1793 made the first manned balloon ascent in the United States, at Philadelphia. His patron for this event was President George Washington. In 1808, Blanchard made his sixtieth and last ascent, in Holland; during the ascent he suffered a heart attack. He died early the following year, aged fifty-six, leaving his wife, Madeleine-Sophie, to carry on in his place.

Pilâtre de Rozier, who had hoped to be the first to cross the English Channel, was thwarted by the opportunistic though courageous Blanchard. It was De Rozier's idea to cross from France to England with a new balloon of his own design—actually a combination of both the Montgolfière and the Charlière. This "Rozière," the inventor hoped, would exploit the better features of both types. It

Pilâtre de Rozier, who made the fatal error of combining the features of the Charles and Montgolfier balloons, a mistake that led to the first fatal air accident. (U. S. Air Force)

F. PILATRE DE ROZIER

Premier Navigateur Aérien

Et Pensionnaire du Roi

De Rozier and Romain beginning their fatal voyage, before the balloon burst into flame; the lesson: Hydrogen and flame did not mix. (Musée de l'Air, Paris)

would be simpler to control (for the use of ballast with the hydrogen balloon had not yet been developed to a fine art). However, the combination—the "inflammable air" of the Charlière and the burning brazier of the Montgolfière—could not have been deadlier. With the hot-air balloon on the bottom and the hydrogen on top, the strange new aerostat looked like a ball with a cylinder attached to it. Actually, there was a gap of about five feet between the round hydrogen portion and the cylindrical hot-air segment. So much for the science of safety at the time: The gap, it was argued, would keep the flame from the hydrogen. When all was ready, on the morning of June 15, 1785, De Rozier, with his patron-passenger Pierre-Ange Romain, took off from Boulogne. Swiftly the balloon rose to about five thousand feet, where it burst into flame and plummeted to the ground in history's first aerial disaster. Pilâtre de Rozier tragically acquired another distinction: He had been the first man ever to rise into the air and was the first to die in an air accident. Romain was still alive when witnesses ran to the scene of the crash; he died shortly thereafter. It had occurred not far from the spot where Blanchard and Jeffries had landed just six months before. When he died, De Rozier, France's *premier navigateur aérien*, was only twenty-eight years old.

The deaths of De Rozier and Romain (and of others who followed) prompted re-evaluation of the "aerostat." It was beginning to dawn on some that as a vehicle of the air, the balloon was an aeronautical dead end. It was primarily at the mercies of the wind rather than under human control. Not that it was immediately abandoned, for balloons continued to be used, mainly as a means of entertainment or sport, until the early twentieth century. There were also further attempts to put it to practical use. Given a new device, it seems inevitable that man tries to find some means of turning it to his own destruction. So it was with the balloon. Although it had suffered some eclipse after some of the early fatalities, the balloon was not completely dismissed. Certain minds of a military turn began visualizing the use of the balloon in war. The age-old question, "How can we turn this thing into a weapon?" was applied to the balloon practically from the moment of its birth. Even Benjamin Franklin, no militarist, recognized the military worth of the balloon. Writing in 1783, the day after witnessing the first manned flight of De Rozier and D'Arlandes, Franklin thought it could be used for "elevating an Engineer to take a view of an Enemy's Army, Works, &c; conveying Intelligence into, or out of, a besieged Town, giving Signals to Distant Places, or the like." He also prophesied the paratroopers of the Second World War when he visualized a force of five thousand balloons capable of lifting two men each for a mass aerial invasion. The newborn aerostat was a mere eleven years old before it was conscripted into military service.

The world's first air force, the Première Compagnie d'Aérostiers, was formed in France early in 1794. By this time revolution had come to France, and Louis XVI and Marie Antoinette, who had observed the ascent of the Montgolfière balloon at Versailles, had perished by the guillotine. The new French Republic, revolution-torn and under the Reign of Terror of Robespierre, was subject to invasion from its predatory neighbors. The first Aerostatic Company, therefore, went into action for the first time at Maubeuge on June 2, 1794, when with pilot Jean-Marie-Joseph Coutelle aboard, the hydrogen balloon *L'Entreprenant* rose above the lines to report the disposition of the Austrian and Dutch troops to the French commanders. At the Battle of Fleurus, on June 26, Coutelle ascended again and with a general as observer, and with tactics directed from the air, the French won a remarkable victory. The concept of aerial warfare was born and proved. Its real significance, however, still lay in the future.

The extremes to which an inventor might go were demonstrated by a proposed giant balloon, the *Minerva*. This 150-foot-in-diameter monster

The balloon goes to war at the Battle of Fleurus, 1794. Observation from *L'Entreprenant* led to a French victory. (Smithsonian Institution)

Garnerin entertains the populace in London with its first public parachute demonstration, 1802. (National Air and Space Museum, Smithsonian Institution)

Robertson's conception of the ultimate weapon of the air, ca. 1800. The *Minerva* never flew—in fact, it was never built. Note forward-firing cannon in the prow; almost directly below, marked "E," is the *Minerva's* rest rooms; the crew's recreation area, "G," dangles just to the left of storage barrel. (National Air and Space Museum, Smithsonian Institution)

was the brainchild of one Étienne-Gaspard Robertson, who suggested that the *Minerva*, manned by a crew of sixty, was capable of long-distance voyages of six months, even more. The great aerostat, a veritable floating colony, came complete with recreation areas, a hospital, and rest rooms. A large barrel served as a storage area for food, water, and wine; this supposedly would hold a half year's supply of provisions. Other features were a big gun and a smaller balloon, the *Minerva's* "life-balloon." Needless to say, this conception never materialized. An English satire of the idea appeared in which the *Minerva* was converted into a ridiculous military vehicle for a French invasion of England. It came fully equipped, even to the then-inevitable guillotine. This version of the craft did not come into existence either.

By the turn of the nineteenth century the balloon had regained some of its lost popularity, but less in the field of science and more as a form of entertainment. Balloons ascended over amusement parks, fairs, and parties of the wealthy as part of a spectacular show. Of course, mere ascent and descent would not do, and in time certain "acts" were devised in which trapeze artists were lifted dangling from a balloon; so were a troupe of ballerinas, as were aeronauts, astride horses. When these entertainments palled, new ones were concocted, including night ascents during which the balloonists put on a fireworks display. Out of the "show biz" balloons grew a new development: the parachute jump. The invention of the parachute was undoubtedly the one advance contributed to aviation by the showmen aeronauts. The first man to make a parachute jump was Frenchman André Jacques Garnerin, who, inspired by the experiments of a French physician, Sebastien Lenormard, on October 22, 1797, dropped from his balloon from an altitude of three thousand feet. Garnerin's chute, a crude umbrella thirty feet in diameter, brought him to earth safely, but not without swinging him underneath it like a pendulum. He landed triumphantly but rather air-sick.

In time Garnerin and his followers learned to make a parachute with an opening in the top to permit the air to spill out and to prevent oscillation. Another refinement was to use a material that was not airtight and that allowed some of the air to seep through at a safe rate. Garnerin's parachute jumps became so popular that he took his "act" on tour. Over London, on September 21, 1802, he made the first parachute jump in England, this time from an altitude of ten thousand feet. The great height resulted in a longer time for the swinging motion of Garnerin's little car (modern parachute harness was a much later idea) to become violently frightening. Spectators feared that Garnerin would certainly be tossed out of his chute. But once again he landed, perhaps the worse for wear, but intact. His performances became much in demand, and Garnerin began appearing throughout Europe, traveling as far east as Russia. He also shared the limelight with his wife, Jeanne-Genevieve, who became the first woman to make a parachute descent.

The world's first professional woman parachutist was Elisa Garnerin, niece of André Jacques. Like her aunt and uncle, Elisa traveled across the Continent giving exhibition flights at weddings, *soirées*, pageants, and coronations. Her "act" consisted of an ascent in what appeared to be a conventional balloon. When she reached the desired altitude, Elisa Garnerin yanked on the proper line, which released the basket from the balloon and let her float gracefully back to earth. By this time (she began her career in 1815), her uncle, Garnerin, had devised a system for bringing down a balloon near the spot where it had ascended. He affixed a counterweight to the "north pole" (top) of the balloon. When the chute was released, the weight inverted the balloon, causing the hydrogen to be expended very quickly, thus bringing the balloon down undamaged. Elisa Garnerin continued her aerial career until 1836, when she retired; in the twenty years or so of her active life she had made countless balloon ascents and nearly forty parachute jumps.

The Garnerins had become so renowned that

Garnerin's niece, Elisa, emulating her uncle; between 1815 and 1836 she made numerous balloon flights and dozens of successful parachute descents. (National Air and Space Museum, Smithsonian Institution)

they were appointed by Napoleon as the official aeronauts of France. On one official occasion they constructed a special balloon to celebrate the coronation of Napoleon; it carried a great gilded crown instead of passengers. Lifting off from Paris, this crown-bearing balloon traveled, incredibly, all the way to Rome, where it deposited the crown upon the tomb of the hated Emperor Nero. Napoleon became the laughing-stock of the Italian press, and the Garnerins were relieved of their official position. Their place was taken by Marie Madeleine Sophie Blanchard, widow of the first Channel-crosser.

Madame Blanchard had already made a name for herself as an exhibition balloonist. Having taken over Garnerin's job, she also adopted some of his act, one feature of which was a night ascent and

The widow of balloonist Blanchard becomes the first woman air casualty during an exhibition flight over Paris, 1819. (Musée de l'Air, Paris)

fireworks display. Madame Blanchard, though frightened of riding in a carriage, loved riding in balloons—especially at night. Legend has her taking off at dusk and remaining aloft all night, sleeping in her car, away from the hurly-burly of life on the ground. So it was that on the night of July 7, 1819, Madame Blanchard took off from the Tivoli Gardens in Paris for a night exhibition flight. As she floated over the heads of admiring Parisians, she touched off various spectacular kinds of fireworks: Silver fire trailed like a comet tail beneath her car; she released gold and silver sparkling in slow-descending parachutes. There was a moment of awe when the greatest effect of all occurred—a great burst of flame from the top of the balloon. Soon it became evident that it had not been a part of the entertainment; the hydrogen in the balloon had caught fire. The balloon dropped toward Paris. To break the descent, Madame Blanchard began tossing out ballast, but as the aerostat swooped down low, the car struck the roof of a building in the Rue de Provence and the hapless aeronaut was flung out of the car and down the steep roof into the street, where she died of a broken neck. Marie Madeleine Sophie Blanchard was the first woman ever to die in an air accident.

The balloon, for all its beauty and majesty and despite the fact that it had enabled man to escape the fetters of the earth, was not, literally, going anywhere—that is, no one had been able to devise a working method of control. History, dotted as it is with near misses, is replete with ironies. In 1785, just two years after the first flights of the globular Montgolfière and the Charlière, a French soldier, Jean Baptiste Marie Meusnier, designed an airship—that is, a balloon of elongated form, pointed fore and aft. But the design was never built, and Meusnier himself was killed in battle, cutting short his speculations on the design of what a hundred years later would be called a dirigible—that is, a controllable airship. So the balloon, in quiet, though ill-governed majesty, retained its original spherical form from its birth into the twentieth century. Although the balloon was not entirely the dinosaur of the air age (for it proved continually

A Montgolfier balloon, ca. 1850, in cross-country flight. Though it could free passengers of earthly bonds, it could not take them to any definite destination; the winds determined that. (National Air and Space Museum, Smithsonian Institution)

American balloon pioneer John Wise, who made an early attempt at crossing the Atlantic by balloon. He disappeared during a flight over Lake Michigan in 1879. (Library of Congress)

useful in scientific work as well as in sport and entertainment), it had outlived its day. Man had learned a good deal from Montgolfier's "new-born baby," not the least of which was that the lighter-than-air aerostat was not the solution to the problem of human flight.

One of America's greatest balloonists was John Wise of Lancaster, Pennsylvania. Wise made his first successful ascent in 1835, when he was twenty-seven years old. Although he studied for the ministry, he became fascinated with the idea of flight when news of the Montgolfiers reached America. In a long lifetime devoted to ballooning, Wise made about five hundred ascents. In 1839 he invented a ripping panel for releasing gas should the balloonist wish to make a rapid descent. His particular dedication was to the practicability of long-distance balloon voyages, with a crossing of

Thaddeus Lowe, who introduced the military balloon to the U. S. Army during the Civil War. (National Air and Space Museum, Smithsonian Institution)

the Atlantic especially obsessive. In 1859 he set off from St. Louis in such an attempted flight and covered the remarkable distance of 804 miles to Henderson, New York, before the winds drove the balloon to earth. In 1879, then seventy-one, Wise again attempted a long flight and disappeared over Lake Michigan.

During the American Civil War John Wise attempted to place his ballooning experience at the service of the government. He was, however, beaten by a rival balloonist, Thaddeus Lowe, who formed a balloon observation corps that served as

Inflating Lowe's *Intrepid* which was used for observation by the Union Army during the battle of Fair Oaks, Virginia, 1862. (U. S. Air Force)

an aerial reconnaissance unit for the federal government—Abraham Lincoln having ordered his generals to listen to Lowe's ideas on the subject. The generals did not trust the gas bags. Lowe believed his balloon observations helped save the Union Army from defeat at Fair Oaks. Actually, handling the balloons was a good deal of trouble, and their use was finally abandoned.

Early in the nineteenth century—in 1804, to be precise—the first true aircraft was designed, described—and even more importantly—flown, by an Englishman, Sir George Cayley. A boy of ten when the first Montgolfière made its ascent, Cayley was an inventive and curious youngster. In his early twenties he began experimenting with flying devices; one of the first was a glider, though the term was not yet current, which consisted of a kite affixed to a long rod (these were the wing and fuselage); at the end of the rod was a stick on a universal (movable) joint, at the end of which Cayley had made a tail unit. The universal joint made it possible to adjust the tail to the proper angle for flight. Near the front of the rod (or the nose of the glider) Cayley had placed a metal weight, which could be moved to make adjustments. His drawing, and the actual working model made from it, was the first time anyone had produced the modern configuration of an aircraft—that is, a fuselage, with a lifting wing and tail surfaces for additional lift as well as directional control. Here, in 1804, was the solution to man's quest for wings, but Cayley himself did not pursue it to any final conclusions, nor did anyone else at the time.

Still, Cayley, had a wide influence on others, as his ideas spread throughout Europe and eventually reached the United States. Although he had invented a successful model glider, Cayley was, of course, more interested in powered flight. But in his time there was no engine both powerful and light enough to serve the purpose. He did, however, contribute important theoretical ideas, placing aviation on a solid scientific foundation, in his writings, particularly in three issues of Nicholson's

British aviation theoretician, George Cayley, who conceived the configuration of modern aircraft design. (National Air and Space Museum, Smithsonian Institution)

Model of Cayley's conception of the glider with wing, fuselage, and adjustable tail surfaces. The small weight in the "nose" of the glider could also adjust the balance of the glider. (Science Museum, London)

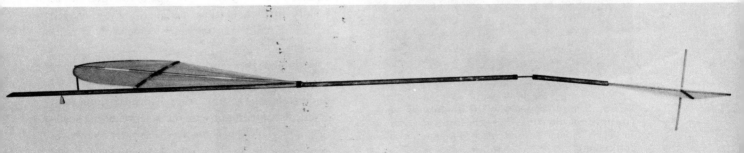

Journal of Natural Philosophy, Chemistry and the Arts (November 1809, February 1810, and March 1810). Cayley's articles, entitled "On Aerial Navigation," set down the foundations of the science of aerodynamics for all who would read.

Directly influenced by Cayley were two other inventive, air-minded Englishmen, William Samuel Henson and John Stringfellow. About a generation younger than Cayley, they benefited from his writings as well as from the stimulation of certain advances in transportation. During the youth of both men the age of steam had come to England and with it the steam railroad, oceangoing steamships, and other new ideas. Both Henson and Stringfellow were in the business of manufacturing lace and both had a practical knowledge of machines. Henson became interested in flight about 1841 and designed (and patented in 1842) what he called his *Ariel*, the Aerial Steamer. To power this aircraft, of no less than 150-foot wingspan, Stringfellow designed a steam engine. In an excess of

William Samuel Henson, the English dreamer who visualized the aircraft as a passenger-carrying vehicle—in 1843. (National Air and Space Museum, Smithsonian Institution)

enthusiasm the two inventors formed an Aerial Transit Company, which they hoped would help to finance the building of the Aerial Steam Carriage and which they hoped would spread flying all over the world.

Needless to say, the Aerial Steam Carriage never flew. There were several reasons for this, the most important being that the engine was incapable of doing its job, and for all the ingenuity of the design, *Ariel* would never have proved to be a safe, stable aircraft. But it was remarkably prophetic, with its advanced wing construction, a tricycle landing gear, and two engines. Although the newspapers ridiculed the Aerial Transit Company out of existence, the widespread attention given to the *Ariel* itself excited an interest in aviation and, no doubt, stirred the imaginations of many air enthusiasts. Henson and Stringfellow never built a full-sized aircraft, but they did make a twenty-foot model, which they launched from a ramp (as was intended with the full-sized plane). They had no success with this model, and Henson, discouraged, gave up and moved to the United States.

Stringfellow, however, continued on his own, and in 1848 he made another model—this one with a wingspan of ten feet—based on the *Ariel*, although with modifications. Equipped with his own steam engine and powered by two fanlike propellers, Stringfellow's plane actually flew for 120 feet before an audience at Cremorne Gardens in London that same year. Strangely, this excited little interest, and Stringfellow, like Henson, was discouraged. "Finding nothing but pecuniary loss and little honour" in the rold of aerial prophet, he forsook experimentation in aviation for the next eighteen years. (In 1868 he again emerged in the history of flight with a model of a three-winged model aircraft—a triplane—which flew successfully.)

Although the work of Cayley, Henson, and Stringfellow was not sufficiently appreciated or understood at the time, they had made important practical contributions to the science of aeronautics. The gist of their message was that if man ever expected to fly in a controllable machine, it would

A contemporary print of *Ariel*, Henson's idea of a passenger aircraft. (U. S. Air Force)

Structural design of Henson's early "airliner." (Smithsonian Institution)

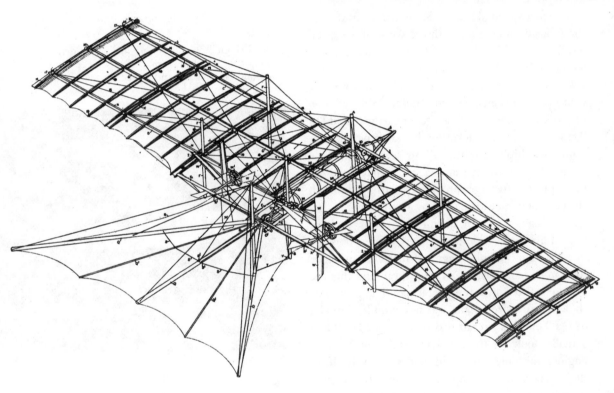

Model of Stringfellow's steam-powered flying machine, which actually flew, 1848. (Science Museum, London)

have to be along the lines indicated by Cayley—that is with a fuselage, a stationary wing, and tail surfaces. Further, this flying machine would have to be powered with a powerful but very light engine, and pulled through the air by a propeller. Control would depend upon movable portions of the machine that could be manipulated by the man in the aircraft so that it would not be at the mercy of the winds. Cayley had pointed the way, and Henson and Stringfellow had followed and refined, but all were ultimately defeated by the lack of an engine of proper weight and power. The ideas of these three great English aerial pioneers were remarkably farsighted.

The focus shifted back to France in the middle of the nineteenth century with the work of a French naval officer Felix du Temple, who conceived an aircraft of birdlike design in 1857. The wings were swept forward and set with a slight dihedral (angled up from the center) for lateral stability—one of Cayley's ideas. The fuselage, or car, revealed Du Temple's nautical background and somewhat resembled a ship's lifeboat. Tail surfaces provided for longitudinal stability, and a rudderlike tail, attached to the fuselage, provided control. Although the type of engine visualized by Du Temple for his aircraft is not known definitely, it was to have turned a twelve-blade propeller. Of interest is the fact that Du Temple suggested that aluminum be used in the construction of the aircraft and that the design called for a retractable landing gear. Although a full-sized plane was never built, a model of Du Temple's aircraft was built (about 1874) and actually took off (powered probably by a steam engine), although it could not sustain itself in flight. As with the English pioneers, the French were handicapped by the lack of a proper engine.

Second claimant to the honor of being the first man to fly in a powered aircraft was Russian Alexander Feodrovich Mozhaisky who, according to Soviet claims first put forth in 1949, designed and flew a steam-powered monoplane in 1882, or 1884, depending upon the reference work consulted. The plane, with one I. N. Golubev as pilot, was launched down a ramp and may very well have

John Stringfellow and his original steam-driven monoplane, which flew in 1848. (Science Museum, London/National Air and Space Museum, Smithsonian Institution)

flown, thanks to the momentum gathered going down the ramp and the slight help of its two thirty-horsepower engines (which turned no less than three propellers). On its trial run, which probably occurred in 1884, the plane (according to one account) lifted slightly off the ground for a moment before falling and smashing a wing. If Mozhaisky

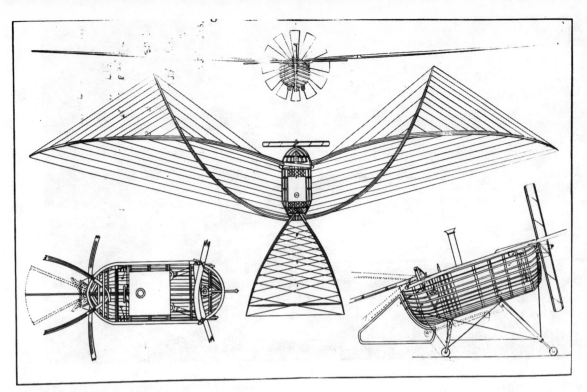

Patent drawing of Du Temple's design, 1857. An
interesting feature was the retractable landing gear. A
model of the craft was built and flown, after a fashion, in
1874. (Musée de l'Air, Paris)

was, indeed, successful in inventing a working aircraft, he certainly disappeared quickly from the
limelight of history.

Another French seaman, Jean-Marie Le Bris,
had become interested in flight around the same
time as Du Temple. No theoretician like Du Temple, Le Bris had been impressed with the flight of
the giant albatross while he was at sea. Almost
simultaneously with Du Temple's patent of a powered aircraft, Le Bris conceived an unpowered craft
inspired by the albatross. Le Bris, however, chose
not to repeat the mistake of earlier bird lovers—he
settled for a fixed-wing design and not the flapping-
wing device, which invariably led to disaster.

Le Bris' first design, built about 1857, was a full-
sized flying glider of about fifty-foot wingspan.
Launched from a cart, it made a short successful
flight with its inventor as passenger. Encouraged,
Le Bris had himself launched over a quarry but was
caught in a downdraft and crashed. The glider was
wrecked, and Le Bris suffered a broken leg. For a
decade Le Bris remained out of the aviation pic-

ture, but in 1867 he came forth with a second
glider, which had been built with funds raised by
his neighbors and friends. Like the first glider, the
second was launched from a cart, and by 1868 Le
Bris had begun testing the machine. The tests were
run with ballast placed inside the needle-nosed
glider rather than with Le Bris himself as pilot. Le
Bris' plan was to run the cart carrying his glider
down a hill with himself in the cockpit, but friends
dissuaded him. When another test was carried out,
the glider rose off the cart, tipped over on one
wing, and crumpled on the ground. This second
failure ended Le Bris' career in aeronautics. As an
early account put it, "His means and his credit
were exhausted, his friends forsook him, and perhaps his own courage weakened, for he did not try
again." History's first glider pilot retired and became a special constable near Brest and "was killed
in 1872 by some ruffians whose enmity he had
incurred."

A young Frenchman, Alphonse Pénaud, who
was denied a career as a seaman because of a hip

Mozhaisky's design for an aircraft that the Russians claim actually flew in 1884, but apparently never again. (Science Museum, London)

LeBris glider of 1868, his second try at creating an albatrosslike flying machine. Its test flight was a failure and closed LeBris' aeronautical career, such as it was. (Musée de l'Air, Paris)

disease, entered the mainstream of the development of aviation in 1870. He was then only twenty years old. The next year, after he had experimented upon a series of model helicopters powered by twisted rubber bands, Pénaud produced a flying model airplane he called a planophore. The major impact of this device, which flew successfully, was to demonstrate Cayley's principle of inherent stability. This was achieved in the planophore by the raised wingtips (dihedral) and the tail planes. An interesting development, too, is the fact that the propeller was placed at the rear of the planophore's fuselage (nothing more than a simple stick). The model was capable of flights of more than 130 feet. Pénaud seems to have discovered the principle of inherent stability independently, for he did not begin reading Cayley's works until after he had developed the planophore.

Five years later, in 1876, when he was twenty-six, Pénaud patented a design he had been working on since 1873—a man-carrying aircraft. This was to have been a twin-engined monoplane amphibian that incorporated a number of remarkable advanced features. One of these was a glass-enclosed cockpit for the pilot, and another was a single control stick (the first joy stick, which controlled the rudder when moved from side to side and the elevators when moved to and fro). The landing gear retracted into the fuselage, which then, theoretically, enabled the craft to land on water. With a crew of two, Pénaud expected that the craft could cruise at about sixty miles an hour. But it was never to be. First, there was not yet an engine (or rather engines, in the case of Pénaud's design) that could power such a machine; second, Pénaud did not have the money to build and test his aircraft. An early aviation historian wrote that he "was criticized, decried, misrepresented, and all sorts of obstacles arose to prevent the testing of his project. He lost courage and hope, his health gave way, and he died in October 1880." Not mentioned is that Pénaud had committed suicide; he was not yet thirty years old. Poor health and his inability to convince others of the value of his aviation experiments had broken him. He was, however, one of the great pioneers of aviation.

In 1890 a Frenchman, Clement Ader, became the first man in history to be lifted off the ground in a powered aircraft of his own design. If this is true—and it is—why isn't Ader credited with the invention of the first successful airplane? Because Ader's flight was a flight to nowhere. His craft, the batwinged *Eole* with Ader seated inside, took off at Armainvilliers on October 9, 1890, and flew a

Alphonse Penaud and his remarkable little "planophore" of 1871. (Musée de l'Air, Paris)

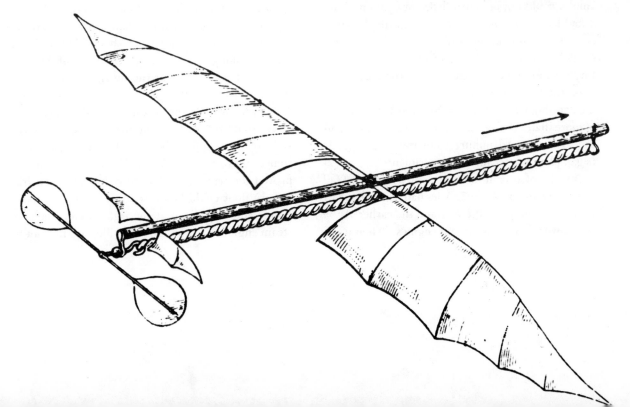

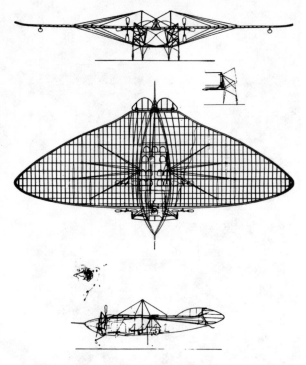

Penaud's design for a passenger-carrying aircraft, 1876. (Musée de l'Air, Paris)

distance of 164 feet before coming down again to wreck the aircraft. Ader, an electrical engineer and inventor (he invented the telephone in France), was not an instinctive airman. His invention, for example, could not be controlled, nor could it—once it had left the ground—remain in the air. Its steam engine was too heavy and simply not powerful enough. Ader also, disregarding the work of the English and French pioneers, chose to base his craft upon the bat. His use of a propeller was wise, but the flapping wing was a step backward. Still a flight of more than 150 feet was quite an achievement and, as Ader emerged unhurt from the wreckage, he began planning for further experiments.

A series of aircraft followed with a history of failure. By October 12, 1897, Ader had constructed his *Avion III*, similar to the *Eole* and the earlier *Avions* but powered with two steam engines. When it was tested, the *Avion III* managed to make only a few tentative hops (although later Ader claimed that the *Avion* had actually flown). Ader's experiments, though interesting, led to a dead end. He had no interest in controlling his craft—an important necessity if it were to be a practical aircraft—nor did he attempt to improve the engines of the period. Ader, with government backing denied him, simply gave up the idea of flying after the failure of *Avion III*. In England, at about the same time Ader was busy in France, a wealthy American expatriate inventor, Hiram Maxim, already famed for his machine gun, began experimenting with the idea of powered flight. Like Ader, he was primarily interested merely in getting a flying machine off the ground—sustained flight, control, were the least of his concerns. Hedeveloped an ingenious steam engine of 350 horsepower, which he hoped would power his multiplane. The engine was constructed so that it could reuse the cooling water that condensed in the steel tubing. Maxim's test rig for this power plant was an elephantine contraption with a wingspan of 110 feet. To achieve stability Maxim had the outer panels of the wing dihedraled. The engine turned two propellers of more than seventeen feet in length. In 1894, after spending four years and thousands of dollars, Maxim was ready to test his invention. The multiplane was placed upon a rail (the craft had four small wheels) and, just to keep it from lifting off the ground too high, outriggers on the bottom wing were attached to two wooden guide rails. Three attempts were made during the year to get the multiplane airborne, and the last was successful, after a fashion. The engines built up enough power to raise the craft off the rails a few inches and to tear the outriggers loose, but broke up some of the guide rail, which prompted Maxim to turn off the steam. He had had enough of aviation (in later years he made rather excessive claims). Although he believed he had contributed something to the progress of flight, he had merely proved the truth of Wilbur Wright's later remark: A barn door could be made to fly with the proper power and if inclined at the right angle. Maxim's steam engine was a kind of contribution, but not to

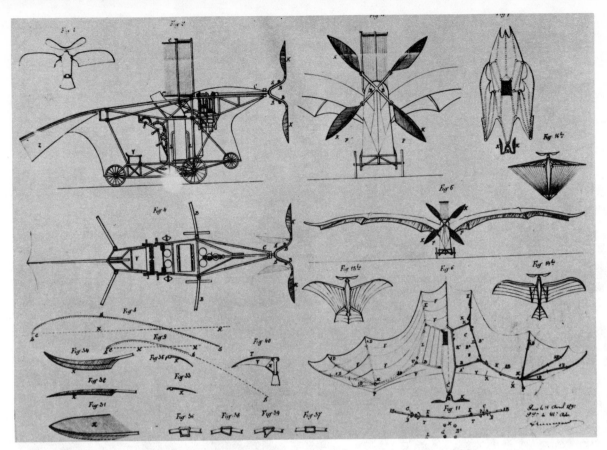

Ader's design drawings for and a model of the *Eole*,
which actually succeeded in becoming airborne—for a
little over 160 feet—in October 1890. It crashed in
falling back to earth. Seven years later he created *Avion
III*, which Ader claimed did fly, but in fact did not.
(Musée de l'Air, Paris)

American-English inventor Hiram Maxim
demonstrating the lightness of the aircraft engine he had
devised to power his multiplane, 1894. (National Air and
Space Museum, Smithsonian Institution)

Maxim's multiplane poised for flight; a third attempt
raised the aircraft off the ground a little but could hardly
be said to have flown. (National Air and Space Museum,
Smithsonian Institution)

flying. Except for a brief return with an unsuccessful biplane in 1910, Maxim abandoned aviation.

Power and control: These were the decisive requisites to be achieved before man would ever fly. These were the concern of the first true airman in history, the most important figure in the history of aviation in the final years of the nineteenth century, Otto Lilienthal (1848–96). An engineer, Lil-

Otto Lilienthal, the great German airman and one of the first true pilots in history—that is, a man who controlled his craft and understood the art of flight. (U. S. Air Force)

Lilienthal and his hang glider, designed in 1891. (National Air and Space Museum, Smithsonian Institution)

ienthal had been a flight enthusiast from about the age of thirteen, when he began reading the science fiction of the period devoted to fantasies of flight. His first, boyish experiments were made with ornithopters—flapping-wing devices that had misled so many early flight-fanciers. Lilienthal, however, was not led astray, although his own work was inspired by the study of bird flight. This work was a brilliant combination of theory and practice.

Like the Englishman Cayley, but unlike Da Vinci, Lilienthal realized that the mere flapping of a bird's wings was not its means of "thrust"; it was, rather, the propellerlike action of its so-called primary feathers. He also studied the structure of bird wings and propounded valuable ideas in regard to wing area and lift—that is, how large a wing surface would be required to sustain an object of certain weight—as it might apply to human flight. Wings for man would not be precisely like wings for birds; but man's wings could be fashioned if the function of birds' wings were understood. The idea was not to reproduce the wing of a bird, but to adapt its function to use by man. Lilienthal put down his ideas in 1889 in a book entitled *Der Vogelflug als Grundlage der Fliegekunst* (The Flight of Birds as a Basis of Aviation). Two years later Lilienthal had built his first glider and began thrusting himself into the air off hills near Berlin. The Lilienthal glider, a graceful object of willow covered with waxed cotton, with a wingspan of about twenty feet, was the first successful glider in history.

Having successfully demonstrated his theories, Lilienthal was encouraged to carry on with further studies of flight. To him, mere gliding was not an end, but a beginning. Methodically, he moved from one step of development to the next. He had proved that cambered (curved) wing cross sections

produced lift, he had proved that imitating birds by flapping devices was fruitless, and he wished to prove that, with control, the glider could be made to fly successfully "with stability and safety . . . Actual trial alone can decide this question, as we must let the air and wind have their say in the matter."

To conduct his trials, Lilienthal had a fifty-foot-high hill raised at Gross Lichterfelde, near Berlin. Wearing his glider, which weighed about forty pounds, strapped to his shoulders, Lilienthal launched himself by running down the incline of the hill. With sufficient acceleration, the glider lifted into the air, and Lilienthal soared into the countryside, sometimes making flights of several hundred feet. Although the control of his machine was paramount to him, Lilienthal depended upon the movements of his body to stabilize the glider in flight. The glider's tail surfaces were fixed in the early glider and played no part in actual control of the machine.

In 1895 Lilienthal began experimenting with a biplane glider, which proved to be an excellent flier. In a fairly strong wind these machines frequently lifted off the top of Lilienthal's launching mound with only the slightest run on his part. His flights, which by 1896 numbered more than two thousand, ranged in distance from three hundred to more than seven hundred feet and at times reached an altitude higher than that of the hill from

Lilienthal testing a biplane glider from the special launching hill he had made for him near Berlin. (National Air and Space Museum, Smithsonian Institution)

Lilienthal coming in for a two-point landing after a successful flight, 1895. A year later Lilienthal was killed when a new glider dived in from an altitude of fifty feet. (National Air and Space Museum, Smithsonian Institution)

which Lilienthal had taken off. His major objective was eventually to achieve powered flight, and by 1896 he had devised a curious monoplane glider whose wingtips flapped by means of a mechanism driven by a carbonic-acid gas motor. He hoped to lengthen his flights with this device and planned to test it during the summer of 1896 in the Rhinow Hills near Stollen. He had also devised a new control device, a movable elevator, which he hoped would make it possible to control the up-and-down movement of the glider easier than with the kicking of his legs. The controls were attached to Lilienthal's head: Lowering his head would raise the elevator, causing the glider to go upward. Moving his head backward would have the opposite effect.

It was while testing this control device in a monoplane glider that something went wrong and Lilienthal fell from a height of fifty feet. The following day, August 10, 1896, Lilienthal died of the injuries suffered in the fall.

During the five years of his experimentation with gliders Lilienthal had been heard to say, *"Opfer müssen gebracht werden"* (Sacrifices must be made). His last flight had proved that. The many photographs made during Lilienthal's experiments had been widely distributed and had fired the imagination of the air-minded all over the world. His death, rather than discouraging his disciples, seems to have only spurred them on. Lilienthal's work—and his final sacrifive—had indeed laid the groundwork for the final conquest of the air.

One of Lilienthal's outstanding disciples was a Scot, Percy Sinclair Pilcher. Inspired by his own early interest in flying and further by reading about Lilienthal and seeing the photographs of Lilienthal in flight, Pilcher began experiments in Glasgow. He was then about twenty-nine years old, having already served in the British Navy and retired to study engineering. During the period of his work with flight, Pilcher also lectured at Glasgow University, as he was qualified in naval architecture and marine engineering. Like his mentor's, Pilcher's eye was upon the future. "The object of experimenting with soaring machines is to enable one to have practice in starting and alighting and controlling a machine in the air," he once told a lecture audience in Dublin in 1897. Gliders, he continued, "are excellent schooling machines, and that is all they are meant to be, until power, in the shape of an engine working a screw propeller, or an engine working wings to drive a machine forward, is added; then one who is used to sailing down a hill with a simple soaring machine will be able to fly with comparative safety." Between June 1895, and early 1896 Pilcher built four gliders, the most successful being the last, which he named the *Hawk*. It was an advanced design, complete with a tiny-wheeled landing gear, and it could be launched with a towline. In the summer of 1897 Pilcher made a flight of nearly three hundred yards in the *Hawk*, as well as several other highly successful

Percy Pilcher, a disciple of Lilienthal, flew his glider the *Hawk* in 1896. A Scot, Pilcher predicted the day of controlled, powered flight. He died in 1899 when the *Hawk* suffered structural failure and crashed. (National Air and Space Museum, Smithsonian Institution)

flights. He had, however, further plans for the *Hawk* type of design. He planned to install a small oil engine with a propeller and make powered flights. He had even helped to form an engineering company that would built this special engine. Pilcher, who was certainly on the brink of powered, controlled flight, did not live to achieve his goal. While demonstrating a triplane glider and the *Hawk* (still without engine), Pilcher crashed in the *Hawk* while only thirty feet off the ground. The *Hawk* had flipped over in the air when one of its rudder stays snapped and fell straight down. Pilcher died of his injuries without ever regaining consciousness three days after the accident on October 2, 1899; he was only thirty-three. Had he lived, it is possible that Pilcher might have been the first man to make a powered airplane.

Lilienthal's first major American follower was a great scientific figure, Octave Chanute. He was a man of sixty, and already a well-known civil engineer when he had begun collecting material on flight. The success of Lilienthal encouraged Chanute, in turn, to encourage others to continue with research into the science. He accomplished this in two ways: Not only did he gather all possible published material on aviation, but also he very unselfishly shared the information with all who expressed an interest. In addition, he published some of his own views on the subject in a book entitled *Progress in Flying Machines* (1894). About two years later he put his preachments into practice when he designed and built several gliders under the influence of Lilienthal's exploits. His initial glider greatly resembled Lilienthal's but proved to be not very successful.

In 1896 Chanute produced his finest machine in the so-called two-surface (that is, a biplane) hang glider, which was tested on the south shore of Lake Michigan, near Chicago. Then sixty-four, Chanute left the actual flying to his assistants, among them Augustus M. Herring. Chanute's main concern was to design a machine with inherent stability which did not need to depend upon Lilienthal's "body control." Although he did not succeed completely in achieving this, Chanute contributed much to the development of aviation in the United

Octave Chanute, patron of aviation. (National Archives)

States, and, later, in a Europe that had become dormant as far as aeronautics was concerned. Chanute's gliders were constructed to be strong (the inventor used his knowledge of bridge construction in bracing the wings) and to compensate automatically for sudden shifts of air pressure, winds, etc. As Chanute himself stated, ". . . a flying machine to be successful must be at all times under intelligent control . . ." He believed that this phase must be thoroughly explored and understood before "the further complications incident to a motor" should be introduced. In a technical sense, then, Chanute did not advance much beyond Lilienthal, and yet Chanute's influence was impressively significant.

It may be that as a propagandizer for aviation and a disseminator of information about aeronautics, rather than for his glider design, that Octave Chanute will be an immortal in the history of flight. It was about 1900 that he began encouraging two young bicycle manufacturers of Dayton,

Ohio, who had become interested in aviation. They were Wilbur and Orville Wright, who had become seriously interested in aviation after reading about Lilienthal's flights in Germany. When the great pioneer was killed, the Wrights were determined to carry his work forward. To learn all that was then available on the subject, Wilbur Wright wrote to the Smithsonian Institution in Washington requesting a reading list. Among the books suggested was Chanute's *Progress in Flying Machines*. Having read the book, Wilbur Wright was prompted to write to its author, thus beginning a long and fruitful friendship. The line of development was carried from Lilienthal through Chanute to the Wright brothers. It is fitting that

the Wrights' first flight experiences should have been made in a design by Chanute. In 1902 the Chicagoan had produced a triplane glider which, though ultimately not as successful as his biplane design, did fly.

Like Chanute, the Wrights were concerned with control, with the mastery of the machine in the air. Like Lilienthal, they were true airmen; although not scientists in the educated sense, they were outstanding intuitive aeronautical engineers—and they were willing to test their theories in actual flight. "If you are looking for perfect safety," Wilbur Wright once said, "you will do well to sit on a fence and watch the birds; but if you really wish to learn, you must mount a machine and become acquainted with its tricks by actual trial."

They rejected Lilienthal's hang glider and "body control" and Chanute's triplane—and had already devised a system of control called "wing warping." This method had been suggested to them by the flight of a soaring buzzard that they observed. When a gust of wind rocked it from side to side, it

Glider designed by an American follower of Lilienthal, Octave Chanute. Tests were made on the sand dunes near Lake Michigan; the pilot: Augustus M. Herring, ca. 1896. (National Air and Space Museum, Smithsonian Institution)

Chanute triplane glider of 1902; the pilot was another Lilienthal disciple, Wilbur Wright. Chanute's greatest contribution to aviation may well have been his encouragement of the Wright brothers. (National Air and Space Museum, Smithsonian Institution)

righted itself by raising the wingtip of the lowered wing (thus giving it more lift) and attaining stable flight again. Testing their idea on tethered kitelike gliders, the Wrights were convinced that their method of control would work—not perfectly, but well enough to encourage their studies. They learned that much of Lilienthal's calculations had been wrong and were determined to rely on their own. The first working fruitful result of their investigations and experiments was their third glider (and their second capable of carrying a man), which they tested on the sands of the Kill Devil Hills (near Kitty Hawk) during September and October 1902.

Glider No. 3, with a wingspan of thirty-two feet, was the prototype of all succeeding Wright aircraft insofar as configuration was concerned. It was a biplane with a forward elevator and a double fixed rudder (when this proved unsatisfactory the aircraft was modified with the addition of a movable single rudder). The rudder was wired into the wing-warping control system. The pilot lay across the center of the lower wing; around his hips was fastened a cradle, which he twisted to right or left to warp the wings, and thus to control the up-and-down movement of the wings. The glider was launched by hand.

The Wrights did not seek out the deserted hills of Kitty Hawk because they were secretive (as has frequently been hinted), but because of the steadiness of the prevailing winds in the area and the comparative softness of the sand for landings. As Wilbur had observed to their encouraging friend Chanute, although it appeared to be dangerous to glide over and land upon the sand, they had found it to be "perfectly safe and comfortable except for the flying sand . . . the machine was not once injured although we sometimes landed at a rate of very nearly thirty miles per hour . . ." and as for himself and Orville, they "did not receive a single bruise . . ."

The pilot operated the forward elevator with his hands by pushing or pulling upon the bent rods.

The Wright brothers' conception of a glider—this is their Glider No. 3 of 1902. Orville Wright is the pilot about to be launched by brother Wilbur and a friend. (U. S. Air Force)

This would raise or lower the flight path of the glider. By moving his hips from side to side, he could control the wing-warping cradle, which would actuate the bending action of the wingtips. Warping a tip down would cause that wing to be raised by the pressure of air striking the tip and pushing it upward.

On October 23, 1902, Orville wrote to their sister Katherine: "The past five days have been most satisfactory for gliding that we have had. In two days we made over 250 glides. We have gained considerable proficiency in the handling of the machine." Glider No. 3 had proved their instincts as well as their aerodynamics correct. As Orville summed up the weeks of experiment and experience: "The flights of 1902 demonstrated the efficiency of our system of control for both longitudinal and lateral stability. They also demonstrated "that our tables of air pressure which we had made in our wind tunnel would enable us to calculate in advance the performance of the machine." In short, they could get into the air, and they could control their flights. They were but a short step away from the goal of airmen everywhere: the invention of a true "flying machine," capable of leaving the ground under its own power and capable of remaining in flight under human control. In reply to a letter from Chanute (in which the latter suggested that the brothers consider taking out patents upon their "improvements"), Wilbur gave a hint of the next step in their plans. "It is our intention," he wrote, "next year to build a machine much larger and twice as heavy as our present machine. With it we will work out problems relating to starting and handling heavy weight machines, and if we find it under satisfactory control in flight, we will proceed to mount a motor."

Meanwhile, in Europe, aviation, so far as the practical powered aircraft was concerned, had all but stagnated since the death of Lilienthal. His one French disciple, Captain Ferdinand Ferber, had not succeeded in improving upon the German pioneer's ideas. European attention was focused upon the airship rather than upon the airplane, thanks primarily to the work of a wealthy Brazilian living in Paris, Alberto Santos-Dumont. He was the first man to mount small engines in his airships, thus achieving a certain degree of controlled, sustained flight. Santos-Dumont built, between 1898 and 1905, a series of fourteen semirigid airships of assorted sizes and shapes. His most characteristic design was an elongated, cylindrical dirigible (that is, capable of directional control in flight). A triangular rudder in the forward section of the airship controlled the directional movement of the ship, and ballast (as in a balloon) was used to control the ship longitudinally. The engine was mounted about midway in the keel; the two-bladed propeller was mounted just below the rudder.

The flights of Santos-Dumont over Paris thrilled

The Wrights testing Glider No. 3 at Kitty Hawk, North Carolina, 1902, with Wilbur as pilot. (U. S. Air Force)

Santos-Dumont flies over the Bois de Boulogne, Paris, in his Airship No. 5, 1901. (National Air and Space Museum, Smithsonian Institution)

the crowds and stirred up enthusiasm for aviation, the airship, and even revived interest in the balloon in sporting circles. Although Santos-Dumont was the first man to produce a reasonably practical control mechanism for an airship, it did not work absolutely and he suffered a few accidents, none of them serious, among the rooftops and trees of Paris. Airship No. 5 was completely destroyed when it crashed into the roof of the Trocadero Hotel. Though the hydrogen in the gas bag exploded and the wreckage was draped and suspended some forty feet in the air, Santos-Dumont coolly manipulated the brace-wiring until he dropped safely to the roof of the hotel.

Santos-Dumont's most famous airship was No. 6, built immediately after the destruction of No. 5. One hundred and ten feet long, No. 6, with its twenty-horsepower engine, could sputter along at a speed of fifteen miles an hour. Although he was wealthy and had no need of prize money, Santos-Dumont wished to win the Deutsch Prize. This was to go to the first man who covered the distance from St. Cloud to Paris, around the Eiffel Tower,

and a return to St. Cloud—a distance of about nine miles—within thirty minutes. After two unsuccessful attempts, Santos-Dumont electrified Paris on October 19, 1901, when he made the round trip, despite engine trouble and wayward winds, in twenty-nine minutes, thirty-one seconds. The prize money—one hundred thousand francs—Santos-Dumont characteristically shared with the workmen who had built the airship. He presented most of the prize money to the poor of Paris—seventy-five thousand francs. With the winning of the Deutsch Prize, Santos-Dumont became the most celebrated airman in the world. Practically no one heard of the Wright brothers in the sand dunes of Kitty Hawk.

Santos-Dumont was not alone in the development of the dirigible. In Germany an ex-cavalry general, Count Ferdinand von Zeppelin, had also begun experimenting with rigid airships—that is, a dirigible shaped by a metal framework rather than by, as were Santo-Dumont's, the shape of the gas envelope itself. And in France itself, the Lebaudy brothers—Paul and Pierre—introduced their air-

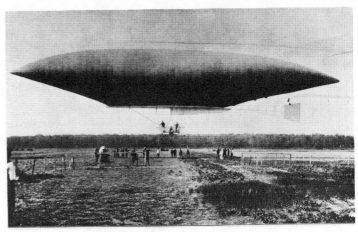

An early successful dirigible, the Labaudy airship, 1902, designed by Henri Juillot. (National Air and Space Museum, Smithsonian Institution)

ship in November 1902 (about the same time the Wrights were testing their Glider No. 3 in North Carolina).

The *Lebaudy*, named for its sponsors rather than for Henri Juillot, the designer, was a decided advance over Santos-Dumont's designs. It was the first truly practical dirigible. Nearly two hundred feet long and driven by a thirty-five horsepower Daimler engine, the *Lebaudy* attained a speed of nearly thirty miles an hour. By 1903 the airship proved itself and had actually flown, under control, a distance of thirty-eight miles in the first cross-country flight by a powered aircraft. Later, Labaudy-built airships carried passengers, even photographers, and made night flights. The epochal cross-country flight was made on November 12, 1903, and could be said to have inaugurated the era of the modern airship. At that same moment, un-

Santos-Dumont's Airship No. 6, with which he won the Deutsch Prize in October 1901. The Eiffel Tower was the Paris pylon of the nine-mile flight. (U. S. Air Force)

Another French-designed dirigible, the *Clement-Bayard* V. (U. S. Air Force)

known and unsung, Wilbur and Orville Wright had returned to Kitty Hawk with a new aircraft, which they called the *Flyer*. It was destined to change the course of the history of aviation. Ironically, just as the Lebaudy airships and the later, somewhat more sophisticated, Clement-Bayard series had evolved to open up a new epoch in flight, the Wrights' *Flyer* would emerge to cut that epoch short—at least for a while. The advent of the "flying machine" would place development of the airship in jeopardy, although many dreamers clung to the concept for years.

One such dreamer was the American journalist-designer Walter Wellman who, even after the Wright brothers had flown at Kitty Hawk, visualized the airship as a superior means of transportation. It was the news of the success of the Lebaudy dirigible that impressed him with the airship's potential: Wellman's wish was to fly over the North Pole. In 1907, he made a trip to Paris, where he ordered a gas bag for the polar flight and eventually made several unsuccessful attempts in 1907 and 1909. Undaunted, Wellman had an even grander dream. The original airship was redesigned by his mechanic, Melvin Vaniman—an American he had met during his trip to France. Vaniman, a musician, opera singer, and photographer, appears to have had little training in engineering or aerodynamics. He had apparently worked well during the polar failures, and Wellman respected him enough to permit him to alter the configuration of the airship.

Named the *America*, the airship was nearly 230 feet long, was powered by two eighty-horsepower engines (turning four giant propellers), and carrying beneath airship's control car a lifeboat, provisioned and equipped with wireless—just in case. Beneath the lifeboat, in turn, dangled what Wellman called an "equilibrator," a device made up of three hundred feet of steel tubing, which served a dual purpose: It carried fuel and it was supposed to keep the *America* from gaining too much altitude. The equilibrator was designed to drag along the surface of the water, its lower tip buoyed up by wooden blocks. Should a change in temperature

Walter Wellman, newspaperman-balloonist and Melvin Vaniman, jack-of-all-trades but no aeronautical engineer. The two men headed a crew that hoped to cross the Atlantic by air. (National Air and Space Museum, Smithsonian Institution)

The *America*, the Wellman-Vaniman airship, in trouble off the bow of rescue ship *Trent*, 1910. Wake of equilibrator can be seen in water below lifeboat. (Library of Congress)

cause the airship to rise, the equilibrator would rise, lifting the wooden blocks out of the water. No longer floating, the weight of the blocks would pull the *America* down to a proper altitude. Or so the theory went. Wellman managed to get the backing of the New York *Times* and the London *Daily Telegraph* for no less than an Atlantic crossing.

There was much hoopla and delay—no fault of Wellman's, though the rivals of the *Times* and the *Daily Telegraph* suggested the whole idea was a promotional stunt for the sponsors. Weather, in fact, was the cause of the delay. Scheduled for mid-September, the flight was launched on October 15, 1910. Three days later, it was over. The weather over the Atlantic was typically miserable for that time of the year and the equilibrator was, in a word, a drag indeed. "Dragging behind us," one of the crew noted in the log, "it tries to pull our nose in the

The crew of the *America* await transfer from erratic *America*, ending Wellman's Atlantic crossing attempt, October 1910. (Library of Congress)

water. It drives us forward on our nose till the waves splash over the lifeboat." Lashed by the wind, the *America* bounced over the Atlantic, damaging the lifeboat. A sudden break in the clouds brought out the sun, which heated up the gas and lifted the *America*, crew of five, and equilibrator up to a height of three thousand feet. Wellman released some gas to bring the airship down and then, when the sun was hidden and the gas cooled, the *America* dropped to rest practically on the surface of the Atlantic. Much equipment was frantically jettisoned and the *America* remained airborne and as well as almost afloat.

Wellman was ready to give up, and ordered the crew into the lifeboat—although the still rough seas and the whipping equilibrator made the move rather hazardous. The equilibrator also injured two crewmen and holed the lifeboat. With engines off (initially to save fuel, but eventually because they were useless), the *America* drifted aimlessly only a few feet above the Atlantic. In this sorry state it was spotted by the lookout of a ship, H.M.S. *Trent*. After a chase the hapless aeronauts (plus their mascot, a kitten) were rescued from the drifting *America*, which, relieved of its burden, disappeared over the horizon.

By the afternoon of October 19, Wellman and crew were safely ashore in New York and, despite their failure, were welcomed as heroes. The failure however cured Wellman's flying fever and he returned to the lesser exertions of writing. Vaniman, on the other hand, did not lose his enthusiasm; he continued to fly and eventually became captain of his own airship, the *Akron*. Two years after the failure of the *America's* flight, Vaniman and four others died when the *Akron* exploded shortly after leaving Atlantic City.

Despite their failures Wellman and Vaniman proved several things with the *America:* an airship was capable of staying aloft for an extended period of time—the flight had broken the world's record for continuous powered flight at the time. They kept the dream of crossing the Atlantic by air alive. There was one major negative contribution: no one needed an equilibrator.

It remained for the Wright brothers to show the way, without fanfare, without an ambitious grand design, but merely with hard, and hard-headed, methodical work.

3 EARLY BIRDS

Writing in the 1890s, American humorist Bill Nye expressed popular attitudes toward aviation in an essay entitled "Flying Machines," which purported to be a history of flying. The irrepressible Nye was a decade ahead of his time, for his "history" expressed the mood and views of the era in which the Wright brothers introduced their *Flyer*.

"A Frenchman," Nye wrote, "invented a flying machine, or dofunny, as we scientists would term it in 1600 and something, whereby he could sail down from the woodshed and not break his neck. He could not rise from the ground like a lark and trill a few notes as he skimmed through the sky, but he could fall off an ordinary hay stack like a setting hen with the aid of his wings . . .

"In England," he continued, "during the present century, several inventors produced flying machines, but in an evil hour agreed to rise on them themselves and so they died from their injuries. Some came down on top of the machines, while others preceded their inventions by a few feet, but the result was the same. The invention of flying machines has always been handicapped, as it were, by this fact . . ."

He even introduced "technical" terms, always of interest but invariably mystifying, to the layman. "In 1853," Nye pointed out, "Mr. J. H. Johnson patented a balloon and parachute dingus which worked on the principle of a duck's foot in the mud. I use scientific terms because I am unable to express myself in the common language of the vulgar herd . . ."

As for the workable flying machine, Nye concluded that "Such an invention would be hailed with much joy, and the sale would be enormous. Now, however, the matter is still in its infancy. The mechanical birds invented for the purpose of skimming through the ether blue, have not skum. The machines were built with high hopes and a throbbing heart, but the aforesaid ether remains unskum as we go to press. The Milky Way is in the same condition, awaiting the arrival of the fearless skimmer.

"Will men ever be permitted to pierce the utmost details of the sky and ramble around among the stars with a gum overcoat on? Sometimes I trow he will, and then again I ween not."

As if to validate Nye's views, as well as those of the scoffers who agreed with him, certain experiments were made with a flying machine in October 1903, which, despite the high-mindedness of the machine's inventor, might have had an unfortunate effect upon aviation's future in the United States. In fact, it did, at least on a personal level. Samuel Pierpont Langley (1834–1906), although largely self-taught in the sciences, had been a professor of physics and astronomy at what is now the University of Pittsburgh before he was appointed secretary of the Smithsonian Institution in 1887. By the time of his appointment, which lasted until his death in 1906, Langley had begun experimenting with rubber-band-driven model airplanes similar to those of Pénaud. When one of Stringfellow's steam

Samuel P. Langley, who built a successful flying model airplane, but not a man-carrying full-sized aircraft, as later claimed. He did, however, contribute to the evolving science of aeronautics. (U. S. Air Force)

Langley's steam-powered model in flight, 1896. (U. S. Air Force/National Archives)

engines was presented to the Smithsonian, it served as a further spur to Langley's experiments. He began delving into aerodynamics to determine those laws that applied to sustaining inclined planes in the air and to thrust—as supplied by an engine-driven propeller. By 1891 Langley began building steam-driven model airplanes, and within five years he had produced one capable of flights of nearly a mile at a speed of thirty miles an hour. Langley's was the most successful flying model built up to its time. He called his constructions aerodromes, and longed to produce a full-sized, man-carrying machine.

Although Langley had been criticized for playing with his flying toys, with the outbreak of the Spanish-American War in 1898, their military possibilities—for aerial observation—were brought to the attention of the United States Government. Langley was then given $50,000 with which to build an aerodrome that could carry a pilot: This would mean an aircraft with a wingspan of forty-eight feet, five inches and a fuselage length of fifty-two feet, five inches. With pilot, it would weigh 750 pounds. A quarter-sized exact scale model was

built and, powered by a gasoline engine, actually flew on June 18, 1901. But making the full-sized *Aerodrome* proved more difficult for the classic reason: There was no suitable engine available. This problem was solved when Langley's assistant, Charles M. Manly, redesigned an engine originally constructed for Langley by Stephen M. Balzer. The Manly-Balzer engine was a remarkable advance in 1903. It was the first "radial" engine—its five cylinders were arranged, starlike, around the crankshaft—and could produce a thrust of little more than fifty horsepower with a weight of less than four pounds per horsepower. Gasoline was used as fuel; it marked the end of the heavy steam-driven aircraft engine even if, as it proved, it was not yet the ultimate solution to the problem. Even so, Langley believed that he was ready for the test flight, with Manly as pilot. As with the earlier models, the full-sized *Aerodrome* was designed to be launched from a catapult mounted atop a house-boat in the Potomac River. The date set was October 7, 1903.

On the first test something went wrong with the launching mechanism, and Manly suffered a short,

Langley Aerodrome on its launching site, Potomac
River, 1903. (U. S. Air Force)

mortifying, dampening flight. As one reporter
phrased it at the time, the *Aerodrome* "simply slid
into the water like a handful of mortar." Luckily
Manly was uninjured, a miracle considering the
proximity of two propellers (each turning nearly a
thousand revolutions a minute) to his cockpit. Nor
was the *Aerodrome* beyond repair. Both pilot and
machine were retrieved from the Potomac, and
with opprobrious laughter—particularly from the
press—ringing in his ears, Langley undauntedly
prepared for another flight. This occurred about
two months later, on December 8, with Manly
again as test pilot and the houseboat in mid-Poto-
mac. A photographer of the Washington (D.C.)
Evening Star captured the moment of Langley's
greatest humiliation when on that day the *Aerodrome*, suffering structural damage when the tail
crumpled, once again fell into the Potomac. Nye-
like, a Boston writer commented: "Perhaps if Professor Langley had only thought to launch his airship bottom up, it would have gone into the air instead of down into the water." With its tail
damaged, the plane turned onto its back and
splashed into the Potomac, again taking pilot with

The Aerodrome at launching, December 8, 1903, as it is
about to fall into the Potomac with pilot Manley going
down for the second time (he had also been dunked in
October). This concluded Langley's experiments with
the flying machine. (National Air and Space Museum,
Smithsonian Institution)

it and again the miracle: Manly escaped injury.

Even so, it was the end of Langley's experiments with flight. The government, no longer concerned with war, had lost interest, and there were criticisms in the press and in public of the waste of public funds in the "useless quest" of human flight. Disappointed, Langley gave up any further experimentation and died three years later. He had missed an opportunity, but, in fact, like others before him—Chanute, Ader, Maxim—he had no real grasp of the concept of flight. He had little idea of the need for control of aircraft. He did not truly understand the structure of aircraft, and, finally, for all its advanced features, the engine he had used was underpowered. Also, depending upon water to provide a soft landing area for his *Aerodrome* (since the craft was not equipped with wheels or landing skids) foredoomed it to a dunking even if it had flown. Langley, a great man in many ways, was one of aviation history's might-have-beens.

There was a tawdry sequel to the story of Langley's *Aerodrome*. Langley himself withdrew from aviation, and the plane itself was again salvaged and placed in the Smithsonian. Langley's successor, Dr. Charles D. Walcott, anxious to bring glory to the Smithsonian and to his predecessor, began a curious campaign sometime around 1910. Although this incident is out of place chronologically, it belongs here as a footnote to Langley's experiments rather than in the mainstream of aviation's history.

The Wright brothers, as is well known, succeeded where Langley had failed, only nine days after the *Aerodrome* had dipped into the Potomac for the second time, Langley and the Wrights had enjoyed cordial relations during his lifetime—and one of their major accomplishments was to prove that Langley's belief in human flight had not been the dream of a crackpot. He was right, and the Wrights had proved it. But for some reason, a few years later, Dr. Walcott wished to discredit the Wrights and went about it in a curiously unscientific manner. He gave permission to Glenn Curtiss, the Wrights' chief rival who had lost a patent-infringement lawsuit to them, to "test" the old 1903 *Aerodrome*.

Since that time a good deal of knowledge about the science of flight—flight control (the subject of the Wright-Curtiss lawsuit) and engine construction (a good deal of it because of the work of the Wright brothers)—had accumulated. Curtiss made a number of changes in the *Aerodrome*. He added pontoons, he changed the position of the cockpit, he installed a single propeller in the front of the fuselage, and he made other extensive modifications. Consequently, during May and June 1914, Curtiss actually flew the modified *Aerodrome* off the waters of Lake Keuka, near Hammondsport, New York, in five-second hops. As far as he was concerned, Curtiss was satisfied that Langley had built a flyable flying machine *before* the Wright brothers had flown their plane. The point was obvious: He

Glenn Curtiss airborne in his redesigned version of the Langley Aerodrome, which was successfully flown in 1914 (when it was also possible to mount a more powerful engine in the plane), in an attempt to discredit the Wright brothers. (U. S. Air Force)

wished to discredit the Wrights' claim and perhaps have the decision in the lawsuit reversed. And then he had gratuitous backing from Dr. Walcott and the Smithsonian. In the Institution's annual report of 1914 it was stated that the *Aerodrome* had "demonstrated . . . with its original structure and power [neither true], it is capable of flying with a pilot and several hundred pounds of useful load [also false]. It is the first aeroplane in the history of the world of which this can be truthfully said [another lie]."

The next year the report contained further references to the *Aerodrome*, concluding with another dig at the Wrights: "The tests thus far made have shown that former Secretary Langley had succeeded in building the first aeroplane capable of sustained flight with a man." Such distortions could not stand up under any kind of study, for the differences between Langley's 1903 original and Curtiss' 1914 modification were strikingly obvious. But Walcott stood by his false guns. He succeeded only in confusing the historical picture for a time and alienating the Wrights and the Smithsonian. The falsifications were ultimately cleared up by Walcott's successor, Dr. Charles G. Abbot—in 1942. By then the historic aircraft was no longer in the United States. Disappointed and hurt by their treatment by Walcott and the Smithsonian, the Wrights had presented the plane to the Science Museum in London. That was in February 1928, after Orville Wright gave up on the obdurate Walcott. The Wright plane was returned to the United States in 1948, in time for the forty-fifth anniversary of the Wrights original flight—by which time, too, both brothers were dead.

Despite the inexplicable efforts of Dr. Walcott, credit for the invention of the first successful aircraft in history undeniably belongs to the Wright brothers. They were the sons of a minister but were mechanically rather than spiritually inclined. Wilbur (1867–1912) and Orville (1871–1948) had

Orville (left) and Wilbur Wright, American bicycle mechanics, who gave man wings. (U. S. Signal Corps/National Archives)

The birthplace of the first successful flying machine, Dayton, Ohio, 1903. (U. S. Air Force)

shared a longtime interest in flight when, about 1899, they began experimenting with aviation. They were then quite successful in the manufacturing of bicycles. Their shop in Dayton, Ohio, is to aviation what the log cabin once was to the American presidency. In this small, humble building the Wrights dreamed of flight, tested their ideas and calculations, and finally designed their gliders and Flyers.

Wilbur Wright, four years older than Orville, took the lead in their experiments. Wilbur wrote to Chanute and to the Smithsonian for advice on aviation literature, and generally led the way. In time, the brothers worked so closely, they welded into a team so perfectly matched, that to divide their contributions would be pointless. They were

methodical, careful, scientific (although not trained scientists), and persevering. They were courageous and had complete confidence in their work (in which they discovered that certain earlier pioneers—Lilienthal, Langley—had miscalculated), but they tested their theories on kites and pilotless gliders before taking any risks themselves.

Following the successful flights of Glider No. 3 at Kill Devil Hills in the winter of 1902, the Wrights spent the summer of 1903 in designing and building their powered *Flyer*. In order to fulfill that requirement, they also designed their own twelve-horsepower engine. A larger machine than the No. 3 glider, the *Flyer* had a wingspan of forty feet, four inches. Crated up, it was shipped from Dayton, Ohio, to Kitty Hawk, North Carolina, in September 1903. At Kitty Hawk the Wrights constructed their camp, the largest building of which was the hanger where they assembled the *Flyer*.

The *Flyer* was not ready until December 12, but then the wind died down. Two days passed before the weather was right for flying. Because they wanted witnesses should their efforts be successful, the Wrights raised a signal flag inviting a few Coast Guard men stationed at nearby Kill Devil to watch the flight, if any. A coin was tossed to see who would make the first attempt; Wilbur won, lay down on the wing, and started the engine, which drove the two propellers. As the Coast Guard men and Orville watched, the plane sputtered into the air, dipped on one wing, and fell into the sand. Disappointed, the witnesses left, and even more disappointed, the Wrights set to work repairing the *Flyer*. On December 17, 1903, the flag was raised again, and five men and a boy arrived to watch the new attempt. This time it was Orville's turn—and this time the Wrights proved that man could fly, that he could achieve powered, sustained, and controlled flight. It was the first of four flights that day and lasted for 12 seconds and covered a distance of 120 feet. In the second flight, Wilbur covered 195 feet in 11 seconds; Orville followed with a fifteen-second flight in which the plane flew more than 200 feet. About noon Wilbur took off again and remained aloft for nearly a minute, during which he

The Wrights carefully studied various possible flying machines, including birds, before attempting to try their wings on man. Kites were important to their studies; in this rare informal photo, Wilbur Wright makes adjustments to a kite that belonged to the son of Frank T. Coffyn, one of the Wrights' first student pilots. Bayside, New Jersey. (National Air and Space Museum, Smithsonian Institution)

The Wright camp, Kitty Hawk, North Carolina, November 1903. The Flyer, newly arrived from Dayton and assembled, awaits final testing before flight attempt. (U. S. Air Force)

Man with wings: Orville Wright in the Flyer, with Wilbur standing by, in a photograph by Coast Guardsman John T. Daniels, December 17, 1903. (U. S. Air Force)

traversed a distance of 852 feet. Later in the day a gust of wind overturned the *Flyer*, damaging it too much to repair in the primitive hanger at Kitty Hawk. This ended the tests, but they had flown.

Although they did not court publicity, the Wrights thought that the press might be interested in the fact that they had actually solved the age-old problem of human flight. Orville Wright, in a succinct telegram to their father, told of their "Success four flights Thursday morning . . ." and asked him to "inform press." Except for a garbled story, which had been leaked out of the Norfolk telegraph office, very little appeared about this epochal flight in the newspapers. With Langley's recent failures still fresh in their minds, the general newspaper attitude was one of cynical skepticism. To most, the Wrights were only two more in a long line of crackpots who claimed they could fly. Only three newspapers in the entire country ran some mention of the flight, but the home paper, the Dayton *Journal*, did not even bother, in their early editions, and the later ones were all wrong. The world did not beat a path to the Wrights' door.

In May 1904, the Wrights were ready to test a second *Flyer*, this time in a pasture near Dayton made available to them by a friend, Torrence Huffman. Newspapermen arrived, but the *Flyer II*, and the wind, proved balky, and the gentlemen of the press, unimpressed, left the scene more skeptical than ever. The *Flyer* went on to make more than a hundred flights. Nor could the Wrights interest their government in the plane until 1908, during which four-year interval they continued to improve their Flyers. By 1905 they were certain they had solved the problems of flight, control, and dura-

The Wright Flyer is introduced to European airmen. Wilbur takes off before a French audience in a demonstration that galvanized French aeronautical thinking—and, finally, won recognition and admiration for the Wrights in Europe. (Musée de l'Air, Paris)

tion. But no one expressed any real interest in their machine. When the U. S. War Department turned down their offer, the Wrights approached the British War Office; the reaction was the same. A second offer in October 1905, to the U. S. War Department, misunderstood as a request for money to develop a practical aircraft, was made with the same lack of results.

For 2½ years after that the Wrights did not fly at all (although time was spent on improving their engines) and then, unexpectedly, their fortunes took a turn for the better. Early in 1908 the War Department signed a contract for a Wright Flyer, and in March, the next month, a plan was instituted for the formation of a Wright company in France. Wilbur Wright went to France to demonstrate the Flyer there while Orville remained to carry out the U. S. Army tests. Wilbur electrified Europe, where the skeptical French newspapers exclaimed that his flights presented "one of the most exciting spectacles ever presented in the history of applied science." French aviation pioneers agreed with René Gasnier, who said, "We are as children compared with the Wrights." In his own country Orville Wright caused a sensation also. The craft used by both brothers was the most modern Flyer known as the Wright Model A. Its wingspan was just a fraction greater than the original Flyer (now forty-one feet); the control system was refined a bit, but still depended upon wing warping. The Model A was capable of carrying a passenger, who, like the pilot, sat up instead of lying across the bottom wing.

The flights by Wilbur in France and those of Orville in the United States were actually the first real public demonstrations by the Wrights of what they had accomplished five years before. Having done this before witnesses, they had become news all over the world. Even Orville's flights in the United States were reported in Europe. Wilbur, in the words of the secretary of the Aeronautical Society in Britain, was "in possession of a power which controls the fate of nations . . ." He, in turn, could write to their sister Katherine in Dayton: "Tell Bubbo that his flights have revolutionized the world's beliefs regarding the practicability of flight. Even such conservative papers as the London *Times* devote leading editorials to his work and accept human flight as a thing to be regarded as a normal feature of the world's future life."

What he neglected to say, in typical modesty, was that he was accomplishing the same thing in France. Orville began his series of flights on September 3, 1908, at Fort Myer, breaking every known flying record (including those of Wilbur and one of their archrival Glenn Curtiss) up to that time. Until tragedy struck, Orville made ten successful flights, the longest of which lasted for an hour and fifteen minutes. This was the longest time man had remained aloft in a powered aircraft up to that time. On one flight he reached a new altitude record of 310 feet (Wilbur later reached 360 feet and remained up for more than 2 hours). Three times he even carried passengers.

Orville had proved the Wrights' claims for their invention by September 17, when the tests were abruptly ended. On the third passenger flight he took up Lieutenant Thomas E. Selfridge as an observer. They were making the fourth round of the field when one of the propellers developed a crack, which in turn caused it to flatten and lose thrust, making the plane vibrate violently. A propeller tore loose and snagged into wires bracing the rudders. Although Orville cut the engines and tried to bring the plane under control—it had staggered from a height of about 125 feet to 50 feet—it dived straight into the ground. Orville was seri-

Orville Wright impressing the folks back home—Fort Myer, Virginia, September 1903. (U. S. Air Force)

First heavier-than-air fatality: wreckage of the Wright plane after crashing. Spectators are trying to remove the body of Lieutenant Thomas E. Selfridge. At right others attend to the seriously injured Orville. (U. S. Air Force)

The Army's Wright Flyer over Fort Myer, 1909. (U. S. Air Force)

ously injured (fractured thigh and ribs), and Selfridge was killed. This was the first fatal crash of a powered aircraft. Despite the accident, the U.S. Signal Corps observers were sufficiently impressed with the plane's performance to agree to purchase one for $25,000.

Since the fatal accident canceled further tests of the proposed Army Flyer—and any flying by Orville for the rest of 1908—the final tests were postponed until June 1909. Orville, recuperating, joined Wilbur in France in December 1908, and then both returned in the spring after tributes in London, Paris, New York, and Washington. On June 28, 1909, Orville—now completely recovered from his injuries—took up the Army tests where he had left off the previous year.

By the end of July all Army tests had been successfully completed and the Wrights were awarded their $25,000 contract for the plane. They even received an additional $5,000 as a bonus because they had exceeded the Army's speed specification—40 miles per hour—by 2.5 miles per hour. In 1909 they had finally succeeded in ushering in the age of flight.

By 1911 the Wrights had made the final modifications on their Flyers. They had come around to the European idea of using wheeled landing gears instead of skids, and they had moved the elevator from the front outrigger—which did not assist stability or handling—to the rear of the aircraft. These were small refinements compared with the impact of their real contribution and influence. The rest was up to others who followed. As for the Wrights, they seemed to come full circle in 1911 with the return to gliding at Kill Devil Hills near Kitty Hawk. Orville that year designed a new glider on which he had hoped to test a new automatic stabilizer. In this glider Orville set an endurance record of nine minutes, forty-five seconds on October 24, 1911, which stood as a record for the next ten years. Wilbur by this time had not flown for quite a while. He died of typhoid fever in 1912; he was only forty-five years old. Orville lived into his middle seventies and lived to regret many things (among them the treatment by the Smith-

The Wrights return to Kitty Hawk after convincing the U.S. Army that man could fly. New concepts for the future were being tested in the glider of 1911 (a year before the death of Wilbur Wright). Orville was the pilot in this series of photos, which includes a slight mishap with the winds of Kitty Hawk. (U. S. Air Force)

John J. Montgomery (left) and cousin, Bishop George Montgomery, with John Montgomery's glider, Santa Clara, California, April 1905. The bishop refused to bless the machine, calling it "an instrument of destruction." Even so, it was successfully flown that day—although the Wrights had done all that, and more, long before. (National Air and Space Museum, Smithsonian Institution)

sonian and lawsuits), especially the perversion of their invention into a formidable weapon of war. He died in 1948 at the age of seventy-seven.

A career that roughly paralleled that of the Wrights was that of a California teacher, Professor John J. Montgomery, who was frequently called America's "Forgotten Glider Pioneer." Some even used his career as a weapon against the Wrights, claiming more for Montgomery than he himself would have. Although interested in building gliders since the late 1880s (under the influence of Lilienthal), Montgomery did not succeed in building a working glider until 1905. By this time the Wrights had already flown in a powered machine, but since Montgomery worked in a scientific near vacuum, he knew nothing about it. Montgomery's glider was a tandem-wing design (two wings on the same level, not with one above the other, as in the Wright gliders), which resembled Langley's ill-fated *Aerodrome*. On April 29, 1905, with a professional parachutist, Daniel Maloney, as pilot, Montgomery had the glider lifted up to an altitude of 3,500 feet by a hot-air balloon. At that height Maloney cast himself free of the balloon and, before a large crowd at Santa Clara, California, made a successful flight and landing.

The obvious audience appeal of the glider and balloon combination was exploited by Montgomery and Maloney and soon posters were plastered about California advertising the "Most Daring Feat Ever Accomplished by Man" and informing people that it afforded them the "Only Chance to Witness This Marvelous Scientific Wonder." Maloney began giving exhibition flights similar to the first one, in which he was raised by the balloon and then floated to earth, performing spirals and dives on the

The Montgomery glider, with pilot Daniel Maloney, being lifted by a balloon for an exhibition flight. Maloney had been the successful test pilot of the April flight; he died in a crash in the same craft later, in July 1905. (National Air and Space Museum, Smithsonian Institution)

way. On July 18, 1905, Maloney was killed attempting this feat after the glider had become slightly damaged during the takeoff.

Montgomery continued to design and add refinements (such as wheels) to gliders of excellent flying quality until 1911 although not truly advancing aviation, as claimed by the detractors of the Wrights. Like the Wrights, Montgomery withdrew from aviation briefly, but then attempted a comeback. In October 1911 he himself was killed in his machine. Although a courageous and honest experimenter, Montgomery, like Langley, is generally remembered in aviation history in comparison with the Wrights and for what he failed to accomplish.

If the Wrights had suffered, to some extent, as prophets without honor in their own country, they were widely influential in Europe. They were not, of course, embraced without question, for their claims were frequently challenged by skeptics who failed themselves attempting to emulate the Wrights. Aviation in Europe had not advanced much since the death of Lilienthal in 1896. The emphasis remained upon the airship and the glider, with tentative but unsuccessful attempts at powered flight. Word of the Wrights' experiments began to filter into France, thanks to the work of Octave Chanute, who spread the word. Among the first to receive that word was Captain Ferdinand Ferber, an ex-Lilienthal disciple, who abandoned the Lilienthal glider for the design of the Wrights. Chanute arrived in France in March 1903 with the latest report on the Wright Glider No. 3, drawings of the machine, and photographs that further inspired Ferber as well as other early French pioneers—Ernest Archdeacon, Gabriel Voisin, and Robert Esnault-Pelterie.

The influence of the Wrights, however, was not absolute, and the designs inspired by or copied from the Wright gliders did not always work out in the air. Nor did European designers fully grasp the Wright concept of controlling aircraft. Even if successful, a glider that could not be controlled by its pilot, was little more than an oversized toy. Nor were the French anxious for the Wrights to succeed. Esnault-Pelterie was not too unhappy to an-

Montgomery's 1911 glider on a takeoff, Evergreen Valley, California. Test pilot Joseph C. Vierra is in the cockpit. Montgomery spelled Vierra as test pilot and was killed in his glider in October. (National Air and Space Museum, Smithsonian Institution)

nounce that he had built an "exact copy" of a Wright glider (he had not), and since it did not fly, he doubted that the Wrights were quite what they were cracked up to be. Archdeacon expressed the general mood when he exclaimed, just a few months before Kitty Hawk, "Will the homeland of the Montgolfiérs have the shame of permitting the ultimate discovery of aerial science to be realized abroad?" Ferber was even more succinct: "The aeroplane must not be allowed to be perfected in America!" Even when word of the Kitty Hawk flights came through scientific circles, the tendency was to disbelieve or ignore it. Still it was inevitable that eventually Europeans would fly. But the honor for making the first official flight did not go to those pioneers hoping to beat the Wrights into the air, but to daring airshipman Alberto Santos-Dumont.

Santos-Dumont had switched from airships to heavier-than-air flight after hearing of the Wright flights of 1905; also, Archdeacon had offered a trophy to anyone who made the first flight of twenty-five meters (eighty-two feet), and the French Aero-Club offered prize money for the first flight covering one hundred meters. (The Wrights

Santos-Dumont in the cockpit of *14 bis*, preparing for takeoff, September 1906. (Musée de l'Air, Paris/Air France)

by this time were making flights of nearly twenty-five miles.) To accomplish his mission, Santos-Dumont produced one of the oddest aircraft in history, which he called *14 bis*. Since the contraption he devised had been tested underneath his airship No. 14, the heavier-than-air craft was considered by the inventor as a further extension of the airship. (*Bis* means "encore" or "again" in English.) Before he attempted to fly it under its own power, Santos-Dumont tested its engine, designed and built by Léon Levavasseur, one of the great aero-engine pioneers. He also tested the machine's controls, such as they were. The *14 bis* was a *canard*, meaning it flew tail forward, the tail looking like a box kite. The

wings, with pronounced dihedral—which endowed the craft with some inherent stability (something the Wright planes lacked)—also looked like box kites. The pilot, Santos-Dumont himself, stood in a wicker basket; the engine was mounted behind him. The propeller, which looked like two canoe paddles fastened together at the end of the handles, whirled around behind the wings, and pushed the contraption forward. Santos-Dumont took off in this aircraft for the first time on September 13, 1906, at Bagatelle near Paris; he covered all of seven meters. By October 23 he had captured the Archdeacon prize, and on November 12 he managed to stay aloft for a little more than twenty-one seconds to cover

The *14 bis* airborne, with Santos-Dumont in control; the craft flew tail first, wings—and pilot—following. (Musée de l'Air, Paris)

a distance of 722 feet, which won him the Aero-Club prize. Once again Santos-Dumont became the hero of the hour, and his "hops" (for that is what they really were) were hailed as a great step forward in aviation. It was not, of course, although the excitement it generated led to even greater things.

Three years later Santos-Dumont again appeared on the scene with a new design, the so-called *Demoiselle* (the twentieth in his series of aircraft designs and, except for minor modifications in two that followed, his last). The *Demoiselle* was Santos-Dumont's contribution to light-plane design for the sportsman: a small, inexpensive flying machine. He freely circulated the plans hoping that it would encourage Everyman to take up the sport of flying. It did not quite work out as the inventor hoped, although the plane was an interesting design, with a wingspan of only eighteen feet. It could remain aloft for only about ten minutes and was a tricky craft to fly, reaching speeds in excess of fifty miles an hour. Controlling the *Demoiselle* called for exceptional skill, not to say daring, and it could be flown only under the most favorable weather conditions.

By 1910 Santos-Dumont had begun to reveal symptoms of an illness (later diagnosed as multiple sclerosis) that ended his flying career. He spent the rest of his life as a near invalid. Those final years were bitter for a man who believed he had been the first to fly (he actually flew *in public* before the Wrights) and saw his "invention" turned into a weapon of war. In his final years he returned to his homeland, Brazil, where he was dealt the ultimate blow. Brazil had erupted in a civil war, and one day, shortly after his fifty-ninth birthday, he was plunged into despair when he saw aircraft used to bomb his own countrymen. On July 23, 1932, Santos-Dumont committed suicide.

A more substantial contribution than that of Santos-Dumont was made by the Voisin brothers, Gabriel and Charles. A graduate architect, Gabriel revealed an early interest in aviation when he served as a glider test pilot for Archdeacon in 1903. Eventually Voisin began thinking about powered machines, by which time he was joined by Charles in the first aircraft manufacturing firm in France. Their early designs were little more than massive, powered box kites.

Although Santos-Dumont had beaten the Voisins into the air, the Voisins were to have a greater, more lasting influence upon aviation than the tragic Brazilian. There were two reasons for this: The first was that the brothers had evolved, despite limitations, a viable design, an aircraft capable of flight and development. Santos-Dumont, particularly in his *14 bis*, reached a dead end in the very beginning. The other reason for the wider influ-

Demoiselle, Santos-Dumont's contribution to, he hoped, the widespread use of the airplane by almost everyone. The tiny plane was actually extremely difficult to fly, except by a most experienced pilot. There were a few of those in 1909. (Musée de l'Air, Paris)

Brazilian-born Alberto Santos-Dumont, air pioneer who contributed to the excitement of aviation in France. (Musée de l'Air, Paris)

Gabriel (left) and Charles Voisin. (Musée de l'Air, Paris)

ence of the Voisins was that they designed and built aircraft for several early French flight pioneers who themselves contributed to aviation. Among these were Léon Delagrange, Henri Farman, and Louis Blériot. In testing the machine made for Delagrange, Charles Voisin became the first native-born Frenchman to fly, on March 15, 1907. It was only a hop flight of sixty meters (about 190 feet), but it qualified as a flight. Later, both Delagrange and Farman went on to become celebrated aviators (although the flying career of Delagrange was cut short in 1910, when he died in an air crash).

The Voisin planes, with a few variations, retained the same general configuration for several years. The wing resembled an extended box kite set on its side—the side curtains introduced in later models were added for greater stability. The pilot sat in a squared-off bathtublike fuselage with the engine and propeller behind him. Another box kite on extended booms served as a tail unit. It provided lift only for the after section of the plane and did not serve in any way for directional control. The only control surface was a winglike structure attached to the front of the fuselage. This controlled the up-and-down movement of the plane. There was no real lateral control—that is, unlike the Wright plane, the Voisin, like all other early European aircraft, could not bank: It could not tip to the right or left to make a circular turn. In fact, flying one of these planes was somewhat like driving an automobile in the air. Turning was a complex maneuver made up of wobbling skids and yaws. Despite these limitations, the Voisin became a popular plane and inspired other designs and improvements.

The Voisin biplane ca. 1908–9. (Musée de l'Air, Paris)

A remarkably advanced-looking aircraft was introduced in France in 1907, concurrently with the Voisin. This was the REP monoplane, designed by Robert Esnault-Pelterie. It marked a European divergence from the Wright brothers' plane in its single-winged design. The REP was the first aircraft with a completely enclosed fuselage constructed of welded-steel tubing. The wings drooped downward (anhedral), and there was no rudder. It was a difficult plane, therefore, to keep under control, despite its futuristic details. One of its most remarkable features was the seven-cylinder engine (in two rows) designed by Esnault-Pelterie himself. A later model of the REP appeared with a rudder and somewhat improved performance. A serious crash ended Esnault-Pelterie's flying days in 1908. Although he continued as a designer, Esnault-Pelterie left the flying to others and eventually sold out his factory to the Farmans. He had introduced a number of innovations—steel-tubing construction, pneumatic shock absorbers, hydraulic brakes—of lasting value.

One of the great airmen of all time was Harry Edgar Mudford Farman (1874–1958). Born in Paris of English parents, he grew up in France (although he did not become a citizen until 1937). But he must have thought of himself as French, for the Harry eventually became Henry, frequently Henri, and he spoke very little English. Farman had intended to become an artist but abandoned that to take up the sport of auto racing. When he suffered a nearly fatal accident in 1905, he decided to forsake the sport in favor of one he regarded as safer—aviation.

After several experiments with model planes and homemade gliders, the next step was with a powered aircraft that Farman ordered from the Voisins. A born pilot, Farman began making modifications on his Voisin—he removed the vertical panels between the wings, for example. Although these had improved lateral stability, they also served to "drag" (that is, slow) the plane and in a crosswind caused the plane to drift sideways. Farman also improved the tail surfaces, the landing

Esnault-Pelterie's futuristic REP, October 1907, the first
aircraft designed with an enclosed fuselage. (Musée de
l'Air, Paris)

gear, and eventually devised a set of early ailerons—four flapping surfaces on the rear wingtips
of both wings top and bottom—for control in
banking. He also experimented with various engines that improved the performance of his aircraft.
Eventually Farman so altered the original Voisin
conception that his planes were called Farmans.

He made his first important mark in aviation
when, on January 13, 1908, he won the Deutsch-
Archdeacon Prize of fifty thousand francs for making the first circular flight in Europe. He took off
between two posts, yawed around another post
about five hundred meters distant (he had not yet
conceived his ailerons, nor was the Wrights' wing-

Henri Farman, British-French airman, here photographed at an American air meet, 1908. (U. S. Air Force)

By 1909 Farman introduced his own plane (produced partly because of the various changes he had made on the Voisin and mostly because the Voisins had secretly sold a plane they had promised to him to another pilot, English pioneer J. T. C. Moore-Brabazon). The cumbersome tail unit of the Voisin had been eliminated; a four-wheeled skid landing gear was installed, and a new engine, a Gnome rotary, which whirled with the propeller, was also installed. It proved to be an extraordinarily flyable plane and was one of the most popular of the early pre-First World War aircraft.

French ingenuity was responsible for the solution to the problem of water-based aircraft. With so much water around, it seemed that rivers and lakes, even oceans, might provide excellent takeoff and landing surfaces for planes. Inventor-aircraft designers turned to watercraft soon after the Wrights flew at Kitty Hawk. Gabriel Voisin designed a glider with floats for Archdeacon in 1905, which they attempted to lift off the surface of the water by pulling it behind a motorboat. In July the

Farman crossing the finish line at Issy to win the Deutsch-Archdeacon prize, January 13, 1908. (Musée de l'Air, Paris)

warping method known in Europe at the time), and returned to the starting point. In all he had covered a distance of about a mile in a minute and twenty-eight seconds. The historic flight was made at Issy-les-Moulineaux from an Army parade ground on the left bank of the Seine near Paris. Issy was to become the first aerodrome in Europe, the later scene of many subsequent historic flights as other airmen followed Farman and built hangers on the field. Farman continued flying and winning prizes—and refining his ideas on aircraft design. In July of the same banner year, 1908, he made a flight of twenty minutes, the longest made in Europe up to that time. (The record was broken by Wilbur Wright, who arrived in France that same summer.) Farman chalked up another mark for European aviation when he made the first cross-country flight—sixteen miles between Bouy and Reims—on the Continent.

Early French designs for aircraft that could operate from water: the Voisin-Archdeacon glider, which was pulled into the air by boat, but was not terribly air- or seaworthy. The craft with the strange wings was Bleriot's attempt and, though powered, the Bleriot III never flew. (Musée de l'Air, Paris)

Archdeacon actually rose off the Seine River, but without power there seemed little future in the float glider. Shortly after, Voisin designed a similar craft for another aviation enthusiast, Louis Blériot, which also employed a motorboat as its source of power. This glider, too, lifted off the Seine, but dipped into the river and nearly drowned Voisin. He then decided to abandon the idea of operating aircraft off water.

Blériot, however, continued in the pursuit and, in 1906, designed a curious-looking craft into which he mounted an engine that drove two propellers. Blériot dubbed it the Blériot III. While it was indeed a handsome design, Blériot could never get it to fly, even with later modifications.

In the United States, meanwhile, Glenn Curtiss also toyed with the idea of a seaplane, so to speak, and with characteristic Yankee pragmatism began by mounting one of his planes on a canoe. He had as much success as Voisin and Blériot.

It remained for an unknown French marine engineer, Henri Fabre, to complete the work of the better-known aviation pioneers. He designed a winged contraption with a fifty-horsepower Gnome rotary engine mounted behind the wing. Since the seven-cylinder Gnome had no throttle, the engine could not be controlled beyond being either on or off. With the engine mounted in the rear, it was possible to position the plane in the water and still have the engine accessible to an assistant who could start it from the dock. Three flat floats, slightly canted upward, sustained the craft on the water. Though beautifully designed and built, Fabre's "seaplane" did not look like anything that would fly. Of interest, too, was the fact that Fabre had never taken flying lessons, nor had ever flown before.

Despite all the odds, Fabre placed the machine into a lake in southern France, near Marseilles. Someone turned over the engine and he took off. He apparently quickly taught himself to fly and, after a flight of about fifteen hundred feet, he safely landed the plane. Encouraged by success, Fabre made several flights before he stalled on a turn and splashed into the water. He was unhurt, but the plane was broken up. Fabre had had enough: He

had proved the feasibility of operating aircraft from water if sufficiently powered and if fitted with efficient floats. This accomplished, Fabre returned to marine engineering and never attempted to fly again—nor to dabble in the design of aircraft.

Louis Blériot (1872–1936) represented another line of development in European aviation—the belief that the monoplane represented the most efficient type of aircraft. Blériot, a wealthy manufacturer of headlights for automobiles, father of six children, hardly seemed to fit the role of the daring young man in the flying machine. He began experimenting (with an unsuccessful ornithopter) in 1901 and later commissioned Gabriel Voisin to build him a glider. Eventually Blériot broke with Voisin after a series of not very conclusive experiments and in 1907 began developing his own designs.

Henri Fabre, the first man to design and fly a seaplane.

A marine engineer, Fabre flew his contraption on March 28, 1910. Having proved his point, Fabre returned to his original line of work. (Smithsonian Institution/Musée de l'Air, Paris)

Louis Blériot in his cross-country *Blériot VIII* of 1908. Blériot was a consistent advocate of the monoplane, now the standard aircraft configuration. (Musée de l'Air, Paris)

Blériot (right) with an early student, Hubert Leblon and, in the background, a portion of a Blériot monoplane. Not one of history's outstanding pilots, Blériot must have been a better flight instructor. (U. S. Air Force)

achievements with a cross-country flight on October 31, 1908. This machine was not quite the same one that had begun flying in June, for during the various tests Blériot had made modifications to improve flight characteristics. The wing was reduced slightly, and a fixed lifting tailplane was added to the top of the rear fuselage, just in front of the elevator. Also, elevons were added to the wingtips for additional control. The Léon Levavasseur-designed Antoinette engine furnished fifty horsepower to the four-bladed metal propeller.

Blériot was more "intrepid pilot" than born aviator, for he suffered many accidents in his various designs. Out of the wreckage of one plane arose not only a miraculously unhurt Blériot, but also an improved model of another Blériot monoplane. With success his, Blériot began competing with the Voisins and began manufacturing airplanes and teaching others how to fly.

Also in the monoplane tradition was the Antoinette, one of the most beautiful aircraft ever flown. It was designed by an artist turned engineer, Léon Levavasseur, who had developed the engine that had powered so many of the early planes. In February 1908, Levavasseur turned also to the design of aircraft, which were named Antoinette for the young and pretty daughter of the head of the firm, Jules Gastambide. The company was known as *Société Antoinette* and was formed first to manufacture Levavasseur's engines and, by late 1908, the Antoinette monoplanes. The first in the aircraft series—named the Gastambide-Mengin in honor of the two men who commissioned it—with its four large spoked wheels looked like two bicycles, side by side, with an engine, wing, and tail attached. By late 1908 and especially by the summer of 1909 the classic form of the Antoinette had evolved: the long, graceful fuselage (with a triangular cross section), a cambered (that is, curved) wing section, beautifully flared tail, and, of course, the fifty-horsepower Antoinette engine.

The most celebrated Antoinette pilot was Hubert Latham (1883–1912), who, like so many of the early birdmen, was independently wealthy. After completing his schooling, he seems to have devoted

Whereas the Voisins and Farman preferred the biplane, Blériot favored the monoplane. The result was the prototype of practically every modern single-engined monoplane since: fuselage with the engine in the front of the plane, a wing about a third of the way back, and movable tail surfaces. Interestingly the fuselage was entirely covered with fabric so that the 1907 plane looked very modern—although in fact it was not very successful. However, in June of the next year Blériot unveiled his new design, the Blériot VIII, which made several flights during the rest of the year, capping its

his life to that of the professional sportsman: He hunted big game in Africa, he indulged in an obsession with speed in motorboats (powered with the Antoinette engine), and he generally sought out danger and adventure. Certainly one of the reasons for Latham's preoccupation with risk was the fact that he had tuberculosis and his doctors had given him little time to live.

Through his neighbor, Gastambide, Latham became associated with the Antoinette firm and quickly became its chief pilot when he mastered the Antoinette plane and became, with Blériot, the chief exponent of the monoplane type of aircraft.

The Antoinette control system was not one of Levavasseur's most inspired conceptions, being rather clumsy and not as natural to manipulate as the later developments of joy stick and rudder bar. For a time also the Antoinette employed crude ailerons—triangular shapes at each wingtip that banked the plane. But Levavasseur abandoned those in favor of a wing-warp system. These disadvantages did not discourage Latham, who began breaking various records with the Antoinettes. His trademarks were a checked cap and cigarette holder.

Leon Levavasseur, an artist who turned to aircraft and engine design. Besides producing a reasonably reliable engine, Levavasseur created one of the most beautiful aircraft ever flown, the Antoinette. *Antoinette VII* of 1909 is depicted. (Musée de l'Air, Paris)

Hubert Latham in the cockpit of his Antoinette. His hand rests on the wheel that actuated the elevator controls. A similar wheel, on the other side of the cockpit, worked the wing warping for banking the plane. A rudder bar inside the cockpit made directional control possible. (Musée de l'Air, Paris)

Latham, racing with Blériot and other French pilots, hoped to be first to fly the English Channel to win the London *Daily Mail*'s prize. His two attempts ended in the Channel waters. (Musée de l'Air, Paris)

Although Latham had gathered several world records with the Antoinette, by the summer of 1909 he had his eye on the prize, offered by the London *Daily Mail*, of five hundred pounds to the first airman to cross the English Channel in a powered aircraft. There were other eyes on the prize also, namely Santos-Dumont's (until friends convinced him that crossing the Channel in the diminutive *Demoiselle* was foolhardy), and a few others, among them Count Charles de Lambert in England, who had learned to fly with Wilbur Wright and had a couple of Wright Flyers built for the purpose. He cracked up one of them, and before the second was ready, the contest was over.

Latham soon appeared to be the man in the lead and, following several delays, set out from Sangatte, France, in an Antoinette IV (one with ailerons) on July 19, 1909. Although the Antoinette engine was the best of its time, it was not perfect, and about two miles out the engine sputtered out. Latham had to land the plane in the sea, where he was later picked up nonchalantly seated on the wreckage smoking a cigarette in his long holder. The seamen who pulled the Antoinette out of the Channel only added to the damage. Unperturbed,

Latham placed an order for another. Word had come to him that Blériot had begun talking about attempting the flight in one of his monoplanes and, besides, Latham had made a bet that he would cross the Channel before August 1. With a new plane, this time an Antoinette VII, he set out again on July 27 and was within sight of the Dover cliffs (about a mile from making a landing) when engine trouble once again cheated him of arriving at his goal. He was doubly cheated, for he was already two days late: The Channel had already been crossed by air.

Despite his propensity for accidents, Louis Blériot had gone on with his flying, winning several minor prizes between mishaps. By July, when Latham had already announced his intentions, Blériot had suffered two quite serious burns of the left foot from his plane's exposed exhaust pipe. These accidents had occurred in his Model XII Blériot, so he decided that for his Channel attempt he would use the earlier Model XI.

One important change had been made: For the original REP engine, Blériot had substituted a new, three-cylinder, radial, air-cooled power plant. It was the invention of Alessandro Anzani, an Italian motorcycle manufacturer living in Paris. Because holes had been drilled into the cylinders to cool the engine, it did have an unfortunate characteristic of swallowing oil in great quantities and splashing out the unused oil through the cylinders into the face of the pilot. Although he wore goggles, Blériot was forced also to carry a wad of cotton attached by a string to his goggles to wipe them clean. When he arrived at his chosen takeoff site by train (the plane had been shipped by rail), he did not present a very impressive figure of a fit aviator. He arrived in Calais on crutches because of the severe burns on his left foot. Now both he and Hubert Latham awaited good weather for their flights. Newspapers began speculating: "Who Will Be Ready First, Latham or Blériot?" French and British naval ships plied the treacherous waters of the English Channel as the excitement mounted. While Latham slept on the morning of July 25, 1909, Blériot was awakened by a friend with the news that the weather promised fair. By the time Latham could ready his new Antoinette, the wind had turned against him, and Blériot was well over the Channel. He had taken off at sunup—about 4:40 A.M.—and pointed his little monoplane toward the cliffs of Dover. He managed a speed of about forty-two miles per hour and at an altitude of about 250 feet flew over the water.

Without a compass, Blériot succeeded in crossing nearly twenty-five miles of water despite having been lost for about ten minutes. Finally, at five-twenty or so, he brought his plane down near Dover Castle after some thirty-six minutes in the air. His usual luck held: In coming in, he smashed the landing gear and broke a propeller blade. But he was the first man to cross the English Channel in a powered aircraft. Although he was greeted as a hero by the English, the fact that Blériot had succeeded meant the end of British dependence upon the sea as a factor in defense. The era of the ship was coming to an end; there were, in a popular phrase of the time, "no islands anymore."

The Blériot monoplane, after the Channel crossing, became the reigning single-winged plane in Europe, and one of the most popular and widely

Louis Blériot approaching Dover, England, July 15, 1909. (Musée de l'Air, Paris)

A typical Blériot landing: the pilot is being welcomed by Britishers, including Bobbies, near Dover Castle, after completing the first English Channel crossing in a heavier-than-air craft, 1909. (Air France)

built aircraft of the early years of powered flight. Although the Antoinette shared some of the Blériot's popularity, the company itself went into bankruptcy before the First World War. (Levavasseur, the inventive genius behind the company, died poor in 1922 at the age of fifty-nine.) Sales that might have gone to the Antoinette firm went after the summer of 1909 to Blériot; more than a hundred Model XI's were ordered. The little planes were very popular even in the United States, home of powered flight. The Blériot was a small plane, its wingspan stretching a mere twenty-eight feet (the Antoinette's was forty-six feet). Although Blériot is generally credited with its design, much of the conception was that of designer Raymond Saulnier.

Compared with the rival Antoinette, the Blériot XI was an ugly duckling. More than half of its rear fuselage was uncovered. The nose, with its curious bedspringlike landing gear, was a conglomeration of steel struts and wire. The wheels looked like the wheels from a small bicycle. Different models were powered with different engines, ranging from the three-cylinder Anzani of the original Channel crosser to one of eight cylinders set onto the cylinder block in a "V"; other Blériot XIs were powered by the Gnome rotary with the propeller mounted be-

hind the engine. In this arrangement (as with all rotaries) both engine and propeller revolved at tremendous speed. This created a great centrifugal force in the nose of the plane, which made flying it a test of skill. The fact that Blériot successfully made the Channel crossing that July 25 could be as readily attributed to simple good luck as to the efficiency of the aircraft or Blériot's flying skill. The fact that Blériot had actually made the flight (the rather unhappy landing was forgotten in the excitement of the feat) was enough to establish him and his plane as one of the classic aircraft of all time.

European aviation truly energized during the closing months of 1908, which could be credited to the presence of Wilbur Wright in France from August to December. Especially inspiring was the Wright concern with control of the plane in the air, something Europeans had tended to overlook. Wilbur's flights revolutionized European aviation (and ended once and for all the slanders that the Wrights had been better liars than fliers) and renewed interest in powered flight, which resulted, in France, in the advances of the Voisins, Farman, Levavasseur, and Blériot-Saulnier. They were independent thinkers and not slavish imitators, however. But the fact of the Wrights' accomplishment was enough for the European pioneers and encouraged

Various engine mountings in Blériot types. The plane with the four-paddled propeller used a cumbersome water-cooled powerplant, complete with radiater directly underneath. The Gnome rotary that rotated with the propeller was lighter but required skilled flying to master. The mass of whirling metal in the nose of the plane frequently threw it out of control in turns. (U. S. Air Force)

them to improve their own designs and to make their own contributions.

In England, too, self-conscious about its laggardly progress (practically none since the death of Pilcher) and especially embarrassed by French superiority, the sound of wings—and engines— stirred the air. Strangely, the first powered flight in Britain was made by an American, Colonel Samuel F. Cody (who became a British citizen in 1909). Cody, no relation to the western hero "Buffalo Bill," was a showman traveling in England with a production entitled *The Klondyke Nugget* when he first revealed an early interest in flight. This took the form of man-lifting kites that were pulled into the air over the English Channel by ship. Seven years later Cody had graduated to aircraft, and on October 16, 1908, he he made the first official powered flight at Laffan's Plain, Farnborough. His plane resembled the Wrights' Flyer, from which it was obviously derived; it remained aloft for twenty-seven seconds, covering a distance of nearly five hundred yards. Encouraged by this flight, Cody went on to produce several other aircraft. By 1910, he had received the Michelin Trophy for a flight of four hours, forty-seven minutes, during which he covered a distance of 185.5 miles.

Cody's most famous design, the Cody 3, was

Samuel Franklin Cody, American-born British citizen, who made the first powered flight in Britain in October 1908. He poses with his Michelin Trophy in 1910. (U. S. Air Force)

come a great figure in British aviation. In 1912 he won the British Military Aeroplane Competition with a Cathedral type of plane. By August 1913, Cody had produced his seventh design. He was killed in this plane, which broke up in the air.

It is likely that the first powered flights made in England were made by Alliott Verdon Roe in June 1908, some months before Cody. Since these flights were not "official," he was not given credit for them. The plane, a biplane, was abandoned by 1909 by Roe in favor of a triplane, Bull's-eye. The triplane was a successful plane, but Roe was denied the honor of being the first British-born airman to fly over his homeland (he was beaten by J. T. C. Moore-Brabazon in a Voisin). Roe, however, was one of Britain's outstanding air pioneers and pilots and, after building several triplanes, he switched to biplanes and produced several great aircraft called Avros. Along with Roe, Moore-Brabazon, and Cody, British aviation had begun to spurt ahead with the work of such pioneers as Charles S. Rolls (of Rolls-Royce), Francis K. McClean, George Cockburn, and Geoffrey de Havilland.

also called the Flying Cathedral. One of its most interesting features was the between-the-wing aileron for lateral control. Although this was not yet the final aileron, it was to some extent an improvement on wing warping. By this time (1909–10) Cody, who dressed like a movie cowboy, had be-

Aviation in the United States, also spurred on by the Wrights, began coming to life again in 1908. It

Cody's Flying Cathedral, 1909, a very successful design. In 1913, however, Cody was killed when a later model of the plane disintegrated in flight. (U. S. Air Force)

was at this time that a name that rivaled that of the Wrights emerged: Glenn Hammond Curtiss (1878–1930). Like the Wrights, Curtiss shared a natural affinity for mathematics and mechanics; from an early age he had also been associated with bicycles. By the age of nineteen Curtiss was winning bicycle races in his hometown, Hammondsport, New York. This naturally led to the faster, more exciting motorcycle, with which he set several speed records. He began experimenting with light, fast engines and as early as 1904 had devised his "Windwagon," a three-wheeled vehicle driven by propeller. His excellent work with engines brought him to the attention of scientist Alexander Graham Bell (inventor of the telephone). Like his friend Langley, Bell was fascinated by the idea of flight. He had experimented with kites, and as early as 1903 (before the Wrights had flown at Kitty Hawk) had said that "an aeroplane kite could carry the weight of a motor and a man." In Curtiss, Bell believed he had found both the engine and the man.

In the summer of 1907 Dr. Bell, at the suggestion of his wife, Mabel Hubbard Bell (who supplied $25,000 in funding), formed the Aerial Experiment Association. Bell was president (without salary), Curtiss was enlisted as director of experiments; the secretary was the U.S. War Department's Lieutenant Thomas E. Selfridge (who died the next year in the Wright plane crash at Fort Myer); chief engineer was Frederick W. Baldwin, and his assistant was John A. D. McCurdy. The last two were Canadians fresh out of engineering school. The aim of the association was to pool their various talents "upon the construction of a practical aerodrome driven by its own motive power and carrying a man."

At the time Curtiss was not particularly interested in flight; the construction of motors was his primary interest. The first design was assigned to Selfridge and completed by March 12, 1908. Officially called *Aerodrome No. 1*, the aircraft was named *Red Wing* by its designer. When tested over iced-over Lake Keuka (near Hammondsport, New York), *Red Wing* managed to get into the air—

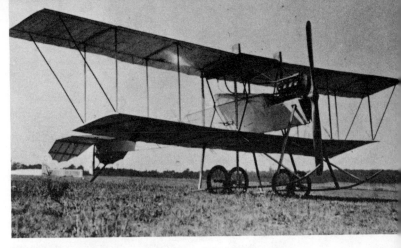

Early (1909–10) designs by one of Britain's great aviation pioneers, Alliott Verdon Roe. The designer called them Avroplanes. (U. S. Air Force)

Glenn H. Curtiss, great American airman and rival of the Wright brothers. He is seated in his *June Bug*, powered by his eight-cylinder air-cooled engine. This plane was the third in the series produced by Bell-financed Aerial Experiment Association. (U. S. Air Force)

The short, unhappy flight of the *Red Wing*, Lake Keuka, Hammondsport, New York, March 1908. The plane had been designed by Lieutenant Thomas E. Selfridge. (U. S. Air Force Museum)

Baldwin was pilot—but it was not really airworthy. After a flight of a little more than three hundred feet, at an altitude of about six to eight feet, the plane stalled and crumpled onto the ice. Baldwin escaped serious injury, but *Red Wing* was a total loss. Learning from this mishap, Bell made several suggestions to his young airmen for the improvement of the design of the next plane. He emphasized the need for some form of landing gear to make smoother landings possible, controls that depended to some degree upon a man's natural movements ("instinctive motions"), and the need to devise some form of "movable surfaces at the ends of the wing-piece."

Bell's valuable ideas were incorporated into the design of *Aerodrome No. 2, White Wing*, which was primarily the responsibility of Baldwin but to which Curtiss contributed a good deal. Curtiss, like Selfridge, had picked up a number of ideas, freely borrowed, from the Wrights. Even so, *White Wing* revealed some innovations, among them a tricycle landing gear, hinged ailerons at the wingtips, and quite sophisticated controls, including a

wheel for the rudder. Baldwin himself flew *White Wing* for the first time on May 18, 1908, at Stony Brook Farm near Hammondsport, for a distance of ninety-three yards. This was an improvement over the performance of *Red Wing*, but not over that of the Wright Flyer III, which four days before had covered a distance of five miles. *White Wing* suffered a number of minor landing damages and underwent repair work and small modifications. On May 22, Curtiss made an exceptionally good flight of 1,017 feet in nineteen seconds, coming down—intact, for a change—in a nearby field. Competition with the Wrights was now under way.

Aerodrome No. 3 was the Curtiss-designed *June Bug*, so called because it was completed in June

The *White Wing*, second in the Aerial Experiment Association series of designs—this one by Frederick W. Baldwin and flown by him in May 1908. (U. S. Air Force)

1908. Although the third in the Aerial Experiment Association's series of aircraft, it followed the basic design of the earlier planes. *June Bug*, had been improved somewhat by Curtiss with a box-kitelike tail, ailerons, and a light V-8 air-cooled Curtiss engine. Preliminary tests impressed Curtiss and other association members with *June Bug's* potential, so they decided to try for the *Scientific American* trophy donated to the Aero Club of America. It was to go to the first powered plane to cover a kilometer (3,280 feet) in a straight-line flight. (The Wrights had, of course, already done this, but not under "official" observation.)

On July 4, 1908, a large crowd assembled at Stony Brook Farm to watch the bid for the trophy. The weather proved unco-operative most of the day, and Curtiss was unable to make his official attempt before late in the afternoon. Taking off in the damp, darkening sky at about seven in the evening, Curtiss made his bid. At an altitude of about twenty feet Curtiss not only covered the required kilometer but also continued on until his total distance measured nearly a mile at a speed of almost forty miles per hour. Curtiss had made the first officially recorded flight in the United States and was awarded the *Scientific American* trophy. But his triumph was brief, for within a few days he received a letter from Orville Wright informing him that the wingtip ailerons used in the lateral control of *June Bug* were, in fact, infringements upon patents held by the Wrights. Since Bell had suggested the ailerons—which were not precisely the same as the Wrights' wing warping—Curtiss felt Orville's allegation was an afront to Bell's scientific integrity. Curtiss did not believe the Wrights had a case. The result was a long, acrimonious, tedious litigation that embittered the Wrights and Curtiss. (The decision was made finally in favor of the Wrights in 1914.)

Only one more flyable plane came out of the Aerial Experiment Association, John McCurdy's *Silver Dart* which flew successfully late in 1908. The association disbanded shortly after, each of its members going his own way. Selfridge was dead by this time and Curtiss, in company with Augus-

The most successful product of the AEA: Curtiss' *June Bug*, in which Curtiss made early record-breaking flights, 1908. (U. S. Air Force)

tus M. Herring, formed the first aircraft manufacturing firm in the United States.

Although as he admitted, he was "not a professional aviator," Curtiss was to become one of the most famous aviators of his time. More aggressive

The birth of the aircraft carrier, November 14, 1911. Eugene Ely takes off and lands on the deck of a converted battleship ii in a Curtiss biplane. (U. S. Air Force/U. S. Navy)

than the Wrights (to whom he owed more than he was ever willing to admit, in court or out), Curtiss accrued a number of "firsts" during his active career in aviation. He opened the first flying school in the country, at Hammondsport, and trained several of the most celebrated American pilots of the early years of aviation. He was the first American designer to show an interest in seaplanes and has been called the "Father of Naval Aviation" since he introduced the idea of the aircraft carrier late in 1910.

Curtiss-trained pilot Eugene Ely demonstrated the feasibility of this idea when he took off from a specially constructed flight deck on the cruiser *Birmingham*. The plane was typical of the product of the Herring-Curtiss Company and was based upon the *June Bug*, the primary difference being the placing of ailerons between the wings instead of at the wingtips, pending the outcome of the Wright infringement suit. Two months later, on January 18, 1911, Ely made another demonstration flight. After taking off at San Francisco, he made a landing on the cruiser *Pennsylvania*, the first ever made on a "carrier." It marked the true beginning of naval aviation.

Having successfully flown over the water, Curtiss again turned to what he called the "hydroaeroplane." He abandoned his early plane-in-a-canoe concept and began evolving float designs. After some failure and some success, Curtiss actually took his plane off the water—he had moved his operations for these experiments to North Island, near San Diego, California—on January 26, 1911. Although Fabre, in France, had preceded Curtiss by a year, Curtiss is generally credited with developing the first true hydroplane. He continued to refine the craft, improving the design of the pontoon, even adding wheels, making it capable of movement in the air, on water, and on land (he named this amphibian the Triad). Having impressed the U. S. Navy with the possibility of the aircraft carrier, Curtiss proceeded to sell the traditionally conservative high command the seaplane. This required a lot of doing and flight demonstrations, but with a little high-level help, including

The Curtiss "hydroplane" of 1911—the first successful American seaplane, at North Island, California. (Historical Collection, Title Insurance and Trust Co., San Diego)

that of the hero of Manila, Admiral George Dewey, Curtiss broke down upper-echelon Navy resistance, and in July 1911 the Navy Department ordered its first aircraft, a Triad. Curtiss soon established himself as the foremost manufacturer of seaplanes.

Following the renewed activity in aviation that began in 1908 and the developments that followed in Europe and the United States, it was inevitable

that a great aerial competition would take place. The first great international air meet (more officially La Grande Semaine d'Aviation de la Champagne) began on Sunday, August 22, 1909, and ended on Sunday, August 29. The setting was the plain of Bethany, 3 miles north of the city of Reims in the Champagne region of France. Here assembled the most celebrated aviators of the day: Blériot, fresh from his Channel triumph the month

Reims, 1909. Paul Tissandier, a student of the Wrights, is ahead in his Wright Model "A." Trailing in a Voisin is French pilot Louis Paulhan, who later wrecked his plane, although escaping serious injury. The photo was taken on the first day of the Reims meet, Sunday, August 22. (U. S. Air Force)

Voisin biplane, piloted by Paulhan, rounds a pylon. (Musée de l'Air, Paris)

before; Latham, recovered from his Channel failure (in which he suffered a face injury); Farman; and the unknown quantity and only American, Glenn Curtiss. Absent were the Wrights (busy completing Army tests at Fort Myer); Santos-Dumont, testing his newest *Demoiselle*, was unaccountably absent. Esnault-Pelterie had been forced to withdraw because of an injury he had suffered—in a boxing match. The Wrights were represented by three planes, however, flown by a trio of their pupils. Paul Tissandier was the first pilot to get off the ground (when the first plane, an REP, failed). Tissandier also participated in the late-afternoon speed trials (the day's flying having been postponed by poor weather).

The star of Reims was Henri Farman, who flew despite minor injuries suffered in an accident before the meet. Plagued also by engine trouble, Farman received permission from the judges to install a new engine—a Gnome rotary—in his plane. Farman went on to win a second-place prize in the altitude contest, and a first in the *Prix des Passengers* for taking up two passengers (his being the only plane capable of lifting three men). On Friday, August 27, Farman won the Grand Prix de la Champagne et de la Ville de Reims for the longest nonstop flight (112 miles in a little over 3

Henri Farman (in cap) at the Reims meet, 1909. Farman took three prizes at the meet, including the Grand Prix for distance—112 miles nonstop. (U. S. Air Force)

Blériot entering the cockpit of his plane for the Gordon Bennett trophy—the speed competition at Reims. (Musée de l'Air, Paris)

hours), making him the top prize-winner of the Reims meet.

While the Grand Prix was the biggest money prize (100,000 francs donated by the champagne industry and the city of Reims), the most coveted prize was the *Coupe Internationale d'Aviation*, better known as the Gordon Bennett Trophy. Distance was fine, but speed—that was the glory of aviation. James Gordon Bennett, publisher of the New York *Herald*, expatriate American, and sponsor of several speed prizes on the sea, land, and air, found such undertakings good for his newspapers. The Bennett Trophy drew a great number of entrants, no fewer than twenty from France itself. England had but one representative, George Cockburn, as did the United States: Glenn Curtiss. After preliminary contests the French contestants were narrowed down to three, any one of whom was expected to be the winner of the trophy: Blériot, Eugene Lefebvre (in a Wright plane), or Latham in an Antoinette.

The field in the Bennett Trophy race narrowed down quickly: Cockburn's heavy Farman could not

Eugene Lefebvre, representing France in the Gordon Bennett race, rounding a pylon in a Wright biplane. A landing that ended up in a haystack eliminated him from the race. (U. S. Air Force)

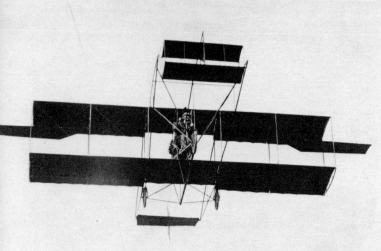

Curtiss pilots his *Golden Flyer* at the Reims air meet on August 29, 1909, the final day of the competitions, to win the Gordon Bennett Trophy for the United States with an average speed of forty-seven miles per hour. (Musée de l'Air, Paris)

Glenn Curtiss at Reims, preparing for a flight. (Smithsonian Institution)

get up the speed to make him a winner, he was unable to complete even a single lap of the race. Upon landing, he ran into a haystack. Eugene Lefebvre was next in his Wright Model A. Despite Lefebvre's remarkable handling of the biplane—he won a reputation as the daredevil of the meet with his aerobatics—he could not do better than thirty-five miles an hour in the race. (A week after the Reims meet, Lefebvre became the first pilot fatality of aviation—Selfridge had been a passenger—when another Wright plane he was testing crashed with jammed controls.)

With the elimination of Lefebvre from the race, Latham suffered a mishap and then the contest narrowed down to Blériot and Curtiss. Blériot flew the fastest single lap, thus winning the Prix du Tour de Piste (the Piste was the racetrack over which the races were flown). Curtiss won the Bennett Trophy (the Bennett race covered the Piste course twice). Curtiss' entry into the Reims meet, at the behest of the Aero Club of America, had been a last-minute decision. Curtiss had won the *Scientific America* Trophy for the second year in a row, which made him the outstanding American airman and a natural representative of his country in the meet. When the invitation came, the meet was only a month away. Curtiss immediately began construction of a new aircraft, which he named the Golden Flyer (it was painted yellow), and a new V-8 fifty-horsepower air-cooled engine.

The *Golden Flyer* was similar to its predecessor, *Gold Bug*, with a wingspan of twenty-eight feet, nine inches, a typical tricycle landing gear, and large between-the-wings ailerons for lateral control. Each aileron measured six feet long by two feet wide and jutted out beyond the wingtips. The engine made the difference in Curtiss' winning flight, although several other planes were also fifty horsepowered (the Wrights' were only thirty horsepower). Curtiss also employed Yankee common sense: "I climbed as high as I thought I might without protest, before crossing the starting line— probably five hundred feet—so that I might take advantage of a gradual descent throughout the race, and thus gain additional speed. I cut corners as close as I dared and banked the machine high on turns . . . the air seemed fairly to boil. The machine pitched considerably, and when I passed over the 'graveyard,' where so many machines had gone down and were smashed during the previous days of the meet, the air seemed literally to drop from under me." Curtiss averaged forty-seven miles an hour in the two laps and became the first winner of the Gordon Bennett Trophy. He had

proved that it was possible for a biplane to beat a monoplane (Blériot's) in a speed race—though he had won by the slender margin of six seconds.

The final Sunday—August 29—provided ideal weather and the meet's most spectacular accident, luckily not fatal. Curtiss and Blériot continued their duel for speed prizes in a three-lap race. Blériot brought out his most powerful machine, which was pulled by an eighty-horsepower engine. Curtiss had already flown when Blériot took to the air. At the far end of the course he suddenly brought his monoplane in for a landing; it burst into flame. An overheated fuel pipe had ruptured and spilled fuel onto the exhaust. Blériot had seen this while still in the air and had quickly landed, but not in time to prevent the fire. The Blériot burned so quickly that Blériot himself was burned, and the plane was a total loss. It was but another in the series of Blériot crashes. The "intrepid" airman, however, eventually read the writing in the sky. He had once explained his philosophy of the crackup by saying , "A man who keeps his head in an aeroplane accident is not likely to come to much harm. What he must do is to think only of himself, and not of his machine; he must not try to save

The wreckage of Blériot's plane after it burned at Reims on the last day of the meet. (Musée de l'Air, Paris)

both. I always throw myself upon one of the wings of my machine when there is a mishap, and although this breaks the wing, it causes me to alight safely." The following December, during an exhibition flight over Turkey, he suffered one of his "mishaps." His plane fell onto a rooftop, crumpling the wings and cracking several of Blériot's ribs. Taking the hint, Blériot never flew after December 1909, and devoted himself to the manufacture of aircraft instead.

Hubert Latham, who had won second place in the Grand Prix at Reims, had been eliminated from the Bennett Trophy race. His Grand Prix flight was made with the Antoinette IV (entry No. 13), the same plane in which he made his first Channel attempt. In an Antoinette VII, similar to this one but without the wingtip ailerons, Latham took the Prix de l'Altitude with a flight that reached 155 meters (508.5 feet); Farman was second with 110 meters. Latham's climbing achievement was especially notable because he admitted to becoming dizzy at great heights, and in 1909, 508 feet was considered a great height. Latham's win brought the Reims meet to a triumphant close—a meet that, though afflicted with its full share of accidents, had no fatal crashes. As the English magazine *Flight* pointed out in its issue of September 4, 1909, the Reims meet had marked the true arrival of aircraft. "Now that they are matters of history," the comment ran, "none can gainsay that journeys of over a hundred miles in length can be made by aeroplane without pause; or that the same machine can fly to great heights, or that it can carry comparatively great weights as represented by three persons aboard." Reims had definitely proved that the flying machine had come to stay.

The great success of the first major air meet at Reims (earlier ones were not in the same category) was unquestioned. It had attracted, according to one estimate (and that supposedly conservative), no less than a half million spectators. Most, of course, were French, but there were also contingents from Britain and the United States running into the thousands. Never before had so many aircraft— thirty-eight, of which twenty-three actually flew— been assembled in one place. Twelve different types of planes were seen, flown by twenty-two pilots. Reims represented a high point in early aviation history and inspired a number of pre-First World War air meets that followed. It also marked the first true, feverish interest in aviation by the layman. As one of the spectators, England's David Lloyd George, later observed, "Flying machines are no longer toys and dreams; they are an established fact." Although this seemed true enough, flying in general was left to sportsmen, and for most laymen it was a spectator sport. A rash of air meets ensued in Italy, Germany, England (with several through 1910–11), and France (also with several—at Juvisy, Cannes, and Nice). Colorful posters heralded these meets, attracting the public for the thrilling show and the airmen for the generous prizes.

The first "aviation meet" in America was held

Hubert Latham rounds a pylon in his Antoinette IV at Reims; he took second place in the Grand Prix in this plane. In another Antoinette he took the prize for altitude—all of 508.5 feet (155 meters). (U. S. Air Force)

Period poster heralding a "Meeting d'Aviation" at Nice, a sequel to the successful Reims meet. (Musée de l'Air, Paris)

MEETING D'AVIATION
NICE
10=25 AVRIL 1910
P.L.M.

BILLETS D'ALLER & RETOUR
INDIVIDUELS & DE FAMILLE A PRIX REDUITS
TRAINS EXTRA-RAPIDES DE JOUR & DE NUIT

CH. BSOR

near Los Angeles on the old Dominguez Ranch from January 10 through January 20, 1910. Promoting the meet was a showman-actor, Dick Ferris. Although it was not as impressive as Reims, great crowds (well over twenty-five thousand arrived by streetcar, automobile, and horse) saw flying machines they had never seen before. Among these were the French Farmans and Blériots. Curtisses and Wrights represented the United States. Curtiss himself was present and took several prizes and set a new speed record carrying a passenger (a speedy fifty-five mph). The star of the meet, however, was French flier Louis Paulhan, who set a new altitude record (4,165 ft.) and made a seventy-five-mile cross-country record flight in just under two hours which won him the ten thousand dollar grand prize. Also on hand, although as pilots of dirigibles, were Roy Knabenshue and Lincoln Beachey, whose names would mean something in the future development of American aviation.

An even more impressive meet was held near Boston in September in the Harvard Aeronautical Society's competition. The competitors were American and English, and the spectators flocked to Squantum Field in their autos to see the flying machines. The leading English pilot was Claude Grahame-White. His teammates were Alliot Verdon Roe and Thomas O. M. Sopwith, neither of whom did very well in the meet but who, later, designed outstanding aircraft. Grahame-White nosed out Glenn Curtiss to win the Boston *Globe*

Prize (ten thousand dollars) in a race around Boston Light.

As a sequel to his performance at the Harvard-Boston Meet Claude Grahame-White gave the residents of Washington, D.C., a thrill when, on October 14, 1910, he flew an airplane into the capital. Taking off from nearby Benning Race Track in his Farman, he brought the plane down onto West Executive Avenue, between the White House and the building that housed the War, Navy, and State departments. After a brief visit with officials of the War and Navy departments Grahame-White nonchalantly took off.

Grahame-White remained in the United States after the Harvard-Boston Meet to participate in what was to be the most splendid American meet of all. Held during the final week of October at Belmont Park racetrack on Long Island, the meet was the American equivalent of Reims. It capped all the year's aviation events and was as well, one of the season's social highlights. Pilots, a total of twenty-seven from three nations—France, England, and the United States—competed for the prizes, including the second running of the Gordon Bennett race. In addition to throngs of common men—and women—the spectators included a number of glittering social names—Drexel, Mackay, Whitney, Gould, Vanderbilt, and Ryan. Thomas Fortune Ryan, in fact, donated a prize of ten thousand dollars for a race from Belmont Park around the Statue of Liberty and back.

One of the star performers of the first great American aviation meeting was Curtiss pilot Charles F. Willard, here demonstrating a spot landing. (U. S. Air Force)

Spectators watch English pilot Claude Graham-White's Farman at the Harvard-Boston Meet, September 1910. (U. S. Air Force)

Englishman Grahame-White, flying a Blériot, won the Gordon Bennett Trophy with a speed of sixty miles per hour (as compared with Curtiss' forty-seven miles per hour of the previous year). The improvement in aircraft in the short time between Reims and Belmont Park was even more dramatically demonstrated in the altitude contest, won by American Ralph Johnstone, flying a new Wright plane, with an effort that reached 9,714 feet (compared with Latham's 508.5 feet at Reims). The Statue of Liberty race, although initially won by American John B. Moisant in a borrowed Blériot (his own having been wrecked just before the race began), was finally decided in favor of Grahame-White. Disqualified on a technicality (because he had taken off after the stipulated time for the race), Moisant lost out on the prize.

Belmont Park, New York, October 1910. Latham, in his Antoinette, during the Bennett Trophy race in which he came in fourth. (National Air and Space Museum, Smithsonian Institution)

Claude Graham-White taking off from West Executive Avenue, Washington, D.C., October 14, 1910. This was the first flight into and out of the capital. (U. S. Air Force)

Although Grahame-White was the star of the show, as he had been at the Harvard-Boston Meet also, it was Latham and his Antoinette that most captivated the American spectators. His plane inspired numerous model-airplane kits for the next Christmas season. Two weeks later Latham had the consolation of winning the $5,000 offered by the Baltimore *Sun* for the first flight over the city. The flight brought Latham and the Antoinette more laurels, and invalid R. Winans, a millionaire, his first glimpse of a flying plane—the major reason for the prize offer. In January Latham made the first flight across the Golden Gate at San Francisco.

Another form of aerial tournament, generally encouraged by generous prizes, was air races between specific cities. One of the first of the famous interurban races was one between London and Manchester for the prize offered by the air-minded London *Daily Mail*. It was won in April 1910 by French pilot Louis Paulhan, who covered the 183 miles in five and a quarter hours, winning over the English favorite, Grahame-White. When the prize was first offered in 1908—ten thousand pounds (nearly fifty thousand dollars) to the first pilot who covered the distance within twenty-four hours of takeoff—rival papers mocked the *Daily Mail* for its foolishness, and humor magazine *Punch* offered a like amount to the first pilot who went to Mars and back within a week. To the skeptical, either flight appeared as feasible.

Other such flights followed: In May 1910, Curtiss made the first flight between New York and Albany; the Angers to Saumer (France) race followed in the next month; in September, in conjunction with the Milan Air Meet, a prize was offered for the first crossing of the Alps. It was won by Peruvian Georges Chavez in September, but suffering from the cold from the high-altitude flight, Chavez crashed when landing and died two days after winning the prize. And so it went, with a succession of air shows and air races.

One of the memorable flights of the prewar period was the Paris-to-Madrid contest sponsored by the newspaper *Le Petit Parisien*. One of France's most colorful airmen, Jules Védrines, was the lone

A new world's speed record was set at the Belmont meet by France's Alfred Leblanc, whose Bleriot achieved an average speed of 66.22 miles per hour. His flight ended badly for, while landing, he struck a telephone pole in half. Miraculously, LeBlanc survived and would fly later for France. (Library of Congress)

Louis Paulhan, winner of the Manchester-to-London race, April 1910. (Musée de l'Air, Paris)

entrant—of the 4 who took off—to complete the distance of 842 miles (in fourteen hours, fifty-five minutes, eighteen seconds). When the contest opened, there had been twenty-nine entrants, most of whom were eliminated through various mishaps (including one that killed a spectator and injured several others).

Védrines was a ruthlessly aggressive flier and hounded his fellow contestants. As one of them said, "He was always at my heels, pursuing and menacing. . . . After a while I heard and saw him in my sleep." Védrines' racing style was disconcerting to his rivals, to say the least, and may have served to eliminate them as much as mechanical defects in their quirky machines. (His courage served him well during the war that would come within a few years; he died in an air crash in 1919 while demonstrating the possibilities of an airline linking Paris with Rome.)

The cross-country, international flights became fashionable in 1911. French pilot Jean Conneau became the first man to fly from Paris to Rome in May; in June he also finished first in a Circuit of Europe (Paris–Liège–Spa–Utrecht–Brussels–Roubaix–Calais–London–Paris) race, a meet that was marred by no fewer than three fatal accidents. Conneau wound up the flying year by winning again, this time in a Circuit of Britain in July; Conneau's chief rival in this race was his own countryman, Védrines. Védrines flew a Morane-Saulnier, and Conneau a Blériot. Interestingly, one of the rules of the contest was that replacements of parts on competing planes should be minimal, and five essential parts (carefully stamped by the Royal Aero Club) could not be changed at all. The point was to encourage improvement of the design of aircraft. Conneau completed the circuit—a distance of 1,010 miles—in twenty-two hours, twenty-eight minutes, nineteen seconds: The redoubtable Védrines came in an hour later. Soon after the Circuit of Britain, there were also circuits of Germany and Belgium. Though not as spectacular as the British race, the German race revealed that the German airmen were not solely devoted to the airship. Such little-known names as Taube,

Jean Conneau, French pilot and chief rival of Vedrines. (Musée de l'Air, Paris)

Another aviation first: Latham's Antoinette over San Francisco, January 7, 1911. This was the first successful crossing of the Golden Gate by air. (Library of Congress)

Jules Vedrines preparing for takeoff at Issy-les-Moulineux in the Paris-to-Madrid race, May 1911. The plane is a Morane-Borel, which Vedrines borrowed after his original craft was damaged in an accident. Assistants hold the plane while the engine—a Gnome rotary—builds up speed. Vedrines won the race; he was also the only entrant, all others having been eliminated by accidents. (U. S. Air Force)

Aviatik, and Albatros came to light in the German race, names that in a few short years would have a dreadful ring.

The United States lagged behind Europe in the aerial tournaments; nor were money prizes as lavish and plentiful. The Gordon Bennett Trophy was returned to the United States in 1911, won by Charles T. Weyman, flying a speedy Nieuport—a French design. Then, in August, the long-distance record was broken by Harry N. Atwood, flying a recent Wright plane, in which he traversed a distance from St. Louis to New York (1,256 miles) in twenty-eight hours, fifty-three minutes in the air. (He took off on August 14 and landed on August 25, having made eleven landings in between.)

The epic cross-country flight of the era, however, was made by Calbraith Rodgers, a six feet four former college football player and automobile racer who had learned to fly only a month before his flight. The prize was fifty thousand dollars, offered by publisher William Randolph Hearst to the first man to fly across the United States within a period of thirty days. Hearst had offered the prize in 1910 to publicize a meet in California; the single stipulation was that the flight must be completed by October 10, 1911. Rodgers had bought a Wright Model B Flyer and with backing from J. Ogden Armour, a meat tycoon, Rodgers decided to try for the Hearst prize. Naming the Wright Flyer *Vin Fiz* (for a new soft drink that Armour was producing), cigar-consuming "Cal" Rodgers took off from the Sheepshead Bay racetrack, Long Island, New York on September 17. By evening he had reached Middletown, New York, a distance of 105 miles from New York City. At the same time a special train carrying his mother, his wife, his manager, three mechanics, and enough spare parts to construct a new plane, moved across the country with him. He would need them—the spare parts, that is—and the mechanics. His mother, wife, and manager went along for the ride.

The magnitude of Rodger's undertaking will be realized when it is understood that in 1911 there were no airports, no landing fields, no radios, no weather information, no ready source of supplies except the accompanying five-car train. Landings and takeoffs had to be made from convenient (and at times, inconvenient) fields and farms. Landings were fairly precipitate for Rodgers, and landing did not always require as much room as taking off. However, in order to find a suitable takeoff site, Rodgers recruited the help of accommodating natives who often carried the plane a mile or more to an open space for takeoff. The Model B Wright (actually the *Vin Fiz* was the Model EX, a single-seater version of the B) was smaller than the earlier Flyers. It was equipped with wheels and had no forward elevator.

In crossing the United States, Rodgers came to earth no less than seventy times. Besides the usual mechanical problems—faulty spark plugs, broken fuel lines, etc.—Rodgers had to contend with weather, terrain (ranging from desert to mountains), and souvenir hunters who gathered up bits of the plane after a poor landing. There were also such prosaic obstacles as trees, barbed-wire fences, and a chicken coop—all of which Rodgers plowed into. The mechanics had daily work to do on the plane—and Rodgers did not always walk away intact from his landings either.

An early Nieuport of 1911 of the type in which Charles T. Weyman won the Gordon Bennett Trophy. (Musée de l'Air, Paris)

The *Vin Fiz*, Calbraith Rodgers at the controls, takes off in a rural setting trailing a little hay in the tail skid. One of the many stops in Rodgers' cross-country flight in 1911. (National Air and Space Museum, Smithsonian Institution)

By the time he reached Chicago, Rodgers (who had been delayed by an injury) was no longer in the running for the Hearst money. But he had beaten Atwood's distance record and proposed to continue on, even though there would be no prize at the end of the flight. On November 5 he landed at Pasadena, California, just a few miles from his goal, the Pacific. In taking off for the final leg, the Wrights' engine quit, and the plane dived into a field. Rodgers was pulled out of the wreck with two broken legs, a broken collarbone, and a brain concussion.

One of Rodgers' nineteen not so good landings, after which the *Vin Fiz*—and sometimes Rodgers—were repaired and the flight continued. (National Air and Space Museum, Smithsonian Institution)

The *Vin Fiz* after one of its smoother landings being carried to a suitable takeoff spot by townspeople of Elmira, New York. The plane was carried three quarters of a mile through a woods and a swamp. (National Air and Space Museum, Smithsonian Institution)

Cal Rodgers, on crutches, after his arrival at Long Beach, California, December 10, 1911. Rodgers was the first man to cross the United States by air—New York to California beginning on September 17 and ending December 10. (National Air and Space Museum, Smithsonian Institution)

Charles K. Hamilton, a Curtiss graduate and one of the early American exhibition fliers. (U. S. Air Force)

After a stay in the hospital, Rodgers, indomitable, was ready to push on on December 10. With crutches lashed to his plane (of which now the only remaining pieces of the original were one of the vertical rudders and a single strut), he took off from Pasadena and landed at Long Beach so that the wheels of the *Vin Fiz* could, symbolically, touch the Pacific. In eighty-four days Rodgers had covered 4,321 miles, having spent eighty-two hours and two minutes in the air. Although he had missed out on the prize, he had made the longest flight up to that time and had become the first man to cross the United States by air. Upon receiving the Aero Club's Gold Medal in December, he predicted a day when flights from New York to California would be made in aircraft flying "around a hundred miles an hour," although he did not visualize that happening "until some way is devised to box in the passengers against the wind." (This fascinating airman died on April 3, 1912; while stunting near Long Beach, the *Vin Fiz* fell into the Pacific.)

The era immediately preceding the outbreak of the First World War was one of near stagnation in the United States for aviation. Sport, exhibition flying, "show business" seemed the concern of Americans rather than the further development of aircraft. This is understandable for many reasons: Airplanes could not carry passengers as a ship did, or even like an automobile (which, thanks to Henry Ford's mass-production methods, were beginning to multiply like beetles). In other words, to the practical American, of what use was a flying machine except for some fool to fly in? Someone had thought of flying the mail by plane as early as 1911, but that was hardly more than a stunt. Still, the Wrights and Curtiss in the United States (as well as the Voisin brothers, the Farman brothers, and others in France) were turning out aircraft that people bought. They were the daredevils, who flew in competitions or concocted exhibitions to bring in spectators. One of the early professional fliers, who had learned to fly with Curtiss, was Charles K. Hamilton. In the summer of 1910 Hamilton first made headlines when he made the first long cross-

Charles Hamilton demonstrating the Multiplane, the invention of Israel Ludlow. Unpowered, the Multiplane was towed into the air by automobile. Demonstration flights invariably drew great numbers of small boys. (U. S. Air Force)

country flight in America (New York to Philadelphia and return) and later went on to make a career of exhibition flying.

Hamilton was, in a phrase current at the time, "game," but he realized that the exhibition circuit was not conducive to long life. "We shall all be killed," he was heard to say, "if we stay in this business." There was little satisfaction in performing for the gawking crowds that assembled to watch flying exhibitions. Before long they became so blasé, at least the pilots believed, that they only came hoping to see a spectacular crash. Hamilton

had begun his career as a trick bicyclist, later graduated to parachuting, gliding, and ballooning. He later joined, about 1911, a group of pilots who called themselves Moisant's International Aviators and toured the United States giving exhibition flights. Hamilton's boast was that he had, during the course of his work, broken every bone in his body. Despite his willingness to expose himself to all sorts of dangers, Charles K. Hamilton was not killed while flying (although several of his contemporaries were); he died in bed of pneumonia in 1912.

That the desire to experiment with new forms of flying machines was not dead in the United States was amply evidenced by the invention of John F. Cooley of Rochester, New York. Two years in the making, Cooley's machine was a quite advanced design for its time (1910), with practically no wing,

An advanced—though nonflying—design for its time:
the Cooley machine of 1910. Inventor John F. Cooley
stands (on left) before his craft. The two sixty-
horsepower Elbridge engines did not get the craft into
the air. (U. S. Air Force)

twin propellers, a long sleek fuselage—with radiators, much like those on the Antoinette, running just above the windows. It did not concern Cooley, obviously, that the pilot should be able to see where he was going. But then, Cooley's plane, as it eventuated, did not go anywhere anyway.

In France, where the aviation industry was bustling, various means of flight were under investigation, among them the old challenge of vertical flight in the helicopter. These seemed to work as toys but not as a full-sized man-carrying machines. However, as early as 1907 (three years before Cooley's failure), Paul Cornu constructed a strange device that looked more like a multiple bicycle accident than an airplane. But, powered by an Antoinette

engine, the thing actually lifted him off the ground. Not high, but off—the first time an aircraft rose vertically in free flight. Later, the machine lifted not only Cornu but also his brother to an altitude of about five feet before settling back to the ground. Although Cornu's flights did not usher in an era of helicopters, it did point in the direction of the potential of vertical flight.

In the United States, meanwhile, the emphasis was on stunting and exhibitions. Even these, however, contributed to the improvement of aircraft and engines as the aviators—called birdmen by the newspapers at the time—acquired more experience, and, no doubt, suffered many a mishap. Hailed as the "World's Greatest Stunt Flier" was

An early, little-known, and reasonably successful helicopter design by French inventor Paul Cornu. On November 13, 1907, Cornu succeeded in getting the helicopter into the air. (U. S. Air Force)

Lincoln Beachey, "the World's Greatest Stunt Flier," began his flying career as a balloonist and was taught to fly by Curtiss and soon became noted as a fearless exhibition pilot. Among his feats was a dangerous, drenching flight over Niagara Falls and under the Falls Bridge in June 1911. (Library of Congress)

American Lincoln Beachey. Beachey's daring kept interest in aviation alive in the United States after appetites had become jaded with exhibition flying. His specialty was the "death dive." Shutting off the engine of his Curtiss at five thousand feet, Beachey would dive the plane nearly vertically and land with breathtaking precision—generally before a crowded grandstand—in a previously selected spot. He also, in June 1911, created a stir by flying over Niagara Falls, under the arch of International Bridge, and through the Gorge before 150,000 spellbound spectators and for five thousand dollars. A nerveless stunt flier, Beachey could pick a handkerchief off the ground with his wingtip, he looped, he rolled, and he "turkey trotted." One writer at the time compared him with the poet Milton and the pianist Paderewski and called him "the greatest artist of the aeroplane." Another

Beachey specialty was to race his Curtiss against the greatest auto racer of the time, Barney Oldfield, for the "Championship of the Universe." Beachey generally won.

Beachey's last flight occurred at his hometown, San Francisco, when during an exhibition flight his specially made monoplane lost its wings in a dive and Beachey fell to his death in San Francisco Bay (March 14, 1915). He had finally met the "Silent Reaper of Souls" of whom he had written so often. He once told a newsman that when the end did

Beachey had a keen instinct for showmanship (and an undisguised contempt for his audience); in 1912 Beachey staged an auto vs. flying machine competition between himself and celebrated racing driver Barney Oldfield. Beachey won by a nose. (National Air and Space Museum, Smithsonian Institution)

come "I wanted to drop from thousands of feet. I wanted the grandstands and the grounds to be packed with a huge, cheering mob, and the band must be crashing out the latest rag. And when the ambulance, or worse, hauled me away, I wanted them all to say as they filed out the gates, 'Well, Beachey was certainly flying some!' "

Women too were intrigued by flying in the fledgling years of aviation. In the United States the most fetching proponent of aviation was writer Harriet Quimby. Trained at Moisant Flying School, she became the first licensed woman flyer in the United States, in 1911. (The first woman to pilot a plane in the United States, though not licensed, was Blanche Scott, who had been trained by Curtiss. The first woman to pilot a powered aircraft was French Baroness Raymonde de la Roche, who flew a Voisin in 1909.)

Harriet Quimby was determined to make women important contributors to the development of aviation. She wrote widely on that subject—even predicted a day when the United States would have airports and regularly scheduled airliners (perhaps even with women pilots). She made her first mark in history when, in April 1912, flying a Blériot, she became the first woman to cross the English Channel by air (from England to France). She made this through a fog-enshrouded overcast with the aid of a simple compass.

After her Channel flight, Harriet Quimby became the most famous woman aviator in the world and began making exhibition flights to spread her gospel of women in aviation. This fame was not fated to last for very long. She appeared at the Boston Meet in July 1912 and took up her manager, W. A. P. Willard, as a passenger in her Blériot. Unstable at best, the Blériot was even worse with a passenger. Caught in turbulent air, the plane tossed out both Willard and Harriet Quimby, who fell a thousand feet into the Atlantic. Harriet Quimby, in her brief life as "The Dresden China Aviatrice" (as she was called because of her beauty), had brought feminine grace to flying. She designed her own fashionable flying clothes, which always interested her readers, but even more (de-

Lincoln Beachey, who boasted that if anyone could fit a barn door with an engine he would fly it. One of his crowd pleasers was the loop; during one, Beachey's plane lost its wings and fell into San Francisco Bay, killing the twenty-eight-year-old pilot. (National Air and Space Museum, Smithsonian Institution)

Harriet Quimby, writer, feminist, and pioneer of flight. (Library of Congress)

Harriet Quimby's *Blériot XI*, the plane in which she crossed the English Channel in April 1912. (National Air and Space Museum, Smithsonian Institution)

Matilde Moisant in the cockpit of a Blériot; the barograph strapped in the rear fuselage measured altitude in the Wanamaker Trophy competition. In 1911, the same year in which she received her pilot's license, Matilde Moisant won the trophy. (National Air and Space Museum, Smithsonian Institution)

The end of Matilde Moisant's flying career. Just after landing after a flying exhibition at Wichita Falls, Texas, Moisant was horrified to see that the spectators were rushing toward her still-moving Blériot. To avoid cutting through the crowd she gunned the engine enough to pull the plane into the air and over the crowd, before it stalled into the ground and burned. Pulled from the wreckage with her clothing and hair aflame, Moisant was not seriously injured. But she gave up flying at twenty-six, upon the urging of her family. (National Air and Space Museum, Smithsonian Institution)

spite her tragic death), she had proved that women were the equal of men as pilots.

The second licensed woman flier in the United States was petite Matilde Moisant, sister of pioneer aviator John Moisant. Organizer of the famous Moisant's International Aviators (actually comprised of fliers from several nations), Moisant had made headlines when he carried a passenger in a cross-Channel flight in August 1910, and nearly won the Statue of Liberty race in October at the Belmont Meet. On tour with his aviators, Moisant was thrown from a Blériot (they did not bother with seat belts in those days) at an altitude of fifteen feet and died of a broken neck. When his brother Alfred opened up a flying school in 1911, among the first students were Harriet Quimby and their own sister Matilde. Apparently undaunted by her brother's death, Matilde kept the famiy name alive in aviation by joining Harriet Quimby in exhibition flights and her own exhibition solo flying. She became the first woman to receive the Altitude Prize in the United States in 1911, with a record of 2,500 feet. Matilde Moisant became a famous exhibition flier, but by 1912 she decided to give it up after surviving four serious crashes (the last in flames). She lived to be 85 before her death in 1964.

Ruth Law was the third American woman to be issued a flying license after having learned in a Wright Flyer. She later used a Curtiss in her exhibition flights equipped with Wright controls. A daring pilot, Ruth Law was the first woman to loop a plane; in 1915 she piloted her plane up to an altitude of 11,500 feet to break the then-current record. The next year she attempted a flight from Chicago to New York.

Although she came down somewhat short of her goal, she covered a distance of 512 miles nonstop (in late November, in freezing weather, in an open plane). She then held the record for distance in the United States, which had been newly made only a couple of weeks before by Victor Carlstrom (452 miles before engine trouble forced him down). When war came to the United States in 1917, Ruth Law, as well as other women pilots, offered their services to the U. S. Air Section of the Signal Corps, but were, needless to say, rejected. After the war (during which, at least, she had been permitted to make exhibition flights in bond-selling tours), Ruth Law formed her "Flying Circus." In 1922, after an accident in which a young member of her troupe fell to her death, Ruth Law retired from flying.

The Stinson sisters, Katherine ("Kitty") and Marjorie, learned to fly at the Wright Aviation School at Dayton, Ohio. Kitty learned first (and was not accepted by the conservative Wrights until she had brought written permission from her parents) when she was barely nineteen. She began illuminating the Stinson name by making exhibition flights and stunting fearlessly. She later toured the Orient, the first woman to fly there, and returned to the United States in time for the First World War. Refused as a pilot, she served in the Ambulance Service in France, where she contracted tuberculosis and was forced to give up flying. Marjorie, also a Wright pupil, returned to her home in San Antonio, Texas, and with her brother Edward Stinson (later the designer of sport planes) started a flying

Ruth Law, who began flying in 1912 and quickly gained fame as a daring pilot and record breaker. (U. S. Air Force)

One of Ruth Law's most famous "acts," looping at night with flares attached to her plane. She also made early altitude record and long-distance flights. She volunteered for air service in the First World War—and was permitted to make fund-raising and recruiting flights. She quit flying in 1922 when one of her women stunt pilots was killed while trying to transfer from a moving car into a plane. (National Air and Space Museum, Smithsonian Institution)

The Stinson sisters: Katherine in her flying outfit, and Marjorie. Both proved to be excellent fliers, Katherine (or "Kitty" as she was best known) with exhibition flights in the Orient, and Marjorie as a flying instructor and an early air mail pilot. (U. S. Air Force)

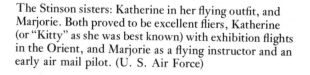

school. As early as 1914 she was sworn in as a mail carrier to become one of the first airmail pilots. During the war she was a respected instructor and taught dozens of military pilots to fly. Both Stinson sisters lived to ripe old ages.

Production of the airship did not stop with the introduction of powered flying machines. Ballooning was still a popular sport of the wealthy in the United States as well as in England and on the Continent. After Santos-Dumont's success with a dirigible, the controllable airship became the more practical form of lighter-than-air craft.

The American pioneer in the development of the airship was "Captain" (an honorary rank) Thomas Scott Baldwin. In his earlier years Baldwin had been a showman providing aerial entertainment with parachute jumps and balloon ascensions. With the advent of the airship, he visualized another, more spectacular form of entertainment using the dirigible. When Curtiss came onto the aviation scene with a good light engine, Baldwin (who, incidentally, was not related, to Curtiss's colleague in the Aerial Experiment Association, Frederick W. Baldwin) approached him. The result was Baldwin's *California Arrow*, introduced at the Louisiana Purchase Exposition at St. Louis in 1904. With the Curtiss engine, Baldwin could produce successful dirigibles. In 1908 the team of Curtiss and Baldwin sold the first airship to the U. S. Army for $10,000. Known as *Signal Corps One*, it was ninety-six feet long and nineteen in diameter, and flew for the first time at Fort Myer, Virginia, on August 18, 1908. The Army's intent was to use the airship in reconnaissance. It was a two-man vehicle, and for the Army tests, both Curtiss and Baldwin participated. Curtiss was stationed in the foreward end of the framework, which was suspended under the gasbag; he was the flight engineer in charge of the engine. In the rear, Baldwin worked the controls to maneuver the dirigible. The airship fulfilled the Army specifications by making an initial flight of 2 hours at a speed of twenty miles per hour. It was the first aircraft of what would one day be the U. S. Air Force.

The most famous dirigibles of the prewar—and the war—period were those produced by Count Ferdinand von Zeppelin, who began his work as early as 1900. However, Zeppelin was not alone in manufacturing airships in Germany. An important rival was Dr. Johann Schütte, around whose ideas a company named Schütte-Lanz was formed. Zeppelin's dirigibles were formed by skeletons of aluminum; Schütte's idea was to employ laminated plywood girders because he believed them to be more elastic than those used by Zeppelin. The German War Ministry, hoping to encourage a competitor for Zeppelin, assisted the firm. The first airship, *SL-1*, first took to the air in October 1911. In time, the Schütte-Lanz dirigibles gave way to the superior airships of Zeppelin. Although several were built and used by Germany during the war, the wooden construction was not ideal. Many fea-

The U.S. Signal Corps' first airship, the Baldwin-designed dirigible that was test-flown by Baldwin and Curtiss at Fort Myer, Virginia, in August 1908. (U. S. Air Force)

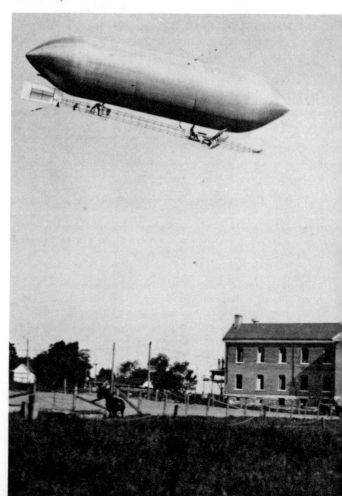

The Schutte-Lanz SL-1 over Mannheim, Germany, 1911. (U. S. Air Force)

The flying machine begins the conversion to a weapon of war. Lieutenant Riley E. Scott, the inventor, prepares his bombsight before a flight. The bomb rack was made of canvas. (U. S. Air Force)

tures of the SL's were eventually incorporated into the Zeppelin designs.

That the military heads of the great nations had begun to take an interest in airships and aircraft was an ominous sign, although few seemed to notice it. Aerial weapons had not proved very formidable in the past, and there was little to indicate that they would be more so in the future. Clumsily inconvenient guns were somehow lashed to struts and fired from planes, but to no great effect. An early bombsight was devised by the U. S. Army's Lieutenant Riley E. Scott in 1911. In January 1912, Scott won a five thousand dollar prize for accuracy in placing bombs with his invention. By this time other forces, political and international, had begun to surface in Europe, which would erupt into a war that would greatly influence, not necessarily to the good, the development of aviation.

Both the U. S. Navy and the U. S. Army set up flying schools at North Island, San Diego, California. It was here that Curtiss had already established a flying school. Curtiss became the first instructor of Navy fliers and contributed to the development of hydroplanes and flying boats.

The main Curtiss center was Hammondsport, New York, where he began producing the first flying boats (aircraft whose fuselage functioned like that of the hull of a ship). The first flying boat flew on January 10, 1912, opening up a new aerial possibility: aircraft that did not require landing fields. Curtiss became the first important manufacturer of water-based aircraft, several of his craft having been purchased by the Army and the Navy by the end of 1912.

But military aircraft, whether landplane or seaplane, did not concern the average American pilot in the innocent, halcyon, prewar years. Nor for that matter did American-made planes. American Supply House on Hempstead, Long Island, for example was licensed to sell the product of Blériot in the United States. Small flying fields began to appear in rural settings throughout the United States; former pastures were transformed into havens for birdmen. The sight and sound of the

Curtiss flying school, North Island, California. Two Curtiss "pushers" are on the right; a more modern 1912 Curtiss is parked to the right. (U. S. Air Force)

A 1912 Curtiss "hydroplane" at Hammondsport, New York. (U. S. Air Force)

planes attracted spectators, who drove to the flying fields to observe the sport and create hazards with their vehicles to the flimsy planes, or to themselves. Eventually areas had to be fenced off for autos and spectators.

Besides the Blériot, which was available in a two-place version as well, the Antoinette was also a very popular plane in America on the eve of the First World War. By this time they had begun to be supplanted by more advanced planes in Europe.

Civil flying before the First World War. Bleriots sold by
the American Aeroplane Supply House. This model did
not employ the rotary engine; it is powered by a Roberts
engine. (U. S. Air Force)

The single-place U.S.-made Bleriot sports flier.

Marcel Prevost's Deperdussin winning the Gorden Bennett Trophy in the Reims meet of 1913. (Musée de l'Air, Paris)

The Deperdussin's design was ahead of its time. (Musée de l'Air, Paris)

The last Reims meet, before the outbreak of war, took place in September 1913. Much had occurred in French aircraft design since the first air show in 1909. New names of aircraft manufacturers as well as the names of new pilots made the news. The big event, as before, was the Gordon Bennett Trophy race, which was won by French pilot Marcel Prévost in a remarkably modern Deperdussin monoplane, the product of the factory of ex-silk merchant Armand Deperdussin. Design of the plane, however, was the work of engineer Louis Bechereau, who produced sleek, streamlined planes of *monocoque* construction. The characteristic of this was that the fuselage was made of strips of plywood around which cloth was wound and then painted over, making the entire structure light and strong and offering the slightest resistance to the wind. Bechereau also enclosed the engine in a cowling, as much to keep the oil from splattering on the pilot as for streamlining.

In his Deperdussin on September 29, 1913, Prévost reached an average speed of 126 miles per hour, the fastest ever in the Bennett race (compared with Curtiss' speed of forty-seven miles per hour only four years before). A comment upon the state of aviation at the time was implicit in the fact that of the four contestants in the Bennett race, three were French and one Belgian; there were no Englishmen, no Germans, and no Americans.

The German aircraft designers, however, were not asleep. Even as the Reims meet was being held in France (unattended by English and American pilots because of lack of backing in the case of the English, and in the case of the Americans, as admitted by the president of the U. S. Aero Club, "because none of our machines are half speedy eough"), the autumn *Flugwoche* (Flying Week) was held at Johanistal near Berlin. One of the types of aircraft seen at Johanistal was the *Taube* (Dove), a birdlike design by Austrian Igo Etrich. The very successful aircraft was eventually produced by the Rumpler Company, which brought out Etrich's

An early (about 1909–10) Taube designed by Austrian Igo Etrich and manufactured by Rumpler. (U. S. Air Force)

patents in 1911. As history developed shortly after, the *Taube* was not to be a dove of peace.

Another name much heard at Johanistal was neither German nor Austrian but Dutch. It belonged to a young mechanical engineer, ne'er-do-well son of a wealthy coffee planter, who had grown up in Java and failed in several schools in Holland, Anthony Fokker. An adventurous practical mechanic rather than a theoretician, Fokker had been inspired by the flights of the Wright brothers. When he was twenty-one, he earned his flying license in Germany, where he found a better reception than in Holland. Fokker loved flying and spent a good deal of time at Johanistal.

Fokker was twenty when he built and flew his first powered plane, nicknamed *Spider* because of its weblike wiring. Although completed in late 1910, *Spider* was given its first true flight in May of the next year. Soon Fokker moved his operation to Johanistal, where he began manufacturing aircraft

Dutch designer Anthony Fokker aloft in his two-place glider. An instinctive pilot as well as designer, Fokker was not strong in theory or paperwork. One of the twin rudders of the glider was, with characteristic Fokker pragmatism, enlarged for improved performance. (U. S. Air Force)

and instructing. He brought publicity to his firm by giving exhibition flights and was the first man to loop a plane over Germany (the first man ever to loop was Frenchman Adolphe Pégoud). Encouraged by the success of his planes (the second was a two-seater version of *Spider*), Fokker approached his own government for orders, but he was turned down. He was also turned down by the Italians and the English. Only the German Government expressed an interest in Fokker's planes and bought two of the two-place design, thus initiating a relationship between Fokker and the German military leaders that would prove fateful within a few short years.

The Russians, too, had begun developing aircraft in the prewar period. The most notable of the early Russian pioneers was Igor Sikorsky, who had come to aviation under the spell of the Wright experiments. His first attempts at helicopter design, in 1909 were not successful (although they would be some years later), and Sikorsky turned to the design of more conventional aircraft. His first biplane followed in the path of the unsuccessful helicopters, but his second, the S-2, actually flew in June 1910. Each successive design revealed new facets of Sikorsky's genius, and by 1913 he had produced a giant four-engined plane, *Le Grand*, which he had visualized as the airliner of the fu-

Fokker in the cockpit of his first plane, the *Spider*. A compass is strapped to the pilot's knee. A seat belt does not appear to be in evidence, an often fatal oversight in early aircraft. (U. S. Air Force)

An example of Russian giantism: the Sikorsky *Le Grand*—with a wingspan of ninety-two feet—in the summer of 1913. Designer Igor Sikorsky at the extreme right in the plane's "balcony." (Sikorsky Aircraft)

ture. It was the largest airplane of its time, powered by four engines and with a wingspan of ninty-two feet. Its enclosed cabin could accommodate eight passengers. The landing gear consisted of both skids and wheels (no less than eight of these).

But *Le Grand* was destroyed in an accident. The accident was not of its own making: An engine fell off a plane flying over, and *Le Grand* was rendered unflyable on the ground) so Sikorsky produced a similar and improved giant plane. This was named *Ilia Mourometz* (for the Russian folk hero), had a wingspan of 102 feet, and flew for the first time in February 1914. On the eleventh of that month the big plane made a flight breaking all records for the time, with no less than sixteen passengers. The airliner potential of the large aircraft was forcibly demonstrated by Sikorsky's *Ilia Mourometz*, but before that idea came to fruition, it would also prove capable of transporting a thousand-pound bomb.

As for the United States, despite the fact that a war had been on in Europe, and dispatches had often mentioned the role of aircraft, the aviation industry and the military seemed to ignore the lessons of the war in Europe. Besides, safe across an ocean, the United States seemed to be immune to Europe's war virus.

American military aviation was not at an absolute standstill. There was a young air service, a branch of the Signal Corps, which those in command visualized as a tool for observation and not as a fighting machine of any value. That the Air Service was not ready for a real war was demonstrated as late in the game as 1916, when the European war had been in progress for almost two years.

The embryonic air force, specifically the 1st Aero Squadron, was sent into action for the first time against the Mexican bandit, Francisco "Pancho" Villa in March-April 1916. Villa and his band of raiders had crossed the border into Columbus, New Mexico in March, leaving seventeen American dead when they left.

Brigadier General John J. Pershing was ordered

to pursue Villa and to bring him back, "dead or alive." Under his command were fifteen thousand troops and the 1st Aero Squadron. This consisted of eleven pilots, eighty enlisted men, and eight planes, the latest Curtiss biplane, JN-4. Pershing's air branch began to suffer from the outset. In the flight from their base, Fort Sam Houston, Texas, to Columbus things went well, but the move from Columbus to Casas Grandes, Mexico, was a nightmare. One plane was forced back to Columbus with engine trouble and three became lost and were forced to make night landings, in which one of the JN-4s was wrecked. The remaining four planes were also forced to land in the dark but managed to do that without mishap.

Finally ready for operations out of Casas Grandes, the squadron suffered its greatest humiliation when it discovered that their planes were underpowered and that the engines could not lift the aircraft over the mountains for their assigned recon-naissance. When the tour of duty ended in April with Villa still at large, only two of the original eight planes remained—and they were unfit for field service and were junked.

Although the pilots had proved capable and resolute, the Curtiss and its engine were found wanting. There was much to be learned about operating aircraft under field conditions. Dust, for example, had clogged engines and the climate affected planes and men. The "Jennys," as the planes were eventually dubbed, were demoted to trainers, or were used to carry messages or to engage in observation, provided the hills were not too high. Nor did the Jennys carry guns.

European military aviation after only two years of war was far ahead of American military aviation in 1916. War had brought on changes in design, structure, engines, armament, and, of course, the function of aircraft. For the first time in history the flying machine became a weapon.

The *Ilia Mourometz*, Sikorsky's later giant originally designed as a passenger-carrying plane. On February 11, 1914, it took off with sixteen passengers aboard. An interesting feature of the design was the passenger's promenade for walks in the open air. The *Ilia Mourometz* was eventually used as a bomber. (Sikorsky Aircraft)

The First Aero Squadron in Mexico, 1916. The Curtiss "Jenny" in the photo was flown by Lieutenant Herbert Dargue and was stoned by Mexicans when he made a forced landing at Chihuahua. The performance of aircraft in the Mexican incident did little to impress Army commanders with the airplane as a weapon. (National Archives, Signal Corps Photo)

Farman Shorthorn over the Western Front, 1914. (U. S. Air Force)

A BE-2, its propeller stopped by the camera shutter, not its pilot, settles in for a gentle landing. By the onset of the First World War, its day had come and gone. (Imperial War Museum)

4 THE FIRST WARBIRDS

In the summer of 1914 the "crowned heads" and leaders of Europe bumbled into war; years of international rivalry, tension, and simple envy erupted when an Austro-Hungarian archduke was assassinated by a student in Serbia. While the deeper reasons for the outbreak of the war were far from simple, the assassination of Archduke Franz Ferdinand provided reason enough. Soon one nation after the other declared war on one of its longtime rivals in trade, in nationalistic pride, and in military prowess.

The several leaders, though not expecting a great war to result from their declarations, lurched from one debacle to another. Their people embraced the coming of war with a spirit of gaiety and relief. Nothing like a good little war to clear the air, and the air of Europe had been smoldering for decades. Those Germans and Frenchmen marching toward each other's respective capitals sang and tramped blithely into four of the blackest years in man's history. The "good little war" they had counted on did not clear the air at all (in fact, it laid the foundation for an even bloodier war that followed their "war to end all wars").

Most of the patriotic marchers neither reached their enemy's capitals nor returned again to their own homes. When the slaughter began in August 1914, the use of aircraft as weapons was not regarded too seriously by the military leaders. Most of them were old traditionalists, trained in the classic movements of war on the ground. What aircraft they had were a mixed lot whose primary function was observation. The planes at war's outbreak were pretty much the same that any airminded person might have read about since the European visit of Wilbur Wright: Blériots, Deperdussians, Voisins, Farmans, Taubes, Aviatiks, and Albatroses. They were unreliable, slow, and unarmed.

The transition from peace to war in aviation was relatively simple. Since the military regarded aircraft as either a branch of the signal corps (message-carrying) or the cavalry (for reconnaissance), any plane would do so long as it could get up into the air, scout the lines, and return. Among the first of the French planes that went into military service was the Maurice Farman S-11, called the *Shorthorn* because it lacked the forward elevator structure of its predecessor, the S-7 *Longhorn*. The *Shorthorn* was a product of the Henri and Maurice Farman Company, formed by the famed prewar pilot and a nonflying brother. The Farman was intended to be used as an observation plane and was so employed in the first months of the war. Later, it was fitted with guns (by British pilots; the French carried pistols and rifles), which, with the added weight, did not improve its performance. At best the *Shorthorn* could do about sixty-five miles per hour, which made it very vulnerable to faster single-seaters once they were armed. But that came later. The Farmans were eventually used only as trainers, but served into 1917 as artillery observation aircraft and bombers.

The first English aircraft to land on French soil was a BE-2 piloted by Lieutenant H. D. Harvey-Kelly on August 13, 1914. The initials stood for either Blériot Experimental or British Experimental—there seems to be little agreement on that; however, the BE was a product of the government-sponsored Royal Aircraft Factory and had been designed by Geoffrey de Havilland. When introduced in 1912, the BE was quite an advanced design, and achieved records in altitude, climb, and other categories. Its maximum speed was about seventy miles per hour, and like so many early planes of the war, it carried no armament. Its chief function was reconnaissance, although some were used in bombing raids. The BE was also notable for its ability to land at a low speed.

An exceptionally modern design for its time was the Sopwith Tabloid of 1913. It achieved a speed of more than ninety miles per hour, making it the fastest plane of its time. It was also the first single-seater used by Britain's Royal Flying Corps. The military version was fitted with ailerons but, initially, no guns. The Royal Naval Air Service also had a few Tabloids. Some particularly aggressive pilots converted the "scouts" into bombers and, in October 1914, successfully bombed a Zeppelin shed at Düsseldorf, destroying one of the monster airships before it could take off to bomb England.

Also an early nemesis of the Zeppelin was the

Sopwith Tabloid, in an early nonmilitary model (wing warping controls instead of ailerons were still used). (Imperial War Museum)

Early Zeppelin destroyer, the Avro 504. A "modern" craft at the beginning of the war, it served as a bomber and was later used as a trainer as German fighters developed to a dangerous degree. (Imperial War Museum)

Avro 504, designed by prewar sporting pilot Alliott Verdon Roe (later Sir Alliott Verdon Roe). With the Germans threatening Zeppelin raids upon London, the airships became a prime bombing target and only aircraft could reach them in their sheds well behind the lines, out of artillery range. In November three Royal Naval Air Service Avros bombed the Zeppelin sheds at Friedrichshafen after a remarkable flight around Lake Constance and over the Nosges Mountains in order to avoid violating the neutrality of Switzerland.

The backbone of the early German air service was the two-seater observation aircraft, practically all of which were called Taubes by the French. The first civilians ever to see an enemy warplane were the French, and they were the first to suffer the first aircraft casualties. On August 30, 1914, *Leutnant* Ferdinand von Hiddessen dropped bombs for the first time in history upon Paris (probably in an Aviatik, not a Taube), killing three and injuring several others, thus introducing another grim innovation into "the art of war"—the killing of noncombatants by bombardment from the air.

Early in the war the Germans came over in various planes dropping bombs and propaganda leaflets, and soon, blasé Parisians stood around to observe the "Six-o'clock Taube," the name bestowed upon any German aircraft that appeared overhead. Actually, they did little damage and killed few people, but their very presence was chilling: The age of a warfare based upon front lines seemed to be ending.

In the early months of the war the air weapon was not truly impressive. Enemy pilots out on patrol, old prewar flying friends, waved at one another as they passed in the air. Then it dawned on someone that his former friend had been gathering information about his own countrymen's troops. Methods of preventing the return of observation planes were improvised: At first bricks were carried, to be thrown at passing planes, then they were dangled from ropes (and brought in contact with the revolving propeller). Pilots began carrying sidearms for shooting at the enemy, then rifles, and later machineguns. None of these weapons proved terribly effective, although an occasional lucky hit

Clipped-wing birds: A Rumpler Taube (foreground) and an early Aviatik on display in Paris. Initially used as reconnaissance craft, the planes were converted into bombers by carrying a few light bombs, which the observer tossed out in the general vicinity of Paris. All planes with birdlike wing configuration were called Taubes. (U. S. Air Force)

Taubes over Paris, as seen through the result of a previous visit, purportedly a damaged church tower. (U. S. Air Force)

French flying instructors in 1914 and their major teaching tool, the clipped-wing Bleriot Penguin. (Courtesy Paul Rockwell)

Training accident; a little Nieuport 11 has suffered a rough landing. This plane was one of the first modern *chasse* (that is, pursuit) planes. (Courtesy Paul Rockwell)

ended in death for some hapless pilot and observer. Reconnaissance flights proved to be decisive in certain instances, alerting ground commanders to enemy troop movements. One such flight led to the timely withdrawal of British troops from the Mons salient out of the path of the German armies sweeping toward Paris. On these occasions even hidebound traditionalists among the ground leaders admitted that flying machines had some function in the war.

A strange camaraderie arose among the pilots of the warring powers. Their uniqueness—understood, they believed, only by themselves—put them apart from all other types of fighting men. They alone realized what it meant to fly above the earth, what it meant to keep a plane in the air, and what it meant to learn to fly. Learning "to imitate the birds" was another experience shared by all pilots, whether English, German, or French. Blériots were soon converted into trainers called "Penguins." These were standard Blériots, but with clipped wings, which made them practically unflyable. If the student pilot got them going fast enough, they managed to rise off the ground for a few feet but not for long (they were also called "grass cutters"). The Blériot Penguins were used for ground instruction to acquaint the student with the controls of the plane, and to prepare him for the takeoff. Penguins had a strange habit of starting out from opposite ends of a field and, despite the vast spaces, coming to grief by collision somewhere in the middle. Student accidents in Penguins were numerous but rarely fatal.

After graduating from a Penguin, the student advanced to a real plane to test his ability in the air. He went up alone, for in the early days of the war there were no dual-control planes in which the instructor could come along to help the student if he proved to be ham-handed. Getting off the ground was fairly easy; landing was the problem. Learning to imitate the birds was risky for both planes and pilots. After graduating from grass cutters into flying classes, the hopeful pilots passed through a truly dangerous phase. More pilots were killed in training accidents during the early months of the war than in operations or combat.

Typical training-school scene: the Nieuports of two students after a collision at Pau, France. (U. S. Air Force)

That aircraft might serve as observation posts was reasonably obvious; that they could also function as a kind of long-range artillery, dropping bombs upon troops and installations, was equally logical. But what made the real difference was the transformation of a "scout" into a gun platform. The large two-seaters were fitted with guns fairly early in the war, since the pilot could fly the plane while the observer manned the gun. The addition of the gun affected the performance of the plane, adding weight and drag from wind resistance. Also, unless the gunner was careful, he could do damage to his own craft, what with wings, struts, and wires webbing him in.

The solution was, of course, the gun that fired in the same direction as the plane itself pointed. A solution of sorts was devised for Roland Garros, one of the early birdmen of the sporting days of flight. His Morane monoplane had a machinegun mounted atop the fuselage just in front of the cockpit. It would fire in the direction of flight—through the whirling propeller arc. Metal plates were fastened onto the propeller to deflect those bullets that hit it; some, of course, would pass through without striking the propeller.

For a time Garros became the scourge of the front, throwing the German Air Service pilots into

Roland Garros, colorful prewar French pilot. (Musée de l'Air, Paris)

Morane-Saulnier of the type on which Garros mounted his single machine gun. Although he achieved many victories with his innovation, he ultimately succeeded in shooting himself down, and the Germans soon learned how he had done this. (Musée de l'Air, Paris)

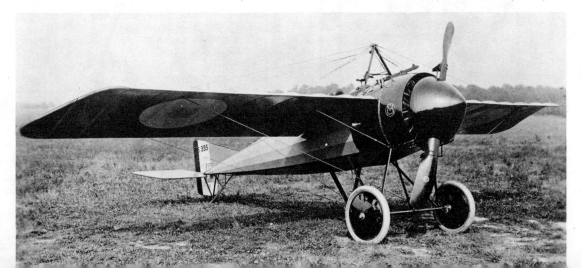

A filmstrip made during a synchronization test, and the business end of the Fokker Eindecker. The machine gun is mounted atop the fuselage and geared to fire through the propeller. (U. S. Air Force)

dismay. His plane approached and shot at enemy aircraft from an until then impossible angle. When Garros was forced down one day behind the lines, his weakened propeller shattered, the plane and its deflector gear fell into German hands. It was, of course, a crude and risky device, but to the inventive Hollander Anthony Fokker (who was ordered to copy it), it suggested a solution. Instead of the crude device of steel plates and bullets striking the propeller, he visualized one that synchronized the firing of the guns with the revolutions of the propeller. The gun (and later, guns) fired only when the blades were clear (others had thought of this idea before Fokker but he was the first to make it work). He installed a machinegun onto one of his *Eindeckers* (monoplanes) and transformed the single-seater aircraft into a formidable weapon: a flying gun.

Outstanding among the early *Eindecker* "aces" were Oswald Boelcke and Max Immelmann, Germany's first heroes of the air war. In their forward-firing Fokkers they quickly took a toll of the slower, more clumsily armed enemy aircraft. Boelcke, the more thoughtful and serious of the two, was an air tactician whose interest lay in preserving the lives of the men he led. Immelmann was more typical of the First World War fighter pilot—headlong, aggressive, a "hunter." Boelcke was beloved and Immelmann was envied.

For their air adventures both were awarded the *Pour le Mérite*. This was Germany's highest form of

A captured Eindecker was a curiosity to the French—on the ground, that is! (U. S. Air Force)

Hauptmann Boelcke.

Oberleutnant Immelmann †

Oswald Boelcke and Max Immelmann, each wearing his Pour le Mérite, as they appeared on the popular picture postcards of the period. The small cross under Immelmann's name indicates that the card was printed posthumously. (Charles Donald Collection)

military recognition. Neither Boelcke nor Immelmann survived the war. Boelcke crashed after a midair collision with a squadronmate, and Immelmann fell when his Fokker (fitted with twin guns) broke up in the air. Probably, but not certainly, this happened because the interrupter gear of the machinegun was out of alignment and Immelmann shot off his own propeller. The resultant vibration tore the engine loose, and he fell to his death. Immelmann's celebrity was so great that he had received fan letters from all over Germany and was called *der Adler von Lille* (The Eagle of Lille). Also, in his honor the coveted *Pour le Mérite* was nicknamed "The Blue Max."

The prime target of the newly armed Fokkers was the Royal Flying Corps' BE-2, the Quirk. Slow, lumbering, poorly armed, the Quirks were the most frequent and numerous victims of the *Eindeckers*. The Fokkers were faster and capable of firing directly at the Quirks, and British pilots suffered—as did the French in some of their outmoded planes. During the period of the "Fokker Scourge" the British had to contend with Immelmann stationed opposite them, while Boelcke was based opposite the French. The view of the harassed British pilots was expressed characteristically when one wrote, "The Hun enjoys things pretty much his

Fokker fodder: A slow, obsolescent British BE-2, the hapless "Quirk," on which German aircraft equipped with forward-firing, synchronized guns preyed during the period of the Fokker scourge, April 1915. (U. S. Air Force)

A rare air-to-air shot of a Fokker Eindecker on the tail (purportedly) of an enemy aircraft (slightly above and to the right). Many air fighting techniques were evolved by Boelcke, who taught that planes were vulnerable from the rear or below. Blind spots provided safe places from which to fire into the fuselage of enemy aircraft, especially from below, as this Fokker is about to do. Although a curious knightly sportsmanship was practiced in early air fighting, it was considered proper to pounce upon an enemy from out of the sun. (U. S. Air Force)

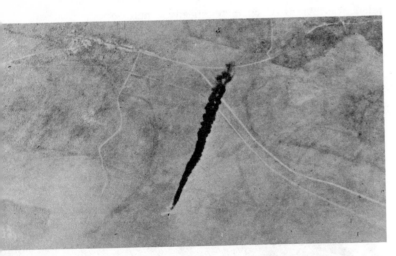

A French Voisin goes down in flames over the Western Front, near Verdun. This is one of the few authentic air combat shots of the war. The victorious German is slightly to the left and above the smoke column; the pilot was supposed to have been Boelcke, but no authentification has been found for that claim. (U. S. Air Force)

own way. When will our side get a synchronized gun, too? Then it will be a jolly good even fight all around." Dispirited RFC pilots referred to themselves as "Fokker fodder."

Three aircraft ended the Fokker Scourge on the Western Front: the Nieuport 11, popularly called the *Bébé* (Baby), had a single Lewis machinegun mounted atop the wing to fire over the propeller. Faster than the Fokker and capable also of firing in the direction of flight, the *Bébé* was more agile in air fighting than the German plane. Structurally, however, the *Bébé* was not much stronger than—if as strong as—the Fokker; the *Bébé*'s lower wing had a disconcerting tendency to snap in violent maneuvering.

The English reply to the Fokker question were two pushers of not very prepossessing appearance, the DH-2 (designed by De Havilland) and the FE-2B (the Fighter Experimental of the Royal Aircraft Factory, known as the Fee to pilots). The Fee was a two-seater. (It was sent to France before the DH with a flexible machinegun mounted in the front cockpit; the pilot sat behind.) Other guns were installed in some models: one between the cockpits, which enabled the gunner to fire at attackers from above and rear (to fire it, he had to stand on the fuselage); the pilot, too, was sometimes furnished with a gun. A powerful (160-horsepower) engine gave the Fee speed and climb advantage over the Fokkers. The DH-2 was a single-seat scout fitted with a forward-firing Lewis machinegun and quickly proved more than a match for the Fokkers.

If the emergence of the airplane as a weapon caught military thinkers unprepared, so did the dissolution of the "art of war" into a degrading war of immobility in the trenches. The machinegun had ended the day of the dashing cavalry charge, and big guns forced men to seek shelter by digging themselves into the earth. The result was stalemate, waste, boredom, and unbelievable misery occasionally worsened by inconclusive charges "over the top" to gain little or no ground. Only aircraft could move over no-man's-land—the vast wasteland between the trenches of the opposing armies. By 1916 it was obvious that it would not, indeed, be a "good little war."

Contributors to the end of the reign of the Fokker Eindecker: the Nieuport 11 *(Bébé)*, with its forward-firing gun (mounted atop the wing); the pilot is an American volunteer, Kiffen Rockwell. The FE-2B (not yet fitted with its machine gun in the front cockpit) and the DH-2. The two British planes are pushers, with engine and propeller mounted behind the cockpits—which mounting frequently caused fatalities in crashes. (Courtesy Paul Rockwell/U. S. Air Force/Imperial War Museum)

A British Fee on patrol over the German lines, 1916. (U. S. Air Force)

The original Lafayette Escadrille, Luxeuil-les-Bains, France, May 1916: Kiffin Rockwell, Captain Georges Thénault (squadron commander), Norman Prince (whose idea it was to form such a unit), Lieutenant Alfred de Laage de Meux (second in command), Elliot Cowdin, Bert Hall, James McConnell, and Victor Chapman (the first of the squadron to die for France). Not shown: William Thaw (standing behind Thénault). Rockwell, Prince, and McConnell also lost their lives before the United States came into the war. (U. S. Air Force)

Unlike his companion in arms, the grubby, abused infantryman, the First World War pilot was a glamorous figure. His exploits were fully reported in newspapers and before long the "scores" of aces (a pilot became an ace after shooting down five enemy aircraft) proved to be as newsworthy as baseball and football scores. What was conveniently overlooked at the time, and still is in that circle that glorifies such scorekeeping, was that those scores frequently also represented the lives of human beings.

The French were the first to begin recognizing the aces. By the time of Pershing's unfortunate experience with the 1st Aero's Jennys, such names as Georges Guynemer, Jean Marie Navarre, and Charles Nungesser were celebrated in France and well publicized in other parts of the world. The German aces captured the imagination, too, and their deeds were known even outside Germany. Among these great names were Oswald Boelcke, Max Immelmann, and an emerging young star, Manfred von Richthofen. The more reticent British even began releasing the names and exploits of some of their air heroes, which began with the advent of the youthful Albert Ball.

Among the most famed of the early air fighters of the early years of the war were the Americans of the Lafayette Escadrille. Not only were they eager, most of them, to "fight the Hun," they were also enamored of flying—the great adventure of it. They—again most of them—believed that fighting for France was tantamount to fighting for America, since they felt that the threat of an imperialistic Germany was a threat to the world. Several of the original members of the Lafayette Escadrille had fought from the war's inception in the French Foreign Legion. The Foreign Legion required no oath of allegiance to France, making it the only avenue to service in the war for Americans at the time without losing American citizenship.

The Lafayette Escadrille was made up of a mixed collection of adventurers, romantics, even one con man (Bert Hall). Many had come from "good homes," and could afford their own uniforms and the niceties of behind-the-lines life. Whatever the background or motivation of the individual, the exploits of the Lafayette Escadrille after its organization in May 1916 provided the folks back home with colorful stories of daring, courage, and sacrifice. Americans were supplied with plenty of tales of romantic aerial jousting over the Western Front (such reports, in turn, attracted more recruits, and temporarily neutral America tended to identify with the Allies more then the Germans—who, in their turn, contributed to their own bad press with the submarine). It might be mentioned that German pilots, especially Baron Manfred von Richthofen, were well treated in the Allied press.

The press did not report, or did not know, of the discomforts of fighting in a cold, hostile environment, often at high altitudes without oxygen; of the illnesses that plagued the young knights of the air (bad nerves, jumpy stomachs): anoxia, the problems connected with inhaling engine fumes (the fuel contained castor oil); not to mention the frailty of aircraft, the infidelity of engines, and the fact that men in other aircraft shot at you.

When the United States came into the war the Lafayette Escadrille was absorbed into the U. S. Air Service as the 103rd Aero Squadron; of its original seven members, three were still alive: Elliot Cowdin, Bert Hall, and William Thaw, who commanded the 103rd.

Pilots of two-seaters (reconnaissance and bomber) were not given the same attention as the single-seater scout pilots since they lacked the glamor of the single man in a tiny plane engaged in individual combat with the enemy. The practice of keeping score of the victories by two-seaters was not encouraged, and observers (many of whom were actually aces according to the folklore of the time) were rather bitter. They often referred to themselves (among the British) as PBOs ("Poor Bloody Observers"). As for the lone pilots in the scouts, they were defined by British Prime Minister David Lloyd George when he said, "They are the knighthood of this war, without fear and without reproach; and they recall the lengendary days of chivalry, not merely by the daring of their exploits, but by the nobility of their spirit." Like all

Mechanics stand by as the Lafayette's Kiffin Rockwell prepares to take off. The Nieuport carries its single machine gun on the wing (very inconvenient when the gun jammed, which they did frequently). The small, round mirror on the right side of the cockpit enabled the pilot to keep his eye on his tail—a favorite position of enemy attack. Rockwell died when he himself dived out of the sun on a German two-seater and, apparently hit by the German gunner, continued his dive into the ground after shedding a wing. He had been one of the Lafayette Escadrille's finest and most dedicated pilots. (Courtesy Paul Rockwell)

French aircrew on a reconnaissance flight over the lines. The observer-gunner is armed with a twin machine gun. The complex wing wiring made firing the guns as hazardous to the crew as to the German enemy. (Établissement Cinématographique des Armées)

Aviatik C2, a widely used reconnaissance aircraft during the early part of the war. (U. S. Air Force)

such grand statements uttered by those who did not share the risk, this one was only partly true. Not all were noted for their nobility of spirit; many experienced, and admitted knowing, fear—but their exploits were often exaggerated and exploited for propaganda purposes.

The Germans used two-seater aircraft for observation also (their pilots, too, were less celebrated than the single-seat fighters). Two of the most widely used in 1916 and for the rest of the war were the Aviatik and Albatros. Both were originally designed for reconnaissance but performed other functions as well. The Aviatik sometimes doubled as a bomber but finally ended up as an artillery observation plane. It was equipped with a radio over which the observer reported back to an artillery battery on the accuracy of its firing. The slow speed of the Aviatik rendered it an easy victim of the faster scouts, however. The slightly speedier Albatros was also used as a bomber on occasion. Both planes carried two guns: a fixed forward-firing machine gun operated by the pilot and a flexible machinegun manned by the observer in the rear cockpit.

Reconnaissance/observation aircraft were the main objectives of the scouts, not other scouts. The

Albatros C-III, two-seater of 1916–17. This one has obviously landed intact behind enemy lines. French soldiers and horses are in the background. (U. S. Air Force)

two-seaters transported military information, and it was the mission of the escorting scouts to protect them from enemy fighter planes. The meeting of swarms of enemy aircraft resulted in great "dogfights," which were romanticized in story and film after the war. The combats broke up into individual duels between enemy aircraft, although it was not uncommon for several planes to gang up on a stray plane. So much for the romance of the Lone Eagle on the Western Front. A pilot imbued with the idea that he could sally forth on his own against an

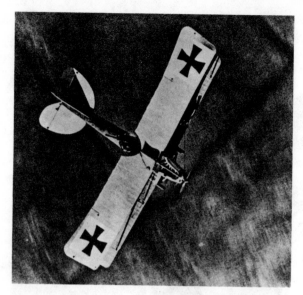

Albatros C-III in flight. Many German aces, among them Manfred von Richthofen, Ernst Udet, and Hermann Göring, began their flying careers in Albatros two-seaters before transferring to the more glamorous fighters. (U. S. Air Force)

The less glamorous reality of air fighting: a German two-seater after a burning crash behind the German lines. In this period pilots did not carry parachutes; many actually regarded it as unsportsmanlike or unmanly. And many died burning, or because of a damaged or malfunctioning plane. (U. S. Air Force)

enemy formation, or even a multigunned two-seater, was doomed to a short life on the Western Front.

Contemporaneous with the German Aviatiks, Albatroses and Rumplers was the British RE-8 (Reconnaissance Experimental of the Royal Aircraft Factory, which crews called the Harry Tate, in honor of an English music-hall comedian). It was an unlovely plane, although very popular with crews (despite an early reputation for spinning easily and disintegrating in a dive). The plane was extensively used from 1916 on as an "art obs" (artillery observation) craft. Like its enemy counterparts, it carried two guns: one fixed, mounted on the port side of the fuselage, and the other at the rear cockpit. Although faster than the German two-seaters of the period, the RE-8 had the advantage of slow speed over enemy scouts, which, in attacking, overshot the plane because the German pilot misjudged the speed. The rear gunner of the Harry Tate then dealt with the German scout.

Another British two-seater was the Sopwith 1½ Strutter (so called because of arrangement of short and long struts at the wing-center section). This was the first Royal Flying Corps aircraft to be fitted with a machinegun firing through the propeller; another gun was mounted on a so-called Scarff ring around the rear cockpit. The Strutter was used as a reconnaissance plane, a bomber, and even as a fighter. It displaced the earlier pusher planes, which were vulnerable to the new German fighters of the period. Eventually the Strutter, too, met its match in the later Albatros fighters when the pendulum of aerial superiority swung to the Germans. This was a characteristic of the air war; each new advance in engine or design placed its originator at a temporary advantage. Then the new plane was countered by yet another new one from the enemy's side and again the scale swung in the other direction. This rivalry contributed to rapid aircraft development in the few short years of the 1914–18 war.

Perhaps the most oversold air weapon of the war was the airship. The climax of the German Zeppelin raids upon England occurred in 1916, although the raids began in 1915 and continued on until 1918.

The Reconnaissance Experimental 8, R.E. 8, "Harry Tate," a product of the Royal Aircraft Factory late in 1916. Its appearance is deceiving; it actually could fly. (U. S. Air Force)

The airships (for not all were Zeppelins) were pre-war commercial designs converted to war. Like two-seater aircraft, they were initially regarded chiefly as reconnaissance craft, particularly in co-operation with the German Navy in the North Sea. But almost as soon as war was declared, the English population lived in fear of the great aerial dreadnoughts slipping through the mists of night to drop bombs upon London. The most active airship units were those of the German Naval Airship Division, under the command of Peter Strasser (who was, ironically, lost in the last airship raid of the war in 1918).

Following the first Zeppelin raid upon England in January 1915, a German newspaper hailed it: "The most modern air weapon, a triumph of German inventiveness and the sole possession of the German Army, has shown itself capable of crossing the sea and carrying the war to the soil of old England! . . . This is the best way to shorten the war, and thereby in the end the most humane . . ." This last statement would become a favorite refrain of warriors through the years. The objectives of the Zeppelins were military targets, not the city of London. But what with wind, imprecise navigation, poor visibility, and crews made miserable by cold and hasty by fear, the bomb-laden airships of Germany did not strike military targets with any accuracy. Typical of airships operations is the story of the L-39, which flew for the first time in December 1916. It made one raid on England and was caught over France by antiaircraft guns while drifting and nearly helpless in the wind. Hit by gunfire, the Zeppelin caught fire, exploded in midair, and fell at Compiègne; none of the crew of seventeen survived. German airships, because of the very cumbustible hydrogen used for lift, were extremely susceptible to fire. As "terror weapons" they were almost as much a source of fear to their crews as to the English civilian. Zeppelins were especially vulnerable to fighter attack from above. It became necessary to place guns on the top of the airship, which were manned during raids over England. Armament consisted of water-cooled Maxim guns. When they were not in use, it was necessary to wrap the guns to keep the water from freezing. The guncrew was also warmly dressed but exposed to the cold and wind atop the moving airship. They were also supplied with parachutes.

Airships, harbingers of "strategic" bombardment, rarely actually hit strategic targets. Although

Sopwith Strutters proved to be formidable over the
Somme in 1916, especially as reconnaissance aircraft.
Equipped with a forward-firing gun and an observer's
gun, they for a time held German fighters at bay. (U. S.
Air Force)

The L-39, of the German Naval Airship Division, in 1916. The airship was shot down by anti-aircraft fire after making its one raid on England on March 17, 1917. (Imperial War Museum, courtesy Alan Dashiell)

A Zeppelin downed over France; a ring of French soldiers keep spectators at a distance. (U. S. Air Force)

A Zeppelin shed at Trier, Germany. Such sheds were a favorite target of Allied pilots; a bomb that could be dropped inside the hangar destroyed both hangar and airship. (Courtesy Reed Chambers)

the German commanders attempted to bomb military targets—the docks, munitions works, etc.—they often bombed the wrong targets because of poor navigation and just as frequently jettisoned bombloads into residential London when attacked by British fighter planes or bracketed by searchlights and under antiaircraft-gun barrage. As a weapon that might have shortened the war, as some German commanders believed, the airship was a failure. The Germans began to abandon the concept of strategic bombardment (which came into its own in the Second World War) following the heavy losses of 1916 and minimal results. Often at the mercy of the weather, especially high winds, and an extraordinarily large target for attacking by faster aircraft, the aerial battleship was little more than a misconception.

By late 1916, despite the Zeppelin raids and the recognition of the military importance of the two-seater reconnaissance planes, it was the single-seater scout (in time called the fighter) that ruled the skies. The evolution of fighters was rapid as

Machine-gun platform on top of the *SL-14* during construction at the Schutte-Lanz factory at Mannheim-Rheinau, August 1916. The *SL-14* participated in only one raid before it was damaged beyond repair and dismantled. (U. S. Air Force)

The *L-53* leaves its shed at Nordholz, Germany. It was the first in the line of airships the British called height climbers—that is, capable of flying at altitudes (16,000–20,000 feet) that enabled them to elude fighter aircraft. Nevertheless, the *L-53* was shot down by British aircraft while on its fourth raid (August 11, 1918). (U. S. Air Force)

Another SL airship, the *SL-20*, a formidable craft indeed. More than 650 feet in length, it might have chilled the populace of London had it not blown up in its hangar without making a single raid. (U. S. Air Force)

London under air attack during a Zeppelin raid in 1916. Searchlights on the Old Lambeth Bridge seek out the mauraders for anti-aircraft crews and specially trained night-fighter pilots. (Imperial War Museum)

Naval airship *L-31* passes over the battleship *Ostfriesland* in the North Sea. The *L-31* was commanded by Heinrich Mathy, who was called the greatest Zeppelin commander of the war, known for his determination and the care with which he prepared his bombing raids. On his eighth mission, on October 2, Mathy and his crew of eighteen went down in flames near Potter's Bar; there were no survivors. (*Right*) The airship had been intercepted by Lieutenant W. J. Tempest in an obsolete BE-2, underscoring the vulnerability of the Zeppelin. The loss of Mathy was a blow to the Naval Airship service. The *Ostfriesland* was later sunk (1921) during the bombing demonstrations in which General Billy Mitchell attempted to prove that bombers were effective against "unsinkable" battleships. (Imperial War Museum/Courtesy Alan Dashiell)

designers attempted to produce aircraft superior to the latest enemy model. Planes emerged that were cleaner aerodynamically, more streamlined, and more powerfully (and all hoped, more efficiently) engined. Sopwith improved upon the Tabloid scout when he introduced the Sopwith Pup in 1916. Although comparatively underpowered (80 horsepower) by this time, its design made it an excellent plane to fly, and its ease in maneuverability made it a dangerous opponent even for higher-powered aircraft. Because of its light wing-loading (the weight of plane as compared with its wing area), it could land in small fields (eventually on carriers) and performed well even at high altitudes.

The French contribution to fighter development in 1916 was the Spad, a name derived from the initials of the company that manufactured it, Société pour Aviation et ses Dérivés. (Originally the company was owned by Deperdussin, who went bankrupt; Blériot then took over.) It was one of the toughest planes to come out of the war. Whereas, its contemporary, the Nieuport, might shed fabric or lose a wing, the Spad could hold up under stress without a shudder. Heavier and faster than the Nieuport, the Spad required more sky for combat aerobatics, but it could climb faster and higher than the Nieuport as well as enemy fighters. The Spad was not an easy plane to fly, for unlike lighter, more stable planes, it could not be permitted to "fly itself." Some planes, like the Nieuport, could be landed with the lightest touch on the controls, but the Spad had to be handled every moment it was in the air. Its structural ruggedness made it a fine plane for rough-riding pilots (provided they had learned to fly the plane), and it could take abuse in the air and in bouncy landings.

Although it was not to appear in great numbers nor even serve as a line fighter, one of the most modern of the 1916 fighters was Dr. Hugo Junkers' E-2, one in a series of the first all-metal aircraft. The first, the E-1, was covered with sheet iron and the name *Tin Donkey* was given to it and to the designs that followed. The E-2 was covered with corrugated dural sheet, which enabled Junkers to produce a remarkably clean configuration. Since

The Sopwith Pup of 1916. (U. S. Air Force)

The French Spad, which came into active service in July 1916. A rugged aircraft, it was a favorite of American combat pilots later in the war. Plane in photo is a contemporary reconstruction. (U. S. Air Force)

A glimpse of the future: Junkers' 1916 all-metal monoplane. The conservatism of German military leaders discouraged its further evolution at the time and only six were built. (U. S. Air Force)

The Siemens-Schukert D-I, a German duplicate of the Nieuport 11. (U. S. Air Force)

Not a flying boxcar but a Siemens-Schuckert Giant. Thirty-nine men stand under the lower wing, with plenty of room for more. Designed as a bomber, the big craft was relegated to a photo-reconnaissance role by 1918. (U. S. Air Force)

the German High Command did not trust the single-wing design, Junkers was not encouraged along these lines, although he pioneered all-metal aircraft design. Later bi-plane types, protected with armor, were employed as ground-attack planes and for artillery observation.

An interesting sidelight of the international aircraft design competition was the Siemens-Schuckert D-l, an out-and-out copy of the Nieuport 11 (*Bébé*). When the *Bébé* appeared late in 1915 to challenge the Fokker *Eindeckers*, it had proved itself superior to the monoplanes. Whereupon the German High Command turned over a captured *Bébé* to the Siemens-Schuckert firm with orders to produce a similar but better-performing answer to the Nieuport problem. The result was an almost exact duplicate, save for a more powerful engine. While the D-1 did outclass the *Bébé*, it, in turn, was outclassed by the Nieuport 17, the Sopwith Pup, and the

Spad. The D-1 did not last very long on the front.

Despite the failure of the Zeppelin strikes against England, the Germans were determined to continue with what in a later war would be called a strategic bombardment campaign. Theoretically, this would pit large, heavy, four-engined bombers against important military and political targets of the enemy. Political targets were difficult to define, for this generally included cities; military targets, if hit and knocked out of the war, logically would eliminate the enemy's ability to continue the war. Or so went the reasoning. To supplant the airships, German designers were put to work by the German Aviation Inspectorate to devise a type of aircraft designated *Riesenflugzeug* (Giant Aircraft). The first of the "R" series, or Giants, were designed and built by Zeppelin and called Staaken, which were manufactured by the Zeppelin-Werke Staakens, in a suburb of Berlin. The Giants had several features

A smaller Giant, the Friedrichshafen G-III, built by
Zeppelin in 1917. (U. S. Air Force)

The dreaded Gotha, under construction at Gothaer
Waggonfabrik, A.G. Its two pusher engines have not yet
been installed; not a true Giant, the Gotha was still an
impressive bomber, especially when it appeared in
formation over London at night. (U. S. Air Force)

in common, among them wingspans of more than 100 feet, multiengined power, and the capability of flying great distances carrying heavy bombloads. Among the giants was a Siemens-Schuckert with a wingspan of more than 120 feet, four engines (two powering the puller propellers and two the pushers). Siemens-Schuckert produced the largest of the Giants, the R-VIII, with a span of 160 feet. Mere giantism, however, was not enough, for the size meant the bomber was slower than the scouts and vulnerable (for all its armament) to fighter attack. The Giants had arrived one war too soon.

Size was not everything, especially since it interfered with speed and maneuverability. This German bomber had been forced down by enemy aircraft. This A.E.G. (Allgemeine Elektricitats Gesellschaft) was classified as a heavy bomber (*Grossflugzeug*) like the Gotha and the G-III, though smaller than either. (U. S. Air Force)

More effective than the Giants were the less impressive heavy bombers, such as the Friedrichshafen G-III (also a product of Zeppelin). Its wingspan spread seventy-eight feet, and it used only two engines with pusher propellers. Armament consisted of machineguns in the nose and the rear cockpit. The pilot sat in the center cockpit. The G-III, along with the more notorious Gotha, formed the backbone of the German heavy bombardment force, Bomber Squadron No. 3, the famous *Englandeschwader*. With a span of seventy-seven feet, the Gotha, like the G-III, was powered by two engines of the pusher type. As with the Taube, a generic name for any and all large bombers was adopted by the general public. In England it was the Gotha, whatever the type of plane.

Because they had appeared before their time (before engines were powerful enough), the heavy bombers suffered a rather high mortality rate. Many were destroyed by the English defenders, but more were lost through accident. Many fell to English antiaircraft fire and to fighters.

Britain's answer to the *Grossflugzeug* (heavy bomber) challenge was the Handley-Page 0/400, in fact the first of the long-range strategic heavy bombers. It was powered by two Rolls-Royce engines, was heavily gunned, and had a wingspan of a hundred feet. It was capable of remaining airborne for eight hours, which made it possible to strike at targets inside Germany. By May 1918, an even larger (126-foot wingspan) Handley Page had been flown (the V/1500) with four engines. This plane would have been used to bomb Berlin had not the war ended. The Handley Page bombers were the direct ancestors of the bombers of the Second World War.

Although not as spectacular in size as the heavy bombers, the DH-4, a two-place day bomber, was widely used and manufactured in larger numbers. It was popularly known as the Flaming Coffin

The Handley Page 0/400, the first long-range strategic bomber; only the Armistice canceled its mission: the bombing of Berlin. (U. S. Signal Corps/National Archives)

The infamous Flaming Coffin, the de Havilland DH-4; a fuel tank installed between pilot and observer was its major danger spot; otherwise it was a reliable aircraft. (U. S. Air Force)

because of its tendency to burst into flame in the air. Despite this, it was used to bomb targets inside Germany during the final year of the war. It could fly higher and faster than most German fighters and was reasonably capable in combat. The DH-4s and the Handley Pages were to have formed the backbone of what was called the Independent Air Force under the command of General Hugh Trenchard for strategic bombing of Germany. Trenchard believed that the Air Force deserved to function on its own and not in direct co-operation with ground forces. He found a disciple in this view in American airman William Mitchell, who commanded American air units in France.

British pilots referred to April 1917 as Bloody April. The balance of air power had swung back to the Germans when they introduced a new fighter, the Albatros D-III, to the Western Front around the first of the year. It proved to be more than a match for the old BE-2s and the FE-8s, particularly in the skilled hands of such German air leaders as Manfred von Richthofen, who led his packs against the hapless British. The era of flight formations had dawned, and the day of the lone air fighter was over. The dogfights of April alone cost the English more than 350 aircraft, most of them falling to the new Albatros.

One of the first victims of Richthofen's Jasta 11 Albatroses (the pilots plural was invariably Albatri) was a plane that, in fact, was superior to the German plane. This was the Bristol F2B Fighter, known as the Brisfit. When it went into combat early in April 1917, the Brisfit was used like any two-seater, maintaining formation rather than dogfighting with the German attackers. As maneuverable as the Albatros, the Brisfit had the further advantage of a second gun in the rear cockpit. When the Germans returned to their bases to report that the new English plane was "inferior to the Albatros," they doomed great numbers of their fellow pilots to a flaming death. Once it was realized that the Brisfit could handle like a fighter, it wreaked havoc among the Albatros formations.

The English introduced another formidable "scout" in April 1917, the SE-5 (Scouting Experimental from the Royal Aircraft Factory). A tough,

Albatros D-III, which ushered in the bloody April of 1917. (U. S. Air Force)

The Bristol F-2B Brisfit, which eventually challenged the reign of the Albatros in 1917. (U. S. Air Force)

stable aircraft, it had the added advantage of being armed with two guns, one laid on the top left of the fuselage and the other atop the wing on a Foster mounting to fire over the propeller. What the SE-5 lacked in maneuverability it made up in speed (120 miles per hour) climb, and sturdiness to withstand power dives without breaking up. Its appearance on the Western Front, along with the Bristol fighter, heralded the end of Bloody April. One of the SE-5's major features was the in-line, instead of the

The SE-5, one of Britain's best fighter aircraft of the First World War. (U. S. Air Force)

whirling rotary, engine—a French-built Hispano-Suiza.

The summer of 1917 brought a new Sopwith single-seat fighter, the Camel, into the battle over the Western Front. The first British fighter equipped with two synchronized machine guns (mounted on the "hump" forward of the cockpit, which gave the plane its nickname), the Camel was an exceptionally maneuverable fighter. This was an asset as well as a liability, for while the sudden, darting movements of the Camel confused German pilots, its tendency to whip into a right-hand spin (because of the rotary engine) was often fatal to inexperienced British pilots. But once mastered, and its peculiarities used to advantage, the Camel proved to be the deadliest fighter on the front.

Pilots of both the Royal Flying Corps and the Royal Naval Air Service (combined in April 1918 into the Royal Air Force) flying Camels destroyed 1,281 enemy aircraft during the period of its service—July 1917 to November 1918.

The one plane that might have outmaneuvered the Camel, although it was not as sturdy was the Fokker *Dreidecker* 1, the famed triplane that was designed to replace the outclassed Albatros. It was not the first triplane to go to war, for Sopwith had produced his version of a three-winged fighter during Bloody April; Fokker's emerged in August 1917. While it was a striking aircraft to look upon and remarkably agile in a dogfight (thanks to the gyroscopic force of its rotary engine), and further enhanced by a high rate of climb, it suffered from definite disadvantages. One of them was that in a long dive it tended to shed the fabric of the upper wing; the other was that the wing sometimes snapped and collapsed. Although certain German pilots, among them the first of the triplane aces, Werner Voss, and the "Bloody Red Baron" Richthofen, built up impressive victory scores in the Fokker triplane, its inherent weaknesses caused it to be withdrawn from front-line service before the end of the year. The Sopwith triplane, which apparently fascinated designers, inspired not only Fokker, but also several others (Albatros, Pfalz, Nieuport). The

An Albatros after having met its match. (Jarrett Collection)

The Sopwith Camel, considered by many as the best fighter aircraft of the war. The plane in flight is piloted by Major George Barker, who late in the war fought sixty enemy aircraft in a Sopwith Snipe, a later evolution of the Camel. Though severely wounded, Barker accounted for several enemy planes—and survived. (Jarrett Collection)

addition of wings did not necessarily improve the aircraft, and the idea waned. Fokker even went on to produce a five-winged plane, but it proved to be a total failure. The Fokker triplane, incidentally, was actually devised by Fokker's chief designer, Reinold Platz.

During Bloody April the United States was finally drawn into the Great War, following a series of ship sinkings by German submarines. Generally, American sympathies had been with the Allies from the beginning, although a strict neutrality had been maintained. During the war American aircraft design had not kept pace with that of the fighting powers; nor was there a full-fledged air force geared for war. Nor, further, was there a first-rank American fighter plane extant when the United States entered the war. Its most modern

Fokker's short-lived answer to the Camel and the SE-5, the triplane Dr. I. (Jarrett Collection)

American Jennies in a training flight over Texas near their base, Kelly Field. (U. S. Signal Corps/National Archives)

plane was the Curtiss JN-4, the Jenny of the ill-fated Mexican Punitive Expedition. By 1917 the Jenny could only serve as a trainer. The Jenny did not see combat, although several of these planes were shipped to England and France. Nor did any other American-designed aircraft operate as a fighter or bomber, despite early promises of "clouds of aeroplanes" for "crushing the Teutons."

It took about a year before American pilots (except those, of couse, already serving in the French or British Air Forces) flew into battle. It took time to train pilots and time to establish bases in France for what was called the U. S. Air Service, American Expeditionary Forces. Actually, as early as January 1918, American units began building up in

Nieuport 28 with "Hat-in-ring" insignia of the 94th Pursuit Squadron. Plane in photo is a contemporary reconstruction flown by Cole Palen, Rhinebeck, New York. (U. S. Air Force)

Manhandling a sturdy Spad: American mechanics of the 1st Air Depot, Colombey-les-Belles, France. This later Model XIII was more rugged than the earlier VII. (U. S. Signal Corps/National Archives)

the relatively quiet Toul sector. They had no American-made planes, and their Nieuports bought from France, were not fitted with guns. The first American unit began operations on April 3, 1918. It was the 94th Pursuit Squadron ("Hat-in-ring"), which was later commanded by Captain Edward V. Rickenbacker, the American Ace of Aces. The squadron flew the last in the series of Nieuport fighters of the war, the Nieuport 28. Faster than its predecessors (about 140 miles per hour), it was a frail craft that lost its wing fabric in a dive and at times disintegrated in the air. Although unpopular with many pilots, it was the first fighter plane used by the Americans in France.

Better suited to Americans was the Spad 13, a more powerful version of the 1916 model. It was powered with a 200-horsepower Hispano-Suiza (Spanish-Swiss: Designer Marc Birkigt was a Swiss who had studied in Spain) engine. It carried two synchronized Vickers machineguns and averaged about 130 miles per hour. Like the earlier Spad, it was a rugged craft and could take the manhandling of the less genteel pilot. However, it required a heavy hand on the stick every moment it was in the air; a steep angle of glide required absolute control up to the moment the wheels bumped the ground. Other lighter, more stable planes practically landed themselves.

A curious anachronism used by both warring sides through the entire war was the observation balloon. Captive "kite" balloons floated over the front serving as aerial observation posts from which information was relayed to the ground by telephone. Balloons were raised and lowered by means of a steel cable fastened to a winch in the balloon truck. An enemy balloon was a constant source of irritation, for it could direct artillery fire. From it, troop movements could be reported; so could the approach of aircraft or the location of enemy balloons. The balloon was always fair game for fighter planes.

If an enemy plane were sighted approaching a balloon in time, the balloon truck would quickly haul it down. However, balloon-busting pilots frequently approached from an unexpected quarter (from above clouds, for example, or so close to the ground as to be nearly invisible) to attack. The observers then could do nothing but take to their parachutes. Parachutes were often attached to the side of the basket. The observers wore a harness that was attached to parachutes before jumping. Although balloons were ringed with guns, a sud-

Balloonists prepare to climb into the basket; one parachute container hangs from the basket. (U. S. Signal Corps/National Archives)

The ground crew guides the rising balloon as the truck slowly winches up the cable. (U. S. Signal Corps/National Archives)

den fast swoop by a fighter could bring a balloon down before it could be pulled to safety.

Despite their vulnerability, balloons on both sides (the German balloons were called *Drachen* [kite]) were important in their limited role. They were not popular fighter targets because of the heavy gun positions around them and because they did not burn as quickly as might be imagined. Often several attacks were required, by which time ground gunners filled the air with fire, or protect-

American balloon under German fighter attack; the balloonists have gone over the side just before the enemy plane burns the balloon. (U. S. Signal Corps/National Archives)

An American observation balloon is being prepared to cover a French artillery emplacement, while American engineers, in the foreground, repair the road. (U. S. Signal Corps/National Archives)

Aerial activity fascinated ground troops. French artillerymen on the Meuse observe the fall of a balloon. (U. S. Signal Corps/National Archives)

ing fighters rose up to defend their balloon.

Following the failure of the Fokker triplane, Fokker and his chief designer Platz produced, early in 1918, the plane that might have turned the tide of the war in the air. It was the Fokker D-VII, a biplane that proved to be superior to its competitors—Albatros, Pfalz, Aviatik—and its adversaries—the SE-5, the Spad, the Camel—as well. It was so outstanding that even Albatros was ordered to produce the D-VII. This was a moral victory for Fokker because the favoritism shown Albatros (a German firm; Fokker was Dutch) by the German High Command often denied Fokker access to the better aircraft engines available in Germany. With the advent of the Fokker D-VII, Fokker was permitted to use six-cylinder in-line engines instead of the rotaries with which his earlier fighters had been powered. The Fokker's top speed was about 120 miles per hour, but one of its major advantages was that it could slow down without the pilot losing control (that is, stalling and then snapping into a spin). The D-VII could literally come underneath an enemy plane, "hang on the prop" for a moment while firing, and then quickly dive away. Its construction combined both metal (the fuselage was of steel tubing) and wood. The forward section of the fuselage was metal-covered. The thick wing cross section contributed to its ability to retain control at slow speed—and it was not a tricky plane to fly.

The Fokker D-VII was produced in great numbers for the big offensive that the German High Command hoped to unleash in the summer of 1918. The first D-VIIs appeared in May but were not ready in large numbers until July. By August the Allied toll in aircraft losses had risen alarmingly. By autumn all German squadrons along the front were equipped with the Fokker D-VII, but fortunately Germany had already lost the war on the ground.

Before the Fokker D-VII appeared and generally supplanted it, the Pfalz D-XII went into action against British and French planes in the early months of 1918. It had proved to be a fine fighter in the hands of some of the German aces, but once the Fokker appeared, the Pfalz was abandoned in favor of the easier-to-handle D-VII.

A postwar photo of the Fokker D-VII looping over Long Island, New York. The superiority of the Fokker prompted the Americans to confiscate several for study. Many were flown by American pilots after the war. (U. S. Air Force)

Fokker D-VII. (Jarrett Collection)

The forward fuselage of the Fokker D-VII. (Jarrett Collection)

The Pfalz D-XII, which was supplanted by the Fokker D-VII on the Western Front in 1918. (U. S. Air Force)

A Camel slung under the airship *R-23* as protection from enemy fighter attack. For the pilot, getting into the cockpit during flight must have been a tricky feat. (Imperial War Museum)

Although the British depended primarily on aircraft for the war in the air, they introduced some innovations during the last months of the war. Small airships were used ca. 1915–16 to hunt German submarines in the British coastal waters; they were called Sea Scouts or Blimps and were operated by the Royal Naval Air Service. Later larger airships, called Coastals were used for submarine hunting and in convoy escort across the English Channel. The British gave little thought to converting the airship into a heavy bombardment craft. But having witnessed the frequent distress of German Zeppelins and their vulnerability to fighter attack, the British decided to provide their larger airships with their own airborne escort. A Sopwith Camel was slung under an airship and released when the airship came under enemy attack. This was tested with Lieutenant R. E. Keys, RAF, as pilot and, while it worked, this method of

fighter protection was never used under combat conditions.

A seafaring people, the British eventually improved on the aircraft carrier concept, introduced by Glenn Curtiss in 1916. Among the first operational carriers was H.M.S. *Furious*, which had once been a cruiser. The *Furious* carried twenty Sopwith Pups and, although not a carrier in the later sense, did launch a carrier strike in July 1918. Several of its aircraft took off from the flight deck "somewhere in the North Sea," swooped down on the Zeppelin sheds at Tondern and dropped bombs that destroyed two German airships, the L-54 and the L-60. The *Furious*, with additional conver-

Sopwith Pups on the deck of the carrier HMS *Furious*, 1918. (Imperial War Museum)

A German seafaring warplane, the Dornier Cs-I, an all-metal, low-wing monoplane of remarkable modernity. For a seaplane it was unusually maneuverable and fast. Note the forward-firing gun on upper fuselage. These planes patrolled the North Sea. (U. S. Air Force)

sions, was operated as a carrier in the Second World War.

Although the Royal Naval Air Service operated airships, flying boats, and carrier-borne Pups, it was equipped primarily with landplanes. In the early months of the war R.N.A.S. Sopwith Tabloids carried out a long, hazardous mission to a Dusseldorf Zeppelin shed and destroyed the Z-9. The menace of the Zeppelin was much on the British mind and Royal Navy fliers were entrusted, perhaps because they were good at navigation, to strike the sheds on Germany's coast. They flew the same planes that were issued to the Royal Flying Corps—the "Quirks," the Avro 504A and others, including flying boats. One of its aces, Canadian Raymond Collishaw, favored the Sopwith Triplane. Americans who served for a time with the R.N.A.S. flew in the unpopular DH-4s.

American manufactured, though English-designed, DH-4s finally arrived in France in May 1918 and began operations in August. The major American production achievements of the war were the Jenny and the Liberty engine, a product of the combined minds of the automobile industry and the U. S. Bureau of Standards. The Liberty powered the DH-4s and was planned for use in Handley-Page bombers. The DH-4s, as it eventuated, were the only American-built planes to see combat (about three thousand in all were built by the Dayton-Wright Company), many of them with British and American day-bombardment squadrons.

American bombing units also used the French Breguet 14, the French counterpart to the Bristol fighter. Although not as widely used nor even as popular with pilots as the DH-4—despite the Flaming Coffin sobriquet—the Breguet was one of the most modern of the French aircraft produced near the end of the war. It was of nearly all-metal construction (wing ribs were wood, and it was fabric-covered) and was used as a bomber and for reconnaissance. The sturdy design continued in use by the French Armée de l'Air until 1930.

The romance of aerial dogfighting of the Great War is more folklore than fact, and, after the war, the fabrication of pulp writers and early moviemak-

An American-built DH-4 in France. (U. S. Signal Corps/National Archives)

A Breguet 14 bomber takes off from an American field in France. (U. S. Signal Corps/National Archives)

ers. Like all folklore, however, its legends are rooted in truth. No one can deny the courage and skill of the first air warriors. But no one can claim either, that they contributed much to the advancement of aviation. Their concern was with staying alive, not with the science of flight. It was of course, vicariously thrilling to imagine a dogfight high over the Western Front in which "intrepid" heroes of the air engaged in knightly combat. High above the degrading mud of the trenches, these last

The lesser-known, not-so-glamorous aspects of aerial warfare was carried out by ground crews and mechanics (*mécaniciens* to the French, and Ack-Emmas or A.M.— that is, aircraft mechanic—in military jargon). A ground crew fuses bombs before a mission. American mechanics repair a Nieuport in the foreground. (U. S. Signal Corps/ National Archives)

knights met in the cold, clean air to fight the good battle. Machineguns stuttered, and powerful new engines roared as the little planes twisted and turned. A short burst of gunfire and the battle was over. There was a burst of flame and the aircraft spun spectacularly down until it struck the earth with a flaming, spattering crash. Since there were no parachutes in the tiny fighter planes, pilots had a simple choice: either burn with the plane (if you were still alive) or jump.

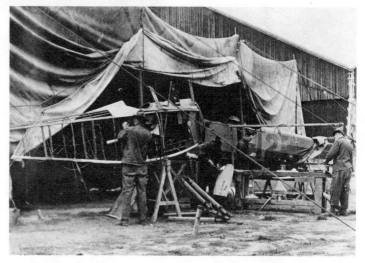

The *ambience* of aerial combat has been beautifully captured by the famous Cockburn-Lange photographs that surfaced after the war, purportedly sold by the widow of the photographer-pilot. The story was that her husband had rigged a camera on the upper wing of an SE-5 and, during combat, managed to snap action photos. Many believed this story and paid goodly sums for copies, and they have since been widely printed as authentic aerial-combat photos. They are not authentic, but used posed model aircraft and background projections, plus retouching. Even so, these fake photos capture the feel of air fighting of the First World War more dramatically than the numerous paintings and drawings of the period. Certainly the one showing Fokkers attacking a British formation seems true; the falling, burning Albatros dramatizes the pilots' fear of being burned alive. Some were known to have leaped from the planes rather than burn. (Jarrett Collection)

Such a way of life—and death—endowed the airmen of the First World War with unique romanticism. They were the last individualists in a new kind of war that had rendered millions faceless and nameless. They were, literally, above it all; they did not battle in mud or cringe in trenches. They lived in comparative luxury, behind the lines, in billets (French homes taken over by the government) or at permanent stations. The British even provided them with batboys to attend to their needs. Some hardly knew how their aircraft functioned or why they flew; they had ground crews and mechanics to attend to such mundane matters. They were the privileged specialists of the war.

Airdromes were exciting, noisy, and busy as mechanics prepared the fliers' "mounts" for battle. Unreliable engines were tested, machine-gun belts prepared, and guns checked while exhausted pilots rested. The condition of their equipment was almost as critical as the health and skill of the pilot. The little-known side of the story is that many pilots were in poor health, suffering cracked nerves and other illnesses very few realized were associated with the pressures of flying. There were those who did not return to their comfortable billets. It was, indeed, a hazardous trade.

A Lafayette Escadrille airdrome, Chaudun, summer 1917. Ground crews ready Spads and, on the right, a Nieuport 28 for patrol. The pilot, dressed for high-altitude warmth, is Kenneth Marr (after the war he became a literary agent). To his left a squadron mascot appears to be unimpressed by the activity. Tents, at left, housed mechanics' working quarters. (Courtesy Paul Rockwell)

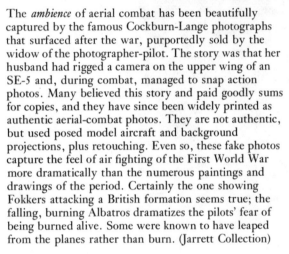

The 229th Squadron, Royal Flying Corps, in a lineup at Oudezeele, France. Behind the SE-5s are their camouflaged hangars. (U. S. Signal Corps/National Archives)

Camels of the American 148th Aero Squadron, August 1918. A more developed airdrome than most, this one provided brick buildings for billets and operations headquarters. (U. S. Signal Corps/National Archives)

A scene in the enemy camp: Triplane pilots of Jasta 10 prepare for flight. Like medieval knights, their preparation for battle required the aid of numerous squires. (Jarrett Collection)

A Fokker D-VII hit by anti-aircraft fire during an attack on an American observation balloon. The plane flipped onto its back when the pilot, Heinrich Marwede, attempted a landing on rough terrain. Not seriously injured, he spent the rest of the war as a prisoner. (U. S. Signal Corps/National Archives)

By around 1917 the early, knightly chivalry was forgotten; airmen flew in packs and had no qualms about attacking single aircraft. The possibility of structural failure, conked-out engine, or jammed gun was also an ever-present danger. The odds for survival were not good. The loser, in the British phrase, "went West."

The most dreaded form of going West was in a "flamer," your plane afire and falling in flames. Fire in the air meant almost certain death, although some pilots were known to have escaped even that. This was accomplished by sideslipping to keep the flames away from the fuel supply, even away from the fabric of the wings. Pilots even left their cockpits and stood on the wing to maintain some control to bring their planes down to a reasonably safe landing. Such an attempt sometimes ended in the pilot falling from his plane; many preferred that to burning.

An ever-present danger in aerial combat (or in training, for that matter) was the possibility of midair collision. With several planes milling around in a comparatively small piece of the sky, the chance of accident increased as the fight grew hotter. The most ironic and poignant death in the air was the flying-school accident, in which a student pilot died without ever having encountered an enemy. This was the grimmer, less romantic aspect of the first war in the air generally ignored by the romantics who counted victory scores, recognized

each variant of every fighting plane, and forgot that men flew and died in them.

The ace of aces of the First World War was Manfred von Rochthofen, whose victory score totaled eighty enemy aircraft before he himself fell in April 1918. If not an instinctive flier, Richthofen was a born hunter and a superb tactician. He believed in formations and generally traveled with a pack which, from time to time, set up a sure "kill" for him. Although probably the most adored man in Germany during his reign as the Red Baron, Richthofen was not noted for his warm personality or for the youthful high jinks associated with pilots. His was a ruthless, businesslike way of making war, and if this method did not fulfill glamorous expectations, it was chillingly realistic.

Although he flew several types of aircraft, including two-seaters, Richthofen is popularly associated with the Fokker triplane. Richthofen did favor this plane and scored several victories in it, including his eightieth. Richthofen met his death in the triplane, a death that continues to be argued after all these years. Richthofen had attacked a green pilot and appeared at the point of adding another kill to his score when Canadian Roy Brown came to the rescue of his squadronmate. At the

A British de Havilland burns after an encounter with an enemy aircraft. (Jarrett Collection)

The tangled wreckage of a midair collision between student pilots, one of whom lies in the foreground. (Jarrett Collection)

same time, as the air battle had worked its way close to the earth, Richthofen came under machine-gun fire from the ground. Either Brown (which was likely) mortally wounded the Red Baron or he was struck from the ground. His triplane broke away from the battle and came to earth in No-man's-land practically intact. Richthofen was dead in the cockpit; he was beyond caring who had fired the fatal shot.

Germany's second-highest-scoring airman was the likable, fun-loving Ernst Udet, with sixty-two enemy aircraft to his credit at war's end. Unlike Richthofen, Udet survived the war. He might not have had he not been spared by one of France's air heroes, Georges Guynemer. The two had fought a battle to a near draw when Udet's guns jammed. Guynemer pulled alongside, realized what had oc-

The ace of aces of the First World War, Manfred von Richthofen. (Jarrett Collection)

Richthofen landing his triplane at this base near Cappy, behind the Somme Front. (Jarrett Collection)

Ernst Udet, Germany's highest-scoring living ace after the war. He later became a stunt pilot, flew in films, and eventually assisted in the rebirth of the German Air force—especially as an advocate of the dive-bombing (Stuka) tactic. (Jarrett Collection)

Captain Roy Brown, believed by many to have shot down the Red Baron when Brown flew to the rescue of a green young pilot under attack by Richthofen. (Royal Canadian·Air Force)

France's top scoring ace, René Fonck. This bemedaled photograph is autographed to Marc Birkigt, designer of the Hispano-Suiza engine that powered Fonck's Spad. (Jarrett Collection)

curred, waved good-bye to Udet, and left the battle. This was one of the few authenticated knightly incidents of the war.

France's top scoring ace was René Fonck, who accounted for seventy-five enemy aircraft and survived the war. Fonck was a superb marksman and, like Richthofen, was a claculating tactician and no romanticist.

More typical of the fighting airman of the First World War, at least as popularly imagined, was the dashing Georges Guynemer. A sickly, slight man, Guynemer was admitted into the French Air Service only because he was persistent and knew the right people. In the air he was a demon and flew with an abandon that made him the darling of France. His method was the headlong attack, a method that destroyed fifty-four German aircraft before Guynemer himself was shot down in September 1917. His plane was then obliterated in a German artillery barrage, and Guynemer vanished from the earth, initiating the legend that "he had flown so high that he could never come down," believed by French schoolchildren for a generation after.

Edward Mannock led the British aces roll with a score of seventy-three. Although he was regarded as too old (twenty-seven) to make a fighter pilot, Mannock somehow managed to sign up with the Royal Flying Corps. In addition, he had one bad eye, which should also have kept him out, but Mannock managed to bluff his way through an eye test as well. A careful tactician, he was a good instructor to young pilots. A realist, he had no interest in a knightly war. He refused to join in toasts to fallen German fliers and was once heard to say of one, "I hope he roasted all the way down." Mannock fell in flames himself after being struck by ground fire.

A Canadian, William Bishop, was the second-ranking British ace, with an official score of seventy-two victories. Combining an unusual blend of the dash of the early air fighters with the science (marksmanship was his major asset) of the later aces, Bishop survived more than 170 combats in the air. He was a notoriously poor pilot, and the legend grew around him that he destroyed as many

Georges Guynemer, France's most colorful fighter pilot (Établissement Cinématographique des Armées)

British ace of aces, Edward "Mick" Mannock. (Jarrett Collection)

Canadian ace Major William Bishop and Mrs. Bishop. (Royal Canadian Air Force)

Allied planes in trying to land as he did enemy aircraft in combat. Between the wars Bishop became a successful businessman and served during the Second World War as an honorary air marshall in the Royal Canadian Air Force.

The American ace of aces was a former racing-car driver, Captain Edward V. Rickenbacker. Like England's Mannock, at the age of twenty-seven

Captain "Eddie" Rickenbacker, American ace of aces, and his Spad. (U. S. Air Force)

Captain "Eddie" may have been considered rather ancient to be a fighter pilot. As commander of the 94th Aero Squadron, Rickenbacker proved to be as outstanding a leader as he was aerial tactician. Despite a brief tour of duty cut short by a painful ear infection, Rickenbacker survived the war as the highest-scoring American airman (with twenty-six official victories) and as the winner of the Congressional Medal of Honor for a single-handed attack upon two formations of enemy aircraft. Rickenbacker saw no romance in the war in the air. He once said, "I can see that aerial warfare is actually scientific murder." He remained in aviation following the war and in the late thrities became president of Eastern Airlines.

Peck's Bad Boy of the U. S. Air Service, AEF was Frank Luke of Phoenix, Arizona. One of the last of the "intrepid airmen," Luke blazed a brief career on the front, which, though it lasted for a mere seventeen days, accounted for twenty-one official victories, most of them balloons. A loner, Luke had little respect for authority or discipline but was permitted to escape serious punishment because of his remarkable knack for burning German *Drachen*. However, had he returned from his last flight (in which he destroyed three balloons), Luke would have been court-martialed. Instead, he was awarded the Medal of Honor posthumously. Wounded and down behind German lines, Luke fought rather pointlessly with German ground troops until he was killed.

One of the classic air battles of the war was fought on October 27, 1918, about two weeks before the Armistice was signed. The lone Canadian

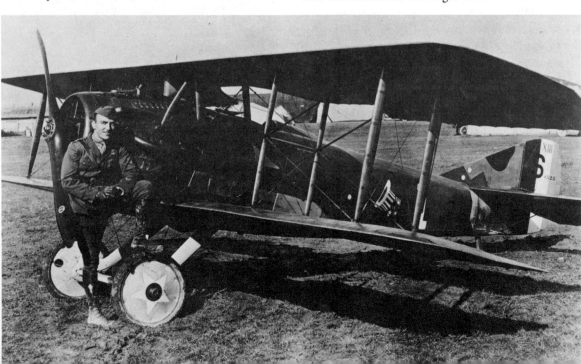

pilot, William Barker (an ace himself with fifty-odd enemy aircraft to his credit), on his way back to England after a tour of duty in France, attacked a German Rumpler on patrol. Although Barker was to have actually proceeded directly to England, he could not ignore the chance of just one more fight. He was piloting one of the new Sopwith Snipes, successor to the Camel. Just a little larger than the Camel (a thirty-foot wingspan as compared with twenty feet, for example), the Snipe was as tough an adversary as the Camel, faster and just as maneuverable (it too was powered with a rotary engine). Upon destroying the Rumpler, Barker was set upon by a swarm of Fokkers which, as the battle evolved, was estimated to number over fifty. Barker single-handedly fought with the swarm, shooting down at least four in flames, and was himself wounded several times before he broke out of the encirclement of wings, guns, and fire. Barker crashed the Snipe in No-man's-land and was unconscious for days. When he awakened, he learned that he had been awarded the Victoria Cross and that the Great War was over.

The dramatic differences in the appearance, construction, and performance between the 1914 Sopwith Tabloid and the 1918 Snipe was enthusiastically summed up when British General Sefton Brancker said, "The progress of aviation during the last four years has been little short of marvelous. War has been the making of aviation." True, but sad. The transition in four years from the ungainly little Voisin to the Gotha or the Handley Page was as dramatic as it was ominous. Only the collapse of the German Army had spared German cities from the bombings planned by the two major Allied air-leader tacticians, Britain's Hugh Trenchard and America's William Mitchell. Trenchard and Mitchell were rare among their military contemporaries in the grasp of the potential of air power. Unfortunately, it proved to be only a temporary deferment. War was not, in fact, "the making of aviation," although rapid developments in design, construction, and engines had occurred. It had been the making of a new kind of weapon, the heavy bomber, not fully understood, nor ever fully ex-

Flying maverick Frank Luke and Spad. (U. S. Signal Corps/National Archives)

Major William George Barker, who fought single handedly in one of the last major air battles of the war. (Royal Canadian Air Force)

Sopwith Snipe, successor to the famed Camel, 1918. (Air Force Museum)

ploited during 1914–18. As a war-sickened world returned to an uneasy peace, this fledgling monster waited in the wings.

The coming of peace found the warring powers with great numbers of warplanes on hand. Despite the restrictions of the Versailles Treaty, Germany was among the first nations to initiate passenger air line services after the war. Germany had led the world in this with its Zeppelins even before the Great War and so drew upon that experience to return to normal. Though restricted in the number of aircraft and forbidden to produce warplanes, the German Government and its airline industry managed to conceal facts from Allied observers and not

only began operations of a passenger airline as early as January 1919, but also secretly began rebuilding a German air force that would emerge later as the Luftwaffe.

Those warplanes not seized by the Allies, or destroyed, were converted into passenger-carrying airliners; former AEG and DFW bombers and fighters were soon carrying passengers between Berlin and Weimar—via Deutsche Luft Reederei beginning on January 19, 1919. Even the once dreaded Fokker D-VII was put to peaceful use with the addition of a passenger cabin, although the pilot remained exposed to the weather. The belief was that a pilot could fly more efficiently,

Symbol of the conversion from war to peace: a "stretched" Fokker D-VII converted into an "airliner," 1919. (U. S. Air Force)

France's Farman bomber in February 1919 became the Goliath passenger-carrying transport. (Air France Photo)

more naturally, if he felt the wind in his face. Anthony Fokker, incidentally, managed to escape from Germany and returned to his native Holland, where his presence would contribute to the development of later Fokker airliners and to the evolution of KLM, the Great Royal Dutch Airlines.

In France the Farman bomber was transformed into a passenger-carrying "Goliath," and set out from Le Bourget Airport on February 8, 1919, for London. The 178-mile flight took two hours, thirty minutes and, with ten passengers aboard (the captain was Lucien Bossoutrot), inaugurated the first international airline. The operator was Lignes Farman, the parent company of today's Air France.

The British soon initiated passenger lines with converted de Havilland DH-4s and 9s owned by Aircraft Transport and Travel; although the company failed in 1920, it did initiate the first of Britain's civil air transport on its London-to-Paris run, August 25, 1919.

Within months after the end of the First World War, its once deadly warbirds had stopped carrying guns and bombs and began transporting cargo and passengers. It promised the dawn of a new air age.

Postwar aerial elegance: the interior of a French transport plane, ca. 1920. (Air France Photo)

Not-so-luxurious postwar air travel, but the beginning of a great airline (today's KLM). A British DH-9 used in the inauguration of the Amsterdam-to-London run, May 17, 1920. (Foto KLM)

Postwar military flying: wing-walking on an airborne Jenny. (U. S. Air Force)

Aviation as show business: midair transfer from one Jenny to another. Parachutes were not part of the costume. (Smithsonian Institution)

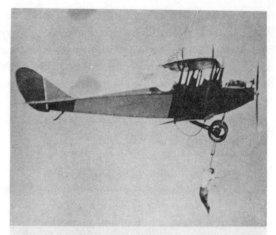

Omar Locklear, dubbed "the first wing walker," demonstrates his specialty. Locklear died in 1920 while stunting for an aviation film. (U. S. Air Force)

5 THE GOLDEN TWENTIES

The dawn of a new air age was rather long in coming to the United States, birthplace of the flying machine. The industry had not boomed, as was expected, during the war, and few companies excepting, such veterans as Wright and Curtiss managed to flourish. The truth was that American aviation manufacturers were not ready with warplane design or manufacturing facilities. Only the Curtiss JN-4, the Jenny, approached in numbers the promised "clouds of planes" that were to "darken the sky" and overwhelm the enemy. The Jenny served only as a trainer and, though a tricky craft at times, was a good, sound airplane. The one battleplane manufactured in the United States during the First World War was the British-designed DH-4, the infamous "Flaming Coffin." And of the less than 200 that finally arrived in France not one was used in combat.

When the war ended suddenly, so far as American manufacturers were concerned, the boom ended before it had really begun. The government immediately canceled millions of dollars' worth of contracts, and some 175,000 workers in the industry were jobless.

So were some ten thousand former military pilots, not all of whom intended to make a career of flying. But the bulk had been bitten by the bug and hoped to exploit their military training to make a new way of adventurous life. Some even remained in the Air Service and would experience a long wait as postwar economy, aversion to war, and governmental and public indifference inhibited the development of military aircraft.

When the war ended the United States had a great number of surplus pilots and aircraft, plus the Curtiss OX-5 and the Liberty engine, brainchild of the automotive industry. The United States had no regular air mail nor passenger airlines, so the most adventurous, inventive (and some would say crazy) out-of-work airmen purchased a surplus Jenny for practically nothing (about five hundred dollars for a new plane; a used Jenny came as low as one-hundred dollars). Replacement parts and engines were available at the same reasonable prices—and they would be needed.

With a Jenny and no job, but with the desire to keep flying, the average ex-wartime pilot became a showman. The public was vaguely aware of the exploits of the aces and associated flying with danger and daring; few had ever seen a real airplane. So began the barnstorming era in American aviation history.

A lone Jenny, or a couple, even a group, would appear in a local cow pasture (there were very few airfields in 1919) to treat the villagers or townspeople to the thrills of skylarking. A crowd would be drawn to the pasture with a display of aerobatics, or wing walking, and then talked into taking an "airplane ride." Jennies were as much a part of county fairs and carnivals as were the fat lady or the pie-judging contest. Stunting for crowds at fairs consisted of wing walking, transfer from one plane to another in flight (too often without parachute), and other feats of derring-do. It was risky, and pilots believed, not without some reason, that the yokels often came to enjoy the inevitable accidents, spectacular crackups, and even the death of an airman. The viewers were not always disappointed, despite the oft-quoted remark of Dick Depew, who once observed that the greatest risk of postwar flying was starving to death.

Still the barnstormers contributed more than the consumption of surplus Jennies to American aviation after the First World War. They impressed a generation of youngsters with flying; many future airmen had their first flights out of a cow pasture in a Jenny. The barnstormers, too, impressed the wary though fascinated oldsters with the flying machine and in a sense kept aviation alive during a low period for the industry in the United States. Few visualized any practical use for the aeroplane.

Not that the United States lacked the traditions, even the experience, in the implementation of aircraft for other than entertainment. As early as 1914 the world's "first scheduled airline" was established to link St. Petersburg and Tampa, Florida. Beginning on January 1, 1914, the St. Petersburg–Tampa Airboat Line made two round-trip flights daily—the twenty-two miles were covered in about twenty minutes. The Benoist flying boat used by the Airboat Line carried only one passenger, and pilot, per trip; passengers weighing more than two hundred pounds were charged an additional five dollars for every hundred pounds. A round trip cost ten dollars. Special trips also could be arranged for a minimum charge of fifteen dollars. "Trips covering any distance over all-water routes," the schedule announced, "and from the waters' surface to several thousand feet high AT PASSENGERS' REQUEST."

But the Airboat Line did not prosper, although some twelve hundred passengers were carried in its short three-month lifetime. It had materialized too soon; but even in 1919 it would have been premature.

The speedy delivery of mail was yet another possible use for the airplane and that, too, was initiated in the United States (military mail was carried between Vienna and Kiev in March 1918, but went out of business with the end of the war). The Post Office Department, with financial help ($100,000) from the Congress, initiated an experimental airmail route between Washington, D.C, and New York, with a stop at Philadelphia. Pilotless and planeless, the Post Office borrowed both from the Army Air Service; Major Reuben Fleet was in charge of men and machines: Lieutenant George L. Boyle was scheduled to inaugurate the route by taking off from Washington and relaying it to Philadelphia. There Lieutenant H. P. Culver would take it on to New York. The total distance of about 218 miles, as the Jenny flies, was expected to take roughly 31/2 hours.

The process was reversed by Lieutenants Torrey Webb and James C. Edgerton on the southbound flights. Same-day delivery of mail was an especially attractive feature of the new venture. However, on the first day a number of things went wrong (not to mention that a number of the first airmail stamps were printed with the Jenny inverted in upside-down flight, inadvertently creating one of the most valuable stamps ever published).

When the great day arrived—May 15, 1918— Lieutenant Boyle found that his Jenny had arrived in several crates and that it would have to be assembled before he could go anywhere. Even as the mechanics and Boyle tightened the wires on the Jenny—its wings finally firmly in place—a black limousine, followed by a diminutive mail truck, drove upon the scene. The President, Woodrow Wilson, Postmaster General Albert S. Burleson,

The dawn of commercial aviation in the United States— a Benoist flying boat at St. Petersburg, Florida, taking off for Tampa, January 1, 1914. (St. Petersburg *City News* Bureau)

Completion of the first round trip of the world's "first scheduled airline." The somewhat bemused man in the middle is St. Petersburg's mayor, A. C. Pheil, who flew as the passenger. To his right is the smiling president of the short-lived Airboat Line, Percival E. Fansler. Pilot Antony H. Jannus stands behind. (St. Petersburg *City News* Bureau)

The inauguration of an airmail service in the United States, May 1918. Postmaster General Albert S. Burleson and President Woodrow Wilson await the final assembly of the Jenny. (United Airlines)

Lieutenant George Boyle ready for takeoff in his flight from Washington, D.C., to Philadelphia. (U. S. Air Force)

and other dignitaries had arrived to witness the birth of a new era. With great ceremony mail pouches were transferred to the Jenny, and a dashingly attired Boyle climbed into the cockpit.

President Wilson, it was noted, wore a bandage on his left hand—a souvenir of the previous week's Great Event, during which he was asked to pose for a photograph fondling a tank. Wilson obligingly placed his left hand on the tank's hot exhaust pipe. Early that morning in May he unsmilingly studied yet another strange vehicle.

Boyle, scheduled to take off at 10:30 A.M., flicked the switch and nothing happened. This continued for some time, aircraft engines being what they were at the time. The cheers that had initially greeted Boyle faded after a few minutes as he attempted to get the Jenny under way. During one of the several silences, the President was heard to mutter, "We are losing a lot of valuable time here." He had a war to get on with, this being the spring of the last year of conflict.

Finally it dawned on one Capt. Benjamin B. Lipsner to make a certain check—and, sure enough: There was no fuel in the Jenny. That corrected, Boyle took off in a satisfying roar of engine and a scattering of dust and flora; the renewed cheers were music to his ears. Having contributed a dignified huzzah, Wilson hurried to his limousine to be rushed back to the White House. A

quick over-the-shoulder glance assured him that Boyle was still airborne and climbing nicely. The Postmaster General beamed. Only the astute Lipsner had reason to cry: The Jenny was flying in the wrong direction.

The fact is that Boyle was soon lost. He made a landing to find out where he was (a farm in Maryland) and cracked his propeller. Not until the next day did Lieutenant Culver retrieve the mail from Boyle for transportation to New York. (Some say that the mail was smuggled back into Washington and put on the next train to New York.)

After that not very auspicious beginning, the Washington-to-New York airmail service improved and prospered; by August the Post Office took over with its own planes and pilots, and the mails were flown back and forth regularly by the end of the year. Out of this small route would grow an impressive nationwide network; it provided some encouragement to American aircraft manufacturers and employment for pilots. By 1925 the Post Office, after passage of the Kelly Act (named for its sponsor, Representative Clyde Kelly), accepted bids from private companies to carry the mails over "feeder lines" that connected the major airmail routes already in operation. These were called Contract Air Mail routes. CAM-1 was operated by the fledgling Colonial Air Transport between Boston and New York. The company's general manager was Juan T. Trippe, who would eventually organize Pan American World Airways.

One of the war-spawned aircraft industries was a Seattle-based company formed by a young engi-

The Post Office goes into the airmail business. Mail bags are stowed into the baggage compartment of a DH-4. (United Airlines)

War surplus de Havilland carrying the mail, early 1920s. (American Airlines)

The first Boeing, the B&W (for Boeing and Westervelt) of 1916. Conrad Westervelt was Boeing's partner in the fledgling company. (The Boeing Company)

The first American international airmail line, connecting the United States and Canada (that is, Seattle, Washington, and Victoria, British Columbia, Canada). Pilot Eddie Hubbard and William Boeing (holding the mail bag) stand before the company's Model C, March 1919. (The Boeing Company)

neer, William Boeing. Beginning with a tiny seaplane, the B&W, the equally tiny company kept alive during the war by turning out designs of other companies for the Navy. The Armistice ended the military contracts, and Boeing sought other sources of revenue. One of his ventures was the inauguration of an "international" airmail line between Victoria, Canada, and Seattle in March 1919. At the

The Boeing B-1, 1919. (The Boeing Company)

Boeing sustained itself by building planes for the U. S. Air Service. The fabric is being affixed to the wing of Thomas Morse MB-3A ca. 1921. (The Boeing Company)

The designs of Dutch airman Anthony Fokker impressed American military aviators. In 1922, when this photo was taken, the U. S. Air Service was flying the Fokker PW-5 (a pursuit plane with a Wright engine), based on Fokker's D-IX. (U. S. Air Force)

same time some sections of the Boeing factory kept going by manufacturing furniture; the aircraft division, near bankruptcy, drew upon its wartime experience with flying boats and branched out with a design, the B-1. The mouse-poor Air Service, under the prodding of air-minded General "Billy" Mitchell, came to the rescue with small orders; the Navy, in time, would follow.

As the feeder lines evolved, less was heard of the British DH-4s, although they continued to fly during the twenties, and such names of new American manufacturers as Stout, Douglas, Ryan, Stinson, Waco, and Swallow were added to those of Boeing, Curtiss, and Wright. Many feeder lines, devoted initially to mail transportation only, eventually evolved into passenger routes; for, example, one of the historic routes, Varney Air Lines (Elko, Nevada, to Pasco, Washington), CAM-5 to the Post Office, was one of the pioneers that became United Air Lines.

Another pioneer line (CAM-4) was Robertson Aircraft Corporation, flying the route, weather permitting, between St. Louis and Chicago. Rob-

ertson was one of the companies using surplus DH-4s. One of Robertson's pilots was an Army-trained ex-wingwalker and barnstormer, Charles A. Lindbergh, who flew the St. Louis–Chicago route as late as 1926; by 1927 his name would be known throughout the world.

Meanwhile, European airlines developed along more sophisticated lines, with emphasis on transporting people as well as things; in Germany, Junkers continued to improve its all-metal aircraft and by middecade introduced a trimotor model—as did Holland's Tony Fokker and the United States' William Stout: the classic plane that would be better known as the Ford Trimotor. Multi-engined aircraft, large and roomy, provided more passenger comfort: wicker chairs, meals served in flight, and Britain's Imperial Airways even promised a bar in its grand giant, the *Argosy;* alas, however, the pilot remained perched in the nose exposed to the elements. Both Holland and France enjoyed an advantage over the British airlines, because of government subsidy. Fokker's designs were a spur to the burgeoning Royal Dutch Airlines. His model F-7 was one of the most successful airliners ever built

One of the classic fighter biplanes of the twenties, the Royal Navy's Fairey Flycatcher. Designed to operate from ship platforms as well as from carrier decks, the Flycatcher was a versatile aircraft during the between-the-wars years and was in use until the midthirties. (National Air and Space Museum, Smithsonian Institution)

Pilot Leon Cuddeback and the Swallow of Varney Air Lines in April 1926. Contract Airmail 5, actually the first scheduled airmail route, was one of the feeder lines that merged into United Airlines. The flight from Pasco, Washington, to Boise, Idaho—a distance of about 490 miles—took 8½ hours of flying time. (United Airlines)

The Swallow of Varney Air Lines en route with the mail. (United Airlines)

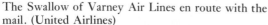

(and proliferated, under licence, practically all over the world).

In Germany, meanwhile, with government aid, Deutsche Luft Hansa was formed by merging the two major competitors, Lloyd and Junkers. By the thirties a great German airline network covered much of Europe, as far south as Barcelona, to Oslo and Stockholm in the north, Budapest in the east, and London in the west. The success of what is now Lufthansa stimulated the German aircraft industry, despite the Versailles Treaty edict forbidding the manufacture of military planes. Initially Junkers and Dornier prospered, to be followed later by Heinkel and Focke-Wulf—all names that now have a decided military connotation.

Despite the rather primitive operating conditions, (although at the time they were regarded as very advanced, indeed), there were remarkably few accidents in the infant years of the airlines. Navigation was not yet a science, and pilots often flew their routes by following railroads (the "iron compass") or highways to their destinations. This technique was responsible for the first midair collision in commercial airline history. On April 7, 1922, a DH-18 took off from Croydon (serving London) for Le Bourget (Paris). Sometime later a Farman

DH-4 of Robertson Aircraft, a St. Louis-based line; the pilot is Charles Lindbergh. (American Airlines)

"Goliath" left Le Bourget bound for London. The two pilots, over France, followed the same road, which would guide them to their respective airports. Flying at the same altitude, the two planes flew directly into one another, killing all seven people aboard.

Meanwhile, in the United States, Boeing Air Transport took a step forward by introducing its Model 40, which not only carried mail (the prime income source) and two passengers; a later Model 40-B, its fuselage slightly "stretched," could accommodate four passengers, although not in the luxurious mode enjoyed by European air travelers. By the middle 1920s the various small companies that would expand into, or be absorbed by, the giant airlines were in operation with various types of aircraft. Boeing eventually elected to concentrate on aircraft design and manufacture, its airline operations were then taken over by United Airlines. Americans were gradually becoming accustomed to the idea of flying, to airports, and to the sound of engines overhead. Still, American commercial aviation trailed that of Europe.

The memorable aviation epic that came to a climax in 1927 was rooted in nationalism, with various nations striving to connect certain key cities, or cross certain natural obstacles, for the first time by air. In the United States there were other compulsions: the feeling among those few who believed there was a future in military aviation (the chief proponent was the Army's outspoken "Billy" Mitchell) that the development of military aircraft was being criminally neglected in the United States. There was one other element, since what money the Congress allocated to the military was niggardly: interservice rivalry. Hoping to catch the attention of the American public and the Congress, the Army and Navy air services competed with one another for attention in the press.

The epoch began less than a year after the end of the First World War; the U. S. Navy won the first round (although the rivalry had not officially begun). The obstacle confronted by the Navy was their own backyard, the Atlantic Ocean. No one had ever crossed the Atlantic by air. The plane

Example of a modern European airliner, the Junkers F-13. The pilot, however, continued to fly in the open air. (Lufthansa)

The Fokker F-7 Trimotor, one of the first successful airliners. (Pan American World Airways)

Fokker F-7A which, in 1924, connected Amsterdam and Java. (KLM Photo)

Symbol of growing German airlines: a Junkers of SCADTA (a line formed and operated by Germans in Colombia, South America) in 1925. The line's proximity to the Panama Canal was a source of worry to American military leaders. (U. S. Air Force)

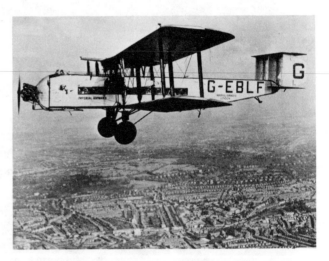

Armstrong-Whitworth Argosy of Imperial Airways on the London-to-Paris run, 1926; the pilot is still out in the cold, though passenger comfort had improved. (British Airways)

The beginning of American passenger transportation, the Boeing B-40 (in flight) and the B-40A. Boeing Air Transport was eventually absorbed by United Airlines. (United Airlines)

The full passenger load boarding Boeing's B-40B, 1926.
(United Airlines)

A lineup of planes at an American airport in the mid-1920s. From left: Fokker Trimotor, Fokker F-14, Boeing B-40B, Boeing 95, Douglas M-2, and a Stearman Junior Speedmail. (TWA)

The Curtiss *America*, a 1914 flying boat designed to cross the Atlantic Ocean. The First World War canceled the attempt for the duration. (Smithsonian Institution)

A Curtiss H boat of 1918, used by the U. S. Navy for patrol and reconnaissance. (Union Title Insurance Company, San Diego)

selected for that task was a Curtiss flying boat, identified as the NC (Navy Curtiss), originally designed for anti-submarine operations. When the war ended the contracts were canceled, but not before four of the NCs had been built. What to do with them?

They had, in fact, been designed for trans-atlantic flight, although never tested. Curtiss, in fact, had such a feat in mind as early as 1914, when he produced his earlier boat, the *America*. Its flight plans were thwarted by the war, although Curtiss turned out numerous flying boats during the war. Under licence his boats were also produced in Britain as the excellent "F" boats. The U. S. Navy by 1918 was flying the improved "H" model. The NCs were even more advanced.

By the time the Navy was ready for its Atlantic attempt in 1919, there was great excitement in the air: the London *Daily Mail* had offered a prize of ten thousand pounds to the first to cross the Atlantic by air. Soon several planes and crews were poised in Newfoundland awaiting the right weather conditions for such a flight—also the pre-

The Navy Curtiss 3 (NC-3), Curtiss' 1918 flying boat designed for the Atlantic crossing. The hull was decidedly shipshape. (Smithsonian Institution)

The jinx ship, the NC-4, the first plane to fly the Atlantic, May 1919. (U. S. Air Force)

vailing winds, west to east, would prove helpful. In time four rivals, all British, were set to contend with the NCs. The Navy wanted no part of a race and made it clear that it was not competing for the prize money. In May 1919, three flying boats left Far Rockaway, Long Island, for Newfoundland (the fourth, the NC-2, had been dismantled to provide replacement parts for the remaining three). The little armada was under the command of Lieutenant Commander John H. Towers, who flew in the NC-3; the NC-1 was under the command of Lieutenant Commander P. N. L. Bellinger (whose pilot was Lieutenant Commander Marc A. Mitscher, one of the Navy's few aviation advocates); the "jinx ship," because of its malfunctions and accidents, the NC-4 was commanded by unsmiling, taciturn, no-nonsense Lieutenant Commander Albert C. Read.

A degree of international ill will greeted the arrival, after some problems, of the NCs at Trepassey, Newfoundland. The British crews looked upon the Curtiss boats with merry scorn, and one pilot, Harry Hawker, whose Sopwith was also

The NC-4 pulling into Lisbon Harbor, May 27, 1919, completing its Atlantic crossing. (Smithsonian Institution)

NC-4 crew: E. Stone; E. Rhoades; W. Hinton; H. C. Rodd; J. Breese, commander of flight; A. C. Read, and naval officer. (Smithsonian Institution)

poised for the flight, looked at the NCs and suggested that it might be best merely to sail the planes across, for it seemed unlikely to him that such a craft could fly. He was proved nearly correct when the NCs, fully loaded, attempted to take off and could not come unstuck.

After jettisoning a couple of cans of oil, the *NC-4* staggered into the air. Read ordered the plane back to see what the plan was and after more jettisoning (including one unhappy, but weighty, crewman), the three planes took off on May 16, 1919. The flight plan had been carefully worked out; there were to be no aerial histrionics, just a businesslike crossing of the Atlantic Ocean. They would not attempt a nonstop flight; first stop would be in the Azores islands before continuing on to Lisbon, Portugal. By the morning of the seventeenth the three NCs were in trouble: fog. The crews could not see to take bearings by instruments nor could

they see the many Navy ships below that marked their path. While the *NC-4* continued on, the *NC-1* and the *NC-3* landed to get their bearings; neither could rise off the water. Both, taking Hawker's sage advice, began riding the waves to port. After five hours the *NC-1* was found by a Navy destroyer, *Ionia*, and the crew taken aboard, after which the *NC-1*, battered by the waves and wind, sank. The redoubtable Towers sailed his *NC-3* into Ponta Delgada, Azores, after more than fifty hours of grueling seamanship covering more than two hundred miles. The *NC-3*, damaged, also was forced to drop out of the flight.

That left only the jinx ship, the *NC-4*. Read had brought it safely into Horta, Azores, on the seventeenth and then proceeded on to Ponta Delgada, where it was expected that Towers, the flight commander, would take over the *NC-4*. But public opinion, obvious to Secretary of the Navy, former newspaperman Josephus Daniels, had its impact. The news of the intact arrival of the *NC-4* had made Read a national hero; to rob him of the try at the full flight might lead to an unfortunate public reaction. Daniels ignored Navy tradition and ordered Read to continue as the commander of the surviving plane.

On May 27, the *NC-4* landed in the harbor at Lisbon: the first aircraft to cross the Atlantic. Continuing with what had become a good-will tour, Read flew on to a brief stopover in Spain and proceeded on to a symbolic landing at Plymouth, of Pilgrim fame. Read and his crew were greeted as heroes in Britain.

Meanwhile, Hawker, accompanied by Lieutenant Commander Kenneth Mackenzie-Grieve, had taken off from Newfoundland, only to come down in the Atlantic a thousand miles from takeoff point. They were fortunately rescued by a Danish ship, *Mary*, although for days, since the ship did not have a radio, it was assumed that Hawker and Mackenzie-Grieve were lost. They too were

Sopwith *Atlantic* in which British pilots Kenneth Mackenzie-Grieve and Harry Hawker planned to cross the Atlantic. The *Atlantic* came down in the ocean, and the pilots (believed lost) were rescued by a passing ship. (National Museum of Science and Technology, Ottawa)

Kenneth Mackenzie-Grieve (left) and Harry Hawker, Newfoundland, May 1919. (National Museum of Science and Technology, Ottawa)

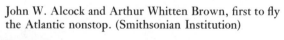

John W. Alcock and Arthur Whitten Brown, first to fly the Atlantic nonstop. (Smithsonian Institution)

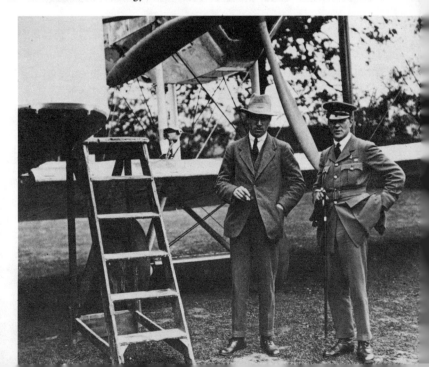

greeted with ceremony and cheers (two days, actually, before Read arrived in Plymouth in the *NC-4*). They were even awarded half the *Daily Mail* prize for "a magnificent failure."

The next attempt was no failure, though it ended rather disappointingly. Captain John Alcock and Lieutenant Arthur Whitten Brown, after assembling their crated Vickers Vimy, originally designed as a bomber, took off from St. John's, New-

Takeoff and landing of Alcock and Brown's Vickers Vimy, a converted bomber. After a harrowing, miserable flight, Brown set the plane down in an Irish bog, mistaking it for smooth, solid earth. (Vickers Limited)

foundland, early in the morning of June 14, 1919. After what at times was a harrowing and uncomfortable flight (Brown clambered out onto the wing to chip the ice that had formed on instruments which, unaccountably, were mounted on the engines), Alcock and Brown were the first to fly the Atlantic nonstop. The flight had taken a total time of sixteen hours, twelve minutes, and ended quite unfortunately in an Irish bog at Clifden, County

Galway, on June 14, 1919. Alcock had selected the landing place, which did not turn out to be very solid ground, and the Vimy ended up with a badly broken nose; neither Alcock nor Brown were injured. Both fliers were knighted for their feat, and Alcock became chief test pilot for Vickers shortly after. In December of 1919 he was killed while flying to a Paris air show. Brown never flew again after their historic flight and, also employed by Vickers, preferred the engineering division.

The British rounded out the year in July when their airship, *R-34*, made the first (and more difficult) east-to-west crossing of the Atlantic. The flight, led by Major G. H. Scott, began at East For-

The *R-34*, first airship to cross the Atlantic both ways. (Smithsonian Institution)

The *R-34* over Long Island after making the difficult east-to-west flight from Britain, July 6, 1919. (University of Georgia)

Liberty-powered LePere biplane (built by the Engineering Division, McCook Field, Illinois), with which the Army Air Service began its record-setting flights. The pilot was Major Rudolph W. Schroeder; his passenger was Lieutenant G. E. Elfrey, who established a new altitude record (31,821 feet) on October 4, 1919. Schroeder, solo, flew even higher on February 27, 1920—more than 33,000 feet. (U. S. Air Force)

Lieutenant J. A. Macready's LePere climbing to a new altitude record in 1921. Using oxygen and a turbosupercharger, Macready rose to 34,508 feet. (U. S. Air Force)

Air enthusiast and military air prophet: comedian Will Rogers (in rear cockpit) and General William Mitchell, outspoken advocate of air power. (U. S. Air Force)

tune, Scotland, on July 2, 1919, with a crew of thirty; 183 hours later the airship appeared over Mineola, Long Island, on July 6. On July 9 it set out again, and after a seventy five hour flight, completed the first round-trip Atlantic crossing. Lighter-than-air enthusiasts were certain that the *R-34's* accomplishment boded well for the future of the dirigible. Their dream was destroyed when, in August 1921, the *R-34* broke up during a test flight (the United States was interested in acquiring it) and fell to earth near Hull, England, killing the seventeen Americans aboard and twenty-seven of the British crew of thirty-two.

In 1919 also the U. S. Army Air Service, led by its assistant chief, Brigadier General William E. Mitchell (his chief was Major General Charles T. Menoher, no airman), initiated a series of aerial premieres, record-making flights that Mitchell hoped would prove his theories concerning air power and aircraft. Military planes broke records in altitude, endurance, distance, and speed flights—the import of which generally eluded Menoher and the Chiefs of Staff. Mitchell even took on the tradition-bound U. S. Navy and proved that his bombers were capable of sinking a battleship in 1921. The point of this was not recognized until the Second World War, lessons painfully learned at Pearl Harbor and Midway, among other far-flung places, when aircraft proved—as had Mitchell—that the battleship was obsolete.

The major weapon employed by Mitchell was the Martin bomber, product of the company formed by Glenn L. Martin, who began as a gypsy flier in his own home-built plane in 1909; Martin produced its first military airplanes in 1913, but not until 1918 was the Martin bomber built—too late for the war. Its later model, the MB-2, succeeded in sinking the "unsinkable" German battleship *Ostfriesland* as well as other ships off the Virginia coast in 1921.

Mitchell's vociferous advocacy of the heavy bomber—like the Martin and others—and, the most outrageous of all, a separate air force, led to his downfall as a military leader and prophet. Always outspoken good copy, Mitchell publically

Proving Mitchell's point: bombers vs. battleships. Although the ships were stationary and, being unmanned, did not fire back at Mitchell's bombers, no one in the Navy expected that they could be sunk. In this photo Martin bombers have attacked the obsolescent American battleship *Alabama* on September 1921. (U. S. Air Force)

aired his views, which were quickly printed in the newspapers of the time. When he accused certain military leaders in both the Army and the Navy of "incompetency, criminal neglect, and almost treasonable administration of national defense," he had gone too far. Mitchell was court-martialed in 1925, an event well covered by the press, and was found guilty; he thereupon resigned from the Army before the verdict could be officially carried out. Mitchell went into farming in 1926 and died ten years later; in 1945 he was posthumously promoted to major general—his permanent rank at the time of his court-martial was colonel—and awarded the Congressional Medal of Honor in recognition of his

Martin bomber, 1919, of the type that participated in the Army-Navy ship-bombardment tests. (U. S. Air Force)

Martin bomber on a peacetime mission: bombing an iced-over Platte River in Nebraska. (U. S. Air Force)

"service and foresight in aviation." Tragically, it took the Second World War to prove that Mitchell had been a perceptive pioneer in the definition of the term "air power."

One of Mitchell's favorite concepts was strategic bombardment, never truly attempted during the First World War—although the Zeppelin did carry out a kind of ineffectual strategic bombing. Plans for dispatching formations of heavily laden bombers to Berlin, an idea Mitchell held in common agreement with Britain's own advocate of heavy bombardment, Major General Sir Hugh Trenchard, were formulated in 1918. The mission was

Army Keystone LB-10 bombers passing over Newark, New Jersey, a demonstration of the vulnerability of cities from the air. (U. S. Air Force)

"Mitchell's Folly," the Barling XNBL-1, one of the first heavy bombers. Its size and slow speed would have made it a sitting duck for the faster pursuit planes of 1925, when it was finally abandoned. (U. S. Air Force)

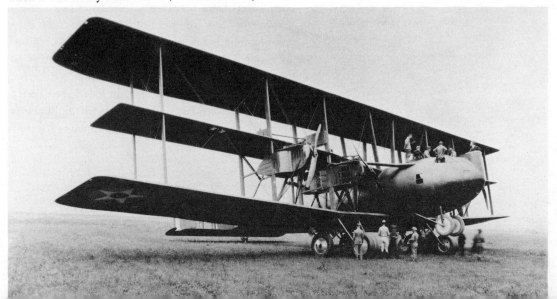

James H. Doolittle, during a refueling stop on his cross-country flight, September 1922. (Doolittle Collection)

Fokker F-IV (Air Service designation T-2) in which Macready and Kelly crossed the United States nonstop in twenty-six hours, fifty minutes, May 1923. (U. S. Air Force)

canceled by the Armistice, but neither air leader forgot it.

While he served as the American Army Air Service Commander (his superiors, in general, were figureheads so far as aviation was concerned), Mitchell encouraged the development of what, by the Second World War, would emerge as a true heavy bomber, capable of long-distance flights with heavy bombloads to attack military objectives behind the enemy lines—or to attack an invading enemy before it could land on American shores (an idea the Navy did not like at all, its commanders being most covetous of the waters around and near the United States). The twenties saw the development of the American heavy bomber by several manufacturers—Curtiss, Martin, Keystone, and even one that came out of the Army's own engineering division and named the Barling bomber, in honor of its designer, Walter H. Barling. A massive triplane powered by six Liberty engines, the Barlin appeared before the engine it required existed (ordered in 1920, it was not completed until 1923). The big bomber flew for the first time on August 22, 1923, in what was described as "a beautiful flight" lasting all of twenty minutes. Theoretically, the Barling had a range of 335 miles—and a top air speed of sixty-one miles per hour. Under-powered and plagued by structural deficiencies, the Barling bomber—which soon became known as "Mitchell's Folly"—was flown for the last time in 1925, the year of Mitchell's court-martial. Its final ignominious function was to serve as a grounded target for fighter attack practice.

During, and after, the Mitchell era the U. S. Army Air Service continued its program of advancing aviation and attracting public attention and approbation. In September 1922 a young lieutenant, James Doolittle, crossed the country coast-to-coast, the first to accomplish this in less than twenty-four hours; this flight was the first nationally noted event of a flier-scientist who was to contribute much to American aviation, both civil and military. The next year, in a larger plane, a Fokker T-2, two Army fliers made the flight across the continent nonstop. It took Lieutenants John A.

Macready and Oakley G. Kelly nearly twenty-seven hours to make the 2,520-mile flight in the Fokker transport. That same year the first successful attempt at refueling in the air was carried off by two Army pilots, Captain Lowell H. Smith and Lieutenant John P. Richter in a DH-4B, proving that it was possible to remain aloft for hours with the new technique (one, incidentally, still in use). By June of 1923, Doolittle's solo cross-country record was broken by Lieutenant Russell L. Maughan in a famous "dawn to dusk" flight in a small Army Curtiss pursuit. He covered 2,670 miles (making five refueling stops) in twenty-one hours, forty-eight minutes.

The climax of the Army "spectaculars" during the Mitchell period was the first round-the-world flight by Army fliers. It began in the early morning of April 6, 1924, as four Douglas DW-4s took off from Lake Washington, near Seattle, and two returned there on September 28. In 175 days the two surviving "World Cruisers," as they were called, had covered more than 26,000 miles. Of the two planes lost during the flight, the flagship *Seattle* crashed into a mountainside in Alaska (with no loss of life), and command of the mission was assumed by Lieutenant Lowell Smith, Pilot of the *Chicago* (and veteran of the 1923 endurance-refueling flight). The second loss, the *Boston*, occurred during a homeward-bound leg heading for Iceland when the plane was forced down with a faulty fuel pump. The *Boston* was abandoned at sea, and the *Chicago* and *New Orleans* proceeded to complete the circle. The entire mission was most carefully planned, despite the two losses.

An interesting sequel: Following the completion of the flight the airmen were greeted with honors by the populace of Seattle, but when it came time for them to return to Dayton, Ohio, Major General Mason M. Patrick (who had succeeded Menoher, who had proved incapable of dealing with Mitchell) ordered them to return—by rail.

Less spectacular though no less newsworthy was the Army's Pan American Good-will flight—a 22,-000-mile tour of Central and South America. It was flown in Loening COA-1 amphibians, five of

Maughan at the beginning of his flight after taking off from Mitchel Field, New York. His average speed was 156 miles per hour. (U. S. Air Force)

First midair refueling; Smith and Richter remained aloft for more than thirty-seven hours, August 1923. (U. S. Air Force)

Lieutenant Russell L. Maughan and the Curtiss PW-8 pursuit in which he crossed the United States in a heralded "dawn to dusk" flight, June 1923. Maughan flew from New York to San Francisco in twenty-one hours, forty-eight minutes. (U. S. Air Force)

Douglas DW-4s, the 1924 World Cruisers, in which the U. S. Army Air Service planned the first round-the-world flight. Five of these craft were built and four began the flight. No. 1, the *Seattle*, was quickly eliminated when it hit a mountain in Alaska (without serious injury to the crew). No. 2 was named *Chicago;* No. 3 was the *Boston* (which eventually suffered an accident and was replaced by *Boston II*); No. 4 was named the *New Orleans*. Only the *Chicago* and the *New Orleans* completed the flight. (U. S. Air Force)

Douglas World Cruiser *Chicago* equipped with pontoons for overwater flight. (Douglas Aircraft Company)

A gathering of world fliers: Major John F. Curry; Lowell Smith, pilot of the *Chicago;* Henry H. Ogden; Erik Nelson, pilot of the *New Orleans;* Leigh Wade, pilot of the *Boston* and the *Boston II;* John Harding, and Leslie Arnold. (U. S. Air Force)

Captain Ira Eaker and the Loening COA-1 amphibian, one of five in which the Army hoped to make a good-will tour of Central and South America. As a general Eaker would one day lead the Eighth Air Force. (U. S. Air Force)

The *Detroit*, the *San Francisco*, and the *St. Louis* in formation over Duarte Island en route to Colombia. Over Buenos Aires later, the *Detroit* and the *New York* collided. (U. S. Air Force)

A Loening leaves the land for water and takeoff, Fort de France Bay, Martinique. (U. S. Air Force)

which took off from Kelly Field, Texas, on December 21, 1926, and visited twenty south-of-the-border nations as far south as Chile. Only four planes returned to Washington, D.C., on May 2, 1927. Besides the good will sown by the flight, the fliers had set distance records for the type of aircraft flown, flying in various types of weather, over difficult terrain, operating from both land and water. Some mishaps occurred: a burned-out engine, a damaged landing gear, even a sinking. The most tragic occurred over Buenos Aires, where a midair collision between the *Detroit* and the *New York* resulted in the death of the two airmen, Captain Clinton F. Woolsey and Lieutenant John W. Benton, who had neglected to wear parachutes. The mission commander, Major Herbert A. Dargue, and the copilot, Lieutenant Ennis C. Whitehead, parachuted to safety. Another Loening was acquired, and the little formation arrived at Bolling Field, near Washington, in time for the opening of the Pan American air conferences and a welcome from President Calvin Coolidge.

The U. S. Navy, meanwhile, had begun evolving its air arm more quietly, content after the flight of the NC-4 to leave most of the record breaking to the Army. An attempt to cross the Pacific (San Francisco to Honolulu) had failed in 1925 (the Army succeeded in 1927). But the flying boat, aircraft carrier, and catapult launchings were the subjects of Navy experimentation. Even a plane-carrying submarine was tried and found wanting. By 1927 two battle cruisers were converted into carriers, to join the Navy's first, the *Langley*, and christened the *Saratoga* and the *Lexington*. Small shipboard fighters were developed for carrier operations.

End of the Pan American flight; the crews of the Loenings are greeted by President Calvin Coolidge at Bolling Field near Washington, D.C. Each member of the flight received the Distinguished Flying Cross. Major Herbert A. Dargue, leader of the flight (and one of the men who bailed out of the *New York*), stands to the right of Coolidge, May 2, 1927. (U. S. Air Force)

The United States Navy after the First World War continued to favor flying boats as aerial observation posts for patroling coastal waters. The Curtis H boats developed out of the war and were in use by the Navy in antisubmarine warfare. The Curtiss H-16, powered by two Liberty engines, was completed during the final months of the war. It carried four 230-pound bombs and a half-dozen machine guns. Though Curtiss-designed, they were built in the United States by the Naval Aircraft Factory in Philadelphia. (Navy Department, National Archives)

Among Curtiss' challangers for the flying boat Navy trade was Consolidated Aircraft of Buffalo, New York, Martin of Baltimore and Boeing of Seattle. Boeing's PB-1 undergoes a rear-engine test at the Boeing plant and in flight. It was the only privately manufactured flying boat flown by the Navy in 1925. Its wingspan measured eighty-seven feet. (The Boeing Company)

Consolidated NY-1 ("N" for Navy, "Y" for Consolidated) over Pensacola, Florida. This great naval base trained pilots for the age of the aircraft carrier. Photo was taken in 1927. (General Dynamics, Convair Division)

Both the Navy and the Army continued to explore the potentialities of lighter-than-air craft, with little success. Airships, it was soon learned, were not the most efficient form of air transportation, although they were useful for observation and training. But airships, if filled with hydrogen, were highly volatile and accident-prone. Mitchell, recalling the reign of terror of the Zeppelin during the war, succeeded in talking the Air Service into purchasing an Italian-made semirigid dirigible, *Roma*. Designed by Umberto Nobile, the 410-foot-long airship was the largest of its kind in 1920, when it was delivered to the Army at Langley Field, Virginia. Tests proved that even with its six Ansaldo engines the *Roma* was underpowered, canceling its heralded inspection flight on December 9, 1921; further embarrassment ensued when the ceremonial flight of the twenty-first was also called off. The Ansaldos were removed, Liberties were installed, and a new flight date was set for February 21, 1922—a transcontinental flight was even being discussed. The *Roma* actually did fly that day, but had been airborne for less than half an hour when it suddenly dived from an altitude of about six hundred feet, struck high-tension wires near the ground, and exploded, killing thirty-four and injuring eleven. A study determined that the installation of the heavier Liberty engines may have caused the *Roma's* keel to buckle; but that was not certain. However, the fact that the hydrogen-filled airship burned so instantaneously led to the substitution of helium for hydrogen in American airships; the fate of the *Roma* did not encourage much faith in the airship's future.

The Navy acquired one of its airships from the most experienced, and most successful, manufacturer in the world, Zeppelin. The *ZR-3*, better known as the *Los Angeles* (the German designation was *LZ-126*), was made specifically by Zeppelin at Friedrichshafen in compliance with the postwar reparations agreement. The *ZR-3* was delivered, by air, from Germany to its base at Lakehurst, New Jersey, under the command of a great and skilled airman, Dr. Hugo Eckener. He had left Friedrichshafen on October 12, 1924, and arrived over New York on the fifteenth. Eckener's successful flight inspired a riotous welcome at Lakehurst, and he and his crew were treated like celebrities; the reception by Americans of former enemies contributed much to the improvement of German-American relations.

From the early twenties until 1933 a series of five Zeppelin rigids (ZRs) was built; the *Los Angeles* was the only one, however, built in Germany. The *ZR-2* (which the British designated *R-38*) was based on a German design and built in Britain for the U. S. Navy. During a trial flight in August of 1921 the *R-38* buckled in midair, caught fire, and fell near Hull into the Humber River, with a loss of forty-four lives. The *ZR-1*, meanwhile, had been under construction in the United States, its completion awaiting the erection of a giant million-dollar hangar at Lakehurst. The great airship made its first flight under the name *Shenandoah* in September 1923 and served the Navy as a fine public-relations vehicle, flying about the country visiting state fairs and air shows. While on such a flight from Lakehurst to St. Paul, the *Shenandoah* suffered a structural failure in a storm over southern Ohio and broke in two. The after section fell into a cornfield near Ava, but the nose section was flown as a free balloon by Lieutenant Commander Charles E. Rosendahl, who safely landed it fourteen miles away from the site of the wreckage; fourteen of the crew of forty-three died in the accident.

The destruction of the *Shenandoah* on September 3, 1925, presented additional fuel for Billy Mitchell and the fire he kindled under those he felt were incompetent in the Navy high command. His remarks after the *Shenandoah* disaster led directly to his court-martial.

The last two ZRs suffered the same fate as 1 and 2. The *ZR-4*, the *Akron*, completed in 1931, fell into the Atlantic during a storm, with a death toll of seventy-three. The *ZR-5*, the *Macon*, first flew in 1933; in February 1935, while participating in Fleet exercises the *Macon*, buffeted by high winds, smashed into the Pacific off Point Sur and quickly sank. The loss of life—two—was remarkable, a miracle carried off by the great number of ships in the exercise

An Army blimp, the helium-inflated *TC-3*, flies off into the sunset. The word "blimp" was a combination—"b" for balloon and "limp" because that's what it was before inflation. (U. S. Air Force)

Rescue operation: a blimp lowers onto Horseshoe Lake (Illinois) to retrieve the balloonist whose craft has lost its lift and is settling into the water. (U. S. Air Force)

A further definition of b-limp; losing helium, the Army's *TA-5* settles into the Atlantic off Hampton Roads, Virginia. (U. S. Air Force)

Ever-present hazard: a hydrogen-filled balloon bursts into flame at Fort Sill, Oklahoma. Balloons were used in artillery observation. (Jarrett Collection)

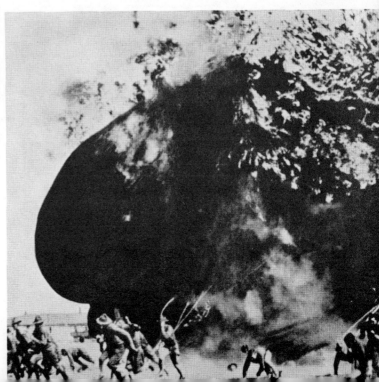

The short, unhappy life of the *Roma*. Built in Italy in 1919, the *Roma* was delivered to the Army in 1920. During the test flight on February 21, 1922, the keel collapsed and the *Roma* fell and burned, killing thirty-four and injuring eleven people. (U. S. Air Force)

Pride of the Navy: The *Los Angeles* hovers over its base at Lakehurst, New Jersey; in the foreground, mooring mast and hangar. Built in Germany by Zeppelin, it was to be the sole survivor of the American airship experiment. (Library of Congress)

Like a straw in the wind, the *Los Angeles* does an embarrassing nose-stand from its mooring mast. (Smithsonian Institution)

The *ZR-1*, *Shenandoah*, under construction; it was completed and commissioned by the U. S. Navy in 1923. (U. S. Air Force)

The *Shenandoah* at Lakehurst, New Jersey. (U.S. Air Force)

area. Eighty-one members of the crew were pulled out of the water. Among the saved was the skipper, Lieutenant Commander Herbert V. Wiley, who had also survived the *Akron* disaster.

While quick Navy action saved lives, the loss of the *Macon* marked the end of the airship. In its "Extra" edition announcing the crash, the San Francisco *Examiner* carried a front page article headed: "Dirigible Doomed As Defense Factor, Officials Say." From Washington, President Franklin D. Roosevelt stated that "there is no thought at the present time of asking Congress for an appropriation for another airship . . ." Admiral William H. Standley, of the Navy Department, was quoted in the *Examiner* as saying, "I have never approved of the use of lighter-than-air craft for other than commercial purposes, and I am more than ever convinced of their unsuitability for military and naval purposes."

The surviving *Los Angeles*, the sole ZR made in Germany, which had been decommissioned in 1933 was eventually scrapped, closing the airship era in the United States.

The 1920s were a time of great aerial adventuring and of advances in aircraft design and power, not to mention foolishness and risk. Men employed the new machine for exploration, for testing new ideas, and they pushed themselves and their craft to what appeared to be new limits of endurance and speed. The two great oceans were ever challenging, although the two antipodes, the North Pole and the South Pole, attracted airmen also.

As early as 1897, an expedition led by a young Swede, Salomon August Andree, disappeared in a balloon while attempting to fly over the North Pole (all three men participating were lost; their bodies, as well as the records of their flight, were not found until 1930).

By the midtwenties there were aircraft capable of reaching the poles, and the honor (questioned by some historians) of being the first over both went to Lieutenant Commander Richard E. Byrd. Retired from the Navy because of an injury that would have kept him from achieving the rank of deck officer, Byrd strenuously applied himself to the challenge of polar flights. Sponsored by automobile king Henry Ford, Byrd flew over the North Pole on May 9, 1926; his Fokker Trimotor for the more than fifteen-hour flight was piloted by Floyd Bennett.

Two days later the great Norwegian explorer Roald Amundsen made the first airship crossing of the North Pole in the *Norge,* commanded by designer-airman Umberto Nobile. Also aboard the *Norge* was a wealthy adventurer, Lincoln Ellsworth, who had failed in a polar attempt the year before. (He would succeed by 1930 in claiming large areas of the Antarctic for the United States.)

The *Shenandoah* at Lakehurst, New Jersey. (U. S. Air Force)

Wreckage of the *Shenandoah* near Ava, Ohio, September 3, 1925. (U. S. Air Force)

Army dramatization of the utility of the airship. To attend a Senate Finance Committee meeting, Senator Hiram Bingham of Connecticut boarded this Army airship at Langley Field, Virginia, and was delivered to Capitol Plaza in time for his meeting, July 1919. (U. S. Air Force)

The *Josephine Ford* returns to the Byrd camp after its 15-hour flight over the North Pole, May 9, 1926. Waiting to greet them is rival polar explorer Roald Amundsen. Byrd had beaten him to the North Pole. (National Air and Space Museum/Smithsonian Institution)

Richard E. Byrd's Fokker Trimotor, named for the daughter of his sponsor, in preparation for North Pole flight; pilot was Floyd Bennett. (Navy Department/National Archives)

Bennett and Byrd on their arrival in New York after
their flight over the North Pole, 1916. (National Air and
Space Museum/Smithsonian Institution)

The *Norge*, the first airship to fly over the North Pole.
Designed and commanded by the Italian airship expert,
Umberto Nobile, the ship carried Amundsen and
Lincoln Ellsworth during its flight, May 11–14, 1926.
(Library of Congress)

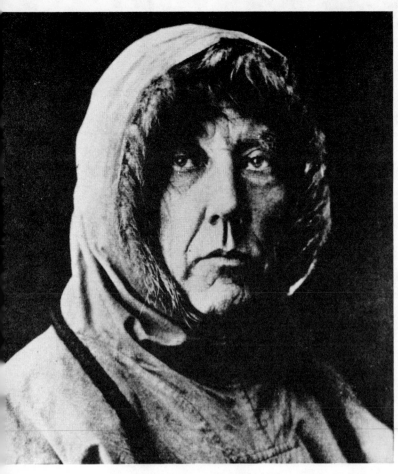

In 1928 Nobile tried another North Pole flight in the balloon *Italia;* the airship crashed on an ice pack, initiating a wide search. Amundsen chartered a plane to help in the search. His plane was also lost and he was never found; however, Nobile and the survivors of his crew were rescued after a three-week search. The *Italia* provided yet another nail for the coffin of the airship.

Design innovations during the twenties were legion in numbers, only a few of which passed the ultimate flight tests. Refinements in aircraft design, particularly military planes, were frequently introduced during the various competitions that burgeoned, beginning in the United States in 1920 with the Pulitzer Trophy race. Perhaps the most exciting, most important aviation event in the country at the time, the Pulitzer races were primarily competitions between the Army and the Navy air services, resulting in the evolution of the modern fast pursuit (later fighter) plane. Although civilian pilots could race for the Pulitzer Trophy, by 1922, because of the high costs involved, the race

Norwegian polar explorer Roald Amundsen. He was the first to reach the South Pole (by dogsled) in 1911 and the second over the North Pole in 1926. He was lost in a search for Nobile in 1928. (National Air and Space Museum/Smithsonian Institution)

Off the beaten track: the Pensute-Caproni, ca. 1922–23. Power was provided by a forty-five-horsepower Anzani engine. Wingspan was about thirteen feet. (U. S. Air Force)

Frenchman Louis Damblanc built this early whirlybird; not only did the "wings" turn, but also wire controls twisted them for lateral control. This craft never left the ground. (U. S. Air Force)

Army P-1 Curtiss Hawks round the pylon during the 1926 John L. Mitchell Trophy Race, 1926. (Mitchell, brother of General Mitchell, died in France during the First World War.) Races such as this, usually flown by military aircraft, advanced their design. Lieut. L. G. Elliot won this race with a speed of 160.4 miles per hour. (U. S. Air Force)

was left to the Army and the Navy. The high-speed, very maneuverable aircraft made a deep impression on the large crowds the races invariably attracted. The last Pulitzer was flown in 1925—won by the Army's Lieutenant Cyrus Bettis, in a sleek Curtiss Racer. The same plane, its wheels replaced by pontoons, won the Schneider Trophy for the United States a few days later.

The Schneider competitions were international and in that sense even more important than the Pulitzer races. The French industrialist Jacques Schneider established the trophy in December 1912 to encourage the development of seaplanes;

The lumbering, but reliable Ford Trimotor entertains at the 1926 air races, Philadelphia, 1926. Three years later Charles "Speed" Holman looped the big plane; Ford's test pilot entered it in the 1930 national air races, and at the '38 Nationals Harold Johnson stunted in it. (U. S. Air Force)

The Navy's "Sea Hawks" (D.W. Tomlinson, W. V. Davis, and A. P. Storrs) thrill the crowd at a 1928 air meet in Los Angeles, in the little shipboard fighter the Boeing F-2B. (National Archives)

the first meet was held in Monaco in April 1913 and was won by one of France's most famous pilots, Marcel Prevost. His trim little Deperdussin won practically by default—the other three competitors, including one American, were forced out of the race by mechanical troubles. Prevost's official winning time was 45.75 miles per hour. The 1914 contest was won by Britain; Howard Pixton set a new speed record in his Sopwith *Tabloid:* 86.78 miles per hour.

The First World War ended the Schneider races for the duration, but once that was over the meet was held, as decreed by the rules, in England, the winner of the last race before the war. Entered were three British entries, two French, and one Italian. The entire race was a comedy of mishaps, none of them serious except that the French were unable to get any of the planes into the air; the British pilots took off unofficially and were disqualified, and Lieutenant Guido Janello, the Italian entry, circled the course in the soupy weather and landed, certain he was the winner. He soon learned that not one

Jimmy Doolittle, U.S.A., winner of the Schneider Trophy race, Baltimore, October 26, 1925. The same type of plane, the Curtiss Racer, with wheels, won the Pulitzer Trophy (flown by Cyrus Bettis) only days before. (U. S. Air Force)

judge had seen him (in fact, he had circled a wrong circuit). Although all agreed that Janello's was a prize-winning feat, the reinstated Schneider race of 1919 was called no contest. As a courtesy, however, it was decided that the 1920 race would be held in Italy—the almost winner. The next year, in fact, Italy did become an official winner, but with qualifications: There were no British or French (or American, for that matter) entrants, and the trophy was won by Lieutenant Luigi Bilogna, the sole pilot whose plane proved seaworthy.

By 1923 the Schneider Trophy had regained its stature—the race of the previous year had been taken by Britain—and attracted entrants from Britain, France, and the United States, represented by pilots of the U. S. Navy. Flying similar Curtiss CR-3 racers, two Navy pilots Lieutenants David Rittenhouse (177.38 miles per hour) and Paul Irvine (173.46 miles per hour), took first and second place, respectively. This placed America on the international scene and proved that Curtiss had developed one of the fastest planes in the world. The setting for the 1924 Schneider would have been the United States, but that was not to be. The Italian entrants, for some reason, withdrew, and the British were having problems with their aircraft. In a fit of sportsmanship, the Flying Club of Baltimore called off the race.

The next year the contest was held, again near Baltimore, and brought entrants from Britain, Italy, and the United States—Navy and Army. On October 26, 1925, Lieutenant Jimmy Doolittle, flying the same Curtiss Racer that had won the Pulitzer Trophy a few days before, won the Schneider Trophy for the United States for the second time (the nation that won it three times running would gain permanent possession). Doolittle had flown a brainy yet daring race, and he pushed the little Curtiss comfortably over the 200-

Postrace congratulations: General Mason M. Patrick, head of the Air Service, in happy conversation with Doolittle and Mrs. Josephine "Joe" Doolittle. (U. S. Air Force)

Second-place winner in the 1926 Schneider Trophy race was this Curtiss racer (officially the R3C-2) flown by Marine pilot Christian Schilt. During this period the races were generally Army vs. Navy events, with an occasional sprinkling of international rivals, also flying military planes. (Navy Department/National Archives)

mile-per-hour mark. The British entry of that year was a beautifully designed Supermarine S-4, which was eliminated by an accident that nearly cost the life of the pilot, Henry C. Baird.

The British passed by the 1926 Schneider, which was taken by Italy in a brilliant contest flown by Major Mario de Bernardi in a splendid Macchi M-39. The Italian plane proved to be superior to the American Curtisses, one of which came in second. Had Marine Lieutenant Christian Schilt come in first, America could have taken the final Schneider race, but the Italian design, superior engine, and De Bernardi's flying blocked that.

The impact of the Schneider competitions upon the development of high-speed aircraft took them out of the realm of sport. While speed was paramount, so were efficiency, safety, and performance. When the various competing nations recognized the Schneider races as a challenge to the prestige of their aircraft industry, the several governments took a hand in assisting the entrants. The United States provided Navy and Army pilots and planes, the Italian Government was most co-operative with funds and pilots. Britain took its first real official interest in 1927—about the time the United States began economizing on its participation. The British, who had won in 1927 and 1929 and were in line for permanent possession, did receive a little private assistance from a certain wealthy Lady Houston. She presented the Royal Aero Club with a hundred thousand pounds, which eventually reached the RAF, the chosen defender of the British claim to the Schneider Trophy. That gift was

Major Mario de Bernardi in the cockpit of the 1926 first-place Schneider Trophy winner, the Macchi M-39, the Italian entry. (U. S. Air Force)

used in the preparation of the 1931 entry, a Supermarine S-6B.

The Supermarine had been the product of a design team headed by Reginald J. Mitchell (1895–1937), one of Britain's greatest aircraft designers. The Supermarine Schneider racer had been refined since the ill-fated S-4 of 1925. An S-5, flown by Flight Lieutenant S. N. Webster, took the trophy in Venice, site of the races in September 1927. There was no race in 1928, which was also the year in which Schneider, a mere forty-nine, died.

In 1929 competition, held at Cowes, England, was also taken by the British and again by a Supermarine, a S-6 flown by Flight Officer H. R. Waghorn. The official winning speed was 328.63 miles per hour, an increase of nearly fifty miles per hour over Webster's prize-winning flight two years before. Mitchell had introduced some modifications into the design: The wingspan was lengthened to 30 feet (from 26 feet, 9 inches), and, perhaps even more importantly, was its new engine, the powerful Rolls-Royce RV-12, capable of revving up 1920 horsepower. By 1931, which would prove to be the last Schneider Trophy race, that horsepower had risen to 2,350, as compared with the Gnome-powered Deperdussin of the first race in 1913, which managed 160 horsepower.

Flight Lieutenant J. N. Boothman flew the new Supermarine S-6B in competition with fliers from Italy and France. He won permanent possession of the coveted Schneider Trophy for Britain, according to the rule set down by the Fédération Aeronautique Internationale. Boothman's Supermarine covered the three laps at Lee-on-Solent, England, on September 13, 1931, averaging a speed of 340.866 miles per hour, a new world's record for any aircraft, sea- or land-based. The S-6B flown by Boothman that day was especially significant in that it was the direct antecedent of one of the most celebrated aircraft of all time, the Spitfire. Before his early death Mitchell had designed the prototype of that classic fighter plane, which flew for the first time on March 5, 1936.

The outright possession of the Schneider Trophy ended a most creative, and at times fatally

The Supermarine S-5, which took the Schneider Trophy in 1927 at Venice. Flight Lieutenant S. N. Webster won with a speed of 281 miles per hour, September 1927. When Britain won the Schneider Trophy for the third time in 1931 they took permanent possession and the Schneider races were over. (National Air and Space Museum)

Supermarine S-6B, the type that won the British final possession of the Schneider Trophy in 1931. (National Air and Space Museum, Smithsonian Institution)

Another kind of race: the first to fly from New York to Paris nonstop. French ace of aces René Fonck was determined to try and ordered Sikorsky to build him the plane that could do the job. Sikorsky's answer was the S-35, ready for flight in September 1926. (Sikorsky Aircraft)

dangerous, era in aviation. The Schneider races, however, contributed more than "thrills and spills," for after it was resumed after the war in 1919 the advancement in aircraft design was rapid. Although the competitions were open only to seaplanes, the lessons learned could be applied to landplanes. Those lessons were applied as well to the general design of the aircraft, of course, but it also led to great advancement in the development of engines as well as the associated attention paid to fuel and the supercharger. Of especial import to military aircraft designers was the evolution of the fast, low-wing monoplane configuration, resulting in the fast, maneuverable fighter plane of a war no one really expected at the time (many believed in the earlier days of aviation that two wings were better than one).

The single most dramatic event in aviation of the 1920s, second probably only to the flight of the Wright brothers, was the transatlantic solo flight of twenty-four-year-old Charles Lindbergh in May 1927. More than any other individual exploit, this lonely achievement rendered the twenties golden for the future of aviation. Even more than the adventures of the warbirds, Lindbergh's single flight truly led to "the making of aviation" internationally and nationally, for it also reawakened the United States to the potential of aircraft.

The lure, superficially, was money: Raymond Orteig, of France, offered a prize of twenty-five thousand dollars to the airman, or airmen, who made the first nonstop flight between New York and Paris. The offer had been made originally in 1919, with a time limit of five years; when there were no takers, Orteig extended the time an additional five years. Around 1926 the world of aviation began to stir, and pilots began considering taking the Orteig prize money. What with improved engines and aircraft design, the idea of crossing the Atlantic nonstop (it had been done, though over a shorter distance, by Alcock and Brown) became more feasible.

Even so, it was no simple undertaking; by May of 1927, when the unknown youth, Lindbergh, was ready for his try, several lives had been lost. In September 1926, France's highest-scoring war ace, Rene Fonck, attempted to take off in a specially built Sikorsky S-35 from New York and crashed during takeoff. In the fire that followed, two of the four-man crew died (although Fonck escaped without serious injury). Even as Lindbergh and more experienced, more celebrated fliers—Richard Byrd and Clarence Chamberlin—prepared to make their tries, one of France's best-loved fliers, also an ace,

Burned-out wreckage of Fonck's S-35, which crashed during takeoff, killing two of the four-man crew. Fonck escaped unhurt, but it ended his plans for a transatlantic flight. (Sikorsky Aircraft)

Coli (with eyepatch) and French ace Nungesser before their fatal attempt to fly the Atlantic in the difficult east-to-west crossing. The plane was a Levasseur PL-8, christened *L'Oiseau Blanc*. On its side was Nungesser's death-tweaking First World War insignia. *The White Bird* took off from Paris on May 8, 1927, and was never seen again. (Musée de l'Air, Paris)

Charles Nungesser, disappeared over the Atlantic with his copilot, François Coli.

Both Byrd and Chamberlin, known quantities in the world of aviation, had made careful and extensive plans; both had large, roomy aircraft whose payload could include a copilot-mechanic, perhaps, food, and other supplies. Byrd had chosen the time-honored Fokker Trimotor, and Chamberlin had a reliable single-engined Bellanca, the plane that Lindbergh originally had hoped to fly. Chamberlin and Bellanca had gotten themselves involved with a fast-talking financier entrepreneur, Charles A. Levine, who hoped to sponsor the New York-to-Paris flight, win the sweepstakes, and exploit it.

Lindbergh had gotten the backing of a group of St. Louis businessmen, who believed in the flier and the future of aviation, and provided him with the funds to purchase the aircraft in which he believed the flight could be successfully accomplished. Lindbergh's first choice was the Fokker Trimotor, but it was rejected by the American Fokker agent because of his youth and inexperience; if he were lost attempting such a flight in the Fokker, it would give the company a bad name.

Lindbergh preferred the Bellanca, but was totally frustrated by the publicity-conscious Levine. Levine was willing to sell the plane to Lindbergh and his backers, provided he—Levine—had final say about the makeup of the crew. He too rejected Lindbergh (for he already had the better-known Chamberlin in mind). Levine, however, was willing to let Lindbergh paint the name of St. Louis on the plane.

Almost in despair, Lindbergh sought elsewhere. The most encouraging response was the one received from a relatively unknown aircraft manufacturer, Ryan, in San Diego, California. When Lindbergh arrived in California, his youth did not put off the generally youthful Ryan personnel. The man who agreed to design a transatlantic plane according to Lindbergh's specifications was himself relatively young—Donald Hall. Working closely with Lindbergh, the Ryan people turned out a small, handsome, single-engine monoplane, which Lindbergh named *The Spirit of St. Louis*, in honor of the home city of his backers. After a series of test flights, Lindbergh, without fanfare, flew the Ryan to St. Louis and then to New York.

Charles A. Lindbergh planning his transatlantic flight in the offices of the Ryan Flying Company, San Diego, California. (Ryan Aeronautical Library)

Fuselage of the Ryan plane being specially built for Lindbergh (the design is a variant on the early Ryan Brougham). Controls and throttle are in place; there is no provision for a forward-viewing windscreen. (Ryan Aeronautical Library)

Wing of the Lindbergh plane has just been lowered from the second story of the Ryan plant for assembly onto fuselage. (Ryan Aeronautical Library)

The fuselage, with engine in place, emerges from the Ryan plant. Second from left is a youthful air enthusiast then working for Ryan, Douglas Corrigan; fourth from left: plant manager Hawley Bowlus, who was also a noted sailplane designer. (Ryan Aeronautical Library)

Fuselage being transported to wing assembly point. (Ryan Aeronautical Library)

Wing and fuselage of *The Spirit of St. Louis* meet for the first time. Lindbergh assists in the group on the left; Corrigan steadies the tail. The X in the plane's license number designates it as an experimental aircraft. (Ryan Aeronautical Library)

Lindbergh, beaming, stands before the completed *Spirit of St. Louis*. (Smithsonian Institution)

Preparing *The Spirit of St. Louis* for tests and for the cross-country flight to Curtiss Field, New York. (Ryan Aeronautical Library)

The Spirit of St. Louis leaving California for St. Louis, New York—and Paris, May 10, 1927. (Ryan Aeronautical Library)

When he arrived unexpectedly at Curtiss Field, he was not regarded very seriously as a contender for the Orteig prize. But his youth, engaging smile, modesty—and the fact that he was planning to make the flight alone—rendered him good copy for the popular newspapers of the time; he was soon dubbed "Slim" (as most of his friends called him), "The Lone Eagle," "Lindy," and later, "Lucky Lindy," and the nickname Lindbergh resented most—"The Flying Fool." If anyone was not a "flying fool," or dependent on luck, it was Charles A. Lindbergh.

While Chamberlin and Byrd awaited perfect weather, Lindbergh kept in constant touch with the New York Weather Bureau. Although Long Island was somewhat fogged in, there was a good chance of clearing and the Atlantic promised reasonably storm-free passage. Eager to take advantage of the break in the weather, Lindbergh hurried to Curtiss Field. The plane was towed to Roosevelt Field, because Roosevelt had a smoother runway, and placed at the extreme west end of it to afford as long a takeoff run as possible. At seven-forty on the morning of May 20, 1927, the (as it proved) efficient, powerful, and trustworthy Wright Whirlwind radial, air-cooled engine spurted into life. Twelve minutes later the heavy plane began its run and for moments appeared, because of the heavy fuel load, as if it might run out of runway. The soft mud was little help, some of it clinging to the plane, adding extra weight. A tractor loomed at the end of the runway, *The Spirit of St. Louis* bumped up, then settled down again, bounced again, cleared the tractor by fifteen feet, lifted over a telephone wire, turned to avoid a small hill, and finally disappeared into the murky sky over Long Island Sound.

To say that the world held its collective breath for the next thirty-three hours would not be abusing the cliché. While Lindbergh flew his lonely way across the Atlantic, people everywhere anxiously awaited word. Lindbergh, without radio, was cut off from that waiting world and fought headwinds, storms, and fatigue (the urge to sleep was all but overpowering). When he finally set *The Spirit of St. Louis* down upon the runway at Le Bourget Airport, near Paris, Lindbergh had become, literally overnight, the most famous man in the world. He had flown the 3,600 miles between New York and Paris in 33½ hours, landing at 10:22 P.M. Paris time, May 21, 1927.

The impact of Lindbergh's exploit upon people's imaginations was no greater than the impress of his character. Poised, genuinely modest, thoughtful (while in France, he visited the mother of the lost Nungesser), he brought an aura of dignity to the American personality—which in the midtwenties was associated in the European mind with gangsters, prohibition, sensational murder trials, and general nonsense. At the time, this aspect of Lindbergh's flight overshadowed his other achievement. In one of his few, always direct speeches, Lindbergh himself assessed his accomplishment. Alluding to the invention of the balloon, Benjamin Franklin's balloon query, "What good is a newborn child?" and Blériot's Channel flight, Lindbergh then said: "Today those same skeptics [who had questioned the value of the accomplishment of the Montgolfiers and Blériot] might ask me what good had been my flight from New York to Paris. My answer is that I believe it is the forerunner of a great air service from America to France, America to Europe, to bring our peoples nearer together in understanding and in friendship than they have ever been."

After his return to the United States, Lindbergh characteristically refused to be drawn into the celebrity racket and to be exploited; not did he himself attempt to cash in on his immense fame. He rejected lavish offers of money from the movies, etc. Instead, he devoted himself to advancing the cause of aviation, particularly in the field of transportation. As an international hero, Lindbergh propagandized for the spread of passenger aviation (in which his own nation lagged behind the rest of the world) flight safety, and a wider public acceptance of the idea of air travel. He also spread the word among the youth of the nation, to whom he was the greatest figure in aviation. These were the days of balsa-wood and tissue rubber-powered

May 20, 1927, Lindbergh, over the Atlantic, begins his flight to Paris. (Smithsonian Institution)

May 21, 1927—Lindbergh in France. (Musée de l'Air, Paris)

Following his epochal flight, Lindbergh refused to commercialize on his fame; instead he set out to promote the future of aviation by making good-will flights in *The Spirit of St. Louis* in the United States and Latin America. In this photo he flies over Gatun Lake, Canal Zone, on January 22, 1928. (U. S. Air Force)

models. The model builders of the twenties and thirties became the engineers and designers (and some, pilots) of the forties and later. Much of the impetus of their interest could be attributed to Lindbergh; and this was true for the youth of the rest of the world.

Lindbergh's major interest lay in the development of passenger aviation. In 1929 he had a new Lockheed Sirius built, and he flew more than 29,-000 miles on a survey trip to Labrador, Greenland, Iceland, the Azores, Europe, Africa, and return. Accompanied by his wife, Anne Morrow Lindbergh, Lindbergh covered many miles for what later became Pan American World Airways. Converted to a seaplane, the Sirius was also used in the Lindbergh's famous *North to the Orient* flight, which blazed the way for the China Clipper of the thirties.

Lindbergh had won the race to Paris, leaving his friendly competitors, Byrd and Chamberlin, behind. With Paris as an objective used up, Chamberlin in his Bellanca switched to Berlin. Backing his flight was an eccentric, young, self-made millionaire, Charles Levine. Having formed the Columbia Aircraft Corporation with ex-Wright designer Giuseppe Bellanca, the thirty-year-old Levine had hoped to sell the plane they had produced to Lindbergh for the transatlantic attempt. Lindbergh finally rejected the plane (he had raised

Inspiring the air-minded. Lindbergh at the 1928 national air races near Los Angeles. Model builders competing for the Mulvhill Trophy cluster around the flier as he is greeted by official Cliff Henderson. (U. S. Air Force)

The Lindbergh Lockheed Sirius, 1929, in which he and his wife, Anne Morrow Lindbergh, surveyed air routes over the Atlantic and Pacific. (Lockheed Aircraft)

the money Levine had demanded but had then found that Levine insisted upon selecting the crew). Finally, after much friction, Chamberlin was selected as the pilot; his copilot remained a mystery.

When the *Columbia* took off on June 4, 1927, the mystery was cleared: Levine was to be the copilot.

In fact, since he had practically no skill as a pilot and none as a navigator, he became the first transatlantic passenger. The Bellanca did reach Germany nonstop, although it was some 118 miles short of Berlin. A forced landing or two delayed them, but they arrived in Berlin on June 7 and were greeted

Bellanca *Columbia*. Clarence Chamberlin is in the cockpit as the plane begins takeoff at Thur, Switzerland. (U. S. Air Force)

Chamberlin is warmly greeted during a good-will tour of Europe after they finally arrived in Berlin on June 7, 1927. Levine is third from the left; next to him is French pilot Maurice Drouhin. (Musée de l'Air, Paris)

Two of Byrd's best pilots: Floyd Bennett and Bernt Balchen; the latter was one of the pilots in Byrd's attempt to fly the Atlantic. (Smithsonian Institution)

with the same wild enthusiasm that Lindbergh had elicited at Paris. Though failing in their original goal, Chamberlin and Levine—and the *Columbia*—had covered 3,911 miles nonstop in forty-two hours, forty-five minutes; it was a new world's record for distance.

Byrd, who followed at the end of the month in the Fokker Trimotor *America*, suffered somewhat the same fate as Chamberlin. Although he and his crew, pilots Bernt Balchen and Bert Acosta, with George Noville as radio operator/flight engineer, crossed the Atlantic, they too fell short of their goal. The *America* became lost in the fog and darkness, and Balchen ditched it into the sea off the coast of Normandy. They had succeeded, but not quite as Lindbergh had. But all had proved that the Atlantic was no longer a barrier to air travel.

The Pacific Ocean was a more formidable "ditch" than the Atlantic; The Pacific's vastness and emptiness for hundreds of thousands of square miles were a challenge, especially to the U. S. Navy. As early as August 1925, the Navy had attempted a flight from San Francisco to Hawaii, but neither of the planes that set out made the complete crossing, although one, under the command of Commander John Rodgers, arrived at the harbor at Nawiliwili, Hawaii, as a surface craft with fabric from the wings as sails. After flying nearly 2,000 miles the plane had run out of fuel. The final 450 miles took nine days to complete. Then in June 1927, no doubt to the chagrin of the Navy (which did not lack for skilled and courageous fliers), the Army again beat them on their own waters. A Fokker Trimotor, *Bird of Paradise*, accomplished this remarkable feat with Lieutenant Albert F. Hegenberger as navigator and Lieutenant Lester J. Maitland as pilot. The key to the entire flight, and the survival of the crew, lay in the science of navigation.

On June 28, 1927, the *Bird of Paradise* left Oakland, California, and headed across the Pacific for the tiny dot, Hawaii. The margin for navigational error was a mere 3½ degrees; if Hegenberger made the slightest miscalculation or if their instruments malfunctioned (which they did), the airmen could end up flying over the Pacific with no place to land.

Bert Acosta, who with Balchen made up the flight crew of Byrd's *America*. (Smithsonian Institution)

The *America* poised on its takeoff ramp; the downhill run would help the heavy plane gain speed. (Smithsonian Institution)

The beginning of Byrd's Atlantic flight. (Smithsonian Institution)

The end of Byrd's flight: the *America* where Balchen skillfully ditched it off the coast of France. They had almost made it, but had become lost in the fog, July 1927. (Smithsonian Institution)

A seagoing aircraft, the Naval Aircraft Factory's PN-9. In this plane Commander John Rogers attempted to fly nonstop from San Francisco to Honolulu in August 1925. The plane flies over Oahu after the trip and repairs. (Smithsonian Institution)

Albert Hegenberger and Lester Maitland, navigator and pilot, respectively, of the Army's *Bird of Paradise*. (U. S. Air Force)

One of the devices used for the first time in this long cross-water flight was a radio beam. This worked intermittently, proving its usefulness, but before the flight was over Hegenberger had to rely upon his own ingenuity to direct the course of the plane. He even took sightings from the whitecaps of waves to determine their course. Twenty-five hours and 50 minutes after taking off in California, they landed at Wheeler Field, near Honolulu, having covered a distance of 2,418 miles.

Lester Maitland performed remarkably as had Hegenberger. Flying the plane for more than a day required constant attention and stamina. The entire flight, in the words of Charles Lindbergh, was "the most perfectly organized and most completely planned flight ever attempted." But there *was* one

The *Bird of Paradise* leaving San Francisco for Hawaii, June 28, 1927. (U. S. Air Force)

Pilot Maitland in the cockpit of the first plane flown nonstop from the mainland to Hawaii. (U. S. Air Force)

Winner of one of the most pointless races of the post-Lindbergh twenties, the Travel Air *Woolaroc*, one of the two planes that completed the flight from Oakland, California, to Hawaii. This was known as the Dole "Pineapple Derby" of August 1927. The race began with twelve entries, several of which were eliminated by crashes or last-minute government inspections. Finally eight set out from Oakland—four of which either crashed on takeoff or, wisely, returned. Two disappeared entirely (so did an Air Corps plane dispatched to look for them). Only the *Woolaroc* and a Breese monoplane, *Aloha*, completed the trip and arrived in Hawaii. The race added nothing to the cause of aviation or to flying the Pacific. (National Air and Space Museum, Smithsonian Institution)

small hitch: All apparently had been ticked off to a T except for their food supply, which they could not find. The entire flight was made on empty stomachs; after landing the men found their soup and sandwiches carefully stowed away under a tarpaulin beneath Hegenberger's plotting board. Otherwise, this Pacific crossing had been perfectly accomplished.

As with Lindbergh's flight, the feat of Maitland and Hegenberger inspired imitation. Two weeks later two civilians, Ernest L. Smith and Emory B. Bronte, attempted the same flight—and almost made it. They ran out of fuel over the Island of Molokai and were forced to land short of Honolulu, their goal; it had been no mean accomplishment, and the two aviators were properly hailed for their flight. Not hailed, however, was the "Pineapple Derby," the first transpacific air race, with a first prize of twenty-five thousand dollars offered by planter James D. Dole. The helter-skelter scramble for money, which became airborne on August 16, 1927, was a disaster from the beginning. Of the sixteen entries, two were killed before the race began. Eventually, only eight planes remained after others were eliminated as unairworthy. Before the prize was claimed, ten fliers were dead from crashes or had been lost in the Pacific during both the race and the rescue searches that followed. The entire mess had proved nothing and caused a good deal of criticism in the press and engendered public suspicion of aviation—and detracted from the accomplishments of such planned flights of Maitland and Hegenberger and Smith and Bronte. Added to their flights was that of Captain Kingsford-Smith the next year. The Australian pilot made the first flight between the United States and Australia in a Fokker F-7 in May 1928. Kingsford-Smith flew from Oakland, California, to Brisbane, with stops at Honolulu and Fiji. While this was an important step, it was still the Atlantic that continued to challenge fliers most.

A rash of "Lindbergh fever" followed in the wake of his epochal New York-to-Paris flight, most of which were aborted, canceled, or ended in the loss of crews and aircraft. While the attempts by Chamberlin and Byrd could have been called qualified successes (though Byrd's ending up in the Atlantic was less than that), thanks to the skill of their respective pilots, the flights that followed were too often amateur displays.

Even an experienced pilot's limited knowledge of navigation and of the tricky weather over the Atlantic contributed little to the success of their flights. By the end of 1927, when the weather over the Atlantic was impossible, two very determined women had lost their lives trying to be first across the Atlantic. In August a Princess Anne Lowenstein-Wertheim (an English aviation enthusiast who had married a titled German) became the first woman to attempt the transatlantic crossing. She was sixty years old, and had the money to buy a

Fokker and to hire two experienced pilots; she made history, for she had the doubtful distinction of being the first woman lost in the Atlantic sweepstakes.

A New Yorker, Mrs. Frances Grayson, also strong of will, also with hired pilots, took off in December. Her Sikorsky, named *Dawn*, disappeared on the first leg of its Christmas Eve 1927 flight, the hop from New York to Newfoundland, the jumping-off spot for the Atlantic tries.

Between the loss of Princess Anne in August and Mrs. Grayson in December, eight unsuccessful attempts were made (not counting those of the courageous ladies). Some were, wisely, canceled— such was the case with the *Royal Windsor*, a Stinson Detroiter that was to have been flown by C. S. Schiller and Phil Wood. The poor weather was the determinant. Only a week later the crew of another Stinson, *Sir John Carling*, took off from Harbour Grace, Newfoundland, and was never seen again. Another plane, a Fokker, had taken off only the day before from Old Orchard Beach, Maine, and, although the wreckage of the plane was eventually found, its three passengers were not. The pilot was Lloyd Bertaud, the copilot-navigator, James D. Hill, and the passenger, reporter Philip Payne, aviation editor of the New York *Daily Mirror* (the flight had been sponsored by publisher William Randolph Hearst). Payne had gone along for the ride and of course the scoop; all he really added was extra weight to an already overloaded Fokker named *Old Glory*. The rash of flights emulating Lindbergh contributed little glory to the history of aviation.

Ever since the loss of Nungesser and Coli in the Atlantic, French airmen had burned with a desire to succeed where the two war heroes had failed. So it was that in October 1927, the world's attention was again drawn to the Atlantic after the futilities of the "Pineapple Derby" when two Frenchmen made the first crossing of the South Atlantic. Captain Dieudonné Costes and Lieutenant Commander Joseph LeBrix took off from St. Louis, Senegal (West Africa), and tackled the problems of the South Atlantic in a single-engined Breguet bi-

Frances Grayson's Sikorsky *Dawn*, in which this very determined lady decided she would cross the Atlantic. With pilot Oskar Omdahl and navigator Bruce Goldsborough at the controls. (Sikorsky Aircraft)

The Stinson *Royal Windsor* on line in the Lindbergh fever flights of 1927–28. Poor September weather canceled out the try. (National Museum of Science and Technology, Ottawa)

Crew of the *Royal Windsor:* Phil Woods, Mrs. Woods, Ada Green, and C. A. "Duke" Schiller. (National Museum of Science and Technology, Ottawa)

Ill-fated crew and plane: another Stinson Detroiter named *Sir John Carling*. Terrence Tulley (left) and James Medcalf took off from Harbour Grace, Newfoundland, on September 7, 1927, and disappeared over the Atlantic. (National Museum of Science and Technology, Ottawa)

The first plane to fly nonstop, east to west, from St. Louis, Senegal, to Natal, Brazil. The Breguet biplane, named *Nungesser-Coli*, was crewed by Dieudonne Costes and Joseph Le Brix. The South Atlantic crossing was made on October 14, 1928. (U. S. Air Force)

plane. Although the Atlantic was narrower at this point between Africa and South America, it was also most treacherous because of unpredictable storms. After more than twenty-one hours in the air, Costes and LeBrix landed their plane, named *Nungesser-Coli* in honor of the lost airmen, at Port Natal, Brazil. They made the first nonstop crossing of the South Atlantic. Like Lindbergh, they were hailed as conquerers of the air and sent upon goodwill tours by their government.

The flight of the *Nungesser-Coli* was the last successful one of the Lindbergh Year, 1927. It was followed by two abandoned attempts and the fatal flight of the determined Mrs. Grayson. The new year opened, on March 13, 1928, with the loss of one of Britain's renowned women fliers, Elsie Mackay, and her copilot, also a veteran, Walter Hinchliffe, in an attempt to make the difficult Europe-to-America crossing. And so, fatally, the next phase of the Lindbergh rash began.

Another east-to-west attempt was made a month after the disappearance of Mackay and Hinchliffe by a mixed crew: one German and one Irish pilot and a German-English-speaking navigator—namely Hermann Koehl, Captain James Fitzmaur-

ice, and Baron Guenther von Huenefeld. Their craft was an all-metal Junkers named the *Bremen* (in which Koehl and Von Huenefeld had made an earlier try in 1927). They took off from Baldonnel, Ireland, on April 12, 1928, and made a rather hard landing (after being lost in the fog) on diminutive Greeley Island, just off the northern coast of Newfoundland. They were the first to make the Europe-to-America crossing—although it could not be said that they had arrived in any style promising future emulation.

Even so, when word was flashed to the outside world that the crew of the *Bremen* had indeed arrived somewhere or other (few knew where, and they were a thousand miles off course), a great race to bring them out ensued. This began even as plans had been under way to bring the three off Greeley Island and to repair the Junkers. Clarence Chamberlin flew up to Quebec to be on hand if needed; "Duke" Schiller, who had withdrawn his *Royal Windsor* from the Lindbergh Derby the previous year, also stood ready. Herbert Bayard Swope, editor of the New York *World*, scooped them all: He managed to borrow Byrd's new Ford Trimotor and to hire two of Byrd's most celebrated pilots, Bernt

Costes (left) and Le Brix are welcomed after their successful flight across the Atlantic. In September 1930 Costes, with Maurice Bellonete, made the first Paris-to-New York flight. (Musée de l'Air, Paris)

British flier Elsie Mackay, who disappeared over the Atlantic with pilot Walter Hinchliffe in March 1928. (National Archives)

Junkers *Bremen*, with crew of three, en route to America from Ireland, April 1928. (Smithsonian Institution)

The *Bremen*, off course, and crumpled after landing on fog-enshrouded Greeley Island. (National Museum of Science and Technology, Ottawa)

The *Bremen* under repair for removal from Greeley Island. (National Museum of Science and Technology, Ottawa)

The *Bremen* crew is welcomed to Washington by President Coolidge for a medal-pinning ceremony. To Coolidge's left: Koehl, Von Huenefeld, and Fitzmaurice. (National Archives)

Balchen and Floyd Bennett, both of whom had just returned from Canada with bad cases of influenza. Despite this, the two men eventually headed back for Canada. During the cold and miserable nine-hour flight, Bennett's condition worsened. He immediately was rushed to a hospital in Quebec with pneumonia.

At this point Lindbergh offered to fly serum to Quebec in a raging snowstorm at night. But to no avail; Floyd Bennett died. Balchen completed the "rescue" in the Ford, how named *Floyd Bennett*. The crew of the *Bremen*, who had not required rescuing, since they could easily have left the island by boat, eventually reached Washington, D.C., to have their feat properly recognized by the President. Some good had come of it, despite the wasteful death of Bennett. Fitzmaurice was promoted to major in the Irish Free State Air Corps, Koehl was offered back the job he had lost with Lufthansa be-

cause the airline officials frowned on the flight (he rejected the offer), and Von Huenefeld, who was dying of cancer, could die with a sense of accomplishment.

Yet another first soon followed after the *Bremen* fiasco: the first flight over the Atlantic by a woman. In June Amelia Earhart went along—"like a sack of potatoes," in her phrase—in a Fokker flown by Wilmer Stultz, assisted by Louis Gordon, in a crossing from Newfoundland to Burry Port, Wales. They landed, they knew not where. Because of her gender, Earhart received the lion's share of attention but insisted that the men had done the work and that one day "maybe I'll try it alone." She was a woman of powerful convictions.

And so it went, a series of flights covering old ground—or old water—as fliers, for reasons best known to themselves attempted redundant or pointless excursions by air. The year ended as it

Amelia Earhart, the first women to cross the Atlantic by air—as a passenger, a distinction she did not like. She was determined to be the first woman to fly the Atlantic on her own; and she was. (U. S. Air Force)

Another victim of Lindbergh fever, Canadian Captain H. C. MacDonald, who hoped to be the first over the Atlantic in a light plane. On October 17, 1928, he set out in a de Havilland DH-60 Puss Moth and became the last fatality of the year. (National Museum of Science and Technology, Ottawa)

The *Question Mark* taking on fuel during its 1929 endurance flight, January 1–7, 1929. (U. S. Air Force)

Major Carl Spaatz, commander of the *Question Mark*, assists in the refueling operation. (U. S. Air Force)

began: Captain H. C. MacDonald, a Canadian, decided he would try to be the first across the Atlantic in a light plane. He took off in his little De Havilland Gypsy Moth on October 17, 1928, and simply disappeared.

The last year of the twenties, the year the Jazz Age came to a close with the Great Depression, U. S. Army fliers took the limelight again with a record-breaking endurance flight. The object was to see how long they could remain aloft and to determine what effect this would have upon man and machine. The plane was a Fokker, similar to the one that had made the California-to-Hawaii crossing; it was unnamed except for a large question mark on its side. In command of the crew of five was Major Carl Spaatz. The plane took off from Los Angeles on January 1, 1929, with a fuel supply of less than a hundred gallons. To keep the plane aloft, a system of midair refueling (pioneered by Lowell Smith and John Richter in 1923) was used.

During the long flight of the *Question Mark* the supply ship made contact with the Fokker forty-three times, transferring 5,205 gallons of gasoline and more than two hundred gallons of oil. Nine of these deliveries were made at night. Besides fuel and oil, various other supplies were passed from one plane to the other in midair, including batteries and food. After nearly a week in the air, the *Question Mark* was forced to land when one of its engines went dead. With the loss of power, the plane dropped from an altitude of five thousand feet to twenty-five hundred feet. The other two engines continued to function, but Spaatz wisely decided to end the flight. After 151 hours the *Question Mark* landed with a world's endurance record on January 7, 1929.

The true legacy of Lindbergh did not lie in the frequent attempts to emulate him; he did not encourage the many poorly planned flights that followed his and that ended as failures or fatally. His accomplishment and demeanor after resulted in a quickening of the American aviation industry and turned the attention of commercial operators from the exclusive transportation of mail and cargo to passengers. Soon the nation was crisscrossed by a network of airlines. By July 7, 1929, when Transcontinental Air Transport launched the first cross-country flights, it was possible to travel coast-to-coast in forty-eight hours (about half the time required by rail). Using the Ford Trimotor by day and the train by night, TAT could offer this great travel innovation. Technical adviser to the airline was Charles Lindbergh, and it became known as the "Lindbergh Line." The trip, incidentally, cost $351.94, which by the end of the year's stock-market crash was a pretty penny. TAT was caught in the Depression and merged with other lines but could be considered one of the parent companies of today's TWA.

The predecessor of the famed "Tin Goose" was the William B. Stout-designed "Maiden Dearborn" (a pun on the usual Made-in-Detroit phrase), which operated beginning in 1925 as one of the small fleet of the Stout Air Transport—later Stout Air Service. Stout's real interest was not in running an airline, but in designing planes. Eventually auto tycoon Henry Ford bought him out, and Stout evolved from this single-engined all-metal plane the Ford Trimotor.

The Ford's leather-covered seats for passengers were an improvement over earlier passenger accommodations (wicker seats without belts, for example). The Ford Trimotor was a wonderfully steady, rugged, reliable aircraft, one of the safest ever flown. Its one major disadvantage was the engine noise, which made life inside the fuselage rather clamorous. Before the day of the stewardess, copilots served the sandwiches and coffee. And for those passengers with airsickness problems (low-altitude flying was a bumpy experience), he supplied the "sick can."

The first midair refueling, January 1, 1929, shortly after takeoff. (U. S. Air Force)

Crew of *Question Mark* after almost a week of flight: Sergeant Roy Hooe, Lieutenant Elwood Quesada, Lieutenant Harry Halversom, Captain Ira C. Eaker, and Major Carl Spaatz. Quesada, Halversom, Eaker, and Spaatz achieved high ranks during the Second World War. (U. S. Air Force)

Pioneer aerial workhorse, or rather "Tin Goose," the Ford Trimotor, designed by William B. Stout and built by motor manufacturer Henry Ford. This was one of the first planes specifically designed for passenger transport. (U. S. Air Force)

An earlier Stout design, boxy, single-engine, but of all-metal construction. The Trimotor variant was to be one of the most reliable aircraft ever built. (U. S. Air Force)

View into the Ford Trimotor cockpit. Metal tags on either side of entrance identify pilot and copilot. A sign above informs passengers, "The members of the crew have been instructed not to accept gratuities." (American Airlines)

Passengers line up to board a Tin Goose. Note folded seat in entrance way. No space was wasted. (TWA Photo)

More than any other aircraft of the late twenties, the Ford Trimotor helped to get aviation literally off the ground in the United States. Other outstanding large commercial aircraft, such as the Boeing 80, followed. Like the Ford, it was powered by three engines but still employed the biplane configuration. The Fords, however, dominated the commercial airline scene when the twenties ended.

The golden era of the twenties seemed to bring some hope to the airship advocates, despite the several tragic events that had marred its history during the earlier years. In 1928 Germany was permitted to build its own first postwar Zeppelin, named the *Graf Zeppelin* in honor of the airship pioneer. The commander of the airship, Dr. Hugo Eckener, set out from Freidrichshafen, Germany, on October 11, 1928, and with twenty-three passengers aboard, crossed the Atlantic to land at Lakehurst, New Jersey, after a flight of some 111 hours, twenty-five minutes on October 15. Forgot-

Trimotor takeoff. (American Airlines)

Boeing's answer to the Ford Trimotor, the passenger-carrying B-80 over Chicago, 1929. The era of the monoplane had not quite arrived. (United Airlines)

A successful round-the-world flight in 1929 by the *Graf Zeppelin* seemed to herald a comeback for the airship. (National Air and Space Museum, Smithsonian Institution)

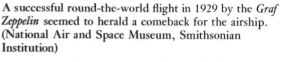

Graf Zeppelin, Friedrichshafen, Germany, 1928. This airship was the first to be built in Germany after the restrictions imposed by the Versailles Treaty. The *Graf Zeppelin's* first major flight was a successful crossing of the Atlantic. (Smithsonian Institution)

ten were the *Roma*, the *R-101*, and the *Shenandoah* in a flurry of "Zeppelin fever" that followed in the wake of the *Graf Zeppelin's* epochal flight. Americans were impressed with the giant airship's 787 feet of length as it slipped effortlessly through the skies.

The great triumph of the *Graf Zeppelin* followed its ocean crossing when, under the sponsorship of newspaper publisher William Randolph Hearst, it set out on a round-the-world flight. Leaving Lakehurst on August 7, 1929, Eckener pointed the ship for Germany again. With him were Sir Hubert Wilkins, the polar explorer, American airship commander Charles E. Rosendahl, and a number of journalists—a total of twenty passengers (some of whom paid nine thousand dollars for the privilege).

Dr. Hugo Eckener, great airship commander. An outspoken critic of the Nazis, Eckener fell out of favor when Hitler came to power. This brought an end to airship development in Germany. Hermann Göring, Hitler's chief airman, despised airships, which didn't help either. (Smithsonian Institution)

The *Graf Zeppelin* in flight; the giant ship was 787 feet long and provided luxurious air-travel accommodations for those who liked to fly but were not in a hurry. (U. S. Air Force)

The crew outnumbered the passengers two to one; some passengers, in fact, were left behind to keep the ship's weight within safety limits. From Friedrichshafen the *Graf Zeppelin* proceeded to Tokyo, and from there across the Pacific to Los Angeles and then eastward to Lakehurst, arriving in the early hours of August 29, having encircled the globe in a total time of twenty-one days, seven hours, thirty-four minutes. The *Graf Zeppelin* became the most honored airship in the world and excited attention wherever it was flown; in 1931 it began a regular service between Germany and South America and made dozens of successful crossings before being retired in 1937. The huge success of the *Graf Zeppelin* encouraged Eckener, with government backing, to develop new airships of even more dramatic proportions. So it was that when the twenties came to a close, the course of commercial aviation, whether by large transport plane or airship, looked promising: To many it appeared as if the Golden Twenties could only lead to aviation's Golden Age.

Not to be outdone by the luxury offered to airship passengers, the American firm of Western Air Express (later to be a component of TWA) showed what was possible with a little use of imagination and a lavish hand. This was introduced in a Fokker F-32 (first of the four-engined landplanes built in the United States), of the Fokker Aircraft Corporation, then a division of General Motors. In the five F-32s purchased, Western Air Express gave the air traveling public of the late twenties a glimpse of the future with its plane rather fancily decorated with tapestried cabin walls, indirect lighting, downy divans—and rather wrinkled curtains. In truth, the Fokker 32, which could carry thirty-two passengers (or sleep sixteen), was not a profit-making aircraft—it could not carry enough passengers and cargo to earn back the cost of maintenance, fuel etc. Also, Fokker's all-wood wings did not hold up well, which made the plane rather risky once rot set in. The F-32 did not last very long as a commercial airliner, but when the twenties ended with a whimper, passenger transport was here to stay.

No, not an interior shot of the *Graf Zeppelin*, but that of the Fokker F-32, flown by Western Air Express in the early 1930s. This monoplane afforded the passengers with the illusion of flying in small rooms. (TWA Photo)

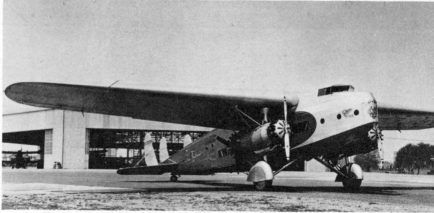

Fokker F-32, luxury airliner. (TWA Photo)

6 THE CLASSIC THIRTIES

Historically, the twenties blended into the thirties. The Great Depression that hit the American economy and spread by the middle thirties throughout the world put a definite period to the end of an age, however. Rarely were historians afforded so clear-cut a definition. (It is unlikely that anyone will ever resolve the division between the Middle Ages and the Renaissance—mainly, perhaps, because in reality there was none. Time merely went on; it was only later that men invented the convenient time divisions.) It was so with the development of aviation. The excitement of the twenties was naturally tapered off by hard economic facts. But the thirties was a time when the new ideas, new techniques, and new types of aircraft spawned in the previous decade were polished (in a technical sense) and perfected. It was a time of refinement rather than dramatic progress. Despite the Depression it was an era of rich development, particularly of commercial aviation, of private flying in the classic aircraft of the pre-Second World War world, of a number of great adventurous flights, of air racing, and of the rise of military aviation. In the days between the shock of the 1929 Depression and the jolt of the 1939 outbreak of war—Hitler's war—a soft summer softness pervaded the air. Men flew in some of the most romantic planes since the years of the early birds.

The formidable Atlantic Ocean, having been proved navigable by air, seemed a likely prospect for airline development. In order for such an operation to be both practical and profitable, the planes employed would necessarily have to be large enough to carry a good number of passengers and a heavy payload of cargo. The first solution, at least so it was thought at the time, came from Germany. Although forbidden by the Versailles Treaty to build aircraft (especially of the type that might be used in war), German aircraft manufacturers got around the treaty by establishing factories in other countries, such as Holland, Soviet Russia, and Switzerland. It was in Switzerland that Claude Dornier built, in 1929, the DO-X, the largest plane of its time. With a wingspread of 157 feet, the giant plane was capable of carrying more than a hundred passengers; its hull—137 feet from bow to stern—was divided into three decks with luxurious passenger quarters. To get this giant airborne required tremendous power—which, in reality, was not available at the time. Twelve engines (six pulling and six pushing back to back) generated six thousand horsepower in the original arrangement (these were later changed to American Curtiss engines for added thrust), but the DO-X had arrived too soon. Its performance hardly approached its impressive appearance. Its very size was against it, for the massive hull and the engine nacelles served to contribute to frontal drag. A headwind was a serious hindrance. Still, the appearance of the massive flying boat in the early thirties was an awe-inspiring sight, like some oceanliner that had sprouted wings. It became the first aircraft in history to carry one hundred people (on one occasion it took up 169); its standard passenger capacity was seventy-two. In November 1930, the DO-X set out

The Dornier DO-X, one of the most impressive aircraft of its time; despite twelve engines it was underpowered and a poor performer. It was the first plane, however, capable of carrying a hundred passengers. (Lufthansa Archive)

The DO-X landing at Norfolk, Virginia, 1931. (Navy Department, National Archives)

for New York, with stops at other ports in a test flight across the South Atlantic. What with problems—fire, winds, fuel consumption (the plane literally gulped fuel)—the plane did not arrive in New York until August 27, 1931, nearly ten months later. With its bulk and its limitations, the DO-X had proved not to be practical at all.

Germany continued in the thirties to expand its airlines and to modernize its aircraft production. A particularly clean design of the period, with its four engines inside the leading edge of the wing (unlike the DO-X's, which contributed heavily to the wind resistance of the plane), was the Junkers G-38. Put into operation in 1931 by Lufthansa, then the leading airline in Europe, the Junkers could accommodate thirty-four passengers, two of whom sat in the nose and three in the huge inner leading edge of the wing (inboard of the engines). The plane was hardly more practical than the DO-X, for only two were built, but both were a symbol of Germany's resurgence as a leading aviation power.

Since the war, it was generally taken for granted that Germany had been militarily maimed and that the Versailles Treaty had made the birth of a new German Air Force impossible. However, for years—since the twenties, in fact—German airmen were trained in secret in Soviet Russia, and new military aircraft were developed inside Russia. In Germany itself certain planes were developed for nominal commercial use, but they could be readily adapted to military use. Such was a so-called airliner, the Heinkel 111 and the Junkers 52, which proved to be an exceptionally good transport plane and was introduced by Lufthansa in May 1933. Of characteristic Junkers corrugated all-metal construction, the Ju-52 carried an average load of fifteen passengers. Like the Ford Trimotor, it was one of the most reliable planes of its time. When war came, the Ju-52 was converted into a military workhorse as a transport for troops and supplies, as a paratroop drop plane, and even as a bomber.

Despite post-World War I restrictions, the German aircraft industry quickly recovered, and new modern airliners were designed—airliners that could be converted into military aircraft. This is the Junker G-38. (Lufthansa Archive)

Junkers Ju-52, which went into passenger service in 1933. One of the best commercial planes of the period, it was used a decade later in the Second World War. (Lufthansa Archive)

A smaller Junkers, the Ju-160, a more advanced design than the Ju-52. (Lufthansa Archive)

The Heinkel He-70, like the Ju-160, was a smaller passenger-carrying aircraft; it carried pilot, copilot, and four passengers. A fast plane, the He-70 was often used by the Luftwaffe high command as a transport. (Lufthansa Archive)

The contrast between the slab-sided Ju-52 and the Heinkel 70, both produced in Germany in the same year, 1933, is interesting. The He-70 *Blitz* (Lightning) was a streamlined, fast transport with a retractable landing gear. Primarily operated as a fast (it could reach speeds of close to two hundred miles per hour) mail carrier, it had room for only four passengers. It was the fastest commercial plane of its time.

Adolf Hitler became Chancellor of Germany in January 1933, before the advent of the Ju-52 and the He-70, although both were in production long before. So were other aircraft of an obvious military nature. Hitler's second-in-command was Hermann Göring, a famous First World War fighter ace with twenty-two enemy aircraft to his credit when the war ended. When that occurred, Göring was in command of the fabled Richthofen squadron. An impractical romantic and a political nitwit, Göring attached himself to Hitler in the early days of the Nazi party because he too believed Germany had been "stabbed in the back." When the party came into full power, Göring, as an airman, was placed in command of the German air force, the Luftwaffe. Next in line was yet another ex-war pilot, Erhard Milch, Göring's opposite: businesslike, shrewd, and intelligent. He was also head of Lufthansa, the German air line, which he helped to establish on a solid footing. Thus, early in the game, were German civil and military aviation conjoined; Lufthansa pilots photographed various areas of Poland, France, and Britain for future reference. Hitler, Göring, and Milch—and their newly resurgent Luftwaffe—would have an impact on the future of the world, if not on aviation.

German air-mindedness among the young was nurtured by Göring through glider clubs, which sprang up all over Germany during the thirties. Since there was no restriction on the construction and flying of such patently peaceful aircraft, the former enemies of the Germans made no objection. Meanwhile, German youths, many young Nazis, were learning to fly, imbued with the idea that one day they would be piloting the real thing, once Hitler was ready to reveal that the Luftwaffe existed.

He-70, nicknamed the Lightning *(Blitz)* in military markings. (Courtesy Heinz J. Nowarra)

Hitler (in long coat to right of center) and entourage attend a Luftwaffe airshow. Field Marshal Hermann Göring stands to Hitler's left. By the midthirties it was obvious that Germany had secretly built a formidable air force. (Jarrett Collection)

German glider, ca. 1937. Future Luftwaffe pilots received early flight training in nonmilitary gliders, thus bypassing Versailles Treaty restrictions. (U. S. Air Force)

Luckily for the world (to some extent at least), Göring placed another ex-fighter pilot at the head of the technical branch of the Luftwaffe: the top-scoring living ace of Germany, Ernst Udet. An adept stunt pilot, Udet was a likable, happy-go-lucky person (he often wore a straw hat when he stunted). While in the United States in 1931, Udet had been so impressed with the performance of Curtiss dive bombers that he ordered some for Germany. This was the real beginning of the Stuka idea, the idea of an air force closely tied to the ground forces. As a consequence, the development of Luftwaffe bombers emphasized the dive bomber instead of the large, heavy, long-range bomber; this development (which was not ignored in the United States or Britain) in reality would decide the outcome of the Second World War. (Udet was betrayed by Göring's, and his own, ineptitude during the war, and in despair Udet committed suicide; his death was announced by the Nazis as having been the result of a flying accident.)

In Italy aviation was encouraged by dictator Benito Mussolini, who aspired to be a twentieth-century Caesar (he was, in fact, Europe's first really powerful leader during the early thirties; he would soon be overshadowed by his future ally, Hitler). Flamboyant, Mussolini enjoyed the grand gesture and encouraged headline-making flights by

American ace of aces Eddie Rickenbacker meets an old adversary, German ace Ernst Udet, at the Cleveland air races, 1931. (U. S. Air Force)

Italian Savoia-Marchetti twin-hulled flying boats after the first mass flight across the South Atlantic, 1933. The planes fly past Chicago's Century of Progress Exposition. (U. S. Air Force)

his airmen. As early as 1931 Italy's best-known airman, General Italo Balbo, led a flight of Savoia-Marchetti seaplanes from Rome to Rio across the South Atlantic. In 1933 Balbo, who was also Italy's Air Minister, topped the earlier effort by leading another mass flight of more advanced models of the Savoia-Marchettis beginning from Orbetello, Italy, and ending at Chicago's World's Fair—the Century of Progress Exposition. Balbo's flight attracted attention and served to bring good will to his various stopping-off points, which included Holland, Iceland, Labrador, and New Brunswick; on the return trip, Balbo stopped off in New York.

Although an impressive public-relations gesture, the Balbo massed flights contributed little to the advancement of Italian aviation, particularly military aviation. Despite the evolution that had been promised by Italy's Schneider Cup-winning Macchi, Italian combat aircraft design was dictated by a conservative General Staff, which dominated the Italian aircraft industry. When a real war came the Regia Aeronautica, despite Balbo, was saddled by obsolete tactics and often inferior aircraft.

In the United States certain developments in commercial (and military) aviation led to the emergence of modern airlines and to the dominance of American aircraft manufacturers in world aviation. For example, in 1930, Boeing Air Transport intro-

Italo Balbo, leader of the mass flight and also Italy's Air Minister. (Smithsonian Institution)

duced the Boeing Model 200, the Monomail. This was the first of the all-metal monoplanes designed for commercial use in the United States. One of its innovations was a retractable landing gear, an anti-drag cowling around the engine, and a low-wing cantilever construction (no wires or struts to hold the wing—all the stress was absorbed by the bridgelike structure inside the wing). The first Monomail was planned for use as a mail and cargo transport.

Later models of the Monomail (Models 221 and 221A) were designed with passenger accommodations for six. The pilot, however, still perched in the wind. The plane, while clean in design and structure, was underpowered with its single engine and was eventually supplanted by multi-engine transports.

Although not an advance aerodynamically, the advent of airline stewardesses (as they were called then) marked a great improvement in air travel. The idea was initiated by a nurse, Ellen Church, who brought it to Steve Simpson, then division

Boeing 221-B, a later evolution of the Monomail. (Boeing)

The Boeing Monomail, first of the modern American commercial aircraft, 1930. (Boeing)

traffic agent for Boeing Air Transport. Simpson then proposed the idea to the company. In his memo he wrote: "Imagine the psychology of having young women as regular members of the crew. Imagine the tremendous effect it would have on the traveling public. Also imagine the value that they would be to us in the neater and nicer method of serving food and looking out for the passengers' welfare. I am not suggesting at all the flapper type of girl. . . ." Simpson suggested that they employ graduate nurses. It took some convincing of both management and pilots (who resented women aboard as crew members), but it was agreed that beginning in May 1930, the air-hostess plan would be given a three-month trial.

The first air hostesses served on the Boeing Model 80 Trimotor, which had begun operations in late 1929. Although Miss Church had designed special uniforms for the stewardesses, they at times wore their regular nurses' uniforms. It had its soothing effect upon nervous passengers. The duties of the hostess included serving refreshments to passengers and keeping them informed of the

Ellen Church, the first airline "stewardess," and S. A. Simpson, who introduced the idea to Boeing Air Transport in 1930, look backward (in 1965). They study a photo of the first group of young women to work as air crew. Ellen Church stands at top left in that photo. (United Airlines)

changes in time as the plane passed through several time zones in the San Francisco-to-Chicago run (with thirteen stops for refueling). A railroad time-table, too, was a necessary piece of equipment in case the plane was grounded. Cleaning the floor was another chore, as was checking baggage, punching tickets, hauling supplies aboard (cold chicken, apples, rolls, cake, vacuum bottles of hot coffee). One of the duties, as noted in a stewardess handbook, was to "watch passengers going to the washroom to see that they do not open the door leading outside." The life of the first "steward-esses" was anything but boring.

One of the first planes designed according to the specifications issued by an airline was the Fairchild 10-A, the Pilgrim. This high-wing monoplane came fitted with an antidrag engine cowling, called the NACA cowling, for the National Advisory Committee for Aeronautics, which had developed it. The NACA was an independent government agency that was made up of members from various official agencies—the War and Navy departments, the Weather Bureau, etc.—as well as informed and

How it was: A "stewardess" serves coffee as passengers enjoy their flight. Nurse's uniform is proper, since the early stewardesses were trained nurses. The plane is a Boeing Model 80. (United Airlines)

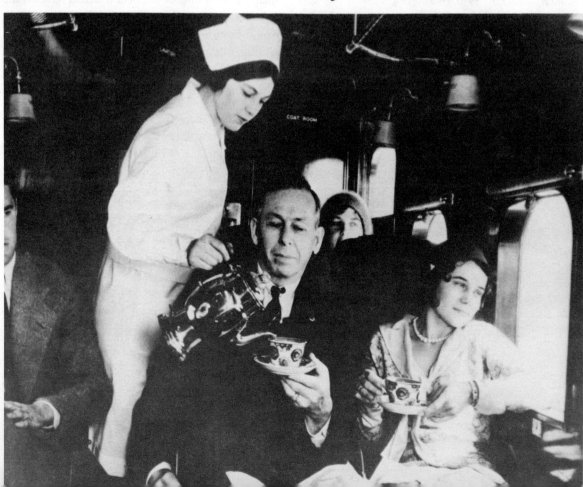

concerned civilians. Its findings were generally available to all. The Fairchild Pilgrim was placed in service by the then American Airways (now American Airlines) in 1931 when the young airline realized that the future of commercial aviation really lay in the transportation of passengers and not in carrying the mails. The Pilgrim was ordered by American primarily for passenger service; it had room for nine. Mail was also carried, but the passenger, at long last, was coming into his own in the United States.

Comfort for the passenger and speed were the two major lines of development in commercial aviation. If the Fairchild Pilgrim represented the first, the Lockheed Orion was an excellent example of the second. For short hops—such as those between Los Angeles and San Francisco—luxury was not as important as time. Consequently such smaller lines as Varney Air Service Limited, which called itself the Speed Lines, employed the fast Orions in its California operations. Carrying from five to seven passengers (often as not Hollywood celebrities of the period) the Orion sped from one point to the other at speeds exceeding two hundred miles an hour.

A major concept in commercial aircraft design emerged in 1933 with Boeing's Model 247, the first all-metal, low-wing, twin-engine transport. Another step in the evolution from the earlier Mono-mail, the 247 was quickly recognized as a superior aircraft and ordered by various airlines. It soon appeared on coast-to-coast runs, making the crossing in 19½ hours at a cruising speed of 170 miles an hour, carrying ten passengers (plus pilot, copilot, and stewardess), mail, express, and baggage. In 1934 one 247 was modified for pilots Roscoe

The Fairchild 10-A Pilgrim, which was built to order for, and to specifications of, American Airways, 1931. The plane carried passengers and mail. (American Airlines)

Varney Air Lines Lockheed Orion, 1931. This plane was transferred to Varney's Mexican branch, was later bought by private owners, and eventually ended up in Spain during its Civil War. (Lockheed Aircraft)

Boeing's contribution to the evolution of the modern airliner, the Model 247, 1933. Inscription on side of fuselage reads: "This plane carried the stars and stripes across the finishing line in the worlds greatest air race." This refers to the MacRobertson Race, in which the Boeing came in third. (United Airlines)

Turner and Clyde Pangborn for participation in the MacRobertson Race (England to Australia). The plane came in third in the race (first-prize winners were C. W. A. Scott and T. Campbell Black, flying a De Havilland Comet) and second in the transport category. The plane was later placed back into commercial service. Its wingspan measured 74 feet and its fuselage length fifty-one feet, seven inches. Not having the engine in the nose, the plane had room for extra radio equipment and four hundred pounds of mail. Also, life inside the cabin was made less noisy than in the Trimotors. With the engines out on the wings and the cabin soundproofed, the Boeing 247 was the most modern airliner of its day.

Airline luxury in 1933 was represented by the interior of the Boeing 247. The stewardess served the traditional meal: a sandwich (usually chicken), coffee, and an apple. The step in the cabin aisle was no decoration but the projection of the wing's main spar, which was constructed from wingtip to wingtip in a single unit. The plane also employed the newly developed controllable pitch propeller (by the Hamilton-Standard Propeller Company

under the direction of Frank W. Caldwell). The ability to change the angle of attack of propeller blades enabled the pilot to adjust its "bite" of the air at different altitudes and for different functions, such as takeoffs when more bite was required, and cruising when less was required. Rubber "boots" on leading edges of wing and tail surfaces prevented the formation of ice. This made the Boeing 247 and all-weather aircraft. By the end of its first year of service, 60 of the planes were in use with various U.S. airlines. Later, 247s went to Germany and China. Unfortunately for Boeing, their advanced airliner had not, as had so many others, appeared ahead of its time. It appeared at a moment when another designer, Donald Douglas, had produced his conception of the modern airliner. For all its superb qualities, the Boeing 247's day was a brief one.

The Curtiss Aeroplane and Engineering Company produced its first passenger plane, the Condor, in 1929. The last of the large biplane transports (wingspan: ninety-one feet, eight inches), it carried eighteen passengers comfortably. A modification of the Condor in 1933 resulted in the first

Interior of the Boeing 247; metal step in center covers the center spar of the wing. (United Airlines)

day-and-night commercial aircraft. Faster, thanks to more powerful seven hundred-horsepower Wright Cyclone engines and a retractable landing gear, the Condor was capable of speeding passengers from place to place night or day. Easily converted, the plane carried from fifteen to eighteen passengers on day routes or could sleep twelve at night. American Airways began the first sleeper service in the United States in May 1934 with the Condor. Besides speed, comfort, and safety, the Condor was also notable for its low operating costs. The economics of airline operation, although not as romantic as the story of the men and machines, were crucial to the success of the airlines. The search was always on for that plane that could transport safely a generous payload (passengers, cargo, and mail) at reasonable cost. This would ensure good wages for the airline's employees and a fair return on their investment to stockholders. By 1933–34 the airlines had become big business, and about this time the plane that made everyone happy came upon the scene. A giant in every sense of the word was the Handley-Page 42, the first four-engined airliner to be placed in scheduled service. This began in June 1931, when they first began flying for Britain's Imperial Airways to replace the Armstrong Whitworth *Argosy* transports.

The Curtiss Condor, the first sleeper aircraft used in the United States. Introduced by American Airways in 1933, the Condor proved that carrying passengers could be profitable. (American Airlines)

Imperial Airways' Handley Page 42, the *Hannibal*, 1931. This marked yet another step in the advance of commercial aircraft, the introduction of four engines. (British Airways)

One model, named the Hannibal (another was named Heracles), remained in operation for at least a decade, giving reliable and comfortable service. It was one of the most popular transports of its time. Powered by four Bristol Jupiter engines, the HP-42 had a wingspan of 130 feet; the fuselage was ninety feet long and housed one of the most comfortable passenger quarters aloft. The size of the plane, the clutter of interplane struts, and the massive wheels subtracted (rather than detracted) from the plane's speed. Top speed was around 130 miles per hour, but a more economical operating—that is, cruising—speed was about a hundred miles per hour. The Hannibal could land at a mere fifty miles per hour and was a steady, stable aircraft—one of the safest of all time. Imperial employed the Hannibal on its eastern run (connecting Karachi and stops between with Cape Town in Africa), and on a western run between London and Paris—a flight that took about 2 hours. On this run it could carry as many as forty passengers, none of whom ever suffered a fatal accident in this remarkable plane.

The single plane which had the greatest impact upon the progress of commercial aviation began as an idea in a letter from Jack Frye of Trans Continental and Western Air to Donald Douglas of Douglas Aircraft. The letter was dated August 2, 1932. In it, Frye asked Douglas if he could produce a multi-engined monoplane capable of carrying a payload of 2,300 pounds at about 150 miles an hour over a distance of a thousand miles. The original request was for a trimotor but with the advance in engine design, Douglas, in conference with his aides, Harry Wetzel and Arthur Raymond, decided that two engines would furnish ample power. The final result was the DC-1 (Douglas Commercial, Model 1), which flew for the first time on July 1, 1933. With its all-metal construction, retractable landing gear, and cowled engines, it was a clean-looking aircraft. Although its engines, one after the other, cut out on its initial test flight (because of a faulty carburetor), the DC-1 (of which only one was built) went on to exceed TWA's specifications: The 145–150-mile-per-hour speed was closer to 180, payload was increased 20 percent, and there was room for fourteen passengers (and crew) instead of the stipulated dozen.

Besides the design and construction of the plane, certain new developments added to its performance, such as the Wright Cyclone engines and the variable-pitch propellers. The sole DC-1, serving as a "laboratory airplane" (as it was called in the newspapers), moved from owner to owner once it had served its purpose and ended up in Spain during the Spanish Civil War. After that war (in December 1940) the plane lost engine power during a takeoff in Malaga, Spain, bellied in for a wheels-up landing, and crashed. Although no one was injured, the plane was a total loss and was eventually dismantled for spare parts, a sad end for one of aviation's most historic aircraft.

The success of the DC-1 prompted TWA to order twenty (and shortly after, an additional twenty, of

The birth of a new age in commercial aviation: the introduction of the Douglas DC-1 in 1933. Only this single DC-1 was built; it was wrecked in a poor landing in Spain in 1940. (Douglas Aircraft)

Second in line, the DC-2 operated by KLM in 1934; this plane flew the Amsterdam-to-Batavia run. (KLM Photo)

the improved DC-2. The improvements were chiefly internal ones, which added to passenger comfort and to the operating efficiency of the plane. The new model, too, began making and breaking records for speed (in the early days of its operations the DC-2 accumulated no less than nineteen American and world records). The reputation for economy, reliability, and potential profitability created a demand for the new Douglas transport both in the United States and abroad. One of the most famous of those bought abroad was the DC-2, which Royal Dutch Air Lines (KLM) entered in the London-to-Melbourne race in 1934. The plane not only entered the race but even attended to its regular passenger service (on one leg it even returned to its previous stop to retrieve a passenger who had somehow been left behind). The KLM DC-2 not only came in second in the race but also was first in the transport category, nosing out Roscoe Turner and Clyde Pangborn in their Boeing 247. Just as his World Cruisers had spread his name in 1924, the prize-

winning DC-2 of a decade later made the name of Douglas one of the most honored in the industry. In 1934 Douglas received the Collier Trophy (given for significant contributions to aviation) from President Franklin D. Roosevelt.

Crosby Maynard of Douglas Aircraft had succinctly written: "Before 1930, commercial air travel for most was generally regarded as a stunt, a rash venture only to be indulged for reasons of novelty, emergency, or to win speakeasy bets. It was, by common consent, a thoroughly uncomfortable experience. The air-travel advice with which pre-1930 voyagers coached their friends touched largely on deafness, gastric distress, cold feet, lack of sleep, and long hours of teeth-rattling vibration." At the end of the line of progress, after its predecessors, the Fokkers, the Fords, and the first true modern airliners, the Boeing 247 as well as the Douglas DC-1 and the DC-2 arrived, and late in 1935, the Douglas DC-3. This was an enlarged version of the early Douglas Commercials: The

Douglas aircraft soon were used by most major airlines; a DC-2 of Pan American flies over the Andes in South America. (Pan American World Airways)

wingspan was lengthened by ten feet, making it ninety-five feet in spread; the fuselage length was stretched a mere two feet, from sixty-two to sixty-four. The passenger load really stretched from the DC-2's fourteen to the DC-3's twenty-one. Not only did the larger wing provide more lift, it also housed two very powerful engines, Pratt & Whitneys, of twenty-four hundred horsepower. The

most modern radio equipment was installed, and so was one of the latest mechanical marvels, the Sperry automatic pilot—"Iron Mike" to crews—which could fly the plane with superhuman sensitivity while the pilot rested on long flights. With the advent of the Douglas DC-3, commercial aviation truly came of age.

The first DC-3 went into operation for American Airlines on June 25, 1936. Soon the DCs replaced the Condor sleepers on long cross-country flights; as a Skysleeper, the DC-3 could accommodate fourteen. It was, in the words of an American

Airlines historian, "a well-nigh perfect air transport, striking a happy balance in speed, gross weight, power, payload space, and wing area." The president of American, C. R. Smith, was more succinct when he said, "It was the first airplane that could make money just by hauling passengers." It was, too, the plane that sold air travel to the world, and it is unlikely that there is an airfield on earth where the DC-3 has not set down. During the rest of the thirties and into the forties it was the most abundant airliner in the air: A total of eleven thousand were built; and by 1939 it was used by every airline in the world. Donald Douglas had revolutionized air travel.

The Douglas transports dominated the long flights, but smaller craft were used in the feeder lines or by smaller airlines. Such a plane was the Lockheed Electra, an all-metal twelve-passenger plane. The plane was popular not only with the airlines but also with private owners. Electras were used also by adventurous pilots such as Jimmy Mattern, Dick Merrill, and Amelia Earhart.

Like the Lockheed Electra, the Bellanca Aircruiser was a solid favorite of the feeder-line operators. Dating back to the pioneering days of the twenties, the Bellanca was used concurrently with the DC-3s and Electras into the thirties. With its span of sixty-five feet, it was the largest single-engined plane of the time. It was not a true monoplane, but a sesquiplane, for some of the lift was provided by the landing gear and wing-support struts, which were airfoil-shaped, like the wing. Powered with one Wright Cyclone engine, the Bellanca carried from eleven to fourteen passengers, some of whose baggage was stored in the wing stubs between the fuselage and the wheel covering (known as pants). The maximum speed was about 160 miles per hour, which was good for a single-engined plane of its size and design.

Culmination of a classic airplane: the DC-3, readied for takeoff. By the midthirties airports were favorite stops for motorists, who gathered around fences to see such dramatic scenes as this and to watch the planes take off and land. (United Airlines)

DC-3 airborne. (American Airlines)

Donald Douglas, Sr., whose concept of an airliner revolutionized commercial aviation. (Douglas Aircraft)

Lockheed Electra under construction, 1934. (Lockheed Aircraft)

An Eastern Airlines Electra in flight on one of its feeder lines, which joined the smaller cities with the large air terminals. (Lockheed Aircraft)

Bellanca Aircruiser on the feeder line between Salt Lake City, Utah, and Cheyenne, Wyoming. (U. S. Air Force)

An interesting line of development in commercial aviation was that of the giant flying boat, stimulated by Pan American Airways in its pioneering of air routes to the Caribbean and South America and later to the Orient. Pan American's predecessor on the South American run was the New York, Rio, and Buenos Aires Air Line (NYRBA), which began its operations in 1929 with a fleet of Consolidated Commodores, a civil version of the U. S. Navy's XPY-1 patrol boat, forerunner of the later famous PBY Catalina of the Second World War. The Commodore had a hundred-foot wingspan and could carry up to twenty passengers. Large flying boats were the solution to the lack of airport facilities in underdeveloped countries and to the necessity to fly across water a great deal. The Commodores had beautifully appointed cabins, roomy and colorfully decorated. NYRBA began

operations luxuriously but, unable to obtain large government mail contracts, was forced to sell out and was merged with Juan Trippe's Pan American Airways in 1930.

Pan American continued with the Commodore but hoped to improve its service by ordering larger, faster aircraft with greater range. The result was Sikorsky's S-40, the largest plane constructed in the United States at the time (1931). Its wingspread was 114 feet (still considerably short of the DO-X's 157 feet). The S-40 was an ungainly-looking aircraft, with its twin booms bearing the tail surfaces (somewhat like the Wright Flyer) and its four Pratt & Whitney Hornet engines hanging below the wing. Even so, it could carry twenty-four passengers at a speed of 115 miles per hour over a distance of 950 miles nonstop. With forty passengers, the range narrowed to five hundred miles. Like the

Pan American pioneers the Latin American mail and passenger market using the Sikorsky S-38 amphibian. Pilot Charles Lindbergh is at left and Pan American Vice President John Hambleton oversees the loading of the mail. (U. S. Information Agency/National Archives)

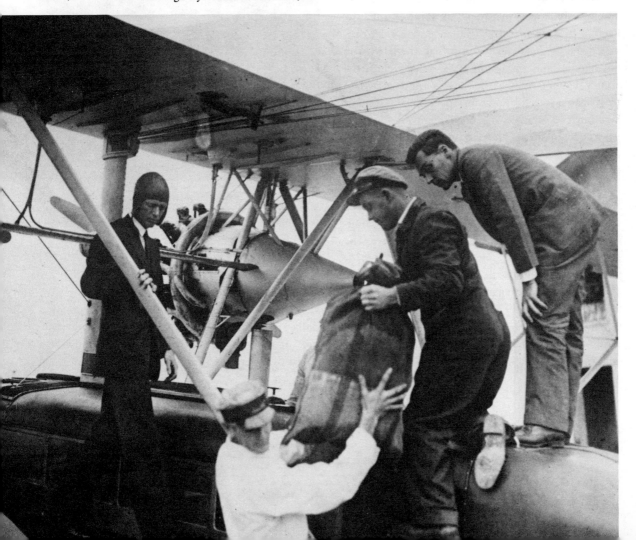

Consolidated Commodore used by the early NYRBA airline and Pan American in the New York-to-Buenos Aires run. (Pan American World Airways)

A further evolution of the Consolidated flying boat, the Navy's P2Y-3, 1933. The engines have been installed in the wing, instead of between, as in the Commodore. (Navy Department/National Archives)

Commodore, the Sikorsky S-40 was a comfortable plane; its reliability and favorable operating costs contributed to the growth of Pan American. The Sikorskys were the first of Pan American's flying Clipper ships.

Having conquered the Caribbean, Pan American ambitiously hoped to extend its services into the Pacific. In answer to this challenge, Sikorsky produced the S-42. A cleaner ship than the S-40—no tail booms, and the engines were faired into the wing's leading edge—the new design met Pan American's specifications for speed and passenger load but at a sacrifice of range. It proved a worthy passenger plane in the Caribbean and, without passengers, surveyed both Pacific and Atlantic routes for the airline.

The Glenn L. Martin Company responded to Pan American's specifications for a large clipper with the M-130, which coincidentally had a wing-spread of 130 feet. The first of the series was the famous *China Clipper*, which made its first scheduled mail flight across the Pacific on November 22, 1935. Passenger service was inaugurated the following year, with scheduled flights to Hawaii and Guam, and Manila in the Philippine Islands. Flights to China began in 1937 and to New Zealand in 1940. The flight to Manila took nearly sixty

Sikorsky S-40, Pan American's replacement for the slower and smaller Commodore, ca. 1931. Three S-40s were built and named *American Clipper*, *Southern Clipper*, and *Caribbean Clipper*. (Pan American World Airways)

hours of flying time (actual time, six days with stopovers) at a cost of $799 (these were Depression dollars). The *China Clipper* was the largest air transport of its time, and although it could cruise at a speed of 130 miles an hour for a distance of 3,200 miles nonstop, it was limited to a dozen passengers (thirty-two if other payload was sacrificed). Even so, also for its time, it was a progressive aircraft because of its all-metal construction, size, speed, payload, and range.

Regular transatlantic passenger service until the middle thirties was dominated by the German Zeppelins and Lufthansa's seaplanes; then both Pan American and Britain's Imperial Airways (later British Overseas Airways Corporation—BOAC) began experimenting with the establishment of such flights. Imperial Airways pioneered the Atlantic crossings with its Short Empire flying boats in the summer of 1937, following that with several scheduled transatlantic flights. Although

handicapped by range limitation—the choice was between carrying sufficient fuel or a paying cargo—the Empire flying boats proved sturdy and long-lived and served over various and far-flung overwater routes throughout the British Empire for more than a decade.

Pan American's great transatlantic plane proved to be the Boeing 314, the largest of the Pan American Clippers. With a wingspan of 152 feet (only five less than that of the DO-X), it was a huge craft of some forty tons. The four Wright engines delivered fifteen hundred horsepower each (and any two could keep the Boeing Clipper airborne); all four of them were accessible to the flight engineer even while the plane was airborne. The 314 was built

Sikorsky S-42, the plane with which Pan American hoped to span the Pacific; though it did not see active service there, the S-42 was used to survey future routes for Pan American. (Pan American World Airways)

Martin's M-130, the classic *China Clipper* of the mid-1930s; with this flying boat Pan American began its scheduled flights to the Pacific in 1935. (Pan American World Airways)

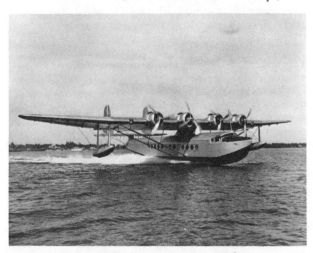

The *China Clipper* leaving San Francisco, flying over the construction of the famous Golden Gate bridge.

Short S-23 Empire Boat after completing a London-to-New York run, July 1937. Powered by four Bristol Pegasus engines, the S-23 was capable of a top speed of two hundred miles per hour. (British Airways)

Experiment in fast airmail delivery: The heavily laden (with fuel, mail, cargo) aircraft is given an assist in takeoff. Once airborne, the seaplane was released to complete the flight from Britain to the United States. This was called the Short-Mayo Composite (because it was the idea of Imperial Airways' R. H. Mayo). The smaller Short seaplane was even faster than the S-32 (which was fast for a flying boat) and assured quick delivery between London and New York. (British Airways)

Boeing's contribution to Pan American's array of clippers, the B-314, which made its first Atlantic crossing in March 1939. (Boeing)

The *California* crossing the shoreline in a test flight. (Navy Department/National Archives)

The Boeing Clippers were used by the U. S. Navy during the war, one of which, the *Yankee Clipper*, was destroyed in a crash. The *Honolulu Clipper*, which was the first of the line, survived, but on a flight from Honolulu to San Francisco it was forced down in the Pacific with engine trouble. While being towed by the seaplane tender *San Pablo*, the *Honolulu Clipper* collided with the ship, smashing bow and wingtip. The Navy sank the *Honolulu Clipper* as a hazard to navigation. (Navy Department/National Archives)

like a luxury oceanliner (including a bridal suite) and could accommodate seventy-four passengers and a crew of from six to 10, depending on the length of the flight. The top speed was close to two hundred miles per hour, cruising speed was 184 miles per hour, and the range was 5,200 miles nonstop. The 314's massive hull was divided into two decks, connected by a spiral staircase: The upper deck housed the flight deck, crew, and cargo; the lower deck, divided into compartments, was for passengers. The Boeing Clipper was an outstanding plane, and only the engineering advances brought about by war made it obsolete before its time. The first Boeing Clipper went into transatlantic service for Pan American in 1939; others were used on the transpacific route. BOAC purchased three of them for its transatlantic service early in the Second World War. When the United States entered the war, the Boeing Clippers were converted into warplanes and used as long-range transports throughout the war. When the war ended, the era of the flying Clippers had also ended.

The late thirties ushered in the age of the four-engined airliner. One of the first was Germany's Focke-Wulf 200, the Condor. It was an excellent plane and carried twenty-six passengers at a cruising speed of two hundred miles per hour. Placed in service by Lufthansa late in 1938, the FW-200 was the first landplane capable of crossing the Atlantic. In August of that year a Condor made a historic flight from Berlin to New York in just under twenty-five hours, and the return flight, three days later, in less than twenty hours.

This was followed in November by a demonstration flight from Berlin to Tokyo which, despite one mishap (which forced a ditching in the water near Manila), the Condor made in forty-six hours, fifteen minutes. Such flights demonstrated that German aircraft design had advanced tremendously since the whalish failure of the DO-X. It was suggested, what with Germany's warlike posturings at the time, that the FW-200 had actually been designed as a bomber and was momentarily disguised as a transport. This was not true. However, after Germany went to war, the Condors were converted into patrol boats and bombers; they proved excellent as long-range reconnaissance planes, but the modifications that made them bombers interfered with performance. About the same time, on the other hand, Germany did have a

Germany's outstanding airliner, the Focke-Wulf 200, the Condor, which made trail-blazing flights to New York and Tokyo in 1938. (Lufthansa Archive)

bomber rather ineffectually serving as an airliner, the Heinkel 111.

French aviation, too, developed during the thirties as new aircraft names began supplanting the wartime Breguets and Farmans. Late in 1933 Air France introduced the fast (170 miles per hour) twin-engined Potez 62 into the Paris-to-London route, popularly called the "Golden Airway" because of its heavy traffic. Although perhaps not as comfortable as the Handley-Page Hannibal, it was a good deal faster. The wing measured seventy-four feet and the fuselage fifty-seven feet in length; the plane held fourteen passengers. The retractable landing gear and streamlining contributed to the speed of the plane.

Air France by 1938 had all but taken the Golden Airway away from the British. This was because the new Bloch 220 could span the distance from Croydon (London's major airport) to Le Bourget (Paris) in seventy-five minutes at a speed of more than two hundred miles an hour. The design of the plane, undoubtedly influenced by the Douglas DC-3, featured all-metal construction, and it could transport sixteen passengers. Air France employed the plane also on flights to Switzerland and Germany.

The symbol of the expansion of Air France up to the outbreak of the Second World War was the

The Paris-to-London liner of 1933–34, the Potez 62. It could carry fourteen passengers at a speed of 174 miles per hour. (Air France)

One of France's great air pioneers, Jean Mermoz. A fine pilot as well, Mermoz made trail-blazing flights across the South Atlantic before joining Air France as an executive. In 1936 he was lost while testing a flying boat on a flight across the South Atlantic. (Musée de l'Air, Paris)

The Bloch 220, used by Air France on its European network: Britain, Germany, and Switzerland. (Air France)

Dewoitine 338, the airliner that connected France with its colonies in the Far East and with South America in the late thirties. (Air France)

The offbeat KLM airliner designed by Frederick Koolhaven, ca. 1931. A trimotor, two engines pulled and one pushed. (KLM Photo)

KLM workhorse, the Fokker Trimotor, Model F-18. This plane, *Pelikaan*, made the flight from Amsterdam to Batavia with the Christmas mail in a hundred hours' flying time. Captain Ivan Smirnoff and crew spent Christmas in Java and were back home in time for the New Year, January 1, 1933. (KLM Photo)

Dewoitine 338, which was used in the Far East (linking Baghdad with Hong Kong) and in South America, to compete with American and German airlines there. The trimotor could carry twenty-four passengers at a speed in excess of 170 miles an hour in great luxury. Its wingspan was ninety-six feet, and its fuselage length was seventy-three feet. On certain routes the passenger load was cut in half to make room for baggage, cargo, and additional fuel. The Dewoitine 338 represented the peak of French commercial aviation on the eve of war.

The Dutch competed with the airlines of France, Britain and Germany—and succeeded in expanding their services into various European cities, including London, Hamburg, Copenhagen, and Paris. By 1930 KLM inaugurated regular weekly flights by Fokker trimotors to the Dutch East Indies. The management of KLM was one of the first in Europe to recognize the advantages of the new Douglas airliners, and with unchauvinistic acumen they abandoned the obsolescent Fokkers. By 1936 the Douglas DC-3, with KLM markings, was flying the airlines European and Far East routes regularly.

The thirties was the time of the rise of the giant airliner and the fall of the dirigible. A succession of tragedies closed the romantic airship era with a loss in lives and in public faith. The first to go during this period was the *Akron*, which was the second American-built rigid airship (the first, of course, was the *Shenandoah*, which had already been lost). Commissioned in 1931, the *Akron* was called "the safest airship every built" by Rear Admiral William A. Moffett, chief of the Navy's Bureau of Aeronautics and popularly known as the "Father of Naval Aviation." Moffett and seven-five other men were aboard the *Akron* when, on April 3, 1933, the ship was caught in a thunderstorm off a fog-enshrouded New Jersey coast. The *Akron* lost altitude rapidly and plunged into the Atlantic; of the seventy-six men aboard only three survived. Among the dead were Admiral Moffett and four men who had survived the *Shenandoah* crash. The loss of the *Akron* was the worst airship disaster in history. Naval and congressional inquiries, how-

U.S.S. *Akron* near Tacoma, Washington, May 1932. (U. S. Air Force)

The *Akron* in the clouds, 1932. Commissioned in 1931, the airship was destroyed in a storm off the coast of New Jersey in 1933. (U. S. Air Force)

ever, could find no structural or technical reason for the crash, and the Navy's airship program continued as planned.

The executive officer of the *Akron*, and one of the three survivors of the ship's fall, was Lieutenant Commander Herbert V. Wiley, who was placed in command of the next Navy dirigible, the *Macon*. Reputed to be the fastest airship ever built (its speed approached ninety miles per hour), the

Macon was commissioned not long after the loss of the *Akron*. Like its sister ship, it cost $6 million, a tremendous outlay in 1933 at the low point of the Depression. Both the *Akron* and the *Macon* were flying aircraft carriers. Little Curtiss Sparrow Hawks (F9C-2), five in all, nestled inside the capacious airship. A special hooking device was built into the upper wing of the airship-based Curtisses. The fighters served as scouts and as protection for

Curtiss F9C-2 Sparrow Hawk about to hook onto the *Macon*. Yoke, upper left, was lowered to steady the plane for lifting inside the airship. (Navy Department/National Archives)

The Navy's *Macon*, commissioned the year the *Akron*
was lost. "T"-shaped opening in underside is the opening
in the hull for the lowering and raising of fighter aircraft.
(Navy Department/National Archives)

their aerial roosts. In February 1935, the *Macon*, on
fleet maneuvers off the coast of California, ran into
a rainstorm. A structural failure occurred at a point
where the fin was attached to the hull. This ruptured gas cells, causing the *Macon* to fall into the
Pacific. And as it fell, further ruptures occurred.
Commander Wiley radioed an SOS, which quickly
brought several ships of the Pacific Fleet to the point
where the *Macon* had fallen. Wiley maneuvered the
airship as long as possible so that it sank into the
water tail first. There was a total of eighty-three
men aboard, and of these, miraculously—and
thanks to Wiley's cool command—only two were
lost. These two men apparently lost their heads as
the ship sank, and jumped while the nose was still
125 feet above the waves. They were killed by the
fall. All the rest of the men were saved, including
one that Commander Wiley had to pull from the
entangled wreckage. But the *Macon* was absolutely
lost; it sank, along with the Navy's airship program.
All three of the homebuilt airships had been lost;
only the German-built *Los Angeles* remained intact.
In 1939 it was dismantled.

Only Germany remained as the one nation with
any kind of faith in the airship. With the *Graf
Zeppelin* in satisfactory operation, the decision was
made (as much a propaganda gesture as it was to
further the cause of the dirigible) to produce the
ultimate airship. The new Zeppelin would be even
larger than the trusty *Graf* and would, it was
hoped, make Germany the leader in commercial
airship travel. There was one other hope: that to
lift this giant dream the United States would re-
consider and rescind the ban on selling helium
abroad. (The fear was that it would be used militarily.) This did not come about, and hydrogen was
used. On March 4, 1936, the *LZ-129* was
launched. Its bulk was awesome: 804 feet long—
the largest aircraft ever built. At first unnamed, the
LZ-129 was eventually and appropriately, in a
Germany turned to militarism again, called the
Hindenburg in honor of a military hero. Soon the
great ship went into operations and proved itself by
making several trips to the United States and South
America during 1936. Its success was so marked
that plans went into motion to form an American

LZ-129, the *Hindenburg*, designed specifically for the North Atlantic crossing, could carry seventy passengers. Built in 1936, it was the largest Zeppelin ever flown. (Smithsonian Institution)

The *Hindenburg* photographed off the shore of New Jersey, May 6, 1937, about an hour before it was to land at Lakehurst. (U. S. Air Force)

Zeppelin Transport Corporation to establish a regular joint German-American airship service across the Atlantic. It appeared that a new airship age had dawned. Another giant, *Graf Zeppelin II*, was built and would be ready for flight in September 1938.

It was on its first of eighteen scheduled flights to the United States on May 6, 1937, that the *Hindenburg*, following a successful transatlantic crossing, passed over New York, heading for its berth at Lakehurst, New Jersey, and came to a fiery end. Aboard were only thirty-six passengers (it could carry seventy) and sixty-one crew members (many of them in training for duty on the *Graf Zeppelin II*). Delayed somewhat by thunderstorms, the *Hindenburg* floated gracefully over New Jersey for some time and then, about seven-twenty in the evening, began its docking descent. All seemed normal until ground crewmen noticed what appeared to be fabric

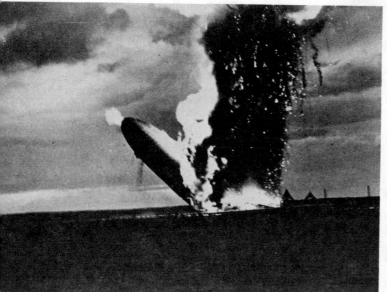

The *Hindenburg* explodes at Lakehurst. These photographs were taken by an amateur photographer. The first photo caught him off guard and appears to have been taken at the moment of explosion. In moments the *Hindenburg* was a flaming wreckage on the ground. Although sabotage was suggested as the cause of the disaster, it is highly unlikely. (U. S. Air Force)

flapping near the tail; then, inside, crewmen noticed a sudden brightness and heard muffled explosions. Spectators, who had come to see the famous airship land, or to meet friends and relatives arriving, were horrified to see a bright glow licking out of the after section of the *Hindenburg*. The hydrogen burst into roaring flame, and the pride of Germany's growing airship fleet, shriveled, bent, and torn, fell burning to the ground.

One of the flaming figures who staggered out of the fire was the *Hindenburg's* captain, Ernst Lehmann, who later died of his burns.

A total of thirty-six (of the ninety-seven aboard) died in the disaster; considering the totality of the holocaust, the number was remarkably small. Most of the casualties were crewmen, caught inside the flaming hull. Several causes of the disaster were suggested, ranging from sabotage to the fact that the *Hindenburg* had made a tight turn on its landing approach, which may have broken a bracing wire, which in turn may have slashed open a gas cell. This would have released the hydrogen. Lightning and static electicity were other possible factors. Captain Lehmann, before he died, said, "It must have been an infernal machine." One theory suggests that a member of the crew deliberately destroyed the airship, and himself along with it. It is unlikely that the true cause will ever be discovered. Airship scholar Dr. Douglas Robinson rightly discounts the sabotage and plot aspect of the disaster. "The one indisputable fact," he has written, " . . . is that the *Hindenburg* burned because she was inflated with hydrogen." Any one of a hundred reasons, accidental or deliberate, would have to be traced back to that one fact.

The destruction of the *Hindenburg* wrote the finish to the passenger airship; it had, in fact, been the last to carry passengers. When the *Graf Zeppelin II* was completed in 1938, it was never put into passenger service, although the Germans did use it once to explore the defenses of Britain before the war began. British fighters encouraged it to leave, and finally Hermann Göring, who detested "those gas bags," had the two remaining airships dismantled for scrap metal and their capacious hangar destroyed. He regarded the hangar as a threat to his fighters. Even in Germany, birthplace of the Zeppelin, the age of the airship was over.

The most colorful pilots and the most beautiful aircraft of the thirties were associated with the annual air competitions that took place in the United States. Britain had its King's Cup races in the thirties also, which like their American counterparts attracted not only airmen but also spectators. France reactivated its Deutsch de la Meurthe Cup. The Schneider Trophy, having contributed to the design of fast seaplanes, was out of circulation because it had gone into permanent British possession. It was replaced by the Thompson Trophy. This prize was established in 1930 by Charles E. Thompson, president of Thompson Products, Inc., of Cleveland. Thompson's hope was to encourage the development of fast landplanes; this was an open free-for-all, which closed the National Air Races at Cleveland. The seed for the annual trophy had been planted in 1929 when the first Thompson Trophy was won by airline pilot Douglas Davis in a Travel Air Model R, also called *Mystery Ship* because it was constantly kept under wraps until the race was run. Then this plane, No. 31 in the race, beat out both the Army and the Navy pursuits by more than fifty miles per hour. From a military point of view this did not look good: a commercial aircraft available to all proving to be superior to aircraft specially designed according to specifications laid down by military "experts."

The National Air Races brought in some of the world's most attractive fliers, even though they competed in segregated events. A special National Women's Air Derby—which to the competitors' disgust was called the Powder-puff Derby in the press—was run for the first time in 1929. This was a cross-country race from California to Cleveland and was open only to women. Winner of the first race was Mrs. Louise McPhetridge Thaden (who, in 1936, was the first woman to win the Bendix Trophy race). In third place was Amelia Earhart, who had made her debut into the history of aviation as a passenger in a plane that crossed the Atlantic in

First-place winner of the first national women's air derby, Louise Thaden in 1929. In 1936 she took first place in the Bendix race. (U. S. Air Force)

Winner of the 1929 Thompson Cup, the Travel Air *Mystery Ship*. Powerful Wright Whirlwind engine, clean design, and streamlining enabled the plane to achieve a speed of more than two hundred miles per hour. (U. S. Air Force)

1928. The fourth-prize winner of the Women's Air Derby was Ruth Elder. The first Women's Air Derby was marred by one fatality: the crash of Marvel Crossen in an Arizona desert. This occurred early in the race and despite public criticism only spurred the other women on to prove they had the courage and stamina to compete in aviation with men. The women later banded together to form the

Ruth Elder, who as early as 1927 attempted to fly the Atlantic (and failed), was fourth-place winner in the 1929 women's air derby. Next to her are national air races organizer Cliff Henderson and official Vic Clark. (U. S. Air Force)

"Ninety-nines," an organization devoted to achieving equality for women in the field of aviation. Ruth Elder, by the way, eventually left flying for a career in Hollywood in the thirties.

Speed was the objective of the National Air Races competitions, which meant the refinement of aircraft design and the perfection of aircraft engines and fuel. An entry into the 1930 Thompson Trophy race was Frank Hawks' Travel Air *Mystery Ship*, with which he had just broken a cross-country record, having flown from Los Angeles to New York in twelve hours, twenty-five minutes. Similar to the 1929 *Mystery Ship*, Hawks' *Texaco No. 13* was forced out of the race with a clogged fuel line. The Thompson Trophy was a closed-course race flown around pylons. The first winner was Charles W. Holman (1930); his official speed was 201.91 miles per hour. For the next decade, until it was interrupted by the war, the Thompson Trophy race was one of the major aviation events of the year. Competition was open to pilots from other countries, but few could manage to make the trip. (In 1936, however, the trophy was won by Frenchman, Michel Detroyat, in a Caudron racer.)

A second major racing event was for the Bendix Trophy. This was a cross-country race open to everyone—men and women—in planes of any size and type of engine. The first race run in 1931 was won by James H. Doolittle, who covered the distance between Los Angeles and Cleveland in nine hours, ten minutes, and then, after refueling, continued on to Newark, New Jersey. The entire trip, coast to coast, had taken eleven hours, sixteen minutes—an hour less than the record held by Frank Hawks. Doolittle then took off again, returning to Cleveland to be awarded the Bendix Trophy and to compete in the Thompson Trophy race. He was forced out of the Thompson when his Laird biplane developed engine trouble.

The winner of the 1932 Bendix race was a fine pilot, Jimmy Haizlip. In a specially designed Wedell-Williams monoplane, Haizlip chopped nearly an hour off Doolittle's record of the previous year, both to Cleveland for the Bendix and to Newark

Frank Hawks' Travel Air, flown under the sponsorship of a fuel company. Hawks made a record cross-country flight in this plane, but was forced out of the 1930 Thompson Trophy race by mechanical problems. (U. S. Air Force)

Jimmy Doolittle lends a hand during the refueling of his Laird Super Solution, in which he became a double record-breaker in 1931: the Bendix and Thompson races. (U. S. Air Force)

for the coast-to-coast flight. The average speed of the Wedell-Williams had been 245 miles per hour; Doolittle's had been 223. In just a short time powerful engines had emerged, and more speed—the aim of the Bendix race—was commonplace. By 1932, in order to qualify for entry into the race, the plane had to go at least two hundred miles per hour. Interestingly, Haizlip's wife, Mae, was also a pilot; using the Wedell-Williams, she placed second in the 1932 Aerol Trophy (open only to women), which was eventually stopped because of a rainstorm that made it impossible to see the pylons. Mae Haizlip, however, became first-prize winner in the Aerol Trophy race the next year.

Doolittle's arrival in Cleveland after his record-breaking Bendix flight from Los Angeles to Cleveland to Newark, and back to Cleveland. (U. S. Air Force)

Haizlip's 1932 racer designed by James Wedell and Errett Williams, both of whom were racing pilots. By this time racing designs generally favored the low-wing monoplane configuration. (U. S. Air Force)

Bendix Trophy winner in the 1932 race, Jimmy Haizlip being congratulated by Amelia Earhart and aviation enthusiast Senator Hiram Bingham. (U. S. Air Force)

A series of wonderful little racers began appearing at the 1930 National Air Races when Ben Odell Howard introduced his *Pete*, a tiny plane he had built himself in his spare time. Powered by only a ninety-horsepower engine, the plane achieved a speed of more than two hundred miles per hour. It won several of the minor closed-course races and close to four thousand dollars for Ben Howard, and in competing against more powerful aircraft, it came in third in the Thompson Trophy race. With

this success behind him, Howard, who worked as a pilot for United Air Lines, designed subsequent little racers, such as the *Ike*, which was flown by William Ong in the 1932 Thompson race. The *Pete* and the *Ike* had a wingspan of only twenty feet; they were seventeen feet in length. *Pete* was powered by a Wright Gypsy in-line engine, and *Ike* by a Menasco. *Ike* was notable for its curious double set of wheels. Streamlining of these was accomplished by pants over the wheels—retractable landing gears were not generally in use in 1932. To the air-minded boy of the thirties, Ben Howard's little racers represented the zenith in speed design.

One of the most spectacular series of racers were the Gee Bees (for Granville Brothers, the manufacturers), designed by Robert "Bob" Hall. With their short, thick bodies, the Gee Bees resembled flying barrels. The *City of Springfield* was completed only a week before the opening of the 1931 National Air Races; consequently it was not thoroughly tested before it flew in the competitions. Hall himself flew, winning the General Tire and Rubber Company Trophy. Lowell Bayles, a stockholder in the Granville Brothers company—and a pilot—won several prizes, the most important being the Thompson

Ben Howard's little *Pete*, which he built around a Wright Gypsy engine borrowed from a friend. (U. S. Air Force)

Ben Odell Howard in the cockpit of *Pete*, 1930. (U. S. Air Force)

Howard's 1932 contender *Ike* (*Mike* was a similar design, but with a standard set of wheels); *Ike* was flown that year by William Ong. *Ike* came in seventh in the Thompson race. Howard admitted that the extra wheels served no real purpose except to attract attention. (U. S. Air Force)

Trophy for 1931. Encouraged by this success, Bayles aimed at breaking other speed records in the *City of Springfield*. In attempting to make a new landplane record, Bayles suffered an accident. (It is believed that the fuel cap on the upper fuselage blew off while the Gee Bee was flying at high speed, and smashed into the cockpit.) The gyrating plane snapped a wing and smashed into the ground, killing the thirty-one-year-old pilot.

The classic Gee Bee was the Model R, which though based on the Z, was not designed by Bob Hall (who had joined another racing group to produce his *Bulldog*). The wingspan of the newer model was increased slightly, from twenty-three feet, six inches to twenty-five feet; so was the length, from fifteen feet, one inch to seventeen feet, nine inches. Even so, the fat, round fuselage made the planes (actually two were built) appear more squat than ever. A much more powerful engine, a Pratt & Whitney Wasp, Senior of eight hundred horsepower, was fitted into the nose of the *R-1*, and the Wasp, Junior, of 550 horsepower, was installed into the *R-2*. It was hoped that the planes would fly at the Nationals, one by Russell Boardman (who owned both planes) and the other by Lee Gelbach. However, Boardman was injured slightly

Robert Hall in the cockpit of the Model Z designed for the Granville brothers. Flown by Lowell Bayles, this Gee Bee won the Thompson Trophy in 1931 at the Cleveland air races. (U. S. Air Force)

James H. Doolittle, Cleveland national air races, September 5, 1932. (U. S. Air Force)

Doolittle's aircraft in the Thompson Trophy competition, the Gee Bee R-1. The big Wasp engine is warming up in the photo. (U. S. Air Force)

in a crackup of another Gee Bee, a Sportster, and the *R-1* was left without a pilot. Meanwhile, James Doolittle was testing his Laird biplane, newly fitted with a retractable landing gear, which he learned, upon being airborne, didn't work. Bringing in the plane with half a landing gear wiped it out of the Nationals for the year. Doolittle was then approached by Boardman to fly the *R-1* in the Thompson Trophy race. He accepted the offer.

Although he had very little time to familiarize himself with the tricky little craft, Jimmy Doolittle quickly revealed himself as one of the great aviators. He flew the Gee Bee to a new landplane speed record (296.287 miles per hour), and then proceeded

to place first in the Thompson Trophy race. Gelbach in the *R-2* finished in fourth place. The two Gee Bees were so similar that about the only way they could be differentiated was by the large number on the side of the fuselage. Gelbach's was No. 7, and Doolittle's, No. 11. The Thompson Trophy race consisted in making ten laps over a total distance of a hundred miles. Doolittle's average speed was 252.686 miles per hour. His prize money for that year's Nationals came to $4,500. Having won so spectacularly, Doolittle announced his retirement from air racing that year. The plane in which he won, later slightly modified with a more powerful engine, was flown in the 1933 Bendix race by Russell Boardman. During a takeoff, the Gee Bee went out of control close to the ground and crashed, killing Boardman. The *R-2* later also went out of control while being flown by James Haizlip (although he managed to survive). Parts of the two wrecks were put together as the *R-1/R-2*, and this plane killed pilot Cecil Allen during a takeoff for the 1935 Bendix Trophy race. The Gee Bees had ac-

Doolittle takeoff in the Thompson race; the Gee Bee's wingspan measured twenty-five feet, and the fuselage was seventeen feet, nine inches long. It was a tough plane to fly. (U. S. Air Force)

Doolittle rounding a pylon in the Thompson race, which he won in 1932 with a record-breaking speed of 252.7 miles per hour, a record that held for four years. (Doolittle Collection)

quired a reputation as killers: Even Zantford D. Granville, founder of the company, died in one. His death in 1934 brought an end to the Granville Brothers; the day of the Gee Bee was definitely over.

Although the stubby Gee Bee attracted a good deal of attention at the 1932 National Air Races, the real stars of the show may very well have been the several Wedell-Williams racers that took first, second, and third places in the Bendix and second, third, and fourth places in the Thompson. The plane was designed by James Wedell, a youthful Texan who never finished high school and was rejected for flying training by both the Army and the Navy. Legend was that Wedell, self-taught, designed his racers by pure intuition. He is supposed merely to have chalked a rough full-sized outline on the floor of his factory, and the aircraft took shape. After the plane was finished according to Wedell's instincts, its dimensions were measured. Wedell flew one of his own designs in several races and won the Thompson Trophy in 1933. He placed second in the Bendix, which was won by Roscoe Turner in his Wedell-Williams. The second name was contributed by Harry Palmerson

Roscoe Turner and the Jimmy Wedell-designed racer in which he came in third in the Bendix Trophy race (Burbank to Cleveland); first place was taken by James Haizlip, also flying a Wedell design. (U. S. Air Force)

Robert Hall in the cockpit of his Bulldog; engine trouble slowed him down—he came in sixth in the Thompson race. (U. S. Air Force)

French pilot Michel Detroyat's Caudron C-460, in which he won 1936 Greve and Thompson races and more than $14,000. The plane's performance was a surprise to the American contestants, who did not expect the French capable of producing such an aircraft. (National Air and Space Museum, Smithsonian Institution)

Williams, a wealthy planter-lumberman, who also contributed the financial backing to the Wedell-Williams Air Service Corporation. Jimmy Wedell died in a plane crash while on a training flight with a student flier in 1934.

Gee Bee designer Bob Hall left the Granville Brothers to design a racer for Russell Thaw. The result was the *Bulldog*, a gull-winged monoplane. Unhappy with the flight characteristics of the plane, Thaw rejected it. Hall then decided to enter the Thompson race (1932) and came in sixth, behind Doolittle's Gee Bee, Wedell's, Turner's, and Haizlip's Wedell-Williamses, and Lee Gelbach's Gee Bee. Hall apparently abandoned the design, for the *Bulldog* was never heard of again.

One of air racing's most dashing figures was Roscoe Turner, who began his flying career during the First World War and later continued as a barnstorming Jenny pilot. As astute a showman as he was a superb pilot, Turner affected a swashbuckling, self-designed uniform: powder-blue riding breeches, Sam Browne belt, and gleaming black boots. He added to the effect with a neat, waxed, and "spiked" (twirled at the ends) mustache, and (at least while Gilmore Oil sponsored him) a lion cub mascot named Gilmore. The aura of the picturesque never obscured the fact of Turner's businesslike airmanship. Beginning in 1929, Turner entered various air races and won several "firsts" as well as top-place prizes. He took first in the 1933 Bendix and was the only pilot to win the Thompson Trophy three times (1934, 1938, and 1939). After his final win, Turner announced his retirement from air racing. "I'm getting old," he said, "and this is definitely a young man's game." He was then forty-three. Turner founded the Turner Aeronautical Corporation; during the Second World War he taught many young men how to fly.

Turner's consecutive Thompson Trophy wins were made in the very handsome *Meteor*, designed by Lawrence Brown with modifications by E. M. "Matty" Laird. With its powerful Twin Wasp, Senior (a Pratt & Whitney engine with two banks of cylinders, seven in each, making it a fourteen-cylinder power plant), the *Meteor* won the 1938 Thompson Trophy with an average speed of a little more than 283 miles per hour. (In one lap, it reached 293 miles per hour.) In 1939, his final race, Turner's average speed was ten miles ahead of the second-place winner's. That year's was the last National Air Races until 1946, the event being interrupted by the Second World War.

Roscoe Turner and mascot Gilmore, named in honor of his sponsor, Gilmore Oil Company. (U. S. Air Force)

One of the greatest pilots of the racing thirties and after was a poor southern girl who loved to fly—and did. She was Jacqueline Cochran, whose specialty was speed. She won the 1938 Bendix Trophy, at the same time setting a new transcontinental record. During the Second World War she helped ferry warplanes to the British; later she led the U. S. Women's Air Force Service Pilots (WASP), which served in several ways, from ferrying aircraft across the Atlantic to flying target-towing planes. Years later she would be the first woman to fly a jet plane.

Another special speed event was for the Louis W. Greve Trophy for aircraft powered by engines of 550 cubic engine displacement or under—that is, for planes with comparatively small engines (displacement of Turner's *Meteor* was 1,830 cubic inches). The Greve Trophy races began in 1934 and ran until the war ended air racing for the duration. The winner of the final Greve Trophy race was the *Goon*, named for a comic strip character in the "Popeye" series. Designed by Art Chester, who also flew it, the *Goon* was powered by a Menasco engine. Its winning speed was 263 miles

Turner's Laird-Turner L-RT *Meteor*, in which he won the Thompson Trophy in 1938 and 1939; after that race he retired from air racing. (U. S. Air Force)

Important women fliers of the late twenties and early thirties: Ruth Nichols and Jacqueline Cochran. Nichols took a year out of college to learn to fly and worked in a bank to finance her flying. In the thirties she made many record-breaking flights for speed and altitude; she failed in an Atlantic solo attempt in 1931. Cochran made many record-breaking flights, not the least of which was winning the Bendix Trophy in 1938 (Burbank to Cleveland). (Smithsonian Institution National Archives)

Art Chester's *Goon*, in which he took first place in the 1939 Greve Trophy race (he came in second the previous year because of an oil leak). These tiny craft appeared to be designed arond the engine and the pilot. The *Goon* was powered by a Menasco C-6S4 engine. Winning speed was 263.39 miles per hour. (U. S. Air Force)

One of the great racing pilots of the twenties and thirties: Alford "Al" Williams. As a Navy flier Williams won the 1923 Pulitzer Trophy. For a time after graduating from Fordham University, Williams considered a career in baseball (he was a fine pitcher); the coming of the First World War led to an enlistment in the U. S. Navy. Williams served for more than a decade, contributing a great deal to the evolution of naval flying (he received the Distinguished Flying Cross in 1929). In 1930 he left the Navy to join Gulf as a flying good-will ambassador. During the Second World War Williams served as a volunteer technical consultant to the U. S. Army Air Force. (U. S. Army)

per hour. In the race one pilot, Leland Williams, was killed when his plane stalled into the ground; the other two contestants fell out because of engine trouble and mechanical problems with a retractable landing gear. Chester continued with the *Goon* to finish and win the Trophy. The mood of the 1939 Air Races was subdued when on September 1, Germany invaded Poland to begin the Second World War.

Although part of the large crowds the great air races attracted undoubtedly consisted of people genuinely interested in aviation, some of the spectators were thrill-seekers. Competing pilots resented this portion of the crowd, and rightly. The death of his friend Douglas Davis (who had won the original Thompson Cup in 1929) in the 1934 Thompson race prompted James Doolittle to comment on the value of the races. "Among people closely associated with aviation in this country," he told the National Safety Council, "there is beginning to develop a feeling that air racing, especially closed-course events, has outlived its usefulness. Air racing originally did promote safety in aviation through testing of materials used in construction of planes and engines, and probably still does. But lately it appears that the value received is not commensurate with the personal risk involved." Once certain developments had arrived, why not stop? Air racing of the thirties had certainly brought about or greatly encouraged the progress of the cantilever monoplane, engine improvements, retractable landing gears, and better fuels and lubricants. But to continue risking one's life merely for money and for the entertainment of the crowd seemed fruitless. Of course, some pilots flew in the races for the simple love of flying and speed. They were aware of the risks they took, but when time ran out, the moment was spectacular and a deep personal tragedy. No mere ticket purchaser was ever worth that.

Vertical flight had concerned the pioneers of aviation from its earliest days and was not overlooked in the thirties. Sikorsky had begun experimenting with helicopters as early as 1909, although these attempts were not initially successful. (He did succeed, however, in 1940.) Among the early successes were those of Spaniard Juan de la Cierva, who began making his "windmill planes" in the early twenties. In 1923 Cierva demonstrated his Autogiro (as he preferred to call his aircraft) near Madrid. Later,

"Is this what you came to see?" Pilots suspected that too many in the grandstands at air shows and races came in anticipation of a spectacular crackup. This one occurred during the Pacific international air races in May 1938. Pilot Ralph Johnson died in the crash of his Waco. Photo by Bolducci Cooley. (Courtesy Robert Dittmar and Harry S. Gans)

about the midtwenties, Cierva established a factory in England in co-operation with A. V. Roe. Cierva's Autogiros were regarded as wonderful craft with a great future, capable of taking off and landing in small fields, simple to control, and safer than conventional planes. Cierva himself came to the United States in 1929 to demonstrate his Autogiro and was a sensation at the National Air Races. The hope was that the Autogiro would become the common man's and woman's vehicle of the air.

An American branch of Cierva's Autogiro venture was begun when a Philadelphia financier became interested in the plane's possibilities. This was the Pitcairn-Cierva Autogiro Company, formed with the backing of Harold F. Pitcairn. The product of the company began appearing in

1931, with some modifications and improvements on the original. The design won the coveted Collier Trophy in 1930, and for the presentation a Pitcairn-Cierva Autogiro landed on the White House lawn. The plane was bought by the Detroit *News* and the U. S. Navy. One was used by Amelia Earhart to set an altitude record. But few others, and certainly not the average man, bought the expensive craft. The Autogiro was the predecessor of the more practical helicopter. Other men, notably Sikorsky, perfected the design of vertical-flight aircraft. Cierva, however, was one of the inspired pathfinders. He died in 1936 when an airliner in which he was traveling crashed while taking off in a fog near London.

One of the classic American planes of the thirties was the Ryan S-T (for Sport Trainer), a product of the same company that had made Lindbergh's *Spirit of St. Louis*. Clean-lined and modern in both appearance and construction, the Ryan S-T was a popular plane with private pilots and student pilots. With its dual seats, it was a fine plane in which to learn to fly. Its cruising speed was 125 miles per

Juan de la Cierva demonstrates his Autogiro at the 1929
national air races, Cleveland; the next year Cierva
formed a partnership with Harold Pitcairn to
manufacture the aircraft its designer hoped would
become as common as the automobile. The Depression
canceled out that dream for all. (U. S. Air Force)

Pitcairn-Cierva Autogiro, still with an "X" for experimental license number, ca. 1931. (Smithsonian Institution)

Classic trainer of the thirties, the Ryan S-T; it was also popular with private pilots who could afford a plane in the Depression thirties. (Ryan Aeronautical Library)

hour, and its landing speed, with the aid of wing flaps, forty-two miles per hour. Single-seat modifications were adapted for military use by the Honduran, Mexican, and Guatemalan air forces in the late thirties. During the Second World War the S-Ts were used widely by the U. S. Air Force as primary trainers (PT-16 and PT-20).

Frequently remembered as the "flivver of the air," the Taylor—later Piper—"Cub" was a popular light plane throughout the thirties. Designed specifically to be powered by the Brownbach Tiger Kitten two-cylinder engine—whence the name Cub—the little plane was economical to fly and easy to handle. In 1931 the cost of the thirty-seven-horsepower-engined plane was $1,325. Although the Taylor Brothers Aircraft Corporation went bankrupt in 1931, the firm was reorganized and refinanced with the aid of one of the original investors, William T. Piper, who kept the little company going through the hard days. By the midthirties, the company began to prosper as hundreds of Cubs appeared at airports all over the country. As Piper himself recalled, "Everyone who was still flying was starved into using Cubs." Earlier models did not have an enclosed cabin. During the Second World War the Cub was extensively used as a trainer by the Air Force and as an artillery spotter by the Field Artillery, where they were generally known as Grasshoppers because they operated so close to the ground. Like the DC-3, the Piper Cub was one of the immortals, (if the word can be applied to a machine) of its time.

One of the most interesting little planes of the thirties, one that its designer, Henri Mignet, hoped would find a roosting place in practically every man's garage, was the *Pou-du-Ciel (Flying Flea)*. Mignet did not patent his design, and he encouraged all who would to build their own copy and to enjoy the "Sport of the Air." It was the designer's contention that "If you can nail together a packing case, you can construct an airplane." He even published a book showing how he himself had done it. The *Flying Flea* was easy to build, but alas, not easy to fly. It was not stable, and some of Mignet's followers suffered fatal accidents in it. One of the problems in the design was the proximity of the wings—and the fact that there was no elevator. The *Flea* had a tendency to go into an uncontrollable

dive, which ended when it crashed to earth. Mignet's idea was good, and his enthusiasm was infectious—"Long Live the Sport of the Air!!!" was his motto—but he was no aeronautical engineer.

Few airports in the United States during the mid- and late thirties did not harbor the famous Piper Cub (this one the model J-3 of 1937). (Piper Aircraft Corporation)

Henri Mignet about to demonstrate his diminutive Pou-du-Ciel. Like Cierva, he hoped that he had produced *the* plane for everyone. He did not, for the Flying Flea was a most difficult plane to fly. Its appearance was more charming than its flying characteristics. (Musée de l'Air, Paris)

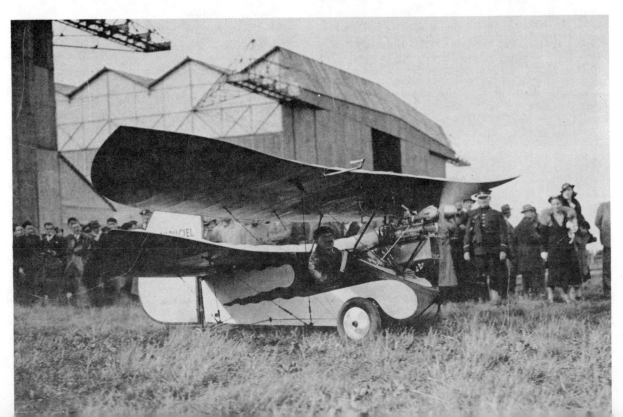

Great flying team: Anne Morrow Lindbergh and husband, Charles, as spectators at the Cleveland air races. Between them: Cliff Henderson and, to Lindbergh's left, Assistant Secretary of Commerce for Aviation Clarence Young. (U. S. Air Force)

Lindbergh survey craft, the specially designed Lockheed Sirius *Tingmissartoq* (Eskimo for "one that flies like a large bird"). In this plane the Lindberghs made survey flights to the Orient in 1931 and across the Atlantic in 1933. Photo shows their arrival in Tokyo Bay on August 26, 1931. (National Air and Space Museum/Smithsonian Institution)

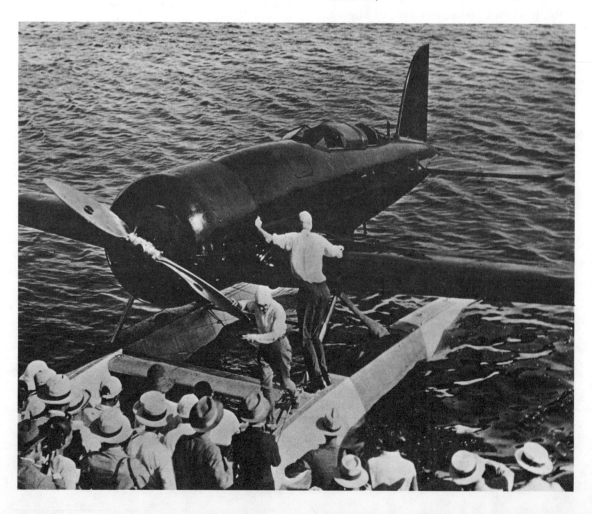

Great flights were made in the thirties, although none were as daring as those of the twenties. The progress in aviation had been so great that the epochal flights of the thirties belonged more to the realm of science than adventure. Transcontinental speed flights were a yearly event, and crossing oceans by air, commonplace; only an air trip around the world held the promise of the old glamor in the post-Lindbergh era. At the vanguard of the scientific approach was Lindbergh himself, who placed his considerable reputation and skills at the service of aviation's commercial advancement. He was joined in his pioneering transoceanic flights by his wife, Anne Morrow Lindbergh, who learned to fly and to operate their radio. In 1931, using their custom-built Lockheed Sirius, the Lindberghs blazed an air trail across the Pacific (crossing the Bering Sea), visiting Japan and China. The Lockheed flipped over in the Yangtze River near Hankow. The plane was returned by ship to the Lockheed plant in California, refurbished, and from July to December 1933, the Lindberghs flew more than thirty thousand miles, surveying possible air routes in the North Atlantic and South Atlantic. Their plane, by then named *Tingmissartoq*, was placed in the Museum of Natural History in New York. The Lindbergh surveys prepared the way for the great airline routes across the Pacific and the Atlantic.

Flying "over the weather" was also pioneered in the early thirties. Storms frequently interfered with the flight of airliners and the mail. Northrop built its beautiful *Gamma* as a high-altitude flying laboratory to explore the possibilities of flying over storms. Speed pilot Frank Hawks flew his *Gamma* on June 2, 1933, from Los Angeles to New York in a record-breaking thirteen hours, twenty-six minutes, fifteen seconds. The record did not stand long in a time when new speed records were made regularly, but the Northrop *Gamma* itself eventually beat its own record (11½ hours) and opened up the stratosphere as a highway in the sky.

Wiley Post, ex-wing-walker and oil-field laborer, did not believe that the answer to air transportation lay in the dirigible. When the *Graf Zeppelin* made

Frank Hawks' Northrop Gamma, in which he made a record-breaking transcontinental flight in June 1933. This plane was proof that it was possible, with proper equipment, to fly over storms—another step forward in the evolution of commercial aviation. (Northrop Corporation)

Wiley Post and his record-breaking Lockheed Vega, *Winnie Mae*, after he had made two round-the-world flights in the plane. (Lockheed Photo)

news with its triumphant round-the-world flight, Post was determined to prove that "a good airplane with average equipment and careful flying could outdo the *Graf Zeppelin*, or any other similar aircraft, at every turn on a flight around the world." Using the compensation money he had received for the loss of his left eye in an oil-field accident, Post bought a plane. Later he received backing from oilman F. C. Hall in acquiring a Lockheed Vega, which was named *The Winnie Mae* after Hall's daughter. Originally *The Winnie Mae* was used by Hall, with Post as pilot, to fly around Hall's various oil properties. When Post won a nonstop transcontinental derby in 1930, Hall gave him permission to use the plane to show up the *Graf Zeppelin*.

Post made his first round-the-world flight in 1931 accompanied by Harold Gatty as navigator. Post proved his point, and he was given *The Winnie Mae* as a gift. Then in 1933 he made a round-the-world flight a second time, covering practically the same ground (New York to England, Germany, Russia, Siberia, Alaska, Canada, and return to New York). Fewer stops were made in the 1933

flight—and Post made it alone with the aid of the Sperry autopilot. It was a remarkable show of stamina, the final stages were grueling. Post kept himself from falling asleep by holding a weight in one hand attached to a string; when he dozed off, the weight fell, jerked his finger, and brought him to wakefulness again.

Following this feat, Post wished to continue with further explorations, only not around but up: the stratosphere. *The Winnie Mae* was equipped with special superchargers, one for the engine and one to supply him, in what appeared to be a man-from-Mars suit, oxygen. Post believed that the winds of high altitudes and the reduced air density (plus certain modifications in engines and propellers) would make it possible to cross the country at much higher speeds than ever before. After some false starts, he again proved himself a prophet when, after dropping *The Winnie Mae*'s landing gear, he flew from Burbank, California, to Cleveland, Ohio, a distance of 2,035 miles, in eight hours, four minutes. He traveled at an altitude of thirty thousand feet and at about twice the normal speed of his plane. Five months later, on August 15, 1935, Wiley Post died in a crash of another plane in which he and air-minded humorist Will Rogers planned to tour Alaska. Both men were killed when the seaplane faltered in a takeoff and turned over onto its back in shallow water.

Women received deserved though belated recognition in the thirties. Laura Ingalls was one of the leading women fliers of the time, and like Wiley Post and other great aviators of the period, she relied on the Lockheed for her record flights. Although she had failed to be the first woman to cross the Atlantic, she was the first woman to cross the United States nonstop. Her greatest flight took place between February 28 and April 25, 1934, when she made a solo circuit of South America in a Lockheed Air Express. Landing in twenty-three countries, Laura Ingalls covered a distance of 16,897 miles; at one point she flew over the Andes (making her the first American woman to cross this formidable mountain barrier). In honor of her flight Laura Ingalls received the Harmon Trophy

Post in stratosphere gear, ready for high-altitude flight in the *Winnie Mae* in 1935; this was before the day of the pressurized cabin. (National Air and Space Museum/Smithsonian Institution)

("most outstanding woman flier of 1934")—she had completed the longest solo flight ever made by a woman flier up to that time. In addition, she became the first flier to make a solo flight around the South American continent.

The first flight by an aircraft from Australia to the United States (with stops at Fiji and Hawaii) was successfully made by Sir Charles Kingsford-Smith and Captain P. G. Taylor in 1934. For Kingsford-Smith this was a reverse sequel to his flight in the *Southern Cross* (a Fokker) in 1928. Taking off from Brisbane on October 22, the two men, in their Lockheed Altair, named *Lady Southern Cross*, arrived in Oakland, California, on November 4. With the flight's completion, Kingsford-Smith became the first pilot to cross the Pacific both ways.

In the thirties Admiral Richard E. Byrd continued to be fascinated by the frigid regions of the earth and contributed greatly to the knowledge of both the Arctic and the Antarctic. A well-equipped expedition to Little America near the South Pole was led by Byrd in 1934–35. Using a Curtiss Condor, Byrd, with Harold June as pilot, mapped some two hundred thousand square miles of the Antarctic during this expedition. Byrd made his

Laura Ingalls and her Lockheed Air Express in which she made a solo flight around South America in 1934, winning the Harmon Trophy for her efforts. (Lockheed Photo)

Kingsford-Smith's *Lady Southern Cross* (a Lockheed Altair), the first aircraft to fly from Australia to the United States, October 22–November 4, 1934. The plane is about to take off from Wheeler Field, Hawaii, November 3, on the final leg to Oakland, California. (U. S. Air Force)

"Little America," Byrd's headquarters for the 1934–35 Antarctic mapping expedition. In the left foreground is a Pitcairn-Cierva Autogiro. Beyond: a Fairchild Pilgrim and the Curtiss Condor that was used for the chart work. (National Archives)

Howard Hughes and his racer, the plane in which he made his record transcontinental flight, January 1937. (Smithsonian Institution)

fourth and last expedition to the South Pole in 1946–47.

Unique among the pilots of the thirties was Howard Hughes. He was also the most taciturn, mysterious, and fascinating. A millionaire before he was twenty (his father had invented a drill for oil wells), Hughes gained a reputation as a "playboy" in Hollywood. He took a fling at film production and made one of the aviation classics, *Hell's Angels*, and introduced Jean Harlow to the world. Genuinely interested in aviation, Hughes became a superb pilot and began breaking records. Because he had the money, he could buy planes readily or have them designed for him. In 1937 Hughes shattered all coast-to-coast (Los Angeles to New York) land-plane records when he crossed the continent in seven hours, twenty-eight minutes at an average speed of 327 miles per hour in his specially designed racer. For this flight Hughes was awarded the Harmon Trophy.

In 1938 Hughes was determined to make a round-the-world flight, to improve on the record then held by Wiley Post. From Lockheed Hughes bought a specially equipped Lockheed Model 14. Setting out from Floyd Bennett Field, New York, on July 10, 1938, Hughes and a hand-picked crew circled the globe in three days, nineteen hours, seventeen minutes, cutting Wiley Post's record in half. Hughes' crew consisted of Lieutenant Hiram Thurlow (on leave from the Air Corps), copilot and navigator; Lieutenant Harry P. Connor, U. S. Navy Reserve, conavigator; Richard Stoddard, radio operator; and Edward Lund, flight engineer. Hughes received the Collier Trophy for this demonstration of the capabilities of modern aircraft to circle the world with the aid of proper navigational and communications techniques.

Hughes H-1, 1935. The plane, designed according to Hughes' specifications by Richard Palmer and D. E. Odekirk, was very advanced for its time. The H-1 had interchangeable wings—a "long wing" for transcontinental flight and a "short wing" for speed racing. The short wing measured a mere twenty-five feet. (Smithsonian Institution)

Lockheed 14, in which Howard Hughes made a record round-the-world flight, July 10–14, 1938. (Lockheed Photo)

The most charming—and one of the most strong-willed—aviators of the classic age of flight was Amelia Earhart. Kansas-born, she began flying lessons while a college student. After a brief beginning in a career as a social worker (by which time she was flying regularly and had a reputation in the Boston area as the wild driver of a car she called *The Yellow Peril*), Amelia Earhart was selected by a group of aviation enthusiasts to represent women in an Atlantic crossing (1928). She was, however, unhappy over being merely "a sack of potatoes," as she phrased it, while pilot Wilmer Stultz did all the flying. The flight made her the most famous woman aviator of the time, and she spent her time,

Aviation stars of the thirties: Amelia Earhart, Wiley Post, and Roscoe Turner photographed while examining the Pratt & Whitney Wasp engine of Post's *Winnie Mae*. (Lockheed Photo)

A.E. and her Lockheed Electra, in which she planned to make her final big flight. Unfortunately, this is what it turned out to be. (Lockheed Photo)

much as did Lindbergh, proving that aviation was here to stay. One additional motive drove Amelia Earhart passionately, and that was that women, as aviators, were the equal of men. As an aviator—she resented the term aviatrix—she proved herself the peer of the great fliers of the time.

Driven by an ambition to be the first woman to fly solo across the Atlantic, Amelia Earhart succeeded in 1932 in a flight that took fourteen hours, fifty-six minutes. She followed this with several others, breaking transcontinental speed records. She was the first to fly solo from Hawaii to California, the first to fly from Los Angeles to Mexico City, among other flights, and she was awarded dozens of medals and trophies for her efforts in behalf of aviation. She was also a popular writer, a lecturer on the staff of Purdue University, and the wife of ex-publisher turned aviation promotor, George Putnam. When she reached the age of thirty-eight Amelia Earhart decided she had gathered all the honors possible and that it was time to "retire from making big flights"—except that she was determined to make one "last flight." Having

flown the Atlantic, the Pacific, and cross-country, she had one other big-flight possibility: around the world. Inspired by Wiley Post's flights, Amelia Earhart decided she would go him one better and circle the earth as close to the equator as possible. (Post had flown his circle in the Northern Hemisphere, where the distance around is less than at the equator.)

For the flight Amelia Earhart acquired a sleek new Lockheed Electra, a twin-engined, low-winged monoplane. A flying laboratory, it was equipped with the most modern instruments of the time. After one attempt, which ended in a crackup, Amelia Earhart, with Fred Noonan, a transport pilot, as navigator, took off again, on June 1, 1937. By the end of the month they had reached New Guinea. On July 2, the weather finally permitting, "A.E." lifted the Electra off the small runway at Lae, flew over the Pacific, and was never seen again. Although some mystery still clings to the disappearance of Amelia Earhart and Fred Noonan, the most likely story is that the plane flew off course, ran out of fuel, and crashed into the sea.

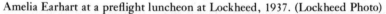

Amelia Earhart at a preflight luncheon at Lockheed, 1937. (Lockheed Photo)

Britain's flying couple: Amy Johnson and James Mollison (to Mrs. Mollison's right: P. J. Saul). (National Archives)

An extensive search by the Navy found no traces of the plane. Another story is that the plane crash-landed off a Japanese-held island and that "A.E." and Noonan were taken prisoner by the Japanese (already, so the story goes, planning a war in the Pacific) and executed as spies. No real proof of this story has come forth; but in 1937 aviation lost one of its most attractive figures.

The affection with which the American public held Amelia Earhart was paralleled by the devotion of the English to their "Queen of the Air," Amy Johnson. She earned money for flying lessons working as a secretary in London. She made her first spectacular flight in May 1930, when she flew a little de Havilland Moth from England to Australia solo in nineteen days. She flew back on a commercial airliner piloted by James Mollison and later married him. Together they crossed the Atlantic in 1933, the flight ending in a crash, although neither of the Mollisons was seriously injured. The friction of competition eventually led to a divorce, and each went on to try for other flying records.

When war came, Amy Johnson joined the Air Transport Auxiliary and served as a ferry pilot. In January 1941, while on a delivery mission, she ran into bad weather near London and was forced to parachute into the Thames River and was drowned.

A touch of the absurd came to aviation in July 1938, when a young California pilot (who had worked as a welder on *The Spirit of St. Louis*), Douglas Corrigan, made one of the most sensational flights of the era. Having flown his nine-year-old, $900 Curtiss Robin to New York, Corrigan fueled up and took off after announcing that he planned to return to Los Angeles. When next heard from, Corrigan and his old plane were in Dublin, Ireland, where he said, "My name's Corrigan. I left New York yesterday morning headed for California, but I got mixed up in the clouds and must have flown the wrong way." And so was born the wry legend of "Wrong Way" Corrigan. It was a likely story, and Corrigan stuck to it to the delight of everyone. He had violated enough rules and regulations to have grounded him for life, but he had so captivated the public imagination that any legal procedure would have caused a furor. So his flying license was suspended for five days (which Corrigan spent aboard an ocean liner, returning to New York for a hero's welcome). After a brief tour with his obsolescent Robin (which had a Department of Commerce "X," for Experimental, license—and even that had been granted reluctantly to the old "flying jalopy"), after writing a book and taking a fling at the movies, Douglas Corrigan settled down to growing oranges in California. His flight, of course, added nothing to the progress of aviation except for a little laughter in a world growing grimmer by the day.

The development of military aviation, like that of air transportation, moved forward during the middle and late thirties. The concern by this time, however, was less with pioneer flights (as it had been in the twenties) and more with the evolution of air power and with the advancement of the warplane rather than of aviation itself. This meant faster, higher-flying pursuit planes. In 1931 Boeing P-12Ds of the 1st Pursuit Group were used in high-

The Mollisons at the Hyde Park home of the President, July 1933. They are still bandaged after a crash landing the week before near Stratford, Connecticut, which ended a flight to the United States from Wales. (National Archives)

Mollison's *Dorothy* (named for a friend after his divorce from Amy Johnson; *Irish Swoop* was its name when flown by James Fitzmaurice in the 1934 MacRobertson race). In October 1936 Mollison made a record west-to-east Atlantic crossing. The plane was built by Bellanca. (National Archives)

Mollison in the cockpit of Amy Johnson's de Havilland Moth, a light plane in which she flew to Australia from England solo in 1930. (National Archives)

Douglas Corrigan gassing up his Curtis Robin in St. Louis following his famous flight to California that ended in Dublin, Ireland. (U. S. Air Force)

Corrigan and the Curtiss named *Sunshine*, 1938; his flight was succeeded by several commercial crossings in 1938–39 (plus three fatal attempts in light planes in 1939). The day of daredevil Atlantic flights was over. (U. S. Air Force)

Boeing P-12 of the Army's 1st Pursuit Group and pilot ready for high-altitude flight, 1931. (U. S. Air Force)

altitude flights, testing pilots and their equipment. Supercharged engines and oxygen masks made it possible for a flight of the aircraft to make a non-stop four hundred-mile trip from Selfridge Field, Michigan, to Bolling Field, near Washington, D.C., at an altitude of twenty thousand feet. Although few realized it at the time, it did mark the end of the open-cockpit-and-goggles era of military aviation. The traditions of the First World War, kept alive through the twenties and thirties, were rapidly becoming obsolete—and so were the aircraft they had fostered.

Heavy-bomber development in 1932 was represented by the Martin B-10, the fastest and most powerful bomber of its time. A modified (mainly more powerful engines) version appeared as the B-12 in 1934, making the Martin bomber, with its 207-mile-per-hour speed, the fastest bomber in the world. It was faster, in fact, than that of most pursuit planes of the time. A further demonstration of its capabilities was carried out in the summer of 1934 when ten Martin bombers, led by Lieutenant Colonel Henry H. Arnold made a test flight to Alaska and back. The object of the mass flight was to determine the feasibility of flying aerial reinforcements to distant points in the event of war.

Beginning of a historic flight: aircraft manufacturer Glenn L. Martin, Assistant Secretary of War Harry H. Woodring, Lieutenant Colonel Henry H. Arnold, and Air Corps Commander Major General Benjamin D. Foulois, Bolling Field (near Washington, D.C.), July 1934. (U. S. Air Force)

Martin B-10s in Fairbanks, Alaska, after an uneventful flight from the United States. (U. S. Air Force)

The 7,360-mile round trip, with various stops en route, went off without a hitch except for one incident. After arrival in Alaska one of the Martin bombers made a forced landing at Cook Inlet, and the plane ended up under water. None of the crew was injured, however, and the plane was later put back into service.

In addition to surveying landing sites along the route, the men in the bombers also made a study of the problems of operating under primitive conditions, of supply, and of the effect of the climate upon equipment. Operating out of Fairbanks, Alaska, the crews photographed twenty thousand square miles of strategic airways—a four hundred-by-fifty-mile strip. On the return trip to Washington, D.C., on August 17, 1934, the Martin bombers made a nonstop flight from Juneau, Alaska, to Seattle, Washington, all of it over water—the first time anyone had flown from Alaska to the United States. The survey was an unqualified success and had proved that the Martin bomber was a superior aircraft and that it was possible to dispatch planes to Alaska from the conterminous United States without flying over foreign territory—namely, Canada. The U. S. Army Air Corps, in other words, had begun to consider seriously the implications of the heavy bomber for war.

It would not be too great an exaggeration to say that in the midthirties, the Air Corps' major adversary was the U. S. Navy. Traditional seamen—and this was true of Army groundmen, too—merely tolerated the noisy planes. The classic sea weapon, they maintained, was the dreadnought, the battleship. But after Billy Mitchell's war with the Navy, the importance of aircraft over water could not be ignored. And while the Navy could not do much about heavy bombers (which required roomy land bases), the various fleets could be attended by aircraft carriers, which carried dive bombers, torpedo bombers, and fighters.

It was Rear Admiral William A. Moffett (fated to die in the crash of the *Akron*) who stated in 1925: "It is the Navy's mission to protect our coasts, our seaborne commerce, and far-flung possessions. Once war is forced upon us we must take the offensive to win it. The Navy is the first line of offense, and naval aviation as an advance guard of this line must deliver the brunt of the attack. Naval aviation cannot take the offensive from shore; it must go to sea on the back of the fleet. I do not believe aircraft on shore can ward off a bombing attack launched, perhaps, from carriers by night from an unknown point for an unknown objective. On the other hand, a fleet with adequate aviation of its own can drive the carriers back out of effective

August 4, 1934, forced landing in Cook Inlet, Alaska. Within a week the Martin was ready for flight again. (U. S. Air Force)

Martin bomber on a mapping flight over Alaska. (U. S. Air Force)

The Navy's answer to long-distance bombers: seaborne pursuits. Boeing shipboard fighters on the deck of the *Langley*. (The Boeing Company)

range. Both for offense and defense the fleet and naval aviation are one and inseparable."

The germ for another disagreement between the Navy and the Army aviation leaders lay in Admiral Moffett's contention that land-based aircraft could not interfere with an invader's bombing attack. The Navy was extremely jealous of all of the air that lay above its oceans. The first U.S. carrier to put to sea (in 1922) was the USS *Langley*, the one-time collier *Jupiter* converted into a carrier. (The

Boeing F2B-1s spotted in the deck of the *Langley*. (The Boeing Company)

Boeing F4B-2 of 1930; it was regarded as the best carrier-based fighter of the thirties. In this close-up, details of the spring landing gear, arrester hook, and swivel tail wheel can be seen. Gun- and bombsights are just in front of the cockpit on the upper fuselage. (The Boeing Company)

F4B-2s in flight formation. (The Boeing Company)

later *Lexington* and *Saratoga* were converted from cruisers; the first carrier built from the keel up was the *Ranger*, commissioned in June 1934.)

The Boeing F4B-2 carrier-based fighter was a classic of the period. Based on the *Lexington*, the F4B-2 was the finest of its time: Powered by a 450-horsepower Pratt & Whitney Wasp engine, it was capable of speeds of more than 180 miles per hour, a range of more than 500 miles, and a ceiling of 28,000 feet. It could carry bombs (in the racks under the wings). Spring landing gear and a swiveling tail wheel helped to make tricky carrier landings a little easier. An arresting hook under the tail dropped to catch heavy cables across the flight deck to stop the plane from continuing its landing run overboard. One of the marks of the early carrier pilots was called instrument face, the flattened nose and loose teeth that resulted from striking their faces against the instrument panel while landing (particularly landing aboard the *Langley*, with its relatively short flight deck).

The Boeing F4B-4 of 1932 (in service until 1938) was Boeing's last biplane. The F4B-4 differed externally from the earlier series models mainly in the larger tail surfaces and headrest. The headrest contained an inflatable rubber life raft and other emergency supplies. The wingspan of the F4Bs was thirty feet, and the top speed of the "4" was about 184 miles per hour (less than that of the Martin bomber of the same period). The range of the plane was doubled by attaching an underbelly fuel tank, which could be dropped when empty. Although the fuselage was all metal and the tail surfaces were covered with corrugated aluminum wing surfaces (except for ailerons) were fabric-covered. The Boeing fighters were extremely maneuverable and rugged aircraft.

The last of the biplane U. S. Navy shipboard fighters was the Grumman F3F, which replaced the Boeing F4B-4 in 1936 and remained in operation until late in 1941, when Grumman monoplanes (the F4Fs) supplanted it. The Grumman F3F was a pilot favorite in its time and was notable for its retractable landing gear. The fast—230 mile-per-hour—F3F was powered originally by a

Cockpit of the Boeing F4B-3, showing stick, foot pedals, gunsight, and bombsight (projecting through the windscreen), and a relatively simple instrument panel: air-speed indicator (top left), altimeter (top right), turn-and-bank indicator (bottom left), and RPM indicator (which measured the propeller speed). (The Boeing Company)

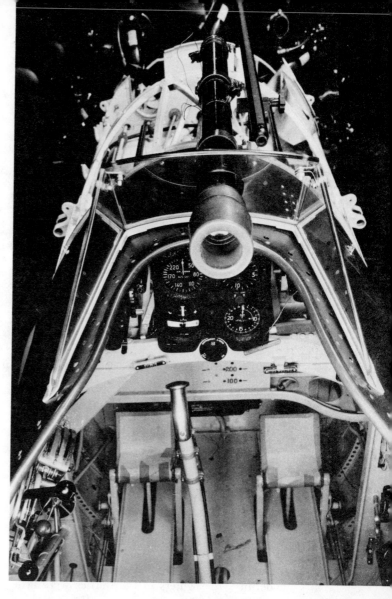

fourteen-cylinder Pratt & Whitney Twin Wasp, Junior, and later by a Wright Cyclone. The F3F was the last biplane in U.S. military service and was eventually replaced when U.S. Army monoplanes, it was learned, could outperform it.

The U. S. Air Corps used biplanes well into the late thirties. The Curtiss Hawk series culminated, in 1931, in the P-6E. The plane's wingspan was thirty-one feet, six inches, and its fuselage length was twenty-three feet, two inches. A Curtiss seven hundred-horsepower engine turned a three-bladed propeller. Top speed was close to, but not quite, two hundred miles per hour. A pilots' favorite, the Curtiss P-6E was one of the Army Air Corps' finest fighters of the thirties.

The Army version of the Navy's F4Bs was the P-12, which supplanted the Curtiss Hawk as a

Last of the line: the Boeing F4B-4 of 1932, here in "outrigger parking" aboard the U.S.S. *Ranger* in 1934. The Boeings were eventually phased out, and replaced by the Grumman biplane in 1936. (The Boeing Company)

Grumman introduced the retractable landing gear to Navy fighter design with its XFF-1 in 1931, a two-place shipboard craft. Later modifications resulted in the SF-2 (the major change: a switch from a Wright to a Pratt & Whitney engine); this Scout fighter was capable of reaching a top speed of more than two hundred miles per hour. (Grumman Aircraft)

292

Grumman F3F, the last of the American military biplanes. Rugged and fast, the F3F was eventually supplanted by the F4F Wildcat of the Second World War. (Grumman Aircraft/Navy Department National Archives)

service fighter in the thirties. Despite the clean design and maneuverability of both these aircraft, they were outperformed in the speed category by the Martin B-10. Theoretically, the planes were designed to stop the bombers, and this would not be possible if they were unable to catch them. And further, theoretically, if the United States had a fast bomber, there was little reason to doubt that any hypothetical enemy had one also. For all their modernity, the fighters of the thirties were little more than extensions of the Great War "scouts," with emphasis upon maneuverability for dogfighting in the classic manner.

The first step toward the new fighter plane was

taken in 1931 when the Detroit Aircraft Company, through its then-subsidiary Lockheed, brought forth an entirely new concept in military aircraft—a low-winged monoplane. The metal fuselage was built in Detroit and the plywood wing in Burbank, California, where the plane was finally assembled. Designer Robert Wood had visualized the new design as a two-place fighter, with the pilot in the front cockpit and a gunner with a flexible machine gun in the rear. The wheels retracted into the wing, and power was supplied by a six hundred-horsepower Curtiss Conquerer engine, a liquid-coooled, twelve-cylinder power plant. The XP-900—later YP-24—cruised at an average speed of 215 miles per hour, which made it a formidable bomber interceptor. The plane unfortunately crashed during tests at Wright Field in October 1931. The Detroit Aircraft Company, a victim of the Depression, went out of business. The XP-900 had died aborning.

Among the last of the U. S. Army's biplanes were the Curtiss P6Es, popularly called the Hawks. These are aircraft of the 17th Pursuit Squadron stationed at Selfridge Field, Michigan, in the early thirties. (U. S. Army)

Boeing pursuits of the 27th Pursuit Squadron, Selfridge
Field. This was the Army version of the Navy's F4B
shipboard fighter. (U. S. Air Force)

The Detroit-Lockheed XP-900 (later YP-24), which introduced the monoplane concept into the Army's fighter aircraft design. In 1931 this was regarded as an advanced aircraft. (Lockheed Photo)

Boeing P-26A, in the markings of the 34th Attack Squadron ("Thunderbirds"), with high headrest modification. (U. S. Air Force Museum)

The first low-winged monoplane went into service with the Army Air Corps in 1933. This was the Boeing P-26. Of all-metal construction, the little (wingspan was twenty-eight feet) fighter was capable of speeds of well over two hundred miles an hour. Affectionately called the Peashooter by pilots, the P-26 was the last Army aircraft with externally braced wings, open cockpit, and fixed landing gear. Eleven P-26As were sold as export versions to China to be used in defense against the Japanese. Although outdated when the war came to the Pacific, the P-26 was among the first of American fighter planes to go into action against the Japanese. The high headrest was introduced with the A model as protection for the pilot in the event of a landing flipover. An early "hot" airplane, the Boeing P-26 had a comparatively high landing speed (eighty-two miles per hour), which was lowered by the addition of flaps (air brakes, in a sense, but actually panels in the underside of the wing that could be lowered to reduce the landing speed).

A more contemporary concept in fighter-plane design was introduced with the Seversky P-35, the sleek work of an ex-World War I fighter pilot turned manufacturer, Alexander P. de Seversky, and designer Alexander Kartveli. With its elliptical cantilever (no external wire bracing) wing, its retracting landing gear, and massive, cowled engine, it was the air-minded youth's dream of the ultimate fighter plane. It superseded the P-26 in the Army's affections as a first-line, fast fighter. Top speed was 280 miles per hour, and the plane was fast on the takeoff. The P-35 went into active service in July 1937. Once the plane became available for private and export purchase, it was used by such racing pilots as Jacqueline Cochran and Frank Fuller, during the late thirties, to win a series of Bendix races. Although itself superseded within a couple of years, the P-35 was notable because it was the ancestor of the wartime P-47 Thunderbolt.

During the same period in which the United States Army Air Corps had encouraged the design

Seversky P-35 banking over its home base, Selfridge Field, Michigan. (U. S. Air Force)

Seversky SEV-3, in civilian guise, equipped with EDO
floats in flight over lower Manhattan. In 1935 this plane
broke several speed records. Initials EDO stand for Earl
Dodge Osborn, founder of the firm that produces floats.
(Robert Kane/EDO)

The Hawker Fury, the standard British RAF fighter of
the late thirties. The Furys were eventually phased out
in favor of the Hurricane and, later, the Spitfire.
(National Air and Space Museum, Smithsonian
Institution)

of faster low-winged monoplanes, development in Europe, and elsewhere, had progressed roughly along the same lines. The British Royal Air Force already had two such aircraft intended for home defense of the British Isles, the Hawker Hurricane and the Supermarine Spitfire. Germany had a similar type in its Messerschmitt Bf-109, but German military aviation had already taken a turn in favor of dive bombers and medium bombers that would co-operate with the ground forces. Typical expressions of German Luftwaffe thinking in the late thirties were such aircraft as the Heinkel 59. The Spanish Civil War (1936–39) was used by Germany, Italy, and the Soviet Union as a testing arena for its aircraft and tactics. It was in Spain that the Stuka idea was first tried and, without serious opposition, seemed to be invincible. Likewise, the Me-109s were more than a match for the planes of the Spanish Loyalists (some of them of Russian manufacture). The performance of the Luftwaffe in Spain impressed Hitler, Göring, and, for that matter, the rest of the world, with Germany's ability to wage modern war. This distorted impression interfered with the full development of German air power and a neglect of the heavy bomber—a fact that would cost Germany the war in the air in the Second World War.

Mitsubishi A5M4, Japanese Navy fighter that saw action over China in the early thirties. (U. S. Air Force)

Classic obsolescence: Polish PZL-6, Polish fighter in 1931 at the Cleveland air races. Evolution of this high-wing monoplane configuration continued until the Second World War eliminated it—and the Polish Air Force. (U. S. Air Force)

At the other end of the Axis, Japan released very little information about its first-line fighters. The tendency in America was to look down upon Japanese aviation design as purely imitative and inferior. From time to time word would leak out from China, with which Japan had been warring since the early thirties. This was an undeclared war, a series of "incidents," until 1937, when full-scale war erupted. One of the aircraft used in the early phase of the war was the Mitsubishi A5M4 (later named the Claude by American intelligence officers). This was a low-winged monoplane with a fixed landing gear; it served on Japanese carriers as a fighter. The A5M4 was a revolutionary aircraft for its time. (It was the first Japanese plane to be equipped with wing flaps. For a time it had a closed cockpit, but this was discarded because pilots distrusted it.) It attained a speed in excess of two hundred miles per hour. Another Navy shipboard fighter that saw combat in China was completely unknown in the West: This was the Mitsubishi A6M Type 0 carrier fighter. These would be named the Zero.

An interesting European design of the thirties was the PZL (the initials stood for Pannstwowe Zaklady Lotnicze: State Aircraft Factory), the "Polish Fighter." One, the P-6 of the series, appeared at the Cleveland Air Races in 1931. By the next year the final plane of this series, the P-11, had evolved and was one of the outstanding aircraft of the midthirties. But by 1939, however, when the Luftwaffe struck, the PZL-11, the first fighter to contend with the Me-109s as well as the German bombers, was outmatched.

As Germany and Japan prepared for war, military strategists of the U. S. Army Air Corps, followers of Billy Mitchell, embarked upon a campaign to establish a heavy-bombardment force. This was a campaign beset with many frustrations, pitfalls, and disappointments. During the thirties few people thought in terms of an offensive war; therefore there was no necessity for a large bomber that could leave the continental United States to bomb targets hundreds of miles away. The Army planners' idea, however, was that long-range bombers might be made that could intercept an enemy invasion force far out at sea. This, naturally, made the Navy unhappy, the sea being its special province. This unleashed arguments about spheres of responsibility and the traditional infighting for appropriations. It was the Boeing Company that began experimenting in 1930 with the type of plane that the Air Corps bomber advocates had in mind. In 1931 Boeing exhibited an experimental twin-engined bomber, the YB-9, an all-metal, low-winged monoplane. With a span of seventy-six feet, the revolutionary bomber could carry a bombload of some two thousand pounds at speeds faster than the fastest pursuit plane of the time.

Next in the evolutionary line of the heavy bomber was the Y1B-9, an improved version of the earlier B-9. Curtiss in-line engines have been substituted for the Pratt & Whitney radials. Wheels were retractable into the wings, a definitely modern touch. But the five-man crew sat in open cockpits as of yore. Armament, besides bombload, consisted of four 30-caliber machine guns.

The last of the B-9s was the Y1B-9A of 1932. The new version of the bomber reverted to the air-cooled radial engine, six hundred-horsepower Pratt & Whitney Hornets. The top speed of the bomber was still 186 miles per hour, and the top speed of the P-26 was more than 230 miles per hour. The B-9 was superseded by the Martin B-10 (the plane

Evolution of a concept: strategic bombardment, which resulted in the Boeing B-17 Flying Fortress. The experimental Model 215, the Army's YB-9, 1931. In flight, the modified B-9, the Y1B-9, with retractable landing gear and streamlined cowlings housing in-line engines. The development of the B-9s necessitated the design of a fighter plane that could counter a high-speed bomber. In the photo the last of Boeing's series, the Y1B-9A, is accompanied by the Boeing XP-936, prototype of the P-26. (The Boeing Company)

that had made the Alaska survey flight in 1934). Boeing, meanwhile, went on with all-metal cantilever-winged aircraft with their 247 transport of 1934.

In 1934 Boeing was awarded a contract by the Army to build the XBLR-1 (Experimental Bomber, Long Range Model 1). Later designated the XB-15 by the Army, the plane was the largest landplane of its time when completed in 1937. Its wingspread was 149 feet, and the fuselage was 87 feet, 7 inches long. Like the Barling bomber and

The Boeing XB-15, in 1937 the world's largest landplane, the introduction of the idea of the four-engined heavy bomber, a direct forerunner of the Flying Fortress, 1937. (The Boeing Company)

Rollout of the Boeing Model 299, July 1935. (The Boeing Company)

Model 299 in the traditional flight past Mount Ranier, Wash. (The Boeing Company)

the DO-X that had preceded it, the XB-15 was ready before the engines that might have powered it were available. Instead of four 1,000-horsepower engines, 850-horsepower motors were installed, which curtailed the performance of the plane. However, since it was produced experimentally, the big bomber did prove the value of the long-range concept and of the four-engined bombardment aircraft. The XB-15 had a range of more than five thousand miles and was capable of lifting heavy cargo loads. (It was never actually used as a bomber.) During the Second World War it served as a transport by the Air Force, when it was designated the XC-105.

About the time Boeing was building the XB-15 in its Seattle plant, an Army specification came through for a multiengined bomber capable of speeds near two hundred miles per hour, with a bombload of a ton and a range of over a thousand miles. The Army had in mind a plane that could meet enemy fleets far out at sea. Taking the word "multi-engined" to mean four as readily as two,

and the example of the XB-15 then in progress, with some ideas from the Boeing 247 transport, the design team evolved what they called Model 299. Smaller than the XB-15, the 299's span was 103 feet, 9 inches; from the tip of the nose to the rudder, it measured 68 feet, 9 inches. It was a remarkably sleek aircraft for a bomber, although its fuselage bulged here and there with gun "blisters." When the big plane was rolled out of the Boeing plant in July 1935, for its traditional (for Boeing) test flight over Mount Rainier, it was so impressive a sight that a Seattle newspaperman, Richard L. Williams, referred to it as a "flying fortress."

The 299 was flown from Seattle to Wright Field, Ohio, to compete in the Army trials with two other designs, the Martin 146 and the Douglas DB-1 (both twin-engined). The 299 surpassed all expectations, with its average speed of 252 miles per hour over the 2,100-mile flight. This was spectacular for this type of plane since bombers were traditionally slow. Test pilot Leslie Tower commented on the plane's ease in handling despite its size.

However, the entire project came to a tragic end—and the Army's program for the heavy bomber could easily have ended with it—when, after completing several tests, the 299 crashed during a take-off. Before the plane took off, someone was supposed to unlock the tail surfaces, but he forgot to do this. (The elevators were locked in a neutral position when the plane was on the ground so that they would not flap in the wind.) The plane crashed and burned, killing test pilot Leslie Tower and the Army's pilot, Major Plower P. Hill. Had the crash resulted from mechanical failure, structural weakness, or some malfunction, "Project 299" probably would have ended right there. But previous flights, as well as the flight from Seattle itself, proved that the 299 was a superior aircraft. The Army decided that, in spite of the crash, it would continue the development of Boeing's innovational design. Had the 299 not been wrecked, incidentally, it would have been designated the XB-17.

Although they did not exist in great numbers during the late thirties the Boeing B-17s began to evolve as successive models underwent various refinements. Different engines were installed (a powerful Wright Cyclone), the fuselage was shortened, lengthened, and finally during wartime, lengthened again. The Army Air Corps used the few bombers they had to make epic flights such as that in February 1938 from Miami to Buenos Aires and back, covering a distance of twelve thousand miles. In May some of these same bombers located the Italian liner *Rex* in a mock interception more than seven hundred miles out at sea. This did not sit well with the Navy, and the B-17s were restricted to operations of no more than a hundred miles offshore. It was a remarkable feat of navigation and flying, and the B-17s had undoubtedly emerged as one of the most formidable aircraft the Army had.

The birth of the B-17 was to change the face of war, although when it was originally conceived, it was designed as a defensive weapon whose function was, primarily, to stop an enemy approaching the shores of the United States. But when the plane was tested in combat, first by the British in 1941 and later by the Americans, it evolved into an offensive weapon, one that would take the war and

Boeing 299 burning after its test-flight crash at Wright Field, Ohio. (U. S. Air Force)

all its destruction to the enemy. To have suggested in 1935, when the 299 first appeared, that the United States had developed a large bombardment aircraft that was capable of flying long distances to drop bombs on foreign soil, would have filled the air with protest, and rightly. But when war struck, war itself became so savage that the idea of shortening it by destroying the enemy's ability to make weapons and to manufacture ammunition appeared to be sound. The B-17 in its offensive role was to have a direct effect upon the outcome of that savage war. It is unlikely that anyone at the time considered the idea of sending great armadas of bombers (since none existed) to bomb great population centers. That horror would come all too soon, and the full impact of air power would be realized in the Second World War.

The import of the potential of such bombers as the B-17 encouraged the kind of aircraft that could counter an enemy bomber of the same type—fast interceptors and pursuit planes—but the general mood was not warlike. News from the Far East seemed merely additional exotica, few understood the civil war in Spain, Hitler appeared to be a vociferous, funny little guy with a Charlie Chaplin mustache, and Mussolini a posturer and blustering clown. In the United States, particularly, few considered war possible. There was more concern with the impact of the Depression on American— and world—economy—with jobs, not military hardware.

Of greater interest to the average man and woman in the United States was the abdication of the British throne by Edward VIII and the subsequent grand coronation of his brother George (who became George VI in May 1937). The event was covered as extensively in the United States as in England. A dramatic quick delivery of coronation photos was accomplished by two Eastern Air Lines pilots, Henry T. "Dick" Merrill and John S. Lambie. Backed by International Photo Service, they made a grim delivery to England on May 9: shots of the *Hindenburg* explosion (the event had advanced their original takeoff date). On May 13, 1937, they left England with the coronation photographs for

Out of the ashes, Boeing continued to develop the Army's B-17s; in flight is the Y1B-17 of the 2nd Bombardment Group. (The Boeing Company)

Grumman XF5F-1, first flown in 1940, was the Navy's first single-seat, twin-engined fighter. Intended for carrier use, it never got beyond the experimental stage. One of its competitors at the time was the Vought XF4U-1, which became better known later as the Corsair. The XF5F, called the Skyrocket, had a top speed of about 350 miles per hour. But its appearance was more impressive than its performance. (Grumman Aircraft)

An experimental Curtiss interceptor, designed to challenge attacking heavy-bomber formations. It was eventually modified and used as a Navy advanced trainer, the SNC-1. (Smithsonian Institution)

delivery in New York the next day.

Although accused of carrying off a "stunt," Merrill had proved the feasibility of round-trip transatlantic flying. He liked to characterize the trip as "a pioneering commercial venture in aviation." This was, in a sense, true—though premature, for the facilities for such flights, regularly, were yet to be firmly established.

Commercial and civil aviation managed to go on, if not prosper, in spite of the Depression. Boeing introduced the first four-engine pressurized air-

liner, the 307, in 1938, making high-altitude flying possible and more comfortable. Short-distance hops were made in smaller aircraft of attractive design, and some people managed to get enough money together to buy, fly, and hangar their Cubs, Aeroncas, and Puss Moths. Skylarking, in those false halcyon days, seemed the one good function for the airplane. Youngsters who haunted airports dreaming of flight would, within a very few years, have their dreams come true. Only the planes they flew had been transformed into weapons—again.

Civil aviation as the thirties came to an end: a Lockheed Electra takes off at the factory in California. (Lockheed Photo)

Jack Lambie and Henry "Dick" Merrill stand beside their Electra, in which they made a speedy round-trip transatlantic crossing in 1937. (U. S. Air Force)

Peacetime aircraft: De Havilland 90 Dragonfly, ca. 1935. It could serve as a five-place light transport. De Havilland aircraft were used by British pilots for long-distance record flights. (Author's Collection)

Typical romantic photography of the late thirties: a light plane, with mountains in the background, outside a hangar at a California airport. (Diane and Art Hofmeister)

The good life: Douglas Dolphin amphibians connecting Catalina Island with the California mainland in the thirties. The Dolphin carried eight passengers. (Douglas Photo)

Junker Ju-87, the most widely used of the Stuka dive-bomber aircraft. It struck the first aerial blow of the Second World War. (H. J. Nowarra)

Heinkel 111, the airliner-turned-bomber during the Spanish Civil War; like the Stuka, it was no match for the British Hurricane and Spitfire. (U. S. Air Force)

Messerschmitt 110, Göring's pet fighter-bomber—here in bombing formation over Warsaw. (Embassy of the Polish People's Republic)

7 THE SECOND WORLD WAR

The outbreak of the Second World War in September 1939 found Germany, the aggressor, with the best-equipped air force in the world. It was, however, geared to short, intensive fighting, in which air and ground forces co-operated in sudden heavy onslaughts on enemy strong points, overwhelming them with a combination of aerial, tank, and armored-car attack followed by fast-moving troops. This was Adolf Hitler's *Blitzkrieg*—a lightning war—which stunned the defenders of Poland first in the morning of September 1, 1939, and within one month had proved decisively effective when Poland capitulated. Hitler had hoped that the victory over Poland would bring an end to hostilities, but to his surprise both Britain and France declared war on Germany shortly after the invasion of Poland began. The Luftwaffe's string of victories, meanwhile, seemed to indicate that as a weapon of war, it was practically invincible. Even Hitler, who distrusted aircraft and had little understanding of planes as weapons, agreed with Göring that the Luftwaffe had begun the war in a blaze of glory—except that it was not designed for a war of long distances and for a war that might linger on for any length of time. Also, the Luftwaffe had gone into the war without one single heavy bomber in service. Its planners, subordinate to the strategists who thought primarily in terms of ground warfare, had become hypnotized by the Stuka concept.

During the years 1939–45 aviation made few advances that could honestly be called progressive; aircraft emerged from these years as a most destructive means of making war. But this could hardly be called an advance in civilization. The changes in aircraft from 1939 to 1945 were more dramatic than were the changes from 1914 to 1918. When World War II began, many military planes were little better than glorified World War I "crates." When the war ended, the aircraft of an entirely new age had arrived, were tested, and had worked—namely, the jet. Luckily the war came to an end before these planes could be widely used. The major part of the fighting of the Second World War was done in conventional, piston-driven aircraft; some of them, the last of their type, became as legendary as the men who flew them.

The Junkers Ju-87 dive bomber, the representative Stuka (all dive bombers were called Stukas, but the Ju-87 was the most notorious) actually struck the first blow of the war when small formations attacked Polish positions on the Vistula River (to prevent the Poles from destroying the bridges that Hitler's armies required in order to cross into Poland at Dirschau). The Stuka was not a beautiful plane. Its fixed landing gear jutted down from a strangely bent wing (for better pilot visibility). With a crew of two the Ju-87 cruised at about two hundred miles per hour, and dived almost vertically. Its attack was frightening, for the pilot could aim the plane at the target and pounce; the shriek of the approaching plane (the noise of which was augmented by special whistling devices in the wing) was terrorizing, caused panic among troops, fleeing refugees, and cavalry horses (cavalry was used in the early days of the war by Poland and the Soviet Union). The Stuka, however, received its come-uppance when the war turned modern and it had to contend with the contemporary fighters of the Royal Air Force.

Whereas the Stuka served as a spearhead for Hitler's Panzers (fast armored cars and tanks), the Luftwaffe's bombers attacked the larger targets, such as cities. The bombers, too, worked in conjunction with ground troops rather than independently. Because of this, the Luftwaffe had no long-range bomber when the war opened—that would prove to be critical during the Battle of Britain and after. The Heinkel 111, the onetime Lufthansa airliner, which began its bombing career (such as it was) during the Spanish Civil War, was an important aircraft in the early phase of the war. It had a top speed of about 250 miles an hour, a range of 1,100 miles, two engines, and—as was learned after the Luftwaffe's winning streak ran out—insufficient armament for its own self-protection and too little armor protection for crews. Because of its speed—fast for its day—it was hoped that the He-111 would prove to be self-sufficient—outrunning enemy fighters and outshooting them. This was true over Spain and Poland, and to some extent over France. But over Britain the skies were dangerously unhealthy for the He-111.

Göring's pet was the Messerschmitt 110, which he regarded as a double-threat fighter-bomber. Faster by almost a hundred miles than the He-111, the Me-110, Göring presumed, could be even more self-sufficient than the Heinkel. The Me-110, he believed, could not only serve as a two-engined escort for the slower bombers, but could also bomb on its own without escort. This may have been true over Poland, but again not over Britain.

Called the wonder bomber because of its versatility, the Junkers 88 was adapted to several roles throughout the course of the war. It was used as a day bomber, night fighter (later in the war), dive bomber, and torpedo bomber. Consequently, it was produced in greater numbers than any other German bomber. Although it did not consistently perform well in its various modifications, it was superior to the He-111 and the Me-110, as was proved during the Battle of Britain in the summer of 1940.

Twenty-seven days after the war had erupted, Poland had been completely overwhelmed (with some aid from Soviet Russia, which had invaded from the east on September 17) and surrendered on September 28. The little Polish Air Force, with its outdated PZLs, was no match for the more modern German Messerschmitts. It was not wiped out on the ground, as has been believed for so long, but moved to camouflaged fields from which it pecked away at the Luftwaffe. The decisive blow to Po-

Junkers 88As, perhaps the best, and the most versatile, of the German bombers at the beginning of the war. (H. J. Nowarra)

Warsaw, September 1939, after a German bombing raid. The Polish Air Force was overwhelmed by the Luftwaffe in numbers as well as quality and was unable to intercept the German bombers and prevent scenes like this. (Embassy of the Polish People's Republic)

land was the heavy bombardment by air of the capital, Warsaw. Ju-87s, He-111s, Ju-88s, and Me-110s laid down a heavy aerial barrage on September 25 with devastating results and hastened the surrender three days later.

Not all German aircraft were designed for fighting or bombing. Another important function was reconnaissance to seek out enemy positions and to photograph them for both ground and air operations. The Henschel 126, a high-wing monoplane with fixed landing gear, was used in such work. The observer doubled also as machine gunner.

Another curious and interesting German noncombatant plane was the prewar Fiesler Storch (Stork). An observation plane and personal transport for high-ranking Luftwaffe commanders, the Storch could, through the manipulation of a complex arrangement of wing flaps, take off from and land in very small spaces. This made it an excellent aircraft for reconnaissance and liaison among troop units.

The most formidable aircraft used by the Luftwaffe at the beginning of the war was the Messerschmitt 109. The fast (well over 300 miles per

A reconnaissance plane, the Henschel 126; in the rear cockpit the cameraman photographs the terrain below. He also doubled as a machine gunner. (H. J. Nowarra)

The Fiesler Stork, which was capable of a near-vertical takeoff. It was introduced to Americans before the war at the Cleveland national air races, where it took off and landed in strictly confined areas. During the war, this was demonstrated by its landing in the Champs-Élysées in Paris (in 1940). (U. S. Air Force/H. J. Nowarra)

A later Me-109—the G model (here in Allied hands in Tunisia in 1943). The twenty-mm. cannon that fired through the nose spinner was a problem because of a tendency to jam in combat. The Me-109G was heavier than the earlier models and not as maneuverable. (U. S. Air Force)

hour; some models reached 400) fighter was heavily armed (both cannon and machine guns) and dealt roughly with the Polish fighters as well as with other Allied bombers and fighters. Like the Polish Air Force, the French Air Force was overwhelmed by the Luftwaffe. After months of a so-called phony war, which followed the conquest of Poland, the German armies and air forces began to move on the Western Front in May 1940. Hitler, meanwhile, had wished that France and Britain would have decided to drop out of the war. His wish did not come true.

The best fighter of the French Air Force (Armée de l'Air) was the Dewoitine 520, but there were too few on hand because between the wars the development of first-line warplanes in France was ne-

The best German fighter plane in 1939, the Me-109, which had few problems dealing with Polish and French fighter aircraft. (H. J. Nowarra)

glected. Rather vainly depending upon its complex Maginot Line, France had fallen into obsolescence as far as its Air Force was concerned. Its bomber force was even more outdated than the fighter branch (Chasse). However, during the brief, tragic Battle of France, the Dewoitine Chasse pilots took a considerable toll of German aircraft.

The backbone of the British Expeditionary Forces air arm was the Hawker Hurricane, which, in fact, could be outperformed by the Me-109. But courageous RAF pilots, in co-operation with their French brothers-in-arms, contested the Luftwaffe over France until French resistance crumbled under the Nazi juggernaut. The Messerschmitt was faster and could fight at higher altitudes than the Hurricane, but the British fighter was more maneuverable, and it was rugged. It was also heavily gunned (ranging, in different models, from eight to a dozen machine guns), which was disastrous for German bombers. However, the Hurricane squad-

Dewoitine 520, France's front-line defense fighter; it proved no match for the Messerschmitts. (Musée de l'Air, Paris)

Hawker Hurricanes, the star of Britain's fighter defense when the Phony War ended and the Battle for France began; the Hurricane, with its eight-gun armament and despite its advanced age, was a tough challenger of the Me-109s and bomber formations. (Imperial War Museum)

Luftwaffe chief Hermann Göring (left) and Ernst Udet—who introduced the Stuka concept into the German Air Force. The romanticism of air fighting of the First World War clouded the thinking of both Göring and Udet—which aided the Allies and hindered the Luftwaffe. (H. J. Nowarra)

rons were overwhelmed to a great extent during the final days of the Battle of France. Winston Churchill, who had been appointed Prime Minister during the *Blitzkrieg* in France, wisely heeded the advice of the Fighter Command leader, Air Chief Marshal Sir Hugh Dowding, and decided not to pour any more fighter squadrons into what was obviously a losing battle. Churchill, and particularly the wise Dowding, wished to preserve the fighter strength for what Churchill called the Battle of Britain.

The glory days of the Luftwaffe—from the opening of the war in 1939 until the escape of the bulk of the British Army at Dunkirk in May–June 1940—brought the glow of great pride and beaming victory smiles to the faces of Hermann Göring, who took full credit for the Luftwaffe's contributions to the speedy thrust through Europe. Another former World War I ace, Ernst Udet, was in special favor in those days, for he had been a stanch advocate of the Stuka, which had wreaked such havoc in the fighting of 1939–40. But as the Battle of Britain impended, the days of the Stuka, and the antiquarian war-making of Göring and Udet, were numbered.

Two of Germany's outstanding Second World War fighter pilots, Adolf Galland (left) and Werner Moelders in discussion with Generalmajor Theo Osterkamp, a First World War ace and Luftwaffe air commander during the Battle of Britain. Moelders was killed in a bad-weather crash during the war; Galland survived despite unpopularity with Hitler and Göring. (H. J. Nowarra)

The result of the Luftwaffe's bombing of Rotterdam, May 1940. (Press and Information Services, Rotterdam)

As a pre-invasion of Britain demonstration of the power of the Luftwaffe, the bombing of the Dutch city of Rotterdam on May 14, 1940, was stunning and shocking to the Dutch and to the rest of the world. Although wartime propaganda exaggerated the heavy toll of Dutch dead and the widespread destruction of the city, it was nonetheless an appallingly devastating bomber attack upon a modern city. Waves of He-111s, most of which had been called back when it was learned that the Dutch were in the process of surrendering, had begun to bomb Dutch strong points in the center of the city. Forty German bombers, however, did not receive the radio message and bombed a concentrated area of Rotterdam. The fires that resulted destroyed 20,000 buildings (78,000 people were rendered homeless), and 980 people died. (The figures released at the time stated that from "30,000 to 40,-000" perished in the bombing, but this was, of course, not true.) What was true was that in a mere 7½ minutes forty He-111s had sown so much ruin and death.

The Battle of France was decided with stunning brevity. In less than two months France capitulated to the German invaders, and as Winston Churchill announced to his people as he rallied

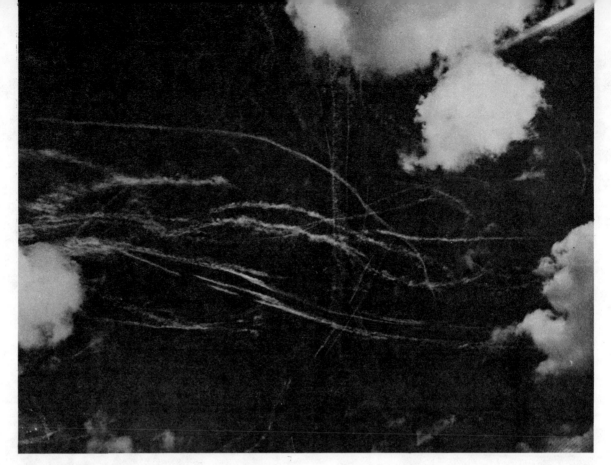

Traceries of the battle: the sky over the county of Kent during the Battle of Britain. British fighters have intercepted a German bomber force. (Imperial War Museum)

them for what he was certain would come next, the Battle of Britain was about to begin. It was the first battle in history that was resolved in the air, where all the fighting occurred. The Germans, based across the English Channel in Occupied France, had to cross the Channel, deliver their bombloads, and return to France. Fighters had to contend with British defenders and also make it back to France as best they could. That the RAF fought for, and over, its own soil was to have a significance in the final outcome of the Battle of Britain. Another unique aspect of the battle was that most of it occurred over England in daylight, and English civilians, merely by looking upward, had a front-row seat (sometimes dangerous, what with falling planes and bombs) at one of the great dramas of history. This was characterized by the vapor trails of the fighting planes as they turned, dived, and fought overhead.

Göring unleashed the Luftwaffe against the RAF in July 1940, promising Hitler that once the Royal Air Force had been wiped out it would be possible to invade England. But Göring was to learn that England was a hornets' nest of air bases, which brought out the planes of Fighter Command to shatter the German bomber formations. The most numerous of Fighter Command's interceptors were the Hurricanes.

Like the Me-109, the Hurricane dated from the early and midthirties, the product of Sydney Camm and a design team of Hawker Aircraft Ltd. The Hurricane flew for the first time in 1935 and was somewhat dated by the time of the outbreak of war. Nonetheless, it proved to be a versatile aircraft and served through the war, from the beginning to the end. Later Hurricanes were fitted with steel propellers; early models had two-bladed wooden propellers. Modifications during the war kept the Hurricane superior to German bombers in general, although the Me-109 and the later Focke-

Wulf 190 were formidable opponents. Hurricanes operated on all fronts, from Europe to North Africa to the tropics of Burma. With antitank guns installed in the wings, it was a powerful "tank buster" in the North African desert against Rommel's Afrika Korps. Although the forward half of the fuselage was metal-skinned, the after section from the cockpit back was fabric-covered.

Companion in arms with the Hurricane in the Battle of Britain stand was the beautiful Supermarine Spitfire, descendant of the famous Schneider Trophy winner of 1931. The Spitfire first flew in 1936 and went into Fighter Command service in 1938. During the ill-fated Battle of France, the Spitfire squadrons were held in readiness in England, and the Hurricanes of what was called the Advanced Air Striking Force and the Air Component of the BEF fought a last-ditch stand. The more rugged Hurricane with its wider landing-gear spread was more suitable for operations from

"Men like these saved England," Winston Churchill once said of the fighter pilots of the Royal Air Force. No one would question that. Here members of No. 242 Squadron are photographed around a Hurricane. Their mixed uniforms are characteristic of the RAF's disdain for regulations and a tendency toward general raffishness. The squadron commander, Douglas Bader, stands in the center in the dark flight suit and checked scarf. Despite the loss of both legs in a prewar accident, Bader was an outstanding pilot and air leader. (Imperial War Museum)

Edgar J. "Cobber" Kain, a New Zealander and colorful pilot. The first British ace of the war, Kain died during the Battle for France while buzzing his own airfield. (Imperial War Museum)

makeshift fields such as were available in France. So the Spitfire was saved for actions above and around Britain itself. Although the Spitfire acquired more fame during the Battle of Britain—possibly because of its name and graceful appearance—it was outnumbered about two to one by the Hurricane at the climax of the fighting. Unlike the Hurricane, the Spitfire was of all-metal construction; like the Hurricane, it was highly maneuverable and flexible so that it could be modified throughout the war's duration to counter new improvements in German fighter planes.

From tip to tip, the wing of the Spitfire measured thirty-six feet, ten inches. (Some, the so-called clipped-wing Spitfires, had thirty-foot spreads.) Fuselage length was twenty-nine feet, eleven inches. The armament varied from mark to mark, ranging from eight machine guns to four twenty-millimeter cannons. These were installed in such a way that the stream of fire converged at a point a certain distance in front of the plane. The impact of this fusillade striking an enemy plane was devastating, as the Luftwaffe bomber pilots especially learned during the battle.

The top speed of the Spitfire, which varied from mark to mark, was about 355 miles per hour. This placed it at a slight disadvantage when contending with the faster Me-109s. However, the Spitfire operated better at the higher altitudes, where much

Brenden "Paddy" Finucane, Irish air leader, who was lost when his Spitfire, hit by ground fire, fell into the English Channel. (Imperial War Museum)

of the Battle of Britain took place. The Messerschmitt handled clumsily at too high an altitude, while the Spitfire retained control and maneuverability. In the battle there was a general division of labor: The slower, more vulnerable Hurricanes attended to the German bombers, while the Spitfire dealt with the fighters. RAF philosophy frowned upon the old World War I dogfighting techniques. What was important was to stop the German bombers from striking their targets, not to accumulate "kill" scores and acedom. The major concern during the Battle of Britain was not the shortage of aircraft, for British factories were producing Hurricanes and Spitfires faster than the Germans could destroy them. The problem was a

Peter Townsend, sporting a "Mae West"; Townsend shot down the first German aircraft that fell over Britain in February 1940; during the Battle of Britain he became an ace. (Imperial War Museum)

Adolf G. "Sailor" Malan, South African air leader and ace. (Imperial War Museum)

Alan C. Deere, the indomitable New Zealand ace (twenty-two victories) and survivor of many air encounters during the Battle of Britain. (Imperial War Museum)

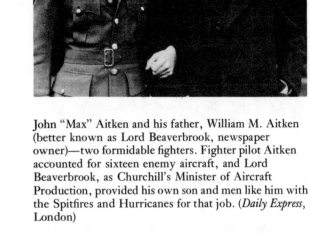

John "Max" Aitken and his father, William M. Aitken (better known as Lord Beaverbrook, newspaper owner)—two formidable fighters. Fighter pilot Aitken accounted for sixteen enemy aircraft, and Lord Beaverbrook, as Churchill's Minister of Aircraft Production, provided his own son and men like him with the Spitfires and Hurricanes for that job. (*Daily Express*, London)

Hawker Hurricanes of No. 245 Squadron awaiting the word for takeoff to intercept German bomber formations. The four round circles in the inboard section of the wing indicate the position of the machine guns, eight in all. An enemy plane caught in the convergence suffered great damage. (Imperial War Museum)

Supermarine Spitfire, one of the outstanding fighter aircraft of the war. AV-R was a Spitfire Mark Vb flown by the famous Eagle Squadron (No. 121), whose membership was made up of American volunteers. The underside shot is of a later Mark XIV; two twenty-mm. cannons project from the wings. The Spitfire in a landing run, with flaps down, is the earlier Mark IIa. It took a skilled pilot to handle the Spitfire; the narrow landing-gear tread frequently led to ground loops or landing accidents on bumpy airfields. (Imperial Air Museum/U. S. Air Force/Imperial War Museum)

lack of pilots, the difficulty of replacing men lost in combat or those who grew fatigued in the daily fighting. Hitler never knew how close he came to winning the Battle of Britain.

As important a weapon as the RAF eight-gun fighters were the radar towers that stretched along the southeastern coast of England. When German bombers and fighters began forming up over France for a raid, the fact was immediately indicated upon the radar screens in the various fighter stations in England. Thus it was possible to meet the German formations over England without the necessity of time-consuming, tiring, and fuel-wasting patrols. Although this did not work with absolute perfection, it worked so well that the German bombers especially suffered terribly during the early—daylight—phase of the Battle of Britain. When the Luftwaffe planned a concentrated attack upon the radar installations, Göring did not believe it was worth the effort. It was another of his major blunders of the war.

The main Luftwaffe target during the first phase of the Battle of Britain was the RAF, either in the air, on the ground, in attacks upon airdromes, or in strikes on factories that contributed to the manufacturing of aircraft. Factories were, of course, situated near cities, towns, and villages. It was in these that it was learned what war from the air could mean. Luton, just northwest of London,

Not-so-secret weapons, radar towers that detected German formations over France and tracked them until British fighters, also aided by the radar, intecepted. (Imperial War Museum)

produced aircraft, tanks, and—its most staple product—hats. German bombing, ironically, did more damage to Luton's hat industry than to those industries contributing directly to the war. Luton lay near the extreme range of the German bombers and especially of the fighters. Having crossed the Channel and southern England, the German planes had little fuel reserve for maneuvering, for fighting, and for getting back across England with its dozens of nests of unmerciful fighters—and, worst of all, for crossing the hated English Channel, whose waters swallowed up many a German plane and crew. Civilians and their homes were attacked as often by accident as design when German bomber crews, harried by British fighters, simply jettisoned their bombs and fled for France. These bombs often fell harmlessly into open fields or, with tragic consequences, into dwellings and city streets.

During August 1940, the Luftwaffe concentrated its efforts against the RAF, which despite the advantage of fighting over its home grounds, had begun to wear down under the constant action. The main objectives had been the airfields of southern England, then came the factories, and then London itself. The first bombing of London had been made in error in the night of August 24–25. The British retaliated with a raid on Berlin; the Germans reretaliated with the first full-scale attack upon London on September 7, 1940. A force of about three hundred bombers escorted by six hundred fighters carried out the attack—among them the vulnerable Dornier 17. This marked the opening of unrestricted warfare upon cities—and on noncombatants, the people of Britain and Germany. The Dornier was a veteran aircraft dating back to the Spanish Civil War. Rather slow (270 miles per hour), it was weak in defensive armament and vulnerable to attack from below and the stern. The switch away from the RAF airfields (Göring, according to reports of his intelligence sources, was certain practically all of Fighter Command had been wiped out) hoped to serve a threefold purpose: to put the finishing touches to the RAF, to sow confusion in the British capital for the coming German invasion

Bomb damage to a dwelling in Luton after a German bombing raid. (Home Counties Newspapers Ltd.)

Overture to the Blitz: Dornier 17s over London's Royal Victoria Docks, September 7, 1940 (lower left). The switch in targets, from RAF installations to the cities, made it possible for an almost exhausted RAF to recuperate. (Imperial War Museum)

("Operation Sea Lion"), and to avenge the bombing of Berlin.

On September 15, 1940, the Germans massed one of their largest daylight raids of the battle, more than two hundred bombers and seven hundred fighters (an admission that the bombers suffered at the hands of the RAF). Göring hoped to deal a deathblow to Fighter Command. Instead, the Luftwaffe suffered one of its greatest defeats. The RAF, which, according to Göring's intelligence sources, supposedly no longer existed, came up in force. (Göring's sources lacked accurate figures of fighter production, and they took at face value the claims of gunners who were certain they had destroyed British planes.) This day, called "The Greatest Day" at the time, the RAF claimed the destruction of nearly two hundred German aircraft (the actual figure was sixty) at a cost of twenty-six Hurricanes and Spitfires (thirteen of whose pilots survived). The losses suffered by the Luftwaffe during August and September brought about yet another switch in strategy: the night bombing of population centers—and the postponement of "Sea Lion." Though no one in the German camp cared to admit it, the Luftwaffe had lost the Battle of Britain, the first true airwar in history. London and other English cities suffered from German night attacks, during the period they called the "Blitz." Although they caused great damage and suffering among the civilians, the night attacks were not militarily decisive. Eventually Hitler lost interest in the Blitz and turned his attention to the Soviet Union. The men of the RAF had for the first time stopped Hitler.

Barrage balloons such as were used during the First World War proved valuable during the Second. For a time, during the Blitz particularly, balloons were practically the only night defense that London had. High above the city, they were hazardous to attacking German planes. Their cables could foul an engine by catching the propeller, slicing off a wing, or damaging the plane in some other way. To deal with barrage balloons, the Germans devised a cable-cutting gadget that was attached to the leading edge of a Heinkel 111. This plane, theoretically, would precede the bombers, clearing the skies of balloon cables. The theory in practice did not always work. There were, of

London smoldering after a German bomber attack. (National Archives)

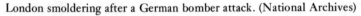

In wartime almost all thought concentrates on the military. Civil aircraft are finished in warpaint and converted to military use. This de Havilland Moth evolved out of one of the most popular British light planes of the between-the-wars period. In wartime it served as a trainer for the RAF. (U. S. Air Force)

Barrage balloons (and three airships) on display at Goodyear; the balloons were manufactured for the U. S. Army. Similar types were tethered over London to break up German bomber formations. (U. S. Air Force)

He-111 equipped to cut barrage-balloon cables to clear a path for German bombers. This one has been shot down over Britain. This device was tested for the first time by Hanna Reitsch, one of Germany's best pilots. (H. J. Nowarra)

A Bristol Beaufighter in American markings—a tough, versatile aircraft. (U. S. Air Force)

Lockheed Hudsons of Coastal Command on patrol over the Atlantic, hunting submarines. (Lockheed Aircraft)

Prewar Short Sunderland, designed for transatlantic travel, in military markings. The roomy Empire flying boats were capable of wide-ranging flights of up to thirteen hours, were heavily gunned, and carried a two thousand-pound bombload. (Imperial War Museum)

course, other defense methods such as heavy concentrations of antiaircraft guns, and later in the war night fighters equipped with radar, which eventually made even bombing by night a very risky business.

One of the deadliest of night fighters was the Bristol Beaufighter, which became operational in the fall of 1940. With a two-man team—pilot-gunner and radar operator—the twin-engined planes became the chief opponents of the German night bombers. Beaufighters operated also in the Mediterranean against Axis shipping. It was a tough, hard-hitting plane.

The sea, too, was a crucial background. Supplies to Britain from the United States had to be shipped over long, dangerous stretches of the Atlantic through which packs of German submarines roamed. The loss in shipping in the Atlantic was an extremely critical problem. RAF's Coastal Command was employed in long overwater patrols seeking out U-boats to bomb or to locate and keep under observation until surface ships could arrive to drop depth bombs. American-built Lockheed Hudsons were converted for the job of patrol-bombing over the Atlantic. Coastal Command also used the Short Sunderland, which had evolved from the Empire flying boat of the late thirties.

When the Soviet Union, thanks to Hitler, became an ally of Britain in the summer of 1941, Britain shared its war materials (some of it American Lend-Lease supplies) with the Soviets. The supply route through the North Sea was as dangerous as that through the Atlantic, and convoys making this run frequently suffered heavy losses to German bombers. One of the German flying boats that patrolled those waters was the Dornier 18.

The Luftwaffe's first modern radial-engined fighter, designed under the supervision of Kurt Tank, was the Focke-Wulf 190. It was one of the outstanding aircraft of its type of the war. Faster than the Me-109 and its adversaries, the Hurricane and the Spitfire (at least the earlier models), the FW-190 was first used in combat in the late summer of 1941. Employed as a fighter-bomber, the plane would sweep across the English Channel

Fairey Firefly, a two-place shipboard fighter-reconnaissance plane. This is the Mark 4, with clipped wings and radomes for tracking enemy aircraft at night. (U. S. Air Force)

Dornier 18, returned from a patrol over the North Sea. The gunner's exposed position in the flying boat's bow was freezingly uncomfortable. Note engines mounted in a single nacelle back-to-back. (H. J. Nowarra)

Focke-Wulf 190, an effective challenger of the Allied bomber formations. (U. S. Air Force)

from bases in France to make hit-and-run attacks upon English coastal towns. But it was as a fighter that the "Butcher Bird" proved most effective, particularly when sent to intercept the day bombers that began striking inside Germany in 1943. It was armed with both machine guns, on the upper engine cowling, and cannons. Some were even fitted with rocket projectors to fire on large bomber formations during the great air battles that occurred over Germany during the final year of the war. Besides being an excellent aircraft to fly, the FW-190 was also designed for quick mass production.

The plane's major weakness was its limited range which, to some extent, was improved by adding drop tanks for fuel.

Also introduced to battle in the summer of 1941 was the de Havilland Mosquito, another remarkable design. Originally intended as a fast bomber, the Mosquito served also as a fighter, reconnaissance plane, mine layer, and "pathfinder" (a plane that marked the bombing zones for the bombers that followed it to the target area). Wartime restrictions upon construction materials forced de Havilland to use wood in manufacturing the Mosquito.

Not only did this enable the British to produce Mosquitos with materials right at hand in the British Isles, but it also made the plane difficult to pick up on radar. With a maximum speed of more than four hundred miles per hour, the Mosquito was also an elusive target even for German fighters. Power was furnished by two Rolls-Royce Merlin engines (twelve-cylinder, liquid-cooled "V") and carried a crew of two—the pilot and bombardier or photographer, depending upon the plane's mission. The bomber version of the Mosquito carried no guns; its only armament was the bombload. The fighter version was armed with four twenty-millimeter cannons. The first Mosquitos (bomber) went into service with the No. 105 Squadron (whose planes were identified by the letters "GB" on the side of the fuselage). This squadron made several remarkable daylight raids upon such distant targets as the Gestapo headquarters in Oslo, Norway, a diesel engine works in Copenhagen, and the main radio station in Berlin. (This last attack interfered with a speech that was to have been made by Göring.)

While the United States kept an anxious eye on the war in Europe and proceeded to assist Britain and the Soviet Union "short of war," one member of Hitler's Axis, long aggrieved by what it had considered poor treatment in the Pacific, had decided to strike. This was Japan, which on December 7, 1941, unleashed crushing aerial attacks upon American ships anchored in Pearl Harbor, Hawaii. This long-planned but surprise attack, like the Battle of Britain, was carried out by aircraft. With this attack, the war became truly worldwide.

A plane totally unknown to aviation "experts" in the United States was the Aichi Type 99 carrier-based dive bomber (the "Val," according to the American system of code-naming Japanese air-

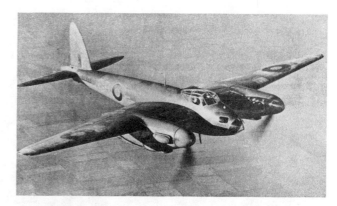

The de Havilland Mosquito—versatile, fast, and deadly. A plane specifically designed for war and one of the most successful. (Imperial War Museum)

A Kate leaving a carrier for Pearl Harbor, December 7, 1941. (National Archives)

A formation of Vals en route to Pearl Harbor. (National Archives)

craft). Although it was designed before the war and had become obsolescent before the war had progressed many months, the Val was a great surprise to Americans when it appeared over Pearl Harbor. It was an efficient dive bomber and, without bombs, remarkably maneuverable for a bomber. A single-engined all-metal monoplane, the Val was' characterized by Stuka-like fixed landing gears. A dorsal fin between the rear of cockpit and the rudder increased stability. Another feature was the dive brakes under the wing. The attack on Pearl Harbor opened with an assault by twenty-five Vals led by Lieutenant Akira Sakamoto.

A Val on the bomb run, with dive brakes down. From a motion-picture film taken by a U. S. Navy photographer. (National Archives)

Japanese photo taken during the Pearl Harbor attack. Battleship Row (foreground) was formed around Ford Island. Torpedoes, just dropped, head for the *West Virginia* and the *Oklahoma*. In the background, aircraft and buildings on Hickam Field burn. (National Archives)

American view, Pearl Harbor, December 7, 1941. A Japanese plane (center, just below white cloud) has made a pass over the submarine base. Black smoke rises over Ford Island's Battleship Row. (National Archives)

The one hitch in the surprisingly successful assault was that the prime targets of the Japanese bombers—the American aircraft carriers—were not in port on the Sunday selected for the opening of the Pacific war. The aircraft carrier, not the venerable battleship, would prove to be decisive in the Pacific sea war.

It was believed, before December 7, 1941, that the Japanese had no first-line aircraft, especially no fighter plane worthy of the name. This false notion was shattered at Pearl Harbor with the perfor-

mance of the Mitsubishi Type 0 carrier-based fighter—the infamous Zero (or "Zeke" in the more or less official code). At Pearl Harbor and in the fighting in the Pacific for the following half year or so, the Zero Sen (fighter) proved to be more than a match for Allied aircraft, such as the P-40, the P-39, and the Hurricane, and it was a close match for the U. S. Navy's F4F (Wildcat). The Zero was light and fast and highly maneuverable. It took some time before Allied pilots learned not to dogfight with it. The heavier, sturdier American planes eventually proved that they could outfight the Zero in a hit-and-run type of battle. American pilots also learned that should the battle become too hot, it was possible to dive away from the Zero at high speed; the flimsier Zero could not follow. In the early months of the war the Zero legend grew out of proportion to the facts. It was a formidable craft in the hands of veteran pilots, but it was also easily ignited by the heavy-gunned American and

Mystery ship: Americans were not aware of the existence of the Japanese Zero at the time of Pearl Harbor, nor of the flying capabilities of Japanese pilots. Planes in the photo show two captured Zekes, the later model of the Zero. (Imperial War Museum)

British fighters. The plane also carried little armor protection for the pilot. Also, attempts at installing leakproof fuel tanks were not very successful, and the plane was highly susceptible to fire.

The Japanese lost only 29 planes during the Pearl Harbor attack (compared with the nearly 200 American, both Army and Navy, planes destroyed or seriously damaged). The raid afforded Americans the first real look at Zeros and Kates. The Kate, an all-metal monoplane, was the first Japanese service aircraft to be equipped with a hydraulically operated retractable landing gear. (Many early planes required retraction of the gear by hand from the cockpit, a wearying and inefficient method.) Kates were equipped with a bombsight on the upper front fuselage, and a modern variable-pitch three-bladed propeller; the engine was a nine-cylinder air-cooled Nakajima Hikari radial. Kates accounted for most of the strikes upon American battleships at Pearl Harbor. The Navy lost ninety-two planes in the attack, most of them on the ground. Very few American planes were able to get into the air during the attack, and most of those that did were obsolescent or in need of repair. The fighters were generally annihilated by the Zero.

Other than a heavy loss of life (2,403 killed), the greatest blow at Pearl Harbor was the virtual destruction of the American Pacific Fleet—eighteen ships were either sunk or seriously damaged (enough to require months of work to restore them to serviceability again). The greatest loss of life resulted when the battleship *Arizona* blew up (with about half of the total casualties). The Japanese attackers concentrated on military installations such as Battleship Row near Ford Island and the various air bases near Pearl Harbor and other locations on Oahu—including Wheeler, Kaneohe and Ewa fields. Damage to the city of Honolulu resulted almost entirely from American antiaircraft fire that went astray during the confusion of battle.

When the United States entered the war, the U. S. Army Air Corps had two operational fighters with which to stand off the Zero. The Bell P-39, with its thirty-seven-millimeter gun mounted in the nose (and firing through the propeller spinner),

Shambles. The Ford Island Naval Air Station hangar burns. Wings of burned-out PBYs litter the ground. (National Archives)

seemed to be a formidable plane, but it lacked maneuverability and was handicapped by an inability to fight at the higher altitudes at which the Zero could operate. During the war the Bell Airacobra proved to be an effective ground-support plane for both American pilots and later the Soviets. The Soviets liked the plane, but American pilots preferred other fighters and nicknamed the plane the "Klunker." Klunkers operated with distinction during the battle for Guadalcanal later in the war.

The second Air Corps fighter is use at the time of Pearl Harbor was the Curtiss-Wright P-40 which, like the P-39, was designed around the Allison in-line, liquid-cooled engine. Already obsolescent (in its earlier models) in 1941, the P-40 bore the brunt of the first days of fighting (it was used also by the British and the French). Various modifications were made on the P-40 during the war (after it had

A lesson in air power. A handful of Japanese carrier-borne aircraft crippled the U. S. Pacific fleet in one brief (and unexpected) attack. Luckily no American carriers were at Pearl Harbor during the attack. (National Archives)

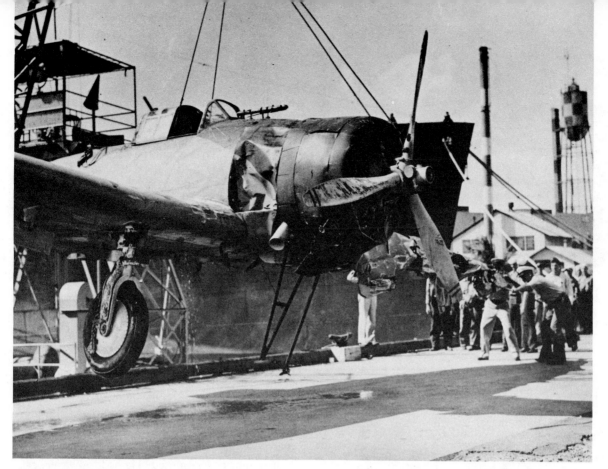

One of the few Japanese aircraft lost in the Pearl Harbor attack. A Kate has just been lifted out of the bay. (National Archives)

Bell P-39 Airacobras, which, as fighters, were outmatched by the more nimble Zero. (U. S. Air Force)

been tested in combat, and to some extent, found wanting), and it passed through various models. The first war model was the P-40B, which gained fame before and after Pearl Harbor as the fighter of the American Volunteer Group, the "Flying Tigers" in Burma and China. Despite the legends, the Flying Tigers did not encounter the Japanese until after December 7, 1941. Once tactics had been evolved, most of them first by the Flying Tigers under the command of General Claire Chennault, it was learned that the Zero was not invincible and that the tougher American planes could be handled in such a way as to exploit their advantages—more weight, more armament, greater diving speed—to win in air combat against the Japanese. The American popular name for the P-40 was Warhawk; the British called it the Kittyhawk.

The U. S. Navy's standard carrier-based fighter was the Grumman F4F Wildcat. This was the

The P-40, an earlier model of which was operational at the time of Pearl Harbor. Although not as maneuverable as the Zero, the P-40 was a more rugged airplane and, in the right hands, could deal with the Japanese fighter. Model depicted is the P-40N of 1943. (U. S. Air Force)

Grumman F4F-3 Wildcat; none participated in the Pearl Harbor battles. Marine Wildcats at Ewa Field were destroyed on the ground, and the Navy F4Fs were at sea aboard the *Lexington*, *Enterprise*, and *Saratoga* at the time of the attack. (Defense Department Photo)

North American B-25 Mitchell, a medium bomber that was used to carry out the famous Doolittle Tokyo raid. Mitchells were used in all war theaters and were one of the outstanding aircraft in their class. (North American Aviation)

Navy's first monoplane shipboard fighter, and it first saw action as early as 1940 as the Martlet with the British Royal Navy Fleet Air Arm Squadron No. 804. A Martlet, piloted by a member of the No. 804 Squadron, was the first American plane to shoot down a German plane (a Ju-88 over Scapa Flow on Christmas Day 1940). A prewar design, the Wildcat had many shortcomings in terms of speed, rate of climb, and maneuverability, which made it a none too effective opponent of the Zero. But as they had with the P-40, pilots developed tactics to get around the deficiencies and used the Wildcat's superior firepower, its ruggedness, and armor protection to combat the Zero. Operating from carriers and from shore bases by both Navy and Marine pilots, the Wildcat, despite its handicaps, helped to smash the legend of the Zero—particularly in the skies over Guadalcanal.

Following the Pearl Harbor attack, Japanese forces appeared to "run wild" in the Pacific just as the chief planner of the attack, Admiral Isoroku Yamamoto, had promised. He had, however, cautioned the warlords that he could promise a series of victories for only about six months. Then, he feared, American industrial potential would begin to be felt by way of a stream of aircraft, ships, guns, and other war materials. The Japanese overran British, Dutch, and American possessions in the Pacific in a dreary, morale-wearying succession of victories. While the Allies fought holding battles or simply lost them, a plan for striking back at Japan was made. This was the raid on Tokyo and other key Japanese cities led by the ex-racing pilot, Lieutenant Colonel James Doolittle. Since there were no Allied bases close enough to Japan from which a strike could be made, the idea came up to use medium bombers (that is, smaller bombers with two engines of lesser range and bombload capability than the "heavy" four-engined bomber), and to launch them from an aircraft carrier. This was a daring plan and, of course, was carried out with courage if minor military result. But it did place the Japanese on edge because it showed that the Americans were capable of striking Japan itself. The plane Doolittle had chosen for this unique mission was the North American B-25 Mitchell. It was not designed for taking off from a short carrier deck, but by careful training, crews were able to do this. All sixteen B-25s took off from the carrier *Hornet*. (The Hornet was referred to as the mysterious "Shangri-la," for it was difficult for the Japanese to conceive of a bomber, even a medium, taking off from a carrier; only some mysterious land base seemed feasible for this feat.) Although it did no great damage, and all B-25s eventually were lost, the Doolittle raid accomplished much for American morale and so disconcerted the Japanese High Command that, despite arguments to the contrary, a decision was made to meet the Americans in a great air and sea battle at Midway.

Within four days of Pearl Harbor, Germany and Hitler, in keeping with their promise to Japan, declared war on the United States. The Allied High Command almost immediately agreed that Germany was the major enemy and that concentration of American effort in conjunction with Britain would be upon Germany. The only way to reach German war production centers, until France could be invaded by the Allies, was by aircraft, specifically the heavy bomber. The RAF's first, and for a time only, four-engined heavy bomber was the Short Stirling, with a wingspread of precisely ninety-nine feet, 1 inch (so that it would fit into the RAF hangers at the time!). It was a little more than eighty-seven feet in length. The Stirling's curiously small wing as compared with its long body endowed the bomber with unusual maneuverability for a plane of its size; but it also handicapped the plane's ability to carry heavy bombloads and limited its ceiling. Still, it was the first RAF aircraft to carry the war to the Germans, and what with its agility and bristling guns (in nose, tail, and upper dorsal turrets) could bomb the industrial Ruhr and take care of itself in battle. Though slower than subsequent British heavies, the Stirling proved itself from 1941 until 1944, when it was withdrawn from operations. It was one of the planes that took part in the famous "thousand bomber" raid on Cologne (May 30, 1942), in which literally a thousand British bomb-

The RAF's first heavy bomber, the Short Stirling; the wing design was determined by the size of the RAF's hangars at the time. The low aspect ratio of the wing (the relationship between chord and span) limited the ceiling of the Stirling, a handicap for a bomber. (Imperial War Museum)

ers of every description proved to Hitler that the British were not beaten.

The outstanding RAF heavy bomber of the war was the Avro Lancaster, a plane that began its

Avro Lancaster, the finest British heavy bomber of the war, Bomber Command's backbone during the most furious months of the war. (Imperial War Museum)

operational life as a twin-engined medium bomber (the Manchester) and that eventually was modified into the four-engined Lancaster. Four Rolls-Royce Merlin engines were substituted for the original (and at the time unreliable) Vultures. The wings stretched to a span of 102 feet, and the fuselage was 68 feet, 9 inches long. Despite its size, according to its pilots, the Lancaster was an easy plane to fly, and it could carry massive bombloads into Germany—even as far as Berlin. The Lancaster was capable of carrying the giant 22,000-pound-bomb ("Grand Slam"), the heaviest bomb used during the war. One of the Lancaster's most famous raids was led by Guy Gibson upon a complex of dams in the Ruhr—the "dam busters" mission of May 17, 1943. Using modified Lancasters that carried specially designed bombs, Gibson's crews breached two of the three dams they set out to destroy and flooded the countryside, disrupting German industries in the Ruhr for weeks. A Lancaster also sank the elusive German battleship *Tirpitz*.

American heavy-bomber theory was represented primarily by the Boeing B-17 Flying Fortress, the design of which had been modified somewhat from the early B-17 of the thirties. Early combat experience by the British, and later combat in the Pacific shortly after the Pearl Harbor attack, revealed that

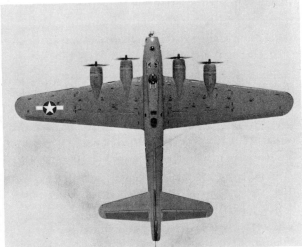

Perhaps the most glamorous heavy bomber of the war, the Boeing B-17 Flying Fortress, with which the American Eighth Air Force initiated its daylight bombing missions on German-held targets. Without fighter escorts even the B-17s suffered great losses under Luftwaffe attacks. The ability of the Fortress to absorb heavy punishment and to continue flying despite serious battle damage made it a favorite among B-17 crews. (The Boeing Company)

some changes would have to be made in order for the plane to be a true flying fortress. One of the most important modifications was the addition of a "stinger in the tail," two fifty-caliber machine guns operated by a tail gunner. There were gun positions also in the fuselage sides, in the belly turret just below the U.S. insignia, and in the top turret behind the cockpit. The radio operator also manned guns from his post from the top of the midfuselage. The B-17E, though formidable, was still a bit weak in firepower in the nose. An increase in the tail surface, plus dorsal fin, improved stability for accurate bomb runs.

The American heavies were designed for high-altitude precision bombing in daylight. The British, having seen how the Luftwaffe suffered during its day raids, preferred bombing at night, which made it more difficult for Luftwaffe fighters to attack the bomber streams. U. S. Air Force commanders contended that such bombing was not necessarily accurate (and it was not) and wasted bombs and German civilian lives. When losses of American bombers grew during the early phases of the bomber campaign, there was always the possibility that daylight bombing would have to be canceled. The argument about day vs. night bombing was the most serious one between British and American airmen. Eventually it was agreed that the RAF would bomb by night and the U. S. Army Air Forces by day.

The second great American heavy bomber was the Consolidated B-24 Liberator, which evolved somewhat later than the B-17. With a wingspan of 110 feet (as compared to the 103.9 feet of the Fortress), the Liberator had the advantage of range over its companion heavy. This made it an especially effective plane for the Pacific theater, where long-distance flights over water were normal daily occurrences. Although the B-24 did not enjoy the fame that the Flying Fortress did, it too was a fine aircraft, although it was not quite as easy to fly as the B-17, partly because of its long, narrow wing. Nor could it fly quite as high as the B-17. On the other hand, the B-24 could carry larger bombloads. Each aircraft had its own special qualities and, combined

B-24 Liberator, the Liberator II in British markings. These were used by the RAF in Coastal Command operations because of the Liberator's great flying range—and because the British did not believe in daytime bombing, for which the B-24, like the B-17, had been designed. In American markings, the B-24J was an excellent warplane. (Author's Collection)

with British aircraft, brought the horrors of modern war to German industrial cities. Like the B-17, the B-24 underwent modifications throughout its operational life. The British Liberator II was an early model roughly similar to the B-24A and was used widely by RAF Coastal Command for overwater flights, sub hunting, transport, and various other chores. A later model, the B-24J, was the more formidable bomber, fitted with power turrets in the nose and tail and a top turret behind the cockpit.

More B-24Js were built than any other model of the Liberator; it was known as the Liberator B to the RAF and the PB4Y-1 to the U. S. Navy. More B-24s, incidentally, were built than any other American warplane.

Liberator and Fortress crewmen continue to argue as to which plane was superior (and B-24 men believe the B-17s got the better press during the war—and still do). The B-24 had a greater range and could carry a heavier bombload than the B-17, but could not fly at the 17's ceiling (out of reach of anything but the most accurate flak); ditching in a B-24 was more hazardous than in the B-17 because of the B-24's high wing and the exposed bomb bay. And some pilots say the B-24 burned easier.

While the Allies amassed their heavy-bomber strength in Britain for the coming offensive against Germany, the Pacific fighting continued, with the Japanese invariably victorious. General Douglas MacArthur had been driven out of the Philippines and had established himself in Australia. From

B-17s of General Kenny's Fifth Air Force attacking Japanese installations during the early phase of the Pacific war. In time the B-24 replaced the Fortresses because the B-17s were needed in Europe. (The Boeing Company)

there he directed the beginnings of the Allied counterattacks against the Japanese in the Southwest Pacific. His air commander was General George C. Kenney, a tough, imaginative airman. Kenney had little to work with when he assumed command of MacArthur's air force (the Fifth Air Force eventually), and a formation of a half-dozen B-17s in 1942 was considered quite large (in Europe fifty or a hundred, and later a thousand, was a normal formation). Zero pilots were wary of the big B-17, although they destroyed many in the early weeks of the war. These were generally the early B-17Ds, which had no tail stinger. When the B-17Es arrived, although not in great numbers, the Zeros were less aggressive in their attacks upon the Fortresses.

The most expansive battleground of the Pacific lay in the skies above water, and this was the province of the U. S. Navy with the aid of British—Australian, New Zealand, English—and Dutch men-o'-war. But the real ruler of the seas was the aircraft carrier, and eventually, battles among ships occurred in which the ships themselves never exchanged a shot. The fighting was done by carrier-based aircraft. One of the most decisive battles of the war in the Pacific was fought from June 3 to June 6, 1942, at Midway. This was the battle that the Japanese hoped would bring out American

Carriers, not battleships, dominated the way of war in the Pacific. Carrier planes, as Billy Mitchell had maintained years before, did sink battleships—and enemy carriers. This photograph was taken during the critical Battle of Midway, June 1942. The *Yorktown* is under attack by Japanese aircraft; black smoke puffs are anti-aircraft fire. The *Yorktown* was lost at Midway—but the Japanese lost four carriers, a blow from which its Navy would never fully recover. (Navy Department, National Archives)

A Marine Brewster F2A Buffalo, no match for the Zero. (Defense Department Photo)

ships in great numbers to be destroyed by an overwhelming force of battleships and aircraft carriers. The Japanese lost four carriers in the Battle of Midway.

Courage was a common quality on both sides in the Battle of Midway, but Marines in such obsolete aircraft as the Brewster Buffalo flew to almost certain death. No match for the Zero, the Buffalo was shot out of the skies as Marine pilots attempted to stop Japanese bombers headed for Midway atoll. Thirteen out of the total of twenty-one of the F2As (as they were known officially) were wiped out in the first encounter with the Japanese. The Marine Wildcats fared somewhat better; the Buffalo had no chance—nor did the pilot who flew it. After the Battle of Midway one Marine captain said: "It is my belief that any commander who orders pilots out for combat in an F2A should consider the pilot lost before leaving the ground."

Grumman TBF Avenger, which made an unfortunate battle debut at Midway. In time it would prove itself, however. (National Archives)

The Grumman TBF (Torpedo Bomber) Avenger made its combat debut at Midway. Six Midway-based Navy Avengers set out for the Japanese fleet approaching the island. Only one returned, and that one was badly shot up by Japanese antiaircraft fire. Not one of the Avengers broke through the heavy screen of fire to hit any of the Japanese ships with their torpedoes. Despite this inauspicious battle debut, the Avenger became a standard Navy torpedo bomber. It was used also as a dive bomber, as well as a conventional level bomber, and operated from carriers and land bases. Originally designed for a three-man crew—pilot, rear gunner, and gunner in a bulge in the lower fuselage—the plane was manned by two in its later modifications (the lower gun turret was eliminated). The Avenger was also used by the British Fleet Air Arm. Wingspan was fifty-four feet, two inches; overall fuselage length was forty feet, eleven and a half inches. The TBF carried a twenty-one-inch torpedo in its fuselage or four five hundred-pound bombs. The wings folded back for storage on carriers.

Dauntlesses on a carrier deck in the Pacific. (Douglas Aircraft)

Both tragedy and triumph merged in the story of the men who flew the Douglas SBDs, the Dauntless, in the Battle of Midway. Wave after wave of the carrier-based Scout bombers were eliminated by Zeros and Japanese antiaircraft fire before the battle suddenly turned. Out of the fifty-one Dauntlesses (including some that operated from Midway), forty-two were destroyed in the fighting. However, during the height of the battle Dauntlesses from the *Enterprise* and the *Yorktown* came upon the Japanese carriers while the planes were on decks being armed for a strike upon American carriers. Dauntlesses broke through the heavy fire, and soon four of Japan's finest carriers—*Akagi*, *Kaga*, *Hiryu* and *Soryu*—had become blazing wrecks. Fuel and bombs in the Japanese planes on the decks added to the inferno. In six minutes the tide of war in the Pacific had changed; the power of the Japanese fleet, its aircraft-carrier strength, was broken. More than three hundred Japanese planes of all descriptions— and their experienced pilots—were lost either during combat or when their home carriers sank into the Pacific. It was a loss from which Japan never recovered, and although the war did not end at Midway, the ultimate end was obvious. Japan could never have won the war in the Pacific after Midway.

A side issue to the air fighting in the Pacific was the problem of what to do when your carrier had been attacked and the deck was damaged or burning when you returned shot up and short of fuel. The solution was to splash into the sea as close as possible to a friendly ship and await rescue. Several such splashes were made at Midway, especially after the *Yorktown* had been bombed by the Japanese. Although the plane was lost, the crew was saved and could fight again. Japanese pilots at Midway were not so fortunate.

The Japanese suffered another serious, though perhaps not so spectacular loss during the Midway operations. While the major elements of the Japanese fleet concentrated on Midway, another made a feint into the Aleutians, hoping to lure the American ships away from Midway. Although this minor action was successful and Japanese troops actually landed in the Aleutians, it contributed little to

Douglas SBDs on patrol with Task Force 58 in the Pacific, during the Marshall Islands campaign. (Douglas Aircraft)

Japanese victory. It was in the Aleutians that the Americans were able to salvage a nearly intact Zero, which had been flown by pilot Tadayoshi Koga, from the marshes of Akutan Island. Koga had mistaken the marsh for solid ground and flipped the plane over on landing, breaking his neck. The Zero was carefully packed, shipped to the United States, repaired, flown, and studied, and then a new plane—the Grumman F6F Hellcat—was specifically designed to outperform the Zero.

Two months after Midway the Marines, still

Dauntless in flight. Gunner covered the tail and flanks. A total of 5,936 Dauntlesses were built; by July 21, 1944, they were withdrawn from combat and replaced by the Curtiss Helldiver. (Douglas Aircraft)

A Dauntless ditches in the Pacific alongside a friendly vessel for rescue. The SBD had returned to the *Yorktown* after a bombing run at Midway to find that the home carrier was aflame. (Navy Department National Archives)

The Japanese cruiser *Mogami*, a shambles after Navy planes had attacked it at Midway. Air power was supreme in the Pacific. (Navy Department, National Archives)

flying Wildcats, proved that the Zero was not the unconquerable plane that post-Pearl Harbor legend had painted. Operating out of Guadalcanal in the Solomon Islands during the late summer of 1942 and the winter of the same year and into 1943, Marines, in co-operation with Air Force fighters (including the P-39 "Klunker"), fought off the Zeros sent to protect Japanese ships attempting to reinforce Japanese troops on Guadalcanal, or that made life a horror for the Marines stationed on Guadalcanal in bombing missions. Marines flying Wildcats took to the air to spoil the legend of the Zero.

Although the aircraft carrier dominated the war in the Pacific and although Japan had lost heavily at Midway, waging the war in the Pacific in 1942 was not a simple matter for the Allies. The American carrier *Wasp*, for example, was torpedoed off Guadalcanal on September 15, 1942. The tide had reversed, but the battle was not over. The Japanese did not abandon Guadalcanal until February 1943, a concession of defeat unusual for them. A month later, in a sequel to Midway (though not on as large

End of a legend: the virtually intact Zero that the hapless pilot Koga attempted to land on Akutan Island in the Aleutians, the diversionary sideshow planned to coincide with Midway. (Navy Department National Archives)

Grumman F4F—the Wildcat—in a revetment at a Marine base in the Pacific. Revetments protected aircraft from strafing attacks. (Marine Corps/Defense Department)

The *Wasp* burning during the fighting around Guadalcanal, September 15, 1942. (Navy Department National Archives)

a scale), land-based aircraft of Kenney's Fifth Air Force destroyed a convoy attempting to reinforce Japanese troops in New Guinea, revealing the ultimate truth of the war: Whoever ruled the air controlled the sea—and the ground.

By the spring of 1943 fairly good numbers of the Lockheed P-38 Lightning began arriving in the Pacific. Designed as a high-altitude interceptor, the big and unusual single-seat, twin-boomed fighter distinguished itself on practically all battlefronts. (It had made its combat debut in the fighting over North Africa in the winter of 1942; the Germans

called it *der Gabelschwanz Teufel* (forked-tail devil). The P-38 was Lockheed's first military design that was initiated to produce an interceptor capable of more than 350 miles per hour at twenty thousand feet. Its twin-boomed configuration made it possible to install heavy armament in the nose of the fuselage pod: four fifty-caliber machine guns and a twenty-millimeter cannon. The P-38 was one of the few successful twin-engined fighters of the war, an added advantage being that the extra engine endowed the plane with extended range (1,500 miles) and extra life should one of the engines (Allisons) be shot out in combat. This made it an especially popular aircraft in the Pacific, and although heavier and less agile than the Zeros, its high speed (eventually more than 400 miles per

Lockheed P-38 Lightnings, one of the heaviest fighter planes of the war. (Lockheed Aircraft)

hour), rate of climb, and range made it a deadly adversary of the Zero as well as of Japanese bombers.

A versatile aircraft, the P-38 also operated as a photo-reconnaissance plane and a bomber. One of the greatest single missions carried out by P-38 pilots was that of the 339th Fighter Squadron, which flew a remarkable close-to-the-water flight of some 550 miles from their base at Guadalcanal to intercept a Japanese transport carrying Japan's great war leader, Yamamoto. With the aid of drop tanks for extra range, the men of the 339th intercepted Yamamoto's plane precisely on schedule and shot it down. The loss of Yamamoto was as great a blow to the Japanese as the loss of Guadalcanal and the disaster at Midway.

The highest-scoring P-38 ace and top-scoring American fighter pilot of the Second World War was Richard Ira Bong of Poplar, Wisconsin. By the war's end, Bong had shot down forty enemy aircraft. He was then taken out of combat by the Fifth Air Force's General Kenney to keep him from being worn out. Thus Bong was able to pass on to student pilots his knowledge of the P-38 and how to fight the Japanese. Though he survived his various air battles, Richard Bong was killed while testing a new jet plane near Los Angeles shortly before the war ended. Bong's closest rival, also a P-38 pilot, was Thomas McGuire, Jr., who destroyed 38 enemy aircraft before he died over Leyte in the Philippine Islands. McGuire had gone to the aid of a friend in combat and did not have

The business end of a P-38; such heavy gunfire could shatter the more flimsy Zero. (Lockheed Aircraft)

Major Richard Bong, P-38 ace of the Pacific, during an interview by the press in New Guinea. (U. S. Air Force)

time to release his drop tank; this caused the P-38 to go out of control and spin into the ground.

Early in 1943 a new Navy and Marine fighter plane appeared in the skies over Guadalcanal, the Chance Vought F4U Corsair. It was the heaviest (8,873 pounds), largest (wingspan of forty feet, eleven inches) fighter designed for operation from carrier decks. Powered by a Pratt & Whitney Double (eighteen-cylinder) Wasp engine, the Corsair was capable of speeds in excess of four hundred miles per hour. To allow for clearance of the large propeller (thirteen feet, three inches in diameter), inverted gull wings raised the nose of the plane high in the air even when on the ground. It was the first plane introduced into the Pacific that outmatched the Zero on practically every point of performance. Mainly used by Marines—among them Gregory Boyington, Joseph Foss, Marion Carl, Ira Kepford—the Corsair rapidly established its superiority as a fighter in the Pacific. When Marine pilots ran out of opponents in the air, they used the F4U in fighter sweeps on Japanese air bases, which resulted in heavy losses of Japanese aircraft on the ground. Most Marine units were land-based; it was not until the end of 1944 that the U. S. Navy accepted the Corsair for carrier operations (early models had a tendency to bounce upon landing, but these bugs were eventually eliminated).

Despite the Navy's suspicions of the F4U-1, the British employed Corsairs in the Fleet Air Arm a year before they were assigned to American carriers. The plane carried a terrifying punch in the nose and wings—no less than six fifty-caliber machine guns (or else four twenty-millimeter cannons). The Corsair could also be armed with eight five-inch rockets. The plane had a characteristic sound contributed by the powerful engine and the air ducts located in the wings (adjacent to the fuselage). Japanese soldiers, who suffered under its ground attacks, called it Whistling Death. American troops referred to the Corsair as the Bent-winged Bird; later in the war, during the heavy fighting closer to Japan, Marines more affectionately called it the Sweetheart of Okinawa. Pilots who flew the plane considered it the best single-seat fighter of the war of any nation.

The Grumman F6F Hellcat supplanted the Wildcat as the major U. S. Navy carrier plane in the summer of 1943. Although not as fast as the Corsair, with which it frequently co-operated in action (the duo were called the Terrible Twins), the Hellcat was also an unforgiving opponent of the Zero. It was only in maneuverability that the lighter Japanese plane excelled the Hellcat and the Corsair. But both American planes were more rugged, could absorb more battle damage, and provided more armor protection for the pilot. Such protection added weight and interfered with performance to some extent, but it did preserve pilots.

The Japanese used other planes besides the Zero, which appears to dominate the history of the air fighting in the Pacific. The Japanese Army and Navy air forces also used bombers, which dropped heavy loads of bombs on American troops in the Pacific, particularly in the Solomons. (These were mainly Navy bombers, which operated from Rabaul.) Heavy bombloads were also dropped on Australian and American troops fighting in New Guinea.

The replacement for the slower Mitsubishi "Sally" was the Nakajima "Helen," which the Japanese classified as a "heavy bomber," but which, according to Allied reckoning, was a medium. Manned by a crew of eight, the Helen was the first Japanese plane to bomb Darwin, Australia, early in the war. It also came equipped with self-sealing fuel tanks and more than usual Japanese armament for crew protection. It was actually a short-ranged plane and carried a relatively light bombload. It was used against American shipping during the fighting in the Philippines in the later phase of the war.

It was the aim of General Kenney to eliminate Japanese air power from the Southwest Pacific by whatever means he could devise. One of the most fiendish methods was to use what came to be called Kenney Cocktails. It was not necessary to meet with Japanese formations in the air to destroy their planes; it was equally efficient to wreck them on

Vought F4U Corsair, which made its combat debut over Guadalcanal in February 1943. The rugged Corsair was an extraordinary battle plane and operated from carriers as well as land bases. (United Aircraft)

Corsairs warming up for a mission on Majuro airstrip, Marshall Islands. (Navy Department National Archives)

Zero nemesis: Grumman F6F Hellcat, which was designed after the Aleutian Zero was thoroughly studied. (Navy Department National Archives)

Gun camera sequence records the end of a Zero. A Fifth Air Force fighter pilot jumped the Zeke pilot, who (in the second frame he has dropped his auxiliary fuel tank for more manueverability) makes a tight turn. But the American again gets on the Zeke's tail and sends it down in flames. (U. S. Air Force)

the ground from the air. Kenney's major objective was the great Japanese air bases on Rabaul, New Britain. Kenney's method was to use low-flying medium bombers such as the North American B-25s, with heavy firepower in the nose. These could swoop down on the Japanese positions with forward-firing guns blazing to discourage Japanese antiaircraft opposition. The B-25s would then drop incendiary phosphorus bombs in parachutes. (This would give the B-25s time to get away before the bombs detonated.) The parachute bombs would drift down upon Japanese planes in their revetments (which protected the Japanese planes from conventional bomb blasts). When the bombs struck, the phosphorus sprayed over a large area and, ignited, clung to the metal of planes, burning them up on the ground.

Another Kenney technique for dealing with Japanese shipping was skip bombing. Medium bombers came in upon Japanese transports and supply ships at mast height and dropped bombs into the water some distance from the target. The momentum of the bombs tossed from the plane skipped

Japanese Nakajima Type 100 "heavy" bombers. Code-named Helen by American Intelligence, it was not an exceptional plane. The Helen's chief claim to fame was that it was the first Japanese Army bomber equipped with a tail gun. (Imperial War Museum)

B-25s of the 42nd Bomb Group lined up on a New Guinea airstrip. Heavily armed, they were often used for sudden, low-level attacks on Japanese airfields with devastating results. (U. S. Air Force)

Parafrag bombs descend on the important Japanese airbase at Vunakanau, near Rabaul, New Britain. Parachutes made it possible to place the bombs accurately and gave the bombers, usually B-25s, time to get away before the bombs detonated. Betty bombers are parked in revetments. (U. S. Air Force)

"Kenny Cocktails" fall on a Japanese radio center at Rabaul. The white-phosphorus bombs, upon bursting, blossomed out in several directions and adhered to anything they touched. They burned fiercely and were most destructive to aircraft, buildings, and humans. (U. S. Air Force)

Skip bombing, another method evolved in the Pacific to cripple Japanese shipping. This Douglas A-20 Havoc has just released its two bombs; one of the bombs from the plane preceding it has bounced into the side of the ship. (U. S. Air Force)

them across the surface of the water; they bounced into the side of the ship. This type of bombing called for skill on the part of the pilot and crew and proved a most effective means of cutting off much-needed supplies to the Japanese troops, who were all but completely cut off from their homeland. The disastrous loss of shipping by the Japanese to Kenney's skip bombers had its effect upon the outcome of the fighting in New Guinea. And delivering Kenney Cocktails to Rabaul, followed up by Marine and Navy fighter sweeps, eliminated that threat in the Pacific.

The great stretches of water of the Pacific called for long-range aircraft that could be used to patrol those waters as well as to rescue pilots and seamen— in addition to functioning as bombers. One of the classic planes of this type was the Consolidated-Vultee PBY (Patrol Bomber) Catalina. These great flying boats were widely used over the seas all over the world by the U. S. Navy, as well as by the RAF's Coastal Command. The Catalina was used also for submarine patrol; its slowness (top speed of about 200 miles per hour) rendered it susceptible to enemy fighters. One of the interesting design features of the PBY was the retractable floats, which merged into the wingtip when raised. The wingspan was 104 feet; fuselage length was a little over sixty-three feet. It was manned by a crew of five.

U. S. Navy ships carried their own scout planes, which were catapulted from the decks and then picked up out of the sea on the mission's comple-

A patrol of Consolidated PBY Catalinas over the Pacific. (Navy Department National Archives)

A Catalina after a forced landing; the rescuer rescued. These craft were widely used over the Atlantic and the Pacific. (Navy Department National Archives)

Mission completed, this Vought OS2U Kingfisher is being hoisted aboard its home ship. It will be lowered back onto a catapult for the next scouting mission. (U. S. Navy)

tion. The Chance Vought OS2U (Observer Scout) Kingfisher was also used for spotting for naval gunners. It would fly over an area under naval gunfire, and its radio operator would report on the effect of the shooting. The Kingfisher was a slow plane (its top speed was about 170 miles per hour). Sometimes it was used as a bomber, but its primary mission was observation.

A later flying boat, after the Catalina, was the Martin PBM Mariner, which was slightly larger (span of 118 feet) and faster than the earlier plane. Mariners were used extensively in antisubmarine patrols in the Atlantic, employing radar equipment and depth charges. Mariners could operate at night and even in bad weather. The later models of the plane used nonretractable floats.

The war in the air over Europe required a generally different approach from that in the Pacific. There was a greater emphasis on heavy bombardment, and insofar as it concerned the American effort, this was dependent on the use of the precision Norden bombsight set in the noses of the Fortresses and Liberators based in England, and later (after the "Torch" invasions in November 1942) in North Africa. The first American heavy-bomber mission in Europe took place on August 17, 1942, when a dozen B-17s bombed transportation targets in France. The mission was a success, all aircraft returned, and it appeared that dependence on the Norden sight for accuracy and on the B-17 for self-protection in large formations was sufficiently demonstrated. This continued for several more missions until bad weather interfered—and the Luftwaffe became accustomed to the B-17.

While American air crews gathered in England, American aircraft production geared up to mass production. Near miracles occurred (such as had proved impossible during the First World War) as aircraft manufacturers co-operated in a mighty effort to produce "clouds of airplanes." Some even switched from turning out their own planes to supplying the Air Force and the Navy with planes designed by other companies. To manufacture the much-needed planes, factories were converted (Ford Motors, for example, made B-24s), new fac-

Martin Mariners of two types; the later models (with floats) fly below and behind. (Martin Information Services)

Scene at Lockheed, Burbank, California. Lockheed Hudsons and Lightnings are joined by Lockheed-built Flying Fortresses. (Lockheed Aircraft)

American war plants operated night and day turning out planes, guns, tanks, and other war essentials in wholesale lots. A night-shift scene in the Douglas plant. (Douglas Aircraft)

tories built, and great numbers of planes began to roll off the assembly lines day and night. When Hitler was informed of this, he refused to believe it, dismissing as mere propaganda.

Before aircraft could appear in large numbers and before crews could be qualified to fly them, training missions during 1942–43 were flown over France, North Africa, Italy, and eventually Germany. The winter of 1943 was a hard one for the now combat-ready U. S. Air Force. By October it had suffered terrible losses, generally because of German fighters. The first of three nearly disastrous missions of 1943 took place on August 1, when Liberators based in Libya, North Africa, took off in a daring low-level attack on the Ploesti oil fields in Nazi-held Romania. Human error, heavy German antiaircraft concentrations, and some Luftwaffe fighters took a deadly toll. Of the 177 B-24s which had taken off on the mission, no less than fifty-four were lost. Although courageous crews pressed on through the confusion that had resulted when the mission commander made a wrong turn toward the target, and about 40 per cent of the Ploesti production capacity was knocked out, the refinery was soon back in production. The mission was flown at an unusually low

Ill-fated mission to Ploesti. Despite a last-minute mixup, the mission was completed and the oil installations bombed, but at great cost to the attacking bomber formations flying at an extremely low altitude. (U. S. Air Force)

Survivor: a Liberator of the 376th Bomb Group arrives at Bengasi, Libya, after the long flight to Ploesti, Romania, and back. (U. S. Air Force)

altitude (to elude radar detection) and used bombs with delayed-action fuses. The smoke of fires from bombs dropped by earlier planes (some of which bombed the wrong targets) and the danger of hitting smokestacks were constant dangers to the crews in the B-24s.

From England, about two weeks after the Ploesti raid, the Eighth Air Force made an unusual mission to Germany—a twin-pronged penetration to Regensburg (where German fighters were produced) and to Schweinfurt (where ball bearings so necessary to war machinery were made). The flight to Schweinfurt meant a two hundred-mile trip each way, into enemy-held skies. The Regensburg flight was a hundred miles farther, but the return flight was avoided by having the B-17s continue on to North Africa rather than risk the return through

aroused fighter formations. Both missions took place, but not quite as planned, and German fighters came out in great numbers. The day's total losses amounted to sixty Flying Fortresses, most of them to very heavy German fighter attacks. The Schweinfurt task force was especially hard hit, losing thirty-six planes (and, of course, 360 men). Schweinfurt was a critical target, since half of Germany's ball-bearing production was centered there. Therefore, despite the losses of the August 17 mission, another was mounted on October 14, 1943. Of the 291 Flying Fortresses dispatched, sixty were lost in the massive air battle that took place over Germany. While the generally accurate bombing did not entirely eliminate the factory, the fact that American Fortresses appeared so deep inside Germany in broad daylight forced the Germans to disperse their factories—although they suffered no shortages of ball bearings during the move. They simply bought ball bearings from Sweden and Switzerland. The great losses over Schweinfurt (had they gone on at such a rate for a week, there would have been no Eighth Air Force

The Norden bombsight, designed to make high-level precise bombing a fact. The sight automatically took into account such elements as airspeed, drift, temperature, and—during the bomb run—even controlled the flight of the aircraft. Although its virtues were overtouted, it was an efficient calculator. (United Aircraft)

SCHWEINFURT
14.10.43
Annotated Print Nº I
Neg Nº 30689

left in England) proved that either the daylight bombings had to stop, as the British insisted, or some other means of dealing with the Luftwaffe had to be found.

The business end of a B-17 was also the weak point in the plane's defense. The Luftwaffe fighter pilots in Me-109s and FW-190s quickly learned that a head-on attack upon a Flying Fortress was not only disconcerting to pilot and bombardier, it also attracted less firepower. Attempts to make the nose of the B-17 more potent resulted in the porcupinelike gun emplacement. Even this meant that only one gun could be trained directly ahead. The

Strike photo taken during the costly Schweinfurt mission of October 14, 1943. Scattered bomb holes (to the right of the letter C) would contradict the pickle-barrel accuracy of the Norden bombsight. Much depended on the individual during a bomb run—when flak might be thick, and bombers damaged by German fighters on the approach, with injured aboard the aircraft. (U. S. Air Force)

The chin turret was used in all models of the final B-17, the G. It was also controlled by the bombardier, but was more formidable than the earlier nose armament. (The Boeing Company)

The bombardier in the nose of a B-17 operated any one of three fifty-caliber machine guns, with assistance from the navigator, also stationed in the nose. The flat panel in the nose (with windshield wiper) marks the bombardier's position; the Norden sight was directly above the panel. (U. S. Air Force)

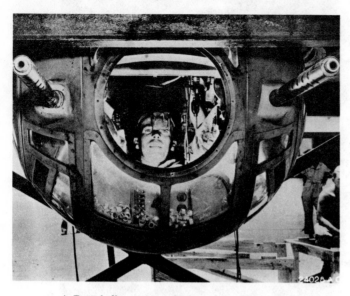

A B-17 belly turret, which projected from under the midfuselage and required a small man with a lot of courage to operate. Electrically operated, the turret had a wide range of fire—front, rear, sides, and down. (U. S. Air Force)

bombardier manned these nose guns, aided by the navigator.

The last wartime Flying Fortress was the B-17G, characterized by the chin turret under the nose in which twin fifty-caliber machine guns were installed. This gun position discouraged Luftwaffe head-on attacks since, in conjunction with the top turret, it could bring four heavy machine guns into action. The B-17G, armed with no less than thirteen machine guns, was one of the most formidable warplanes of its time; it first appeared late in 1942. B-17Gs were produced by Douglas Aircraft, Lockheed Vega, and Boeing.

Although German antiaircraft fire took its toll, it was the fighter that remained the major adversary of Allied heavy bombers. One heavy fighter specifically designed to fight the bombers was the Messerschmitt 410 Hornisse (Hornet), a heavily armed twin-engined fighter, and modification of the failed Me-210. Later models of the plane had rear-firing machine guns installed in the fuselage sides. The Me-410 was also operated as a bomber and for photo-reconnaissance. Despite the increased arma-

ment the Me-410 was outmatched by later Allied fighters, especially the P-51 Mustang.

That precision daylight bombardment was reasonably possible was demonstrated by Ira Eaker's Eighth Air Force when B-17s bombed a Focke-Wulf assembly plant at Marienburg, Germany, on October 10, 1943—just four days before the costly Schweinfurt mission. A high concentration of bombs was placed in the target area, which left factories and other buildings burning along with FW-190s that happened to be in production. On the day of the Marienburg bombing the runway was to have been put into operation with a dedication by Göring himself. The B-17s spoiled the ceremony, along with several aircraft and production facilities.

The ultimate resolution to the high losses of the bomber forces lay in fighters whose range would enable them to escort the B-17s and B-24s to and from the targets. Until such planes arrived, it meant that escort planes had to turn back for England, generally at the most critical point of a mission—when the Allied bomber streams approached Germany, with its dozens of fighter fields within reach. The first Allied plane capable of such missions was the P-38, the Lightning. Most escort work devolved later on groups outfitted with different aircraft. The P-38s, though still operating as fighters, were used most frequently as photo-reconnaissance planes or as fighter-bombers and strafers. As strafers, the big P-38s destroyed trains during the Allied push through France in 1944.

The biggest and heaviest single-engined fighter was the tough Republic P-47 Thunderbolt. Although it first went into action in April 1943, it was not until the introduction of drop tanks carrying extra fuel late in the year that the "Jug," as the plane was called by pilots, could accompany the bombers to Berlin and back. With its massive engine, heavy firepower (from six to eight fifty-caliber machine guns), and rugged construction, the Thunderbolt was a potent fighter, fighter-bomber, tank buster, and all-around combat plane. It could outdive any other aircraft of the time, a maneuver

Example of precision bombing: A 94th Bomb Group B-17 leaves a smoking Focke-Wulf assembly plant at Marienburg, Germany. (U. S. Air Force)

A Messerschmitt 410, designed as a heavy fighter and bomber destroyer, banks away from the wing of a B-17 during a 1944 mission to Brux, an oil target, in the summer of 1944. (The Boeing Company)

A 20th Fighter Group P-38; these planes began flying escort missions in December 1943. (Royal D. Frey/Air Force Museum)

Republic P-47 Thunderbolt, one of the most rugged aircraft of the Second World War. Heavily armed, powerful, the P-47 required an expert pilot's control. (Republic Aviation)

(*Left*) Francis Gabreski, who accounted for thirty-one enemy aircraft in air combat (and two destroyed while strafing) before he himself was forced down and sent to a German *Stalag Luft*. (*Above*) Robert Johnson, one of the first Americans to engage the Germans over Berlin; his victory count at war's end was twenty-eight. (U. S. Air Force)

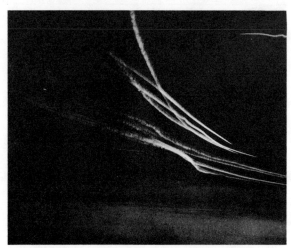

Contrails left by Thunderbolts that have spotted German fighters approaching an Eighth Air Force bomber stream. (U. S. Air Force)

Wingman's view of the end of an enemy fighter. Team fighting became the rule over Europe; fighter pilots flew in pairs to provide mutual protection. A small flame glows in the left wing, as the pilot who fired the shots stopped shooting as his wingman moved in for the kill. The Me-110 soon after burst into flame and crashed. Gun camera photo by Everett M. Stewart, Abilene, Texas; pilot of P-47; John B. Coleman, Milwaukee, Wisconsin. (U. S. Air Force)

North American P-51 Mustang, with wing tank, which enabled it to escort bombers to Berlin and back. The plane in the photo is a P-51D, designated by the British as the Mustang IV. (U. S. Air Force)

that was most helpful when breaking out of combat. The speed of the Thunderbolt was well over four hundred miles per hour. One of the qualities that made the P-47 a favorite of its pilots was its ability to absorb punishment, an admirable quality especially during the latter part of the war in Europe when the "Jug" was used in ground strafing. Rail facilities, trains, and Luftwaffe planes on the ground were the objectives of the strafers, which in turn became the targets of German ground fire. The Thunderbolt was one of the great planes of the Second World War.

Two outstanding Thunderbolt pilots were Francis Gabreski and Robert Johnson. Both men survived the war, although Gabreski spent some of the last months in a prisoner-of-war camp after his "Jug" crashed during a strafing mission on a German airfield. Close to the ground, the P-47's big propeller struck the ground and the plane bellied in. Gabreski served later in the Korean War, made additional "kills," and is now the leading living American ace. Johnson was an exceptionally skill-

ful, aggressive pilot, and was one of the first American fighter pilots to fight the Luftwaffe over Berlin when the first American B-17s attacked the German capital in March 1944. The old World War I tactics of individual dogfighting were at an end by the time of the P-47's advent, and successful air leaders like Johnson and Gabreski rarely flew alone. The lone fighter, without his own wingman to cover his tail and who sought primarily to add to his "kill" score, did not last. Air fighting had become a grim business, and survival depended upon group, not individual effort.

In November 1943, a new American fighter plane, the North American P-51 Mustang, arrived in Europe. Originally designed according to British specifications (as a replacement for the aging P-40), the Mustang was suddenly discovered by the U. S. Air Force and snatched up as a high-altitude, long-range escort fighter. It emerged as one of the finest fighters of the war, with a speed in excess of four hundred miles per hour, remarkable maneuverability at altitudes above twenty thousand feet, and the capability to fly to Berlin and back. Powered by a British Rolls-Royce engine (some of the engines were built by Packard in the United States), the P-51 was a lighter, more delicate aircraft than the P-38 or the P-47. But it could more than equal the FW-190 and the Me-109 in combat. With the appearance of the P-51 especially, in the skies over

Mustang stars: Don Gentile (*Left*) and John Godfrey (*Right*), who frequently flew combat missions as a team. Both began their flying careers with the RAF in Spitfires, later transferring to the U. S. Air Force after the United States went to war. Both belonged to the 4th Fighter Group, which became the highest-scoring group in Europe (1,016 enemy aircraft destroyed in the air and on the ground). Gentile's final score was twenty-three, and Godfrey's was eighteen. (U. S. Air Force)

Germany in the spring of 1944, the challenge of the
Luftwaffe to Allied bombers was met.

The best piston-engine German fighter of the
last months of the war was the FW-190. But with
the arrival of such "little friends" (as the bomber
crews called them) as the P-38, P-47, and particularly the P-51 (which the British nicknamed the
"Apache"), the Focke-Wulf did not command the
air over Germany, nor did the Luftwaffe.

Not a great deal is written, in aviation histories
of the Second World War, about the Regia Aeronautica, the Italian Air Force, and its planes. On the
Axis side, of course, the Luftwaffe dominated in
the story of the air battles with the Allies. The
Italian Air Force took second place to the Germans
insofar as supplies and raw materials were concerned. Not all Italian aircraft (nor all Italian pilots)
were inferior. In the winter of 1941 new units of
Italian fighter planes were stationed in North Africa. Their aircraft was the excellent Macchi-Castoldi 202, which, had it been produced in sufficient
numbers and flown by properly trained pilots,
might have made a difference in the air fighting in
Africa, as well as over the Mediterranean and Italy
itself. The sudden surrender of Italy in September
1943 canceled out the threat to the Allies of the
Macchi-Castoldi 202. Even pilots in the nimble and
lethal American Mustang spoke of the 202 Folgore
(Lightning) with respect. It was highly maneuverable, could attain a speed of well over three hundred
miles per hour (depending on the altitude—at nineteen thousand feet it could do 370). Production of
the Folgore was hampered by a scarcity of engines
(partly owing to the German monopoly of essential
supplies) and to Allied bombing.

By mid-1944 the Luftwaffe, which had appeared
to be so invincible in 1939, was no more. Allied
aircraft ranged over Europe and over Germany

An FW-190 succumbs to the guns of Glenn E. Duncan,
Houston, Texas. Flame shoots out of the wing root and,
in the final frame, smoke fills the cockpit, the wing
buckles, and the landing gear begins descending. (U. S.
Air Force)

Arado 96Bs in a training flight. The war in the air took a toll of Germany's experienced pilots, and dwindling oil supplies, because of strategic bombardment, curtailed training flights such as this. Ill-trained, inexperienced pilots did not last long in the skies over Europe. (H. J. Nowarra)

Fiat CR-42, one of the last biplane fighters, which flew for the first time in 1939 and was purchased by the Italian, Belgian, Hungarian, and Swedish air forces. They were used as escorts in the Mediterranean area and in the Western Desert fighting. The CR stands for Caccia Rosatelli: Fighter Rosatelli, for designer Celistino Rosatelli. (U. S. Air Force)

Macchi C. 202 (the C stands for designer Mario Castoldi), an outstanding fighter that began operations in 1941. Powered by a German Daimler-Benz inline engine, it fought over North Africa and the Soviet Union. It was greatly respected by American fighter pilots. (Aeronautica Macchi)

Upon completing an escort mission this P-51 of the 361st Fighter Group lands as the ground crews wait to prepare the plane for the next mission. (U. S. Air Force)

itself bombing strategic targets, targets associated with the aircraft industry and with the production of oil and fuel. Not that the Luftwaffe was absolutely finished; there were more air battles to come, but the Allies had the tools with which to carry the war to Germany and still be reasonably certain that the majority of their crews would return safely to England.

Despite the efforts of the fighter pilots, bombers fell victim to German fighters that from time to time emerged in aggressive numbers, when fuel was available or if the Allies attacked especially important targets—or Berlin. Antiaircraft fire, directed by radar, took its toll. Even though not absolutely accurate, a direct hit could shear off a wing, flame an engine, or detonate a bombload. When this occurred, unless there was time to take to their parachutes, ten crewmen would perish in the stricken bombers. It was virtually impossible to get out of a gyrating plane. Pilots frequently died

Despite formidable fighter escorts the Luftwaffe managed to break through to the bombers. With bomb bays open and with two engines aflame, a B-17 of the 486th Bomber Group begins its fall. (U. S. Air Force)

Enemy fighters were not the only obstacles that Allied bomber formations encountered. Radar-directed flak took its toll also. Once on the bombing run the aircraft remained on a fixed course; if the flak guns had the correct range and direction, a direct hit could inflict devastating damage. (U. S. Air Force)

Martin B-26 Marauder medium bomber. One of the "hottest" planes of the war, the Marauder had an unearned reputation as a nearly impossible plane to fly. After Jimmy Doolittle proved that untrue (he also recommended better training for pilots), the Marauder was widely used during the war. An unusual feature of the B-26's design was its relatively small wing; the resultant high wing loading initially led to the early landing accidents—and to the nickname "The Flying Prostitute" (because it had no visible means of support). (The Martin Company)

when they remained behind to keep their plane flying level so that the rest of the crew could jump. Although victory was assured by June 1944, when they invaded Normandy, the Allies faced a good deal of fighting both on the ground and in the air.

Medium bombers, too, were used in combat in all theaters of operations. After the invasion of Europe by the Allies, the medium bombers—Marauders, Havocs, and Invaders—were turned loose upon German installations, roadblocks, bridges, and other so-called tactical targets. As in the case of the heavies, this was not accomplished without cost.

Much Luftwaffe equipment was destroyed on the ground toward the end of the war. Denied fuel

by the heavy bombers, its pilots ill trained (also because of lack of fuel for training flights), and its experienced pilots exhausted or wasted by Göring and Hitler, a great number of its planes were destroyed by roaming Allied fighters.

Last-ditch German means of dealing with the heavy bombers that crippled the Nazi war machine came too late. One of the first very fast interceptors was the Messerschmitt 163 Komet. Designed by Professor Alexander Lippisch, the Komet was the first and only rocket-powered aircraft to be used operationally during the war. The idea behind this odd little plane was to send it shooting through the bomber streams at close to six hundred miles per hour, firing rockets from under its wing and the

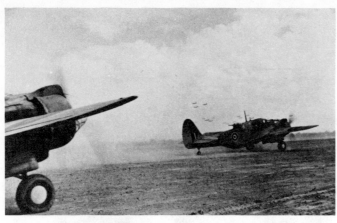

Martin A-30 Baltimores, built to RAF specifications (and based on the earlier Maryland) in North Africa, 1942. These American-built aircraft were used only by the British. (U. S. Air Force)

A French-flown Marauder has been severed by a direct flak hit in the Karlsruhr area on the upper Rhine. To the men of the First Tactical Air Force this target zone was known as Flak Valley. (U. S. Air Force)

Low-level bombing missions were plagued by accurate flak more than the missions at higher altitudes. A Douglas A-20 Havoc has suffered a direct hit. (U. S. Air Force)

A Douglas A-26 Invader, hit by flak on the bomb run before releasing its bombs, falls out of control. (U. S. Air Force)

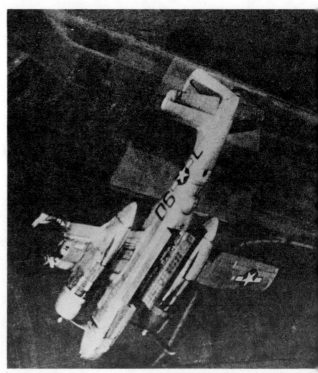

By the spring of 1945 the Luftwaffe rarely challenged the Allied air forces, especially in the air. So fighters ranged over German-held territory strafing Luftwaffe aircraft on the ground. On the day this photo was taken, only three German fighters were destroyed in air combat and 644 more were shot up, like these, on the ground. (U. S. Air Force)

Messerschmitt 163 Komet, one of Germany's desperate attempts to produce a means of stopping Allied bombers from destroying German industial targets and cities. (German Information Center)

Lieutenant General James H. Doolittle, commander of the Eighth Air Force, listens to a pilot after a bombing mission. General Carl Spaatz, commander of Strategic Air Forces in Europe, also listens at left. It was Doolittle's decision, late in the war, that unleashed the American fighter planes (that is, he permitted them to roam away from the bomber streams), enabling them to destroy the Luftwaffe wherever they found it—in the air or on the ground. This controversial decision spelled the ultimate end of the German Air Force. (U. S. Air Force)

cannons in the nose. Endurance was not the Komet's strong point, for its flight lasted only about twelve minutes before fuel was expended. It had yet another drawback: Its rocket fuel was highly volatile and frequently exploded when the plane took off or landed (on skids); the wheels were dropped when the Komet left the ground. It was a dangerous aircraft—to Allied bomber crews as well as to Luftwaffe pilots.

Germany's first operational jet fighter and the first to encounter manned enemy aircraft was the Messerschmitt 262 Schwalbe (Swallow). (The distinction is made because the first operational jet of the war was Britain's Glostor Meteor, which destroyed unmanned German flying bombs before the Me-262 went into action.) The Me-262 was

plagued by many problems, not the least of which was Hitler's idea to use the jet fighter as a revenge bomber against the British. Since it was not designed to be a bomber, this was a handicap. Finally, when Hitler permitted jet fighter squadrons to be formed, it was too late. But with speeds of more than five hundred miles per hour, the Me-262s posed serious threats to both Allied bomber formations and to the fighters. Had they been used earlier in the war, the outcome might have been if not victory for the Germans, at least a much bloodier and deferred victory for the Allies.

A lesser-known German jet was the Arado 234 which, although not produced in great numbers (partly because of Allied bombardment) had the distinction of being the last German plane to ap-

Messerschmitt 262, Germany's first jet fighter. (German Information Center)

Arado 234B, jet-powered reconnaissance bomber. (H. J. Nowarra)

Berlin, 1945. Allied bombers reduced much of the city to rubble. (German Information Center)

pear over Britain during the Second World War (April 10, 1945). The Ar-234 was designed to be used as a reconnaissance bomber. Very few actually reached Luftwaffe bomber units.

The devastation of German cities—Berlin, Hamburg, Dresden (the last two by frightful firestorms), Munich, and others—was evidence of the terrible impact of air power. Another lesson was that when air power is used, there is no such thing as a civilian noncombatant.

Like their Western ally, the Japanese were beaten primarily by air power as early as 1944. But the war continued in order to "save face" of the Japanese military clique. However, in September 1944, during the Battle for Leyte Gulf in the Philippines, it was revealed that Japan was ready to

A strange new war tactic: A *kamikaze* plane crashes into the *Essex*, off Luzon in the Philippines. The desperate, final attempt by Japanese militarists to stop the Allies in the Pacific. (Navy Department National Archives)

take desperate measures in its last-ditch fight. The first *kamikaze* attacks were made. These were fruitless suicide dives made by poorly trained, generally very youthful pilots, upon Allied ships in the hope that it would sway the outcome of the war. The main objectives were the carriers.

The carrier *Bunker Hill* was hit by a kamikaze in May 1945, off Okinawa during the final phase of the Pacific war. In the fires that followed nearly four hundred men of the *Bunker Hill* died. So did the hapless pilot of the plane, which succeeded in breaking through the screen of heavy antiaircraft fire, which frequently destroyed the suicide planes before they did any damage. The *kamikazes* caused severe suffering and wasted lives but contributed nothing to the outcome of the war. The Japanese mystically called their Special Attack Corps the Divine Wind. This was an allusion to an ancient leg-end in which a sudden wind came up and blew away the enemies bent upon invading Japan. The Divine Wind did not work a second time.

In the final fighting on Iwo Jima and Okinawa the Japanese ground troops, like their aerial counterparts, fought to the death. New weapons were developed to deal with Japanese troops dug into caves who often took a tremendous toll in American lives. Rockets launched from a Marine Corsair were fired into caves to assist in the ground fighting on Okinawa. It was this kind of co-operation that earned the Corsair the name Sweetheart of Okinawa. Planes were also used to drop napalm bombs into caves to destroy the Japanese.

A new plane introduced during the final year of the war was the Northrop P-61 Black Widow, which was designed specifically to operate as a night fighter. With a three-man crew, it also served as an "intruder," which dropped down suddenly upon enemy bases to shoot up aircraft and installations. The plane was used in Europe as well as the Pacific; in the Pacific its crews intercepted Japanese intruders which, outnumbered and outgunned during the day, could only venture out at night.

The U. S. Navy was active during the final phases of the war in the Pacific in co-operation with the converging U. S. Air Force. Carrier warfare was a hazardous business. Damaged aircraft often crashed upon landing because of weakened structure. Injured pilots lost control of their planes on touching down. The work of carrier deck crews was also dangerous—and responsible for saving the lives of Navy pilots landing in stricken aircraft.

When Marines began landings on Saipan in the Mariana Islands in June 1944 (and eventually secured it), Japan had definitely lost the war. From the Marianas—Saipan, Tinian, and Guam—the newly formed Twentieth Air Force could reach Tokyo itself by air. The plane capable of this was

Flight deck of the *Bunker Hill*, May 11, 1945. (Navy Department National Archives)

A suicidal Japanese pilot, frustrated in his attempts to shoot down this C-47 (the military version of the Douglas DC-3), rammed into it and succeeded only in killing himself. The C-47 continued on to its base. (Douglas Aircraft)

A Marine Corsair fires rockets into a Japanese stronghold in support of Marines attacking on the ground. Corsairs also delivered the newly developed napalm bombs into Japanese-held caves on Okinawa, where this photo was taken. (Marine Corps Defense Department)

Northrop P-61 Black Widow, which operated over Europe and the Pacific as a most potent night fighter. (U. S. Air Force)

Life aboard an aircraft carrier: Deck landings were rarely simple, but battle damage made them risky. A Hellcat, after a strike on Japanese-held Luzon, lands after being hit by anti-aircraft fire. Severely weakened, the Grumman held together long enough for the pilot to land, leaving a shattered fuselage behind. Another Hellcat, upon landing, lost its auxiliary fuel tank, which burst into flames. Pilot Ardon R. Ives leaves the cockpit. (Navy Department National Archives)

the Boeing B-29 Superfortress, a giant plane with a wingspan of 141 feet, 2 inches, and a length of 99 feet. It was the ultimate bomber of the Second World War, a very heavy, very long-range strategic bomber. Designed, built, and operational in a remarkably short time (not without some growing pains), the B-29 was used to bring the full weight of modern war directly to the Japanese homeland.

Armament consisted of a dozen fifty-caliber machine guns in power-driven turrets. The plane was pressurized (the first U.S. bomber with a pressurized cabin) and required a crew of eleven. The war ended in Europe before the B-29 could be used there. It brought heavy devastation to Japan. In its early missions, what with excessive distances (from bases in China) and strong winds at high altitudes, the B-29 did not quite live up to original expecta-

tions. But it was quickly adapted to employment in a decision by the Twentieth Air Force Commander Curtis E. LeMay that brought the full horrors of war to Japan.

To hit their targets, the B-29s, LeMay decided, would operate at low altitudes at night instead of during the day. This would eliminate, to some extent, the threat of Japanese intercepters. And incendiary bombs would be carried instead of high explosives. Such bombs caused tremendous fires in the highly flammable Japanese cities. The fire raids destroyed about half of Tokyo and nearly all of the city of Toyama, which produced ball bearings, aircraft parts, tools, and other wartime essentials. The B-29s ended Toyama's industrial productiveness in August 1945. Several other, and larger, Japanese cities suffered a similar fate.

A Boeing B-29 Superfortress awaits testing on a flight apron. Rushed into operations, the B-29 was plagued by "bugs," particularly with engines that inexplicably burst into flame. Early operations out of China were not successful, but once stationed in the Mariana Islands, the B-29s devasted the Japanese home islands. (U. S. Air Force)

Sowing the flame. Japanese cities, with their industrial targets, were vulnerable to incendiary bombs, such as these being dropped by a formation of Superfortresses. (U. S. Air Force)

Superfortresses operating from North Field, Guam (in the Marianas), carried heavy bombloads to Japan in the final months of the war. (U. S. Air Force)

High winds over Japan interfered with the functioning of the B-29s; General Curtis LeMay changed tactics and ordered the Superfortresses out at night to bomb from comparatively low level. The result was tremendous destruction to Japanese industrial centers. The photograph shows Toyama (textiles, ball bearings, machine tools, aircraft parts), which was attacked in this manner and 90 per cent destroyed in one attack on August 2, 1945. (U. S. Air Force)

A brave new world? An atomic cloud rises out of Nagasaki, August 9, 1945—the second atomic bomb dropped on a city by the Twentieth Air Force. This began a new era in the tragic history of war and the perversion of the history of flight. (U. S. Air Force)

Air photo of the damage wrought by the A-bomb at Hiroshima; this bombing did indeed bring an end to the Second World War—and the projected invasion of Japan in 1946. (U. S. Air Force)

Two Japanese cities suffered the first destruction by atomic bombardment. Single atomic bombs carried in B-29s struck the city of Hiroshima on August 6, 1945, and when the Japanese refused to surrender, a second was dropped, on Nagasaki on August 9. The devastation of these bombs—more than one hundred thousand human beings were destroyed in Hiroshima alone—supplied the Japanese warlords with sufficient reasons, without too much loss of face, for surrender. After six of history's blackest years, the Second World War came to a frightful end—and the Age of the Atom began. The frail little flying machine of the Wright brothers had evolved in little more than four decades into the most destructive weapon man had ever devised. It had taken all the glamor from war in the air, if in truth there ever was any.

Writing on the wall: Like a sun picture this shadow of a ladder was permanently burned into a metal surface at Hiroshima, August 6, 1945. (U. S. Air Force)

With a Consolidated-Vultee B-36 leading, four veteran aircraft of the war follow: a B-29, a B-17, a Douglas A-26, and a P-51. Designed as a bomber to attack targets in Germany from bases in the United States, the B-36 did not fly until August 1947. With its 230-foot wingspan, 6 engines, and a fuselage of 162 feet, it was the largest landplane in the late 1940s. (U. S. Air Force)

8 SWIFTER THAN THE SUN

Peace, however tentative, ushered in a rich transitional period for commercial aviation, which could take up again where it had been interrupted by the war. The exigencies of the war, as it had during the First World War, inadvertently contributed to postwar progress. The advent of the successful jet engine was one of these contributions, but of even greater importance was that the war had made air travel a common experience for thousands.

By 1945 a vast network of airlines covered the earth. The suspicion (read: fear) of flying was greatly lessened by the wide use of aircraft during the war for other than combat missions such as the evacuation of wounded, transportation, and delivery of cargo.

Almost immediately after the war ended the American aviation industry was capable of making the transition from military to civil aircraft. Airlines required replacement aircraft for their war-worn planes; they needed planes for the new generation of passengers who had become accustomed to fast transportation during the war. With the coming of peace, cold and shaky as it eventually proved to be, a true age of flight had dawned. This resurgence, incidentally, closed the romantic era of the flying boat, which was not as economic to operate as the new generation of airliners with more passenger space and greater range and flexibility.

Manufacturers of light planes hoped that former military pilots might wish to continue flying, and geared up for peace. This great upsurge in private flying did not immediately follow the war, but bloomed in the late fifties. By 1960 some 70,000 private aircraft were in existence in the United States alone—not all, of course, owned by former military pilots.

Some ex-fly boys, especially former bomber pilots, found work with commercial airlines. The transition from peace to war in this instance was somewhat gentler than that which followed the Armistice of 1918. And though the Air Force, as did all military services, shrank in numbers, it did retain a number of pilots who preferred continuing a military career.

Manufacturers of military aircraft were hard hit. Consolidated-Vultee (now Convair), for example, which had turned out B-24 Liberators and PBY Catalinas in great numbers during the war, began closing out satellite factories in Tucson; New Orleans; Allentown, Pennsylvania; Louisville; Elizabeth City, North Carolina, and their San Diego No. 2 plant—nearly half of their satellite divisions. The wartime boom was over and new avenues would have to be explored.

The automobile industry rejoiced; it could shift from turning out aircraft and parts and go back to America's first love: the motor car, whose production and design had lain fallow during the war. Detroit went back to work with a vengeance while the aircraft industry began searching for work. The major aircraft manufacturers, Douglas, Lockheed, Curtiss-Wright, Boeing, were ready with airliner designs the moment the war ended.

A symbol of American commercial aircraft be-

Postwar private flying might be symbolized by this
Luscombe Silvaire, a model dating back to the thirties.
Between 1942 and 1946 Luscombe stopped producing
light planes to fulfill war contracts. New Silvaires began
coming from the plant in 1946 also. (John F. Bartel)

Double dream: Consolidated's Flying Auto of 1947, a
hybrid if there ever was one. Apparently it did fly—but
it never caught on. A year later Aerocar, Inc., was
formed to manufacture a similar vehicle, but only five of
their design were built. (General Dynamics)

Old Faithful: the C-47 (peacetime's DC-3) still in battle paint. Surplus C-47s were sold to newly formed airlines and cargo services that proliferated for a time after the war. (U. S. Air Force Museum)

fore, during, and after the war was the reliable DC-3. Thousands of these Douglas airliners were converted to wartime transport and cargo use, and when the war ended, returned to civil airline work. Wartime surplus C-47s, sold cheaply by the Air Force, were bought up by new airlines that sprang up after the war, often formed by ex-Air Force pilots.

Another war veteran was the Douglas C-54 Skymaster, which had been ready for commercial airline use when war came but was immediately snatched up by the Air Force in 1942 instead. It was nearly three times the size of the DC-3 and served in all theaters of war, flying the "Hump" of the Himalaya Mountains in the China-Burma-India zone as well as domestically. (In 1948–49 it was used again in the Berlin Airlift to carry food to Berliners after the Soviets had cut off other means

of entry into the city.) It was not until 1945 that the Skymaster returned to its original civilian dress as the Douglas DC-4. At a speed of 260 miles per hour, the DC-4 could carry a payload of from fifty-five to seventy passengers (depending on whether it was first or tourist class) or eight thousand pounds of cargo.

Even more advanced than the DC-4, the Lockheed C-69 became the Constellation when U. S. Air Force orders ceased and the plane went into commercial service, for which (in 1943) it had been originally designed. With the Constellation, Pan American Airways flew the first scheduled round-the-world flight in 1949. The last model of the aircraft appeared in 1956 as the Starliner, which although it resembled the original Constellation, was longer in fuselage length (from 95 feet to 113 feet) and span (from 123 feet to 150). The new plane could carry up to ninety-two passengers. Its top speed was 377 miles per hour. Besides being faster than the DC-4, the Constellation carried a

Douglas C-54 Skymaster, a commercial aircraft that went to war before reverting to its original function as the DC-4. (Douglas Aircraft)

Lockheed C-69 Constellation as a civil airliner. (Lockheed Aircraft)

greater payload and its pressurized cabin enabled it to fly at higher altitudes.

The Curtiss Wright C-46 Commando, originally intended, in 1940, as a thirty-six-passenger commercial airliner, became one of the Air Force's major cargo planes during the war. Like its companion planes of the same period, it could quickly be converted back into civil use after the war. In military service the Commando was used primarily as a troop transport; as a civil aircraft, it was used for hauling heavy cargo loads. Its capacious fuselage cross section could handle large containers. The Commando was one of the last twin-engined propeller-driven commercial aircraft of the postwar era.

Boeing's solution to conversion from war to peace was represented by the 307 Stratoliner and the 377 Stratocruiser. Although it may not appear so, the 307 evolved out of the B-17 (the major difference was in the fuselage). The Stratoliner (which also was used by the Air Force as the C-75) was one of the first airliners to come equipped for cabin pressurization. This enabled the plane to fly at substratospheric altitudes (above the turbulent weather zones) without the necessity of having passengers wear oxygen masks. Only ten of these planes were built, being supplanted by Boeing's own Stratocruiser, which went into airline operation in 1949. This plane, the first civil design from Boeing since the 314 Clipper, has some of the B-29

Curtiss Commando taking on cargo. (Pan American World Airways)

Boeing's conversion to peacetime resulted in the
Stratoliner (B-307), which adapted the B-17 wing to a
more roomy fuselage, and the Stratocruiser (B-377), a
descendant of the B-29. (Pan American World Airways)

The last of the piston-engine airliners, the Douglas DC-7, 1955. (Douglas Aircraft)

Vought's unique Flying Pancake (also known as the CV-XF5U-1), an attempt to cross a helicopter with the conventional airplaine. (National Air and Space Museum)

Superfortress in its ancestry: wing, tail, and upper fuselage. The fuselage, in fact, was swollen, so to speak, in the new variant to accommodate passengers. The Stratocruiser was a flying double-decker and featured a lower-deck lounge reached by a spiral stairway from the passenger cabin. With a wingspan of 141 feet, 3 inches, the 377 was the heaviest piston-engined commercial airliner ever built and won the reputation, also, of being the most luxurious. It could accommodate sixty-one passengers in first class, complete with private staterooms and sleeper service on nonstop flights to London and Paris from New York. The 377 was eventually supplanted by the first commercial jets.

Douglas, meanwhile, had been modifying its DC-4, enlarging and refining the original design until it became the DC-7 to meet the competition of Lockheed and Boeing. This was the last of the piston-engined commercial airliners and could carry from sixty-nine to ninety-five passengers. The DC-7C was the first commercial transport capable of nonstop transpacific service. The fuel supply carried by this plane was sufficient to take an automobile six times around the world, and its heating system could warm about sixty average-sized houses. Wingspan was 127 feet, 6 inches; fuselage length was 112 feet, 3 inches.

The coming of peace had a great impact on military aviation as the need for great numbers of such aircraft ended. Of especial significance was the advent of jet propulsion which would end the era of piston-driven planes. Some interesting designs were fostered by the U. S. Navy in the transition years, one being the Chance Vought 173, designed by Charles H. Zimmerman, an advocate of the low-aspect-ratio wing. (Aspect ratio was the relationship between the length of the wing compared with the width.) This plane was popularly called the Flying Pancake. Although it was not developed further, it exhibited unusual flight characteristics, among them an ability to hang on its propellers without stalling and to hover in place. Also, it had a high rate of climb and a wide range of speeds—from 40 to 425 miles per hour.

Another unusual avenue of aircraft design stud-

Convair Pogo, the XFY-1, designed for takeoff from small areas and that first flew in 1954. Lockheed's XFV-1 was another attempt at solving the same problem. (General Dynamics/Lockheed Aircraft)

A Navy Convair Sea Dart making a splashy takeoff; the speed has lifted the craft onto the water skis. (General Dynamics)

ied by the Navy was that of VTO (Vertical Take-off) aircraft. As an alternative to carrier-based fighters, they could operate from small land bases, from cargo decks, as well as from carriers. One of the solutions to this problem was put forth by Convair with its XFY-1, called the Pogo because it took off vertically from tiny wheels set in the wing and tail tips. It could also land in this manner. Once airborne, the Pogo flew conventionally. Although tested, the plane was finally abandoned because the engine did not provide enough power. Another plane of the same type was attempted by Lockheed (the XFV-1), but it like the Flying Pancake, was abandoned also.

The Navy's last seaplane was the Convair Sea Dart (XF2Y-1) its only jet fighter designed to operate from water. The Sea Dart rested on its underside in the water. As speed increased, its wings lifted the plane onto retractable water skis for the takeoff. Only five of these aircraft were built, and finally production plans were canceled. The Sea Dart flew for the first time in 1953 and was intended to be a close-support fighter.

The age of the seaplane was definitely over but the age of the jet plane just beginning. The only Allied jet to see operational service was the Gloster Meteor, which destroyed German V-bombs during the last months of the war. The coming of the Meteor, as well as the Me-262, heralded the end of piston-engined military aircraft. The speed of the Meteor was 590 miles per hour. In 1945 a later version of the Meteor, powered by Rolls-Royce Derwent-V engines, established a new official world speed record of 606.26 miles per hour.

The first American combat jet was the Lockheed P-80 Shooting Star. (The first jet aircraft built and flown in the United States, however, was the Bell XP-59A, powered by a British-designed engine, the work of Frank Whittle.) The P-80 was built around an English motor also, the De Havilland Goblin. Later versions were powered by the General Electric J-33. Although the first Shooting Star was flown in September 1944, none were operational in the Second World War. However, when one element of the Cold War grew hot in Korea in

Royal Air Force Gloster Meteors, descendants of the first Allied jet fighter—also named the Meteor. These vertically climbing Meteors were postwar models. (U. S. Air Force)

1950, the P-80s were used for the first time in combat against Soviet-made fighters. By this time the designation was changed to F-80 (F for fighter).

The Korean War, initially a United Nations problem, was fought primarily by American, Canadian, and Australian forces as allies of the South Koreans. It was a "contained war," one all hoped would not ignite into a world conflict. It might have been called "World War 2.3," for it was fought with a strange conglomeration of old and new weaponry, ranging from the rifle of guerrilla warfare to the modern jet fighter.

Aircraft of the Second World War were adapted for use in Korea alongside the jets. One of the most unusual was the North American P-82, the U. S. Air Force's last propeller-driven aircraft. It was essentially two P-51s joined by a common wing and tail and designed to be flown as a twin-engined long-range fighter with pilot and radar operator-observer in adjacent fuselages. The Twin Mustang was redesignated the F-82 by the time it was used in Korea and credited with the destruction of the first enemy aircraft in that war. (The Twin Mustang was developed near the close of the Second World War as a long-range escort for the Boeing B-29s; this mission was not accomplished until the Korean War.)

Jet aircraft were used in great numbers for the first time in Korea, most of them American-made Republic F-84 Thunderjets, North American F-86 Sabres, and the Lockheed F-80 Shooting Stars, among others which shared missions with the propeller-driven F-82s and the Second World War's B-26s and B-29s. The North Koreans flew Soviet MIGs.

Most jet fighter battles over Korea occurred during escort missions, with the fighters providing protective cover for piston-engine aircraft. The slower speeds of the transports, cargo planes, bombers, and helicopters made them easy prey to the MIGs. The F-86 Sabre consistently outperformed the Soviet jets.

American military jet design was stimulated by German and British jets introduced near the end of the Second World War. The first postwar Ameri-

The first American combat jet, the Lockheed P-80 Shooting Star. First flown in 1944, the P-80 was not used in the Second World War, but saw action against Soviet jet fighters during the Korean War (1950–53) as the F-80. This F-80 is taking off from an American base in Japan; Japanese rice farmers, by the summer of 1950, were quite accustomed to jet noises. (U. S. Air Force)

Grumman F9F Panther, the first Navy jet fighter to see combat (Korea, July 1950). Wingtip tanks were permanently fixed. The range of the Panther was more than thirteen hundred miles. (Grumman Aircraft)

Korean War interceptors: the duo-fuselage F-82 Twin Mustang flanked by two jets, the F-80 (left) and Lockheed F-94 (a two-place version of the F-80). Trailing is the North American F-86 Sabre. (U. S. Air Force)

A Sabre pilot's view of a North Korean Soviet-built MIG-15; Sabre pilots accounted for about 800 of the 1,000 MIGs shot down during the war in Korea. (U. S. Air Force)

Republic F-84 Thunderjet in Korea; fixed armament consisted of six machine guns. The F-84 also carried four thousand pounds of bombs, or missiles, rockets—even a tactical atomic weapon (which was not used, of course)— under the wings. Plane taking off is armed with rockets. (U. S. Air Force)

A Fairchild C-119 Flying Boxcar, one of the several propeller-driven aircraft used in Korea. The C-119 served as a troop and cargo transport. It passes over a battle junkyard. (U. S. Air Force)

can jet fighter was the Republic F-84 which first flew into Korean action in December 1950. A fighter-bomber, the F-84 was heavily gunned and carried heavy loads of missiles (it could even carry a small atomic bomb, which luckily was not used in Korea.)

The outstanding American-made jet used in Korea was the North American F-86 Sabre, the first U. S. Air Force plane with a swept-back wing. The concept was borrowed from captured German jet design data; this proved to be the solution to the problem of compressibility that afflicted high speed aircraft. The speed of the plane, pushing air before it, caused a buildup (i.e. compression) resulting in shock waves which, when tumbling back upon conventional wings, caused severe buffeting and other problems in flight. The swept-back wing and tail surfaces controlled the flow of air behind the Sabre, which was capable of speeds close to 700 miles per hour.

If the jet fighters were given their first true baptism of fire in Korea, the military helicopter came into its own there. Their most remarkable mission was the evacuation of wounded from a battle zone speedily and directly to hospitals. Such quick action saved many lives that might have otherwise been lost. Helicopters were used for troop transportation, artillery spotting, and rescuing pilots downed behind the lines or in the water. So far as aviation is concerned it was the recognition of the helicopter that made the Korean War memorable; little else did.

North American F-86 Sabres on a training flight in Korea, 1953. Sabres were effective as all-weather interceptors and, following U. S. Air Force service, were also used by the air forces of Japan, Greece, Turkey, Nationalist China, Denmark, Yugoslavia, and the Philippines. (U. S. Air Force)

A Bell helicopter in Korea delivering wounded to a waiting World War II veteran, a C-54, for transportation to American military hospitals in Japan. The little choppers worked close to the front lines to pick up the wounded and even over the lines to rescue pilots shot down behind the lines. (U. S. Air Force)

Like a scene from the Second World War, this mission shot of Superfortresses head for enemy targets; only the time is the summer of 1950 and the place is Korea. (U. S. Air Force)

No jet bombers were used in Korea and bomb strikes were carried out by Second World War veterans such as the Mitchells, Invaders, and Superfortresses. The B-29s, on long range missions escorted by jet fighters, bombed North Korean supply lines and troop concentrations, hardly the strategic targets for which the B-29 was designed. When the Korean War ended in 1953, after three frustrating years, the two super powers, Soviet Russia and the United States, had proved the military efficacy of the jet-powered fighter. And, too, there was the emergence of the helicopter, the "chopper," especially as a mercy vehicle, that is notable. The jets indicated the future direction in design for very high speed aircraft; in the United States, probing such possibilities was initiated by the U. S. Air Force.

As it had after the First World War, the U. S. Air Force turned its attention in peacetime to experimenting. The most serious problem was how to control aircraft whose speeds approached that of sound. (The speed of sound varies at different altitudes, faster at sea level and slower the higher up you go. At 35,000 feet, for example, the speed of sound is about 650 miles per hour.) To measure such supersonic speeds, a system was devised by Ernst Mach, an Austrian scientist. The speed of sound at any given altitude is called Mach 1. (In other words, at sea level, it is 760 miles per hour; Mach 2 would then be, at sea level, 1520 miles per hour.) The first plane to fly through the sound barrier (without suffering serious ill effects from compressibility) was the rocket-powered Bell X-1. Piloted by Charles Yeager, the X-1, on October 17, 1947, reached a speed of 763 miles per hour at sea level, thus exceeding Mach 1 at that altitude. The X-1 was used for high-speed, high-altitude experimentation throughout the forties. The highest speed it achieved was 967 miles per hour; the highest altitude reached was 70,140 feet. In 1950 the craft was presented to the National Air Museum, Smithsonian Institution.

A variant of the X-1, the Bell X-1A of the early fifties, continued the Air Force's experimentation. A new high was reached in 1953 when Charles

Bell X-1, the first aircraft to fly faster than sound, over Muroc Air Force Base, California. (U. S. Air Force)

Yeager flew the plane at Mach 2.5 (1,650 miles per hour). In the same plane Arthur Murray reached an altitude of 90,000 feet. The pilots wore specially designed pressure suits, which protected them from the stress of high speeds. At about this same period, the U. S. Navy also began testing experimental supersonic aircraft.

North American contributed the X-15 to the research aircraft program, which by the sixties had begun to probe beyond the earth's atmosphere. It was lifted to an aerial launch point under the wing of a Boeing B-52. Like the X-1, the X-15 was rocket-powered. It was fifty feet long and had practically no wings. Two boatlike objects under the X-15's fuselage were jettisonable fuel tanks. These provided more flying time in which the craft could reach exceptionally high speeds—close to five thousand miles per hour. Pilot Joseph Walker took the plane up to an altitude of 354,200 feet—which is about sixty-seven miles above the earth. The X-15 in 1961 became the first aircraft to reach a speed over Mach 6 (4,094 miles per hour, or Mach 6.04). The pilot was Robert M. White. In 1963 Robert A. Rushworth flew it to Mach 6.06. Only the later astronauts, in spacecraft, would travel faster.

The Bell and North American manned supersonic aircraft placed the United States ahead of other nations in this field. Actually, the British had begun work on the Miles M.52 as early as 1943 to produce a plane that would break the "sound barrier" (the popular name for compressibility) and were, even before the Bell X-1 was ready, on the threshold of supersonic flight. But the official view was that manned flight in speeds as fast as sound were dangerous and the tests and program were stopped in 1946. Even so Britain has been a consistent leader in the development of jet-powered aircraft since the introduction of the Gloster Meteor in the early forties. Also produced concurrently, although not in time to fly operationally in the war, was the de Havilland 100 Vampire. The twin-boomed jet entered RAF service in 1946. Its top speed was 538 miles per hour. In time the Vampire would be used by the air forces of ten different nations, including Switzerland, Sweden, Norway, and Mexico, and in the United States for civil use.

The first British design specifically intended for research into the delta-wing concept was the Avro 707. The success of this configuration confirmed the soundness of using the triangular-shaped wing in very-high-speed aircraft. This concept had been pioneered in Germany and was recognized as valid by British and American aeronautical engineers.

Another step in British delta-wing design was the Gloster Javelin, the first twin-engined jet fighter. It was originally conceived late in 1951; variants of the Javelin were still operational with the RAF into the midsixties. By this time its major function was as a two-man night and all-weather interceptor aircraft.

The largest delta-winged aircraft of the early fifties was the Hawker Siddeley Vulcan, a long-range medium bomber. From tip to tip, the wing measured 99 feet (with an area of 3,554 square feet); length of fuselage was 99 feet, 11 inches. Later marks (or models) manufactured by Hawker Siddeley Aviation, were still operational with RAF Bomber Command at the close of the sixties.

A history-making twin jet in more conventional configuration was the English Electric Canberra, which in August 1952 made a round-trip crossing

Majors Charles E. Yeager (left) and Arthur Murray exchange congratulations; Yeager established a new speed record at 1,650 miles per hour and Murray climbed to an altitude of 90,000 feet in the Bell X-1A, December 1953. (U. S. Air Force)

A North American X-15 being lifted to launch altitude under the wing of a B-52 bomber. This aircraft, if it can be called that (it seems more like a projectile), broke several speed records in the early 1960s. (U. S. Air Force)

of the Atlantic in a single day. Flying from Alder-grove, Ireland, to Gander, Newfoundland, in four hours, thirty-three minutes, the plane turned around to return in three hours, twenty-five minutes. At the controls for the flight over was Roland P. Beaumont; F. L. Hillwood flew the Canberra on the return trip.

Of the Allies, it was Britain that was the pioneer in jet-propelled aircraft. The prototype of this de Havilland Vampire was first flown in September 1943 and went into RAF service in 1946. It was powered by a de Havilland Goblin turbojet engine. (U. S. Air Force)

Avro 707 designed to test the delta wing. Five of these were built between 1949 and 1953, with slight modifications in configuration. (U. S. Air Force)

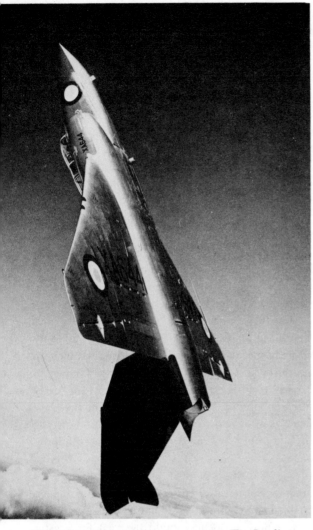

Hawker Siddeley B2 Vulcan, used extensively by the RAF in the late fifties and early sixties as a medium bomber. It was powered by four Bristol Siddeley Olympus turbojets and had a maximum speed of 645 miles per hour at about 40,000 feet. (Hawker Siddeley Aviation)

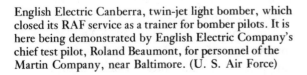

Gloster Javelin, in a dual trainer version. The Javelin was the first twin-engined operational delta-wing fighter. (U. S. Air Force)

English Electric Canberra, twin-jet light bomber, which closed its RAF service as a trainer for bomber pilots. It is here being demonstrated by English Electric Company's chief test pilot, Roland Beaumont, for personnel of the Martin Company, near Baltimore. (U. S. Air Force)

Handley Page Victor of RAF Strike Command.
(Handley Page Ltd.)

In service with RAF Bomber Command from the early fifties until the end of 1968 was the potent crescent-winged Handley Page Victor, one of the most versatile of the early jet bombers. During its long service in Bomber Command (later Strike Command) the Victor was assigned chores as both a high-altitude and low-level medium bomber; it was also used as a reconnaissance aircraft. In its final operational months it was flown primarily as a high-speed refuel aircraft. The Victor's maximum speed approached Mach 1 (650 miles per hour at fifty thousand feet).

Even in the jet age, more conventional aircraft continued to be used for certain specialized jobs. Such aircraft were fitted with engines and propellers—so-called turboprops. These engines utilized the advantages of the jet type of engine (lightness, simplicity, little vibration, efficient operation), which drove a propeller. Such turboprop planes were ideal for aircraft that were not required to fly at great speeds or at very high altitudes. Such an aircraft was the Royal Navy's Fairey Gannet, a carrier-based reconnaissance plane, i.e., an "early warning aircraft." With a crew of three, the Gannet was also used for submarine patrols. Powered by a Bristol Siddeley Double Mamba turboprop engine, the Gannet was pulled by two sets of turboprops that operated independently of each other—that is, alternating while cruising, which enabled the Gannet to stay aloft for as long as six hours. Both propellers could be used for greater power and speed, when required—such as in take-off or under combat conditions.

Another interesting transitional design was the propeller driven Hawker Siddeley Andover, developed from the commercial airliner the HS-748. The Andover flew initially in 1961, by which time Hawker Siddeley (which had absorbed such famous British names in aviation as Armstrong-Whitworth, de Havilland, Gloster, and Avro) was already producing advanced jets, such as the Vulcan, of which more later. The Andover in its military modification was used by RAF Transport Command and could carry forty-four fully equipped men, or eighteen wounded or twelve thousand pounds of freight. The fuselage was "stretched" and the aft section modified for the installation of a loading ramp. Like the Gannet, the Andover was a turboprop-driven aircraft. The commercial model carried from fifty-two to fifty-eight passengers—or three automobiles. It was but one of several commercial aircraft converted to commercial transport use, a common practice of the period.

Unlike their wartime allies, Britain and the United States, the Soviets had no jet designs ready when the Second World War ended. But in the troubled postwar period, the Russians lost no time: they freely "borrowed." For example, the Tupolev Tu-4 was a precise copy of a Boeing B-29 (based on aircraft that had force-landed in Manchuria or Siberia during the war.) Among the German spoils of war that fell into Soviet hands was the German Jumo turbojet engine. Putting the two together— the advanced technology of aircraft design represented by the B-29 and the Jumo engine—inevitably resulted in a Soviet breakthrough that led to the birth of the Soviet jet production, much of which was kept under characteristic Russian secrecy.

That the Soviets were capable of producing formidable jet fighters was not evident until the Korean War when a Lockheed F-80 was destroyed by a MIG-15, designed by Mikoyen and Gurevich. But that was not the earliest of the Soviet jets. As early as April 1946 Aleksandr Yakovlev combined the design of his piston-engined Yak-9 with the German Jumo turbojet engine to produce the Yak-15. This concept went through many modifications, but in general was not in the same league as the Korea fightèr, the MIG-15, with its revolutionary swept-back wing and an engine based on British designs. But Yakovlev persisted and by the mid-fifties unveiled his advanced Yak-25 at a Moscow Air Show. The aircraft was a two-place all-weather night interceptor, which with modifications could also serve as a fighter-bomber. In later generations, with such code names as Flashlight-D, Firebar, Brewer, and the more radically altered Mandrake, the variations on the Yak-25 were used as trainers, light bombers, and fighters.

Fairey Gannet, Mark 4, 1956 (the prototype Gannet first flew in 1949). Besides the Royal Navy, the Australian Navy used the three-place Gannet for submarine patrols. (U. S. Air Force)

Hawker Siddeley Andover transport plane. Rear of fuselage has been modified for installation of loading ramp. Two Rolls-Royce Dart engines, with turboprops, power the Andover. (Hawker Siddeley Aviation)

Yakovlev 25s at a Soviet air show in June 1956, a year after it became operational as a two-place night-fighter interceptor. Radar equipment was housed in the nose. (U. S. Air Force)

Yak-24U Horse helicopter at a Moscow air show. (U. S. Air Force)

The lessons of Korea were not lost on the Russians, whose jet designs continued to evolve with such variants of the MIG-15 as the MIG-17 and, after the war ended, the MIG-19. Nor was the helicopter ignored; there was some initial borrowing from the helicopter pioneer Sikorsky (it was all in the family, since Sikorsky had been born in Russia), notably in the Mi-4 (designed by Mikhail L. Mil). These craft served in as many functions from antisubmarine patrol, transport, etc., as did this type of aircraft in the West. One of the more recent Soviet rotorcraft designs was the Yak-24U, code-named Horse, designed to carry troops into combat zones and the wounded out. Because of initial design problems the Yak-24 came too late for Korea—the U model flew for the first time in December 1957. In its commercial version, introduced in 1960, the Yak-24 carried thirty passengers. This aircraft, and others in the vertical takeoff genre, variable sweep jets have kept the Soviets neck-and-neck, and often ahead, of Western aviation technology since the end of the Second World War.

Not that European aviation has lagged. Its postwar resurgence has introduced new concepts in design, speed, and function—a reminder that the production of aircraft is not dominated by the United States and Britain.

Among the most interesting were military designs of fighter-interceptor types. From Sweden came the SAAB-35 Draken, the standard fighter of the Royal Swedish Air Force until 1970. Two-place models of the Draken served as trainers, while the single-seaters were operational strike aircraft. The 35D model was capable of Mach 2 speeds (1,320 miles per hour at forty thousand feet).

Germany's Luftwaffe was wiped out during the Second World War, and Germany's military production potential was very carefully supervised by East and West, as before. What postwar Luftwaffe power existed in the seventies (as part of NATO) was primarily American-made aircraft. (East Germany, of course, is equipped with Soviet planes.) In 1963, however, an unusual plane designed by Ludwig Boelkow was flown. This was the VJ-101, a vertical takeoff fighter. The engine pods on the

SAAB 35-Draken, single-place interceptor, Europe's first Mach 2 (top speed 1,320 miles per hour at 40,000 feet) fighter. Planes in photo are the 35D model. The initials SAAB stand for Svenska Aeroplan Aktiebolaget. (Saabfoto)

Bölkow VJ-101, a postwar German jet fighter. (Bölkow GMBH)

Dassault Mystère, an outstanding French design of the late 1960s. (Avions Marcel Dassault)

wingtips rotated ninety degrees for takeoff straight up from small places; once in the air the pods move into position for operation. The VJ-101 is capable of speeds in excess of Mach 1.

France's aviation industry made a fine recovery after the war and began producing excellent jet-powered aircraft, among the first being the Dassault Mystère, a single-seat interceptor fighter. This aircraft was used by the Armée de l'Air for several years until more modern planes replaced it. Export models were then sold abroad. The Israeli Air Force used this plane effectively in the June 1967 Arab-Israeli War.

Dassault's Mirage IIIC, a single-seat all-weather interceptor, flies at a speed exceeding Mach 2 (1,-386 miles per hour at forty thousand feet). Like the IIICJ, it served with the Israeli Defense Force/Air Force (Heil Avir Le Israel). This supplanted the Mystère as a first-line fighter in time for the Arab-Israeli War.

One of the most potent French jet-fighter designs was the Dassault Mirage 5, a ground-attack aircraft capable of carrying a tremendously heavy load of weaponry.

An Anglo-French collaboration between the British Aircraft Corporation and Breguet Aviation resulted in the Jaguar, designed as a tactical support and advanced training aircraft. First flown in September 1968 and designed according to specifications of both the Royal Air Force and the Armée de l'Air, the Jaguar became operational with both air forces in 1971–72. Although originally intended for carrier use, the Jaguar proved to be too heavy. The craft is powered by two Rolls-Royce/Turbomeca Adour engines that are capable of producing a top speed of Mach 1.7 (1,120 miles per hour.)

Britain's answer to the vertical-takeoff design problem is the Hawker Siddeley Harrier, an advanced close-support and armed reconnaissance aircraft that went into RAF service in April 1969. Capable of lifting off improvised landing areas, the Harrier looks like some science-fiction insect rising out of a thicket. To rise vertically exhaust gases from the Rolls-Royce Pegasus jet engines are deflected by four rotating nozzles (two nozzles on

Dassault Mirage IIIC. (Avions Marcel Dassault)

Dassault Mirage V, a flying armory. In-flight photo shows a Mirage carrying fourteen bombs (the long, slender objects are jettisonable fuel tanks); the ground shot dramatizes the potential impact of the aircraft. In the foreground, an air-to-ground missile; on either side of that, two pods capable of firing eighteen rockets (these would be affixed under the wing, as are the rocket launchers in position, which were armed with thirty-six rockets). Beltlike object just under the nose of the plane is an ammunition belt holding 250 rounds of 30-millimeter cannon shells. Various other bombs and rocket launchers litter the ground. These were not all carried at once, of course, but were used in various combinations, depending on the mission. The Mirage V was the export version of the Mirage and was used by the Belgian and Peruvian air forces. (Avions Marcel Dassault)

either side of the fuselage just under the wing root). The Harrier can also take off conventionally. Heavily armed with bombs, guns, and missiles, the Harrier can attain speeds close to Mach 1. In level flight without combat load its speed is Mach 1.25. The Harrier is also in service with the U. S. Marine Corps.

Representative of jet development in the U. S. Navy beginning in the late fifties, was the Douglas F-6 Skyray and the Ling-Temco-Vought F-8 Crusader. The Skyray was a single-seat interceptor armed with several types of missiles, bombs, and projectiles, including the Sidewinder missile, two of which were mounted under the wings. The Crusader, like the Skyray, became operational in 1956, and was a carrier-based interceptor originally that was later converted into a reconnaissance craft.

The U. S. Navy's Douglas A-4F Skyhawk was designed in 1954 as a shipboard single-seat attack bomber and went into service operation with both the Navy (carriers) and the Marines (land-based

British Aircraft Corporation-Breguet Jaguar (whose design was based on the Breguet 121), which in its single-seat form is a strike aircraft and in its two-seat variant is a trainer. (British Aircraft Corporation)

Hawker Siddeley Harrier, the first operational military vertical-takeoff-and-landing (VTOL) aircraft. First flown in 1960 (when it was known as the Kestral), a later, modified version went into RAF service in April 1969. (Hawker Siddeley Aviation)

Douglas F-6A Skyray and Vought F-8J Crusader, U. S. Navy carrier craft during the late fifties and early sixties. By 1962 the Skyray was being used by reserve units and as a trainer. The F-8J was a modification of the final Crusader, the F-8E, which was equipped with radar (in the wing center section). (Douglas Aircraft/Ling-Temco-Vought)

Douglas (later McDonnell Douglas) A-4 Skyhawk. Designed as an economical replacement for the A-1 Skyraider, the Skyhawk saw service not only with American air units but also with those of Australia, New Zealand, and Israel. Depicted is the A-4F, the tandem-seat version. The Skyhawk was small enough for carrier storage without wing folding; its span measured twenty-seven feet, six inches. (Douglas Aircraft)

Lockheed F-104 Starfighters in many variants were used by several air forces during the fifties and sixties. It served primarily as an interceptor, but with modifications also carried bombs and various air-to-air and air-to-ground weaponry. The Starfighter was produced in one- and two-place versions, depending on the mission. Its speed exceeded Mach 2 (1,450 miles per hour). (Lockheed Aircraft)

use) in 1956. As late as 1967 additional modifications continued to be made to keep the plane up-to-date. Early models of this plane were flown by Navy and Marine pilots in Vietnam.

Important U. S. Air Force fighters of the late fifties—and still operational in the sixties—were the Lockheed F-104 Starfighter, a Mach 2 interceptor. Eventually cleared for export, the Starfighter became one of the principal aircraft of the postwar Luftwaffe (in a two-seat version). The Luftwaffe alone acquired more than six hundred Starfighter F-104s. Another fighter, the Convair F-102 Delta Dagger, went into operational service in 1956 as a single-seat all-weather interceptor.

An interesting conception was the General Dynamics F-111, a tactical fighter that was designed to be used by both the U. S. Air Force and the Navy. Originally known as the TFX (Tactical Fighter Experimental), the F-111 flew for the first time in December 1964. This was the first aircraft intended for use by two services, since the planes of each generally require different specifications for their respective operational conditions. The outstanding feature of the F-111 was its variable-sweep wing, which endowed the craft with speed versatility. While taking off and landing, the wings are fully extended (slow speed); with the wing swept back, a high speed of Mach 2.5 (1,650 miles per hour at forty thousand feet) is possible. A large

craft for a fighter (the extended wings measure seventy feet), the F-111 carries a crew of two.

A later tactical fighter (one, that is, that does not double as a heavy bomber) was the Ling-Temco-Vought A-7D, the Corsair II, a worthy successor to the World War II Corsair. Besides two twenty-millimeter cannon in the nose, the Corsair II carried a heavy load of small bombs—such as twenty-eight general-purpose bombs (each weighing 250 pounds). Later models of the Corsair II were equipped with Integrated Light Attack Avionics Systems, which include computers, special navigational devices, and high-frequency communications. The Corsair II succeeded the Skyhawk in Navy service and developed out of the earlier Crusader.

By the late sixties various factors affected the design and production of U. S. fighter aircraft. The aircraft industry, especially that branch of it producing airframes, was threatened by the growing interest in the missile—unmanned and most destructive. Also, the costs of even a single-seat fighter-interceptor could be astronomical, what with the sophisticated electronic systems it carried. One airplane costing several million dollars was rather mind- and purse-boggling; a squadron of B-17s could have been acquired for about that during the Second World War. Supersonic fighters were standard on both sides of the Iron Curtain (and tested against each other over Korea and Vietnam). But in the interests of economy, in the United States at least, older models were not phased out and new models introduced willy nilly. (This was true for bombers as well as fighters; consider the long operational life of the B-52.) With each advance in design on one side of the Curtain, new designs were considered on the other. The service life of aircraft was extended through modification;

Convair F-102 Delta Daggers. This aircraft went into service with the U. S. Air Force in 1956; production ended in 1958. The modified TF-102A was a two-place (side by side) trainer that could also be used as an interceptor. (General Dynamics)

General Dynamics' F-111 fighter-bomber, the first "variable geometry" aircraft. The pilot controlled the wing position from the cockpit. For takeoff and landing the wings were in extended position, and were swept back for high-speed (Mach 2.5) performance. (U. S. Air Force)

F-111 demonstrating "variable geometry." (U. S. Air Force)

FB-111, the bomber version of the F-111 fighter of the Strategic Air Command. (U. S. Air Force)

Ling-Temco-Vought A-7D Corsair, designed to replace the A-4 Skyhawk. First flown in 1965, the Corsair saw much service in Vietnam. Plane in photo is armed with twenty-eight 250-pound bombs. (LTV Aerospace)

Grumman A6A Intruder, carrier-borne attack plane, designed especially for "limited" wars, a concept that had grown out of the Korean experience. The Intruder was an all-weather, long-range, low-level attack aircraft equipped with a digital integrated attack navigation system (DIANE). This system enabled the pilot to fly to and attack his target automatically by computer. The A6A went into combat in Vietnam in July 1965. (Grumman Aircraft)

McDonnell Douglas F-15, a sophisticated fighter design of the seventies; the prototype was first flown in 1972. (U. S. Air Force)

General Dynamics' F-16, designed as a lightweight, inexpensive, and versatile fighter. It flew for the first time in February 1974. In 1977 NATO nations Belgium, Denmark, the Netherlands, and Norway had joined the United States in a program to produce the F-16. (General Dynamics)

versatility was emphasized [for example, the F-111, jet trainers and counterinsurgency (COIN)—close support aircraft].

By the late seventies the U. S. Air Force and Navy were still flying many of the planes that had become familiar during the Vietnam War and before. Still, keeping up with the Soviets introduced new designs such as the McDonnell Douglas F-15 and General Dynamics' F-16, the latter capable of more than Mach 2 speed and, according to the Air Force Fact Sheet, it is "a modern and low-cost addition to the tactical fighter force."

Operating concurrently with such advanced aircraft as the F-15 and F-16 are several planes designed for special missions and, in outward appearance at least, seeming to belong to an earlier era— some are even powered by piston engines with propellors. One of the most lethal is the Fairchild A-10, a turbofan-powered, heavily armed, close-support aircraft designed to attack enemy troop concentrations. The A-10 is noted for what the Air Force describes as its "survivability" through "a combination of high maneuverability at low airspeeds and altitudes plus an overall 'hard' aircraft. The pilot is encircled by a titanium armorplate 'bathtub' which also protects the vital elements of the flight control system. Redundant primary structural elements can survive major damage; self-sealing fuel cells are protected with internal and external foam; and the A-10's primary redundant hydraulic flight control system is further enhanced by a back-up 'manual reversion' system which permits the pilot to fly and land the airplane when all hydraulics are lost." By "redundant" the Air Force means that the structure is designed to take a good deal of punishment—for example, triple wing spars, instead of one or two to compensate for damage. The A-10 is also equipped with radar, and devices that jam heat-seeking radar-guided ground-to-air missiles.

Another curious hybrid-like aircraft is a flying radar station, the E-3A, a Boeing 707 modified to carry a sophisticated airborne surveillance and command system. The E-3A has the capability of spotting and tracking airborne targets over land and sea, making it more flexible and superior to

The Fairchild A-10, a close air-support aircraft. Heavily gunned, it is capable of knocking out tanks. The A-10 is powered by twin General Electric turbofan engines. Highly maneuverable, easily maintained, the A-10 first went into Air Force service in 1976. (U. S. Air Force)

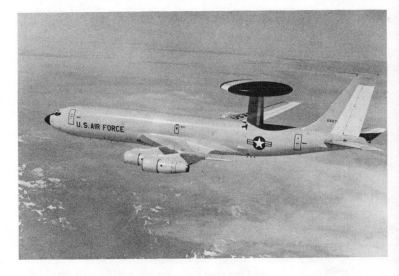

E-3A Airborne Warning and Control System (AWACS)—actually a Boeing 707-320B, with modifications, the most obvious being the rotating radome housing electronic equipment for the detection of aerial attack over land or sea. Actually a flying radar station, the E-3 functions also as an airborne command post. (U. S. Air Force)

stationary radar systems; it is even equipped with a data-processing computer. In peacetime the E-3A keeps surveillance of intruding aircraft and surface vessels.

Yet another special mission aircraft is Grumman's S-2 Trackers and E-2 Hawkeyes, both propeller driven. The Tracker series is powered by a Wright R-1820 air-cooled radial engine and was designed for antisubmarine patrol and, besides carrying electronic detection equipment, also carries various combinations of bombs, torpedoes, and missiles. The most recent model in the series, the S-2D, can remain airborne for a maximum of nine hours and has a range of more than thirteen hundred miles.

The E-2 Hawkeye is powered by twin Allison turboprop engines and operates from carriers as an early warning craft. Carrying a twenty-four-foot circular radome above the center of the fuselage, the Hawkeye has a top speed of four hundred miles per hour. A five-man crew operates a complex electronic tactical data system. The radome scans the search area by slowly rotating, feeding information into high speed computors. The function of the Hawkeye, of course, is to prevent sneak aerial attacks.

American bombardment aircraft have gone through various configurations since the coming of supersonic flight.

The world's first supersonic bomber was the Convair B-58 Hustler, which carried its considerable punch—ranging from nuclear weapons to cameras—in a disposable pod under the fuselage. Length of the Hustler is ninety-six feet, nine inches; wingspan is fifty-six feet, ten inches. Top speed is Mach 2.1 (1,385 miles per hour at an altitude of forty thousand feet). The Hustler was an important element of the U. S. Strategic Air Command (SAC) during the sixties.

Although heavier than any heavy bomber of the

General Dynamics' B-58 Hustler, the Convair Model 4, supersonic bomber whose first flight occurred in November 1956. The disposable weapon pod, slung under the fuselage, originally carried fuel and a nuclear bomb; later the pod housed electronic and reconnaissance equipment. (U. S. Air Force)

The Boeing B-47 Stratojet, the first swept-wing jet bomber. For a time the backbone of the Strategic Air Command, the B-47 was widely used during the Korean conflict. Boeing was joined in its production by Lockheed and Douglas; more than two thousand Stratojets were built. (U. S. Air Force)

Specialized missions require special aircraft with piston engines and propellers, even in the jet age. Late in 1952 Grumman introduced a carrier-borne (also shore-based) antisubmarine aircraft, the S-2A Tracker. This twin-engined plane was used by the U. S. Navy as well as the navies of Japan, the Netherlands, Canada, Argentina, and others. The later (1959) version, the S-2D, was somewhat larger and, besides a crew of four, carried various antisubmarine devices and weapons, including homing torpedoes or depth bombs. (Grumman Aircraft)

The Grumman E-2A Hawkeye, another specialized craft, in U. S. Navy service since 1964. Equipped with a twenty-four-foot circular radome, it was designed as a shipboard early-warning aircraft. An all-weather plane, the Hawkeye serves as detector for its carrier. It is powered by two turboprop Allison engines. (Grumman Aircraft)

Second World War, the Boeing B-47 Stratojet was classified by the Air Force as a medium bomber. Powered by six jet engines, the B-47 was capable of speeds in excess of six hundred miles per hour. It could cover a distance of three thousand miles without refueling. Production of the bomber began in the late forties; the first test plane flew in December 1947. Three years later the B-47s were still in SAC service using a revolutionary technique known as lob bombing, which entailed diving upon targets at maximum speed, releasing bombs at low level, and pulling away in a vertical climb. Pilots then referred to the B-47 as the first six-engine fighter. By the midsixties the plane had passed out of operational service, but it continued to be used by SAC as a reconnaissance aircraft.

The major heavy bomber of the Strategic Air Command during the sixties and seventies is the Boeing B-52 Stratofortress. The first model of its type initially flew in 1952, and various models have served in SAC even since. B-52s have been used in various missions besides their twenty-four-hour-a-day vigil flights over the United States as reconnaissance planes. Powered by eight Pratt & Whitney TF33 turbofan engines (each with seventeen thousand pounds of thrust), the B-52 is a subsonic jet (maximum speed is around 650 miles per hour).

An aircraft designed to phase out the aging B-52 was taken into Air Force consideration in 1961, when exploratory studies were initiated into something called SLAB (Subsonic Low-altitude Aircraft). These studies grew over several years, resulting in a contract being awarded to North American Rockwell (now Rockwell International) to construct their airframe of what was to be called the B-1 strategic bomber. The two engines were

The Boeing B-52 Stratofortress, "the world's largest bomber" (wingspan, 185 feet; length, 157 feet, 6 inches). The B-52 was active in Vietnam. In photo, it carries two AGM-28 Hound Dog missiles attached to inboard pylons. The Hound Dog (no longer used) carried a nuclear warhead, was powered by a turbojet propulsive unit, and had a range of more than five hundred miles. (U. S. Air Force)

Back to square one: the three North American Rockwell B-1s, the last of which was rolled out on January 16, 1976. The first flew on December 23, 1974. The wings are fully extended for subsonic takeoff. With wings swept back the B-1 could fly at a speed of Mach 2.2. Wingspans measured 137 feet (forward) and 78 feet (swept); the fuselage measured 151 feet. (U. S. Air Force)

The Boeing KC-135 Stratotanker, the Air Force's flying gas tank. (U. S. Air Force)

View from a Stratotanker as a B-52 approached below for refueling. The boom has been lowered; winglike gadgets steadied the high-speed boom. (The Boeing Company)

provided by General Electric. Although it was smaller than the B-52, the B-1 could carry almost twice the weapons payload; its swing wing enabled it, like the F-111, to fly at supersonic speeds at high altitude and subsonic speeds at "treetop altitudes." It could take off from comparatively short runways, it was developed not to be an environmental threat—but it ran into serious cost problems. Original cost estimates rose 88 per cent, which made the B-1 controversial whatever its capabilities. Political pressures and fiscal realities of the late seventies led to the cancellation of B-1 development by President Jimmy Carter late in 1977. By this time three of the B-1s had been completed; a fourth still in construction remains in limbo. So for the Air Force this meant staying with the F-111 and the old but reliable B-52.

A B-52 can remain aloft for days if necessary (it would be hard on a crew) by means of inflight refueling furnished by the Boeing KC-135 Stratotanker. Capable of keeping up with jet fighters and bombers at operational altitudes, the KC-135 (a version of the commercial airliner the Boeing 707) can hook up with aircraft in flight for refueling. The refueling boom is tucked under the tail of the aircraft. When the refuel time arrives, the boom is lowered and the two planes join in midair while fuel is pumped into the B-52.

The high speeds of jet-propelled aircraft and the advances in aerodynamic design produced aircraft of unusual appearance. Such a plane is the Lockheed SR-71 (for Strategic Reconnaissance), which flew for the first time in 1964 and was delivered to SAC in January 1966. An aircraft capable of Mach 3 (more than two thousand miles per hour) speeds has scant need for wings—although they do measure about fifty-five feet across. The long, slender fuselage is 107 feet long. With a crew of two, the SR-71 can survey some sixty thousand square miles of the earth's surface (from an altitude of eighty thousand feet) in an hour's flying time. The very sophisticated observation equipment is mounted in a removable pod carried in the fuselage.

Another strange creaturelike aircraft is the North American XB-70 Valkyrie. Although it was originally intended as a strategic bomber, to date, since its first flight in 1964, it has served as an aerodynamic research aircraft. With a slender, projectilelike body mounted on a delta wing (wingspan 105 feet), the XB-70 has served admirably as an experimental plane, testing various innovations associated with supersonic flight. This includes crew safety, extreme heat at high speeds, and the simple matter of coming to a halt after landing (assisted by the old-fashioned parachute). Just stopping the Valkyrie requires the same amount of energy necessary to stop eight hundred average automobiles traveling at one hundred miles an hour. One of the safety features for the crew—four men in this case—is specially designed seats that can be ejected while the plane is flying at maximum speed at seventy thousand feet. The XB-70 is powered by six General Electric J-93 turbojet engines, each producing thirty thousand pounds of thrust. The landing gear alone weighs more than six tons. Total weight of the aircraft is more than 450,000 pounds. As a research craft, the XB-70 requires a crew of only two.

American military designs were put to the test in the war in Vietnam. Like the Korean War, the war in Vietnam was of so-called limited scope—the hope being it would not become World War III. All nations with any sense of survival realize that should the weapons systems actually on hand in the seventies be unleashed, it would mean the wiping out of civilization, if not man himself. So the fighting in Vietnam was a curious and tragic blending of very primitive fighting with the very modern, a mingling of the past and the unhoped-for future. One of the oldest jets in operation in Vietnam was the Martin B-57 Canberra, based on the British plane of the same name. Adapted by Martin, the B-57 was used as a medium bomber in Southeast Asia. Except for a change of engines, modernization, and new weaponry, the B-57 was virtually the same as the Canberra—same configuration, wingspan, and fuselage.

Four Navy fighters refuel from a Convair R3Y-2 Tradewind, transport version of the XP5Y-1. (General Dynamics)

The Lockheed SR-71, head-on view. Engines are Pratt & Whitney J-58 turbojets. (Lockheed Aircraft)

Developed out of the A-11, the SR-71 was designed to replace the Lockheed U-2 "spy plane." Seventeen SR-71s were built for the U. S. Air Force. (Lockheed Aircraft)

With its more than Mach 3 speed capability, the SR-71 has been rightly called "the fastest military aircraft in service." The plane holds several speed and altitude records. The interceptor variant is known as the YF-12A. (Lockheed Aircraft)

The North American XB-70 Valkyrie on completion of its second flight, October 5, 1964, at Edwards Air Force Base, California. (U. S. Air Force)

Close-ups of the Valkyrie on rollout day, May 11, 1964. Canard forward wing and folding wingtip assisted in supersonic flight. (U. S. Air Force)

XB-70 airborne. (North American Aviation)

XB-70 takeoff. High temperatures generated by the speed of this craft necessitated the use of special fuselage construction (welded steel honeycomb sandwich) and titanium in the forward section. (U. S. Air Force)

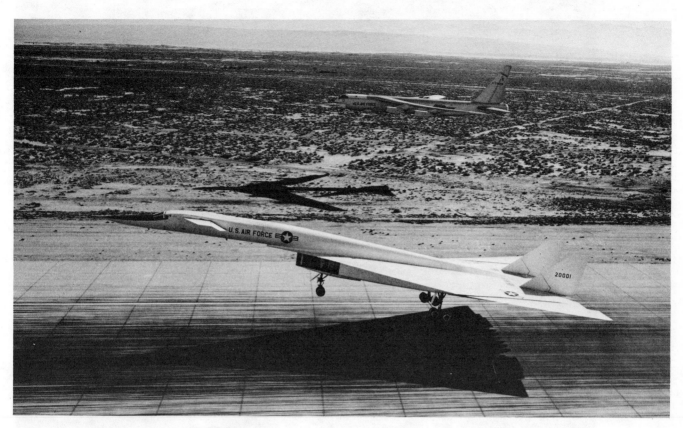

Valkyrie landing; in the background a B-52, which the
XB-70 was designed to replace. Final slow-down stage of
landing required the use of parachutes. (U. S. Air Force/
North American Aviation)

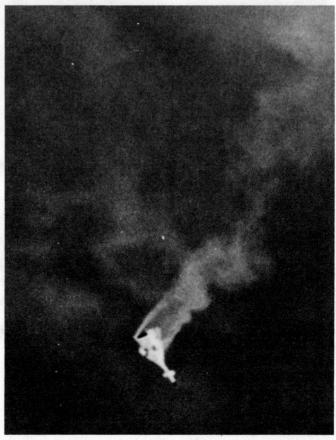

Only two Valkyrie prototypes were built; a third was canceled in 1964. On June 8, 1966, while on a "training mission" (to photograph a formation of fighters with the XB-70), the second prototype was destroyed. The formation consisted of a Northrop T-38, a Navy McDonnell F-4, the XB-70, a NASA Lockheed F-104, and a Northrop F-5. During the flight the F-104 brushed the Valkyrie's right vertical stabilizer. As the XB-70 continued in formation the F-104 exploded, resulting in the death of NASA's chief research pilot, Joseph A. Walker. Then the XB-70 fell out of control and, spinning, crashed, killing Air Force Major Carl S. Cross. The remaining prototype is now stored in the Air Force Museum, Wright-Patterson Air Force Base, Ohio. (U. S. Air Force)

Looking backward: a World War II C-47 on a ground-support mission in Vietnam. Gun position in the side of the aircraft was operated by the pilot, who banked the plane to the left, sighted through a gunsight near his left shoulder, and triggered the guns by a button on the control column. (U. S. Air Force)

The Martin B-57 Canberra, the American version of the British Electric aircraft of the same name. In Southeast Asia the Canberras (here starting engines) were used as tactical bombers. Starting engines with explosive cartridges enabled the Canberras to operate from forward bases without elaborate electric power systems. (U. S. Air Force)

Puff, the Magic Dragon on a night mission; a time-exposure photograph as the AC-47 (the Vietnam War designation of the DC-3) circles a target and streams of gunfire devastate the area. (U. S. Air Force)

Douglas A-1E Skyraiders on a mission, Vietnam, 1965. This prolific (more than three thousand were built between 1948 and 1957) aircraft was durable and versatile and was used in the Korean and Vietnam wars. (U. S. Air Force)

A fully armed Skyraider over Vietnam. Skyraiders were flown by airmen of the U. S. Air Force, Navy, and by the Air Force of South Vietnam. (U. S. Air Force)

An even greater retrogression in aviation than the 1952 Canberra was the Douglas C-47, veteran of the Second World War. The ex-DC-3 was adapted for ground-support missions in Vietnam. Equipped with three 7.62-millimeter guns in the port side of the aircraft, the C-47—called Puff the Magic Dragon—rolled into a left bank over the target area (generally troop concentrations) and the pilot actuated the guns (the sight was located near his left shoulder). It was a primitive form of modern warfare. A crew of seven manned *Puff the Magic Dragon:* pilot, copilot, navigator, two gun-loaders, flight engineer, and a loadmaster to oversee the handling of the guns. The whirling-barrel guns, operating on the principle of the old Gatling machine gun, fired eighteen thousand rounds per minute.

Also widely used in Vietnam in the sixties was the Douglas Skyraider, which dated back to 1948 and had served in Korea. It was initially a shipboard Navy fighter. In Vietnam it operated as a fighter-bomber and dive bomber. The A-1E models of the Skyraider were the last of the series and were produced in 1957. The Skyraider had a long life as an operational aircraft. It was rugged and dependable, and it was the last of the propeller-driven shipboard fighters.

A Skyraider zeroes in on a target spotted by a light observation plane. (U. S. Air Force)

The more lethal, contemporary, aspect of the Vietnam war was represented by such multipurpose aircraft as the McDonnell F-4 Phantom which was flown by the U. S. Air Force, Navy, and Marines as well as British Royal Navy and RAF pilots, the West German Air Force and others. A versatile plane, the Phantom served as a bomber, a fighter, as escort for heavy bombers, and for reconnaissance. In the Vietnam war the U. S. Air Force used the Phantom F-4C in conjunction with ground troops in close-support missions and for interdiction—the destruction of bridges, communications, and any means of interruption of the delivery of enemy supplies.

The Phantom was actually designed by Douglas before that firm merged with McDonnell in 1967. The Phantom, then, is also known as the McDonnell Douglas F-4. First flown in May 1958, the aircraft has been one of the most widely produced since the Second World War. In about a decade more than four thousand Phantoms have been built, some, under license, in Germany and Japan. (One Phantom costs about $3.5 million.) With a speed of Mach 2, the Phantom was fairly evenly matched with the MIG-21 the Soviets supplied to the North Vietnamese. However, it was a more versatile aircraft, since the MIG-21 could only be used as a fighter.

An Air Force Skyraider places a hundred-pound bomb into a Viet Cong position in a jungle. The plane could carry an eight thousand-pound load of ordnance— bombs, rockets, and the notorious napalm. (U. S. Air Force)

Low-level missions exposed Skyraiders to ground fire; this one returns to base with a portion of its wingtip blown away. (U. S. Air Force)

The Republic F-105 Thunderchief was the workhorse of the early jet fighting in Vietnam (it was eventually replaced by the F-4). Neither as fast as nor capable of operating at as high altitudes as the Phantom, the F-105 sometimes fared rather poorly in combat with Soviet MIG-19s and 21s, more modern supersonic fighters. The Thunderchief pilots, however, performed admirably in various types of missions.

Another Vietnam fighter was the Northrop F-5, which was initially designed in the midfifties as a low-cost supersonic fighter for use by smaller nations as a defense aircraft. It was not until 1962 that the plane was ordered by the U. S. Air Force—to be used as trainers for foreign pilots then being trained in the United States. The aircraft was ordered by Taiwan, Greece, Norway, and Turkey, among others. A dozen F-5s were ordered by the U. S. Air Force for use in Vietnam and went into combat in 1966.

The McDonnell F-4C Phantom (originally developed by Douglas) first flew in May 1958. The first models were used by the U. S. Navy. The F-4C went into Air Force service in 1963. (U. S. Air Force)

The Republic F-105 Thunderchief; in the foreground, two 750-pound bombs. Modifications on the F-105D enabled the plane to carry sixteen of these bombs. (U. S. Air Force)

Not all aircraft operated in Vietnam were absolute warplanes. The Military Air Transport Services (MATS) Lockheed C-103—the Hercules—served as an all-around transport in Vietnam. A squat propeller-driven plane that hugged the ground until airborne, the Hercules served as a troop carrier, cargo plane, and as a rescue ship for downed pilots. It could also drop supplies from low level and evacuate wounded.

One of the most used aircraft in Vietnam was the helicopter for combat and, mostly, for rescue missions. Hovering above airmen who have crashed in the jungle or the water, the helicopter was able to reach locations inaccessible to other planes. Likewise, such aircraft are invaluable in the evacuation of wounded from the battlefield itself, thus making it possible to save lives that might otherwise have been lost.

The war in Vietnam provided few, if any, strategic targets in the classic sense of the Second World War. It was anomalistically anachronistic: an eighteenth-century war fought with twentieth-century weapons, hit-and-run guerrillas vs. giant eight-engined jet bombers. The most effective aircraft used in Vietnam by the United States and its allies were the propeller-driven, piston-engined Skyraiders, helicopters, and transports. The Air Force's strategic bombers, the Boeing B-52, were operated tactically, a mission for which they had not been designed. The Stratofortress carried thirty tons of bombs for use against enemy troop concentrations, ammunition dumps, bamboo bridges, and military bases—if they could actually be located in the tangle of jungle and countryside. While such B-52 attacks forced enemy dispersal and interfered with troop movements, it was rarely, if ever, strategically effective. The Stratofortress was slower than the MIGs supplied to the North Vietnamese by the Soviets and had to be escorted by jet fighters on their generally fruitless bombing missions.

Costly jet aircraft (a jet fighter could cost as much as $5 million per plane), not to mention crews, were risked against targets that could easily be repaired (if hit, that is), often within days.

The Northrop F-5 Freedom Fighter. First flown in 1959, the F-5 has been used by several air forces (Greece, Nationalist China, Norway, Iran, etc.) besides the U. S. Air Force in Vietnam. The F-5B is a two seat trainer version of the single-place F-5A. (U. S. Air Force)

The Lockheed C-130 Hercules military transport. First flown in 1954, the Hercules went into U. S. Air Force operation in December 1956. Wingspan is 132 feet, 7¼ inches; length, 97 feet, 9 inches. The C-130 could carry one hundred soldiers or twenty tons of equipment (and later variants even more). (U. S. Air Force)

A Sikorsky HH-3E "Jolly Green Giant" lifting a downed pilot out of the water, Vietnam. These search-and-rescue helicopters were protected by armor plate and were capable of rescuing men from impossible settings that other planes could not land in. (U. S. Air Force)

Carpet bombing (that is, saturating a concentrated area) by B-52s was no more effective than it had proved to be during the Second World War, which often resulted in casualties among friendly troops. In Vietnam it destroyed portions of the country-side that may or may not have contained legitimate objectives.

Techniques that had worked against such an industrial nation as Germany in the 1939–45 war proved ineffective in the war in Vietnam of 1965–75 (although Americans had served there as "advisers" as early as 1954). This history of aviation is not the place to argue the moral questions of American

A North Vietnamese Soviet-built MIG-17 in the sights of F-105 pilot, Major Ralph L. Kuster. At almost point-blank range the Thunderchief's twenty-millimeter cannon strikes the MIG's left wing; a burst of flame and the hit plane, disintegrating, crashes. (U. S. Air Force)

The MiG-21 (NATO code name "Fishbed"), night-fighter version of the Soviet single-seat interceptor. First introduced in 1956, the MiG-21, despite a Mach 2 speed capability, has a lesser range than NATO aircraft. It has been sold to Cuba, Egypt, Finland, India, and Yugoslavia. Designers A. Mikoyan and N. Gurevich account for the MiG. (U.S.S.R. Mission to the United Nations)

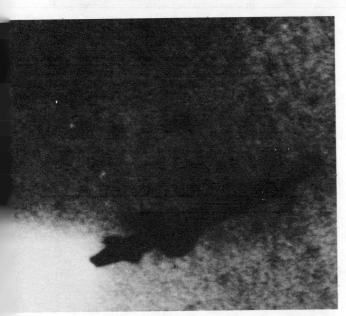

A North Vietnamese surface-to-air missile (SAM)—a more sophisticated form of anti-aircraft projectile than from previous wars—photographed from an Air Force fighter. (U. S. Air Force)

Boeing B-52 Stratofortress striking at a North Vietnamese target with a string of 750-pound bombs. (U. S. Air Force)

"... tragic entanglement ..." A McDonnell RF-101 Voodoo (the reconnaissance version of the Voodoo fighter) lands in a First World War setting at a base in South Vietnam. Originally designed as an escort for the B-36, the Voodoo eventually was modified into an interceptor and fighter-bomber. The F-101 made its first flight in September 1954. (U. S. Air Force)

involvement and performance in Vietnam. But the tragic entanglement was an abuse of humanity and air power.

The haphazard commixture of aircraft was but another manifestation of the frustration of fighting a war few in the United States understood—from the President to the angry or confused man in the street. It was also a war in which few who fought on the American side believed—and that was shockingly brought home with the My Lai massacre, resulting in the death of Vietnamese children, women, and old men. From the air similar outrages were committed in the defoliation and napalm attacks. Entangled in a war without philosophical rationalization, the United States withdrew under a cloud in 1975; it added little to its military stature or to the advancement of aviation.

Civil aviation expanded enormously under the stimulus of jet propulsion—its World War II gift from the military. To produce a suitable jet aircraft took a good deal of planning, thinking, and testing, for the jet meant that an aircraft had to be designed that could travel at speeds at least twice that of conventional airliners and at altitudes undreamed of even during the war. Britain, with its lead in jet-engine technology, was the first nation to produce a postwar commercial jet, the de Havilland Comet,

The de Havilland Comet, the world's first jetliner. (U. S. Air Force)

which first became airborne in May 1952. The advent of the Comet introduced the swiftest and smoothest means of travel, and marked the beginning of the end of piston-engined airliners. But the cost of pioneering marred the history of the first operational commercial jet. For no apparent reason one of the planes disintegrated in the air over Elba, near Rome. (Another had broken up earlier in a severe storm over India.) A few months later, another Comet fell unaccountably. The plane was grounded, and the investigations that followed found the answer: metal fatigue. This was caused by the stress of operations and by the pressurizing and depressurizing of the plane's fuselage for high-altitude flights. The problem was corrected—and noted by aircraft designers all over the world—and the Comet went on to become one of the finest of the early jet planes.

America's first commercial jet was Boeing's 707, which went into service with Pan American in 1958—six years after the Comet flew in England. The 707, since its inception, has spawned several modifications while keeping the same general configuration. Different models have slightly greater wingspans and longer fuselages. The original Boeing 707-121 has a span of 130 feet, 10 inches, and a fuselage length of 144½ feet. Model 707-321, specifically intended for intercontinental flights, was slightly larger, the span being a little more than 142 feet, with length increased to 152 feet. The 707 has a range of five thousand miles and a cruising speed of six hundred miles per hour. Passenger accommodations range from 120 to 177. The 707 is also produced in a cargo-carrying version; it is capable of transporting loads of up to forty tons across the Atlantic nonstop. With the advent of the Boeing 707, American aviation became the world's leading producer of commercial aircraft.

Douglas followed Boeing a year later with its DC-8, which went into service in 1959. It, too, has passed through many modifications, primarily fuselage "stretching" (such as in the DC-8 Super 61, which can carry 250 passengers). The original DC-8 had a wingspan of 142 feet, 5 inches, and a

French-designed Sud-Aviation Caravelle, short- and medium-range jetliner. (United Airlines)

The Boeing 707, the first American commercial jet, in service since 1958. Plane depicted is the cargo-carrying version. The military version is the KC-135. (Pan American World Airways)

The Douglas DC-8—"the world's fastest long-range jet"—in its Series 50 modification, operational in October 1961. (Douglas Aircraft)

fuselage length of 150 feet, 6 inches. In the summer of 1961 the DC-8 became the first transport aircraft to fly faster than sound, at a speed a little more than Mach 1. Like the Boeing 707, the Douglas DC-8 has been widely purchased for use by airlines the world over.

The British and the Americans could not indefinitely dominate the production of jet planes. In 1959 the French aviation firm Sud-Aviation produced a smaller jet, the Caravelle, powered by two jets instead of the customary four, as on the larger airliners. A design innovation was the placement of the two engines (Rolls-Royce Avons) on either side of the rear fuselage. This made for a cleaner wing design—and for extremely quiet flights. The Caravelle was designed for shorter hops than the bigger jets and could carry eighty passengers at speeds of up to five hundred miles per hour. It was the first twin-engined jet to enter U.S. airline service—with United Airlines in July 1961.

Boeing's answer to the short-hop jet was the 727, capable of intercity flights and operating from shorter runways than the giant jets. The 727 became operational in 1963. An interesting aspect of its design is that it is powered by three engines, all located in the rear of the aircraft, two on either side of the fuselage, and a third at the root of the rudder. This placement affords a quieter flight than aircraft with engine pods in the wings. The

idea is an old one actually, dating back to the "pushers" of the early-bird era.

Since not all flights cover the vast distances within the range of such aircraft as the 707, the DC-8, and the Vickers VC-10, smaller jets by the midsixties had become very popular and useful. Douglas produced its DC-9, using the twin jet in the rear design for short- and medium-haul transportation. The DC-9 can be operated by a two-man crew and carries from fifty-six to ninety passengers at a cruising speed of 550 miles per hour.

Britain's Hawker Siddeley Trident, like the Boeing 727, uses three engines in aft installation. The plane was specifically designed for British European Airways as a short- and medium-range transport. The Trident can carry as many as 132 passengers for 2,500 miles nonstop at speeds close

Engine installation and high tail of the Boeing 727. (The Boeing Company)

Boeing's short- and medium-hop liner, the quickly designed and quickly flown 727. First tested in 1963, it went into airline service, with Eastern Airlines, in February 1964. The aircraft can be converted into a cargo plane (from a passenger plane) and vice versa in about two hours. (The Boeing Company)

The cockpit of the Boeing 727; the pilot is seated in the
left seat, while the copilot makes a throttle adjustment.
(The Boeing Company)

The Douglas DC-9, which went into service in November 1965. The Series 30 model's fuselage was 15 feet longer than the prototypes, and measured 150 feet, 6 inches, making more room for either passengers or cargo. The DC-9 in Air Force configuration is known as the C-9 Nightingale. (Douglas Aircraft)

Hawker Siddeley Trident, a design that evolved out of the de Havilland 121. The Trident 2E, in the photo, was modified to increase range and speed. It could carry 115 passengers 2,400 miles at more than 600 miles per hour. The Trident was the first aircraft equipped with automatic landing devices. (Hawker Siddeley)

to six hundred miles per hour. Like many contemporary aircraft, the Trident is equipped with instruments to make fully automatic landings, without special efforts of a pilot.

One of France's many post-Second World War contributions to aviation is the Mystère 20, known as the Fan Jet Falcon. It represents yet another form of jet transportation—the executive, or corporate, transport. These are manufactured for businesses that wish to provide their executives with transportation for fast service between, say, a company's home office and its factories, or for

travel between cities to meet with customers, and for various other private and personal uses. The Falcon, with a span of fifty feet, six inches, and a fuselage of fifty-six feet, three inches, can carry from eight to twelve passengers. Maximum cruising speed is 540 miles per hour, and the average range is about sixteen hundred miles.

Business, or as they are better known, "executive," jets abound also in the United States. Producing aircraft of this type are such nostalgia-laden names as Beech, Cessna, Piper, Grumman with its Gulfstream, and a series of fine aircraft from a relative newcomer and pioneer, the Learjet (named for the company's founder the late William P. Lear.) The purpose of the business jet, of course, is to transport individuals to conferences on a moment's notice, if necessary, speedily, comfortably, and economically. The first Learjet, the Model 23, flew for the first time in October 1963 and went into production the following year (the later Model 24 was virtually the same plane but with a stretched fuselage to increase carrying capacity.) The Learjet is powered by twin turbojets, flies at a speed in the five hundred miles-per-hour range and has a maximum range of two thousand miles. With a crew of two and a passenger capacity of five (some models can carry more), the Learjet is a flying board room.

Typical of more recent developments in business jet design is Lockheed's four-engine JetStar. At a speed of nearly six hundred miles per hour the JetStar can carry as many as ten passengers, plus a crew of two. In a military transport version it can carry seventeen. The smallest four-engined jet, the JetStar has a wingspan of 54.4 feet; the fuselage is slightly more than sixty feet in length. Interestingly, the JetStar, as the C-140, began as a military trainer and transport in the mid-sixties and has been used by the U. S. Air Force as well as West Germany's Luftwaffe.

The Soviets, too, adapted military aircraft to commercial use after the war. By the sixties they produced what was at the time the world's largest commercial aircraft, the Tu-114, a modified Tu-20 Bear, which had originally been a long-range strategic bomber. Produced by Tupolev, the Tu-114 first flew in 1957 and went into production in 1959 and into flight service with Aeroflot in 1961. Plagued with early "bugs," the Tu-114 was long in becoming operational, but proved to be a fine aircraft. The passenger load varied from 170 to 220, depending on the interior design. The Tu-114 was Tupolev's last turboprop design, before the debut of the commercial jet-powered airliner in the Soviet Union.

The United States, however, dominated the field of commercial jets and by the close of the

Production line at Dassault; the plane is the Mystère 20 Fan Jet Falcon private transport. Generally purchased by businesses for use by executives, the Mystère carried from eight to twelve passengers. (Avions Marcel Dassault)

The Learjet, one of the most successful postwar business aircraft. (Gates Learjet Corporation)

Lockheed JetStar (Lockheed C-140), executive transport aircraft. First flown in 1957, the JetStar serves in both private and military capacities. The U. S. Air Force uses it as a transport and trainer. (Lockheed Aircraft)

sixties had produced a remarkable aircraft that can only be described as awe-inspiring. This was Boeing's superjet, the 747. Sometimes referred to as the Jumbo Jet, the 747 was rolled out for the first time on September 30, 1968, the first of the wide-bodied (meaning a large passenger load) jet, and the world's largest civil aircraft. The 747 went into service for Pan American Airways in February 1970 on the New York to London run; since then literally millions of passengers have flown in this great aircraft. The early models carried about 360 passengers at a cruising speed of more than six hundred miles per hour; the range is about six thousand miles. More recent 747s, less luxurious than the initial ones, can accommodate more than five hundred passengers. By the late 1970s some two hundred Boeing 747s were in use by airlines all over the world. Freight carrying 747s can carry one hundred tons of cargo, which is about double that of the more conventional jet freighter.

Lockheed's rival to the 747 cargo plane is the C-5 Galaxy, produced in co-operation with the U. S. Air Force. The Galaxy, which first flew in 1969, is the world's largest airplane: wingspan 223 feet (as compared with the 747's 195 feet), fuselage length 248 feet (the 747 measures 231 feet). From the ground to the tip of the rudder the C-5 towers sixty-five feet.

Tupolev 114 Soviet commercial airliner (NATO code name "Cleat"), which went into service in April 1961. It was the last of the Soviet propeller-driven airliners. The reconnaissance and early-warning version of the Tu-114 is code-named "Moss." (U. S. Air Force)

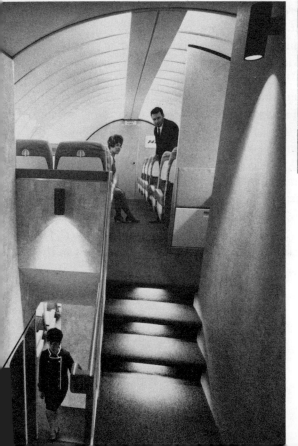

Rollout of the Boeing 747 jumbo jet, September 1968 (first flight took place in February 1969). Still in service in the late seventies, the 747 has undergone many modifications. Overhead shot gives an idea of the size of the plane. The interior view showing the stairway joining the two decks is an early version, for later 747s had spiral staircases. Economic factors eventually subtracted some of the luxuriousness and made room for more than five hundred passengers. (The Boeing Company)

Lockheed C-5 Galaxy, primarily a military transport, in use with the U. S. Air Force since 1970. Despite its bulk the Galaxy has a remarkably short takeoff run (ca. five thousand feet). A proposed civil version of the Galaxy would be capable of carrying extraordinary loads—six buses, as illustrated. (Lockheed Aircraft)

In its initial tests the Galaxy reached a speed of 606 miles per hour, made flights of nine hours' duration, and climbed to an altitude of thirty-eight thousand feet. As a military transport it has been used by the U. S. Air Force since 1971. The capacity of the Galaxy is quite staggering: It can accommodate as many as 345 men, with full field equipment, for transportation from the United States to Europe (or Japan) nonstop (the range of the plane is well over 6,500 miles). In its civilian version, the Galaxy is capable of carrying as many as a hundred automobiles at a time.

In a time of confined, "cold," and, as everyone hoped, small wars, transportation en masse was militarily important for the delivery of troops and their supplies. The two officially nonwarring belligerents—the so-called Free World and the Communist Bloc—were capable of supplying their combating allies (or dupes, depending on the point of view) fighting in some small corner of the world to hold back the tides of communism (or capitalism).

The Soviets, too, produced giant troop and supply carriers, which could be used militarily or commercially. Antonov provided the Soviet Army with efficient transports beginning in the late fifties. The Antonov A-12 was developed from the An-10A, a commercial airliner. In 1962 Antonov introduced an even larger flying weight-lifter, the An-22, in its time the largest flying freighter. The Lockheed Galaxy eventually superseded it in that capacity.

An especially interesting study in aircraft redesign is the Guppy, product of Aero Spacelines. The basic structure of the swollen flying warehouse is the Boeing C-97 Stratofreighter (which in turn had evolved out of the B-29). The G-201 Super Guppy, first flown in 1971, measures no less than twenty-five feet, six inches from deck to ceiling. G. W. Gilmer of Aero Spacelines points out that a "Boeing 747 fuselage section fits nicely inside, with room to spare."

The great aircraft pioneer Igor Sikorsky introduced yet another remarkable cargo transport in 1962, the S-64 Skycrane. The outstanding developer of the helicopter in the United States, Sikorsky, in his Skycrane, had devised a flying moving van. The airframe—it could hardly be called a fuselage—could accommodate the attachment of pod-like freight containers and lift more than seventeen thousand pounds; "people pods" carried ninety plus the crew of two. Originally designed to specifications of the West German Defense Ministry, the Skycrane was also used by the U. S. Army as the YCH-54A troop transport. The later S-65, with fuselage rather than the pod arrangement, was used

"Super Guppy," looking not unlike a whale, quite literally can swallow great payloads for long-distance transport. (Aero Spacelines)

Soviet troop transport Antonov 12 (code name "Cub") taking on paratroopers. Twin twenty-millimeter cannons project from the tail turrets. (U.S.S.R. Mission to the United Nations)

Air pioneer Igor Sikorsky (ca. 1962), who contributed to the design of four-engined aircraft, flying boats, and helicopters. Born in Russia in 1889, Sikorsky died in 1972. (Sikorsky Aircraft)

Sikorsky S-64 Skycrane, without pod. The Skycrane can lift some 20,000 pounds over a distance of 190 miles at 117 miles per hour. (Los Angeles County Fire Department)

by the U. S. Marines as a troop transport and as a flying ambulance.

While the freight-carrying capacity (which meant, with modification, more passengers) was important, the airplane has primarily stood for speed. Military aircraft had broken through the sound barrier—why not commercial airliners?

Around the middle sixties that concept drew the attention of several designers of commercial aircraft. In the United States the race to be first with what was called supersonic aircraft (SST) began with a design competition between two rival giants, Lockheed and Boeing. In September 1966 each offered its conception of such a plane. Boeing was chosen to develop the SST in the United States. However, following the announcement of the results of the design competition and the unveiling of a full-scale model of its SST, Boeing learned that it would not have the expected financial aid from the United States Government and, what with objections to the enormous costs and from environmentalists (who worried what effect supersonic aircraft would have on the atmosphere), the idea was abandoned.

With that idea being noised about, there were others who were also interested in the SST, a plane that would, it was promised, cut transatlantic flying time in half. Despite American leadership in the field, and because the idea received little encouragement before its abandonment, the first supersonic transport was produced in the Soviet Union. The Tupolev Tu-144 flew for the first time in December 1968. The prototype reached a speed of Mach 2.3 (1,518 miles per hour) on one of its test flights. When the Tu-144 was revealed to the Western world in 1971 at the Paris Air Show (a model was displayed in 1965), it was the center of attention.

Unfortunately, disaster struck at the Paris show in 1973; after a demonstration flight a Tu-144 in a landing approach and about 500 feet off the ground stalled, crashed, and exploded in the French town of Goussainville. The crew of six died in the accident, as did a number of townspeople. The loss of the Tu-144 set back the Soviet SST program for several years, and it was not until 1977 that the Soviets announced that the Tu-144 would be brought into commercial service.

Only a year after the Tu-144's maiden flight, a British-French co-operative venture inveiled its SST, the Concorde. Pooling resources, techniques, and finances, the British Aircraft Corporation and Aerospatiale, created the first supersonic transport of the Western world. Capable of flying at Mach 2 (about fourteen hundred miles per hour) with a passenger load of a hundred (the Boeing 747 can carry nearly five hundred) at an altitude of fifty-five thousand feet, the Concorde is capable of flying from London to New York in 3½ hours. Because of the time difference and the Mach 2 speed, it would be possible to leave London at 10 A.M. and arrive in New York at 9 A.M. (local time), a rather bizarre fact of contemporary travel.

But the advent of the SST has not been without controversy. It is expensive to build, not as economical to operate as subsonic jets, and passengers pay more for the luxury of cutting travel time in half. People living in the vicinity of airports have raised objections to the noisy takeoff of the Concorde and to its sonic boom when it slips into high speed. Environmentalists have argued that the plane, flying fast and high, would have a detrimental effect on the ozone layer, which protects us from the rays of the sun, and, that the Concorde's engines would add more pollution to an already contaminated world.

Conservationists contributed their objection: The Concorde was an airborne fuel guzzler.

To all of these complaints the proponents of the Concorde have answers: muffling engine noise, sparing the population sonic booms (which often break windows and cause structural damage to dwellings) by not flying supersonically over populated areas. As for damage to the ozone layer, they point out that military supersonic planes have been in operation for almost two decades with little perceptible effect. The pollution objection was answered with improved engine design. Fuel consumption, it is claimed, is no more than for conventional jets (except, of course, that the Concorde

Boeing's winning SST design 1966, a full-scale wood-and-metal model of the proposed aircraft. This would have been the first supersonic airliner, but had to be abandoned when promised government support was withdrawn. (The Boeing Company)

carries fewer passengers for the same amount of fuel).

In mid-1977 the Concorde was the only supersonic transport in commercial operation, but with serious curbing. Because of the various objections, it was not permitted to land in New York City's Kennedy International Airport for a contentious period of time. New York passengers were forced to travel to Washington, D.C., in order to board a Concorde for Europe. The discord and the temporary ban on the aircraft contributed to some international friction, for British and French aviation industries counted heavily on the revenues that might come from the New York-to-London and New York-to-Paris traffic, the most profitable routes.

Tupolev 144, the first supersonic transport to fly. (National Air and Space Museum, Smithsonian Institution)

The world's first commercial supersonic transport, the British Aircraft Corporation-Aerospatiale Concorde. All SST configurations are basically the same—delta wing (the Boeing initially had a swing wing), "droop" nose to enable the pilot to have a good view of the runway during landing and takeoff, and a complex set of instruments. Other considerations: high operating costs, small passenger loads, and high fares. The Concorde, however, does cut transatlantic travel time in half and, although rather cramped compared to larger aircraft, provides a comfortable flight. (British Airways)

Despite boycotts and traffic tieups in the vicinity of Kennedy Airport by disgruntled residents of the borough of Queens, Concorde test flights in and out of the airport monitored by instruments proved that the plane was less noisy than had been predicted—in fact, it was quieter than some of the older jets. Regular air traffic by Concorde between New York and Europe was instituted. Supersonic commercial aviation is here to stay.

So is yet another fact of contemporary life, although it has not been greeted by angry citizenry, active boycotts, and controversy. None the less, the subject of women airline pilots has been controversial and women fliers have indeed been subtly boycotted and churlishly treated.

Despite a long-time association with the development of aviation and the substantial contribution by women to aviation, deep-rooted male prejudice has denied them the role of airline pilot, especially in the United States. Women were flying commercial planes in England, France, Italy, and the Soviet Union before 1970. Finally, in 1973, the relatively small Denver-based Frontier Airlines hired Emily Warner as a pilot. By 1978 she was a captain and full-fledged pilot. While this giant step opened the door, through which some fifty followed, women did not always find a welcome in the cockpit. Not as pilot, at least. Warner, whose competence and experience are incontrovertible, has found no easy going in the vanguard.

Airline pilot Captain Emily Warner of Frontier Airlines. Captain Warner, a native of Denver, has the distinction of being the first American female command pilot. (Frontier Airlines)

These are not flight attendants, but qualified second officers (that is, copilots). They are, from left to right, Karen Kahn, Claudia Jones, Patricia Toher, Lennie Sorenson, and Mary Hirsch. (Continental Airlines)

"At first, I really felt it," she told interviewer Michael Satchell. "There was cold, unspoken non-acceptance. It's improved, but there are still a couple of guys who don't like to fly with me."

But Captain Warner, pioneer and pilot, had succeeded in breaking new paths in the sky, and by the late seventies fifteen of the two-dozèn major commercial airlines employ women as members of flight crews—sometimes with a little helpful nudge from the Equal Employment Commission and a lawsuit now and then. A mere fifty out of thirty-three thousand is a small beginning, but even more than the supersonic jet (which has yet to pay its way), women are here to stay. They are even prepared to participate in the ultimate air frontier: space.

Father-daughter flight team: Captain Art and Second Officer Debra Ann Powers, Menlo Park, California. A former flight instructor, Ms. Powers is a veteran pilot with more than two thousand hours flying time. (United Airlines)

Flight engineer Debra Ann Powers making a preflight check on her Boeing 747 jet. (United Airlines)

United's first female pilot, Gail Gorski of Prospect, Kentucky. Former inspector pilot for the Federal Aviation Administration, she is now a flight engineer on a Boeing 747. (United Airlines)

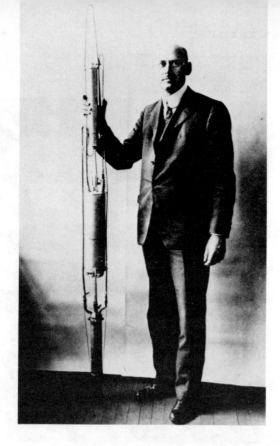

Dr. Robert H. Goddard, American pioneer in rocketry and space flight, with his 1926 rocket. (National Air and Space Museum, Smithsonian Institution)

A German V-2, 1944. The first rocket-powered missile. (National Archives)

9 BEYOND THE MOON

If the mystery of flight engrossed man and vexed his ingenuity, the mysteries of the universe obsess and challenge him. Having studied the stars in space for aeons, man wondered if some form of life not too unlike his own existed on other planets. The earliest speculations imagined that it did—even on the dead and airless moon. The very thought of traveling through space, from the swan-drawn flight of Domingo Gonsales (of Francis Godwin's *Man in the Moone*, 1638) through Jules Verne and the Sunday comic adventures of Buck Rogers and Flash Gordon, was exhilarating. Once man had artificially created wings, he was ready for the greatest adventure of all: to explore the mysteries of the universe, perhaps to unlock the secret of life itself. Before the first steps could be taken in this grand adventure, man had to find some means of freeing himself of earthly gravity, to fly at unimaginable speeds, and to control the vehicle in which he might achieve this. Today's spacecraft had their beginnings in the Chinese war rockets—missiles, actually—of A.D. 1232. The history of rocketry is a long, evolutionary one, commingling weaponry and aeronautics, with various contributions by many inventors from several nations—Britain, the United States, Germany, and Russia. Unfortunately, as seems to be his wont, man first used this new invention chiefly as a means of destruction and the earliest miniature spaceships were hardly more than glorified artillery shells.

As early as 1903 Russian scientist Konstantin E. Tsiolkovsky predicted rocket space flight—the same year, it might be noted, in which the Wright brothers first flew at Kitty Hawk. A physicist and mathematician, Tsiolkovsky published many prescient studies and papers on various aspects of space travel—from proving that a rocket could move through a vacuum to the problems of weightlessness in space travel. All of this was published by 1911. Tsiolkovsky and his ideas, however, were ignored until the late twenties.

The first major step in modern rocket research was made by an American physics professor, Robert Hutchings Goddard. Even as a young man, Goddard began speculating on rocketry and its scientific application. Like Tsiolkovsky, he was generally ignored. An early article (1907) on the subject was rejected by several scientific journals. After years of work he succeeded in publishing his *A Method of Reaching High Altitudes* in 1919. This volume, published by the Smithsonian Institution, opened up a field of study in the use of rockets for research of the upper atmosphere. In 1923, another great pioneer, the German physicist Hermann Oberth, published a work entitled *The Rocket in Interplanetary Space*, in which he predicted that flights from earth to other planets would be possible with liquid fuel.

Three years later, Goddard launched his first liquid-propelled rocket which reached an altitude of a mere 184 feet. But he had proved that it could be done. Encouraged, Goddard proceeded with his experiments—which earned him the popular recognition as "Father of the Modern Rocket." During the Second World War Goddard was the director of research in jet propulsion for the U. S. Navy and was instrumental in the development of JATO (Jet Assisted Take Off.)

Although Goddard's experiments before the war had placed the United States ahead in the field of rocketry, the Germans surged ahead, partly because the fortunes of war had turned on them and the leader, Hitler, wanted revenge. Under the direction of Dr. Walter Dornberger, one of whose assistants was a young scientist named Wernher von Braun, liquid-fuel rocketry was adapted to Hitler's perverted vengeance weapons. In June 1944 the first of these, the V-1 (which the British called the "doodle-bug" or "buzz-bomb") flying bombs began falling on England. Some were launched from ramps across the English Channel or designed to be carried under an He-111 bomber to be launched over the target (these, however, were not used operationally).

Later in the year, von Braun's brainchild, the V-2 rocket, a true missile, began falling on England also. Because of its high speed, the V-2 was difficult to intercept by aircraft, unlike the slower V-1. Officially designated the A-4 (V-2 merely indicated that it was the second of Hitler's Vergeltungswaffen, or Revenge Weapons), the V-2 was the forerunner of all modern space rocketry that followed. The Germans also produced a strange little rocket-powered aircraft, the Messerschmitt Me-163 Komet. Fast (nearly six hundred miles per hour), the Komet was designed to attack Allied bomber formations, but despite its advances it could remain airborne for only eight minutes and its volatile liquid fuel rendered it a dangerous craft to fly. It was not very successful.

After the war many German rocket scientists came to the United States and contributed much to the American space program.

Postwar rocket development took the form of the intercontinental ballistic missile (ICBM) both in the Soviet Union and in the United States, drawing upon captured German V-1 and V-2 information. This, in turn, furnished the base upon which research into man-carrying space vehicles could be

An Air Force rocket of 1962—the Minuteman intercontinental ballistic missile (ICBM). The three-stage, solid-fueled projectile can strike a target 5,500 miles away. (U. S. Air Force)

Sputnik I, the first man-made satellite, which opened the Soviet-American space race and hastened the dawn of the Space Age, 1957. (Smithsonian Institution)

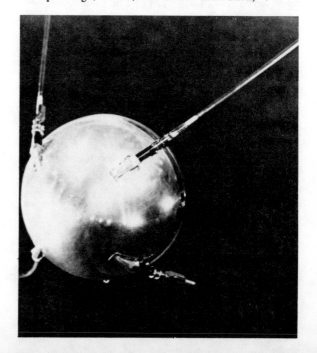

conducted. Such missiles theoretically function defensively as a deterrent; the knowledge that a missile is capable of returning an attack, even a heavy one, acts as a discouraging element to any enemy's "first strike." That making a first attack, even with atomic warheads, does not mean winning a war serves as a powerful deterrent to war makers of all descriptions and "isms." Other so-called interceptor missiles have been developed to interfere with ICBMs, but what with decoy missiles also in use, it is unlikely that all ICBMs could be intercepted. Therefore the existence of both U.S. and Soviet ICBMs means that the only alternative to nearly total extinction is peace.

The peaceful conquest of space, however, retains a full measure of international competition. The so-called space race between the United States and Soviet Russia came out into the open, and the Space Age began, on October 4, 1957, when the Russians launched an artificial satellite, *Sputnik I*, spinning around the earth. This was the first man-made object hurled into space, a twenty-three-inch aluminum ball from which protruded four antennae, sending information back to earth about magnetic fields, cosmic rays, X rays, gamma rays, and gravitational fields.

Before it fell, later in the following year, *Sputnik I* had risen above—or away from—the earth a distance of 558 miles. It was followed in November by a passenger-carrying Sputnik, the passenger being a dog. Meanwhile, what was going on in America? To many preoccupied with the space race, it appeared, very little. Even so, even before the *Sputnik I* was shot into orbit, Operation Man High had occurred on August 20, 1957, when a balloon (this must have appeared to have been a step backward!) was lifted off the ground at Crosby, Minnesota. Inside the balloon's gondola an Air Force scientist, David G. Simons, guided the craft up to an altitude of 102,000 feet—a new world's record. The objective of the flight, however, was not to establish this record but to study the effect of conditions in space upon a man. The gondola, in short, was designed to withstand the heat of the sun's rays as well as other dangerous

Operation Man-high, just before launching as the crew waits balloon to align above the gondola carrying Major David G. Simons. Ascent studied the effects of high-altitude flight. (U. S. Air Force)

rays at the outer edges of the earth's atmosphere. Dr. Simons was subjected to most hazards and discomforts of space travel (except weightlessness, for he was a little more than ten miles up and still within the earth's gravitational field). His record ascent proved that it was possible to construct a man-carrying vehicle capable of withstanding the conditions in space.

The first American earth satellite was *Explorer I*, which went into orbit on January 31, 1958. An important contribution of *Explorer I* was that it discovered the first of two circular radiation belts (then unknown) surrounding the earth. These were the Van Allen radiations (named for scientist James A. Van Allen), which interfered with communications and which could prove dangerous to astronauts unless precautions were taken against them. Later, *Explorer VI* was launched to map the Van Allen radiation belts. Thus was each step outward taken with care and thought, with all possible attention to the safety of the astronauts.

Both Soviet and American satellites and probes began to fill outer space with various whirling gadgets carrying instruments of assorted types during the latter fifties and early sixties. These were the vanguards of man's own reach into the unknown. The Soviet Union's *Lunik II* successfully arrived on the moon, 35 hours after being launched, on September 12, 1959. *Lunik III*, the next month, orbited the moon to take pictures of its hidden side. American probes orbited the sun *(Pioneer IV)*, studied the weather *(Vanguard II, Tiros I)*, and transmitted data of conditions 22 million miles in space *(Pioneer V)*. The first space travelers were, as in the opening of the balloon age, animals, dogs, monkeys, rats, and mice. Finally, on April 12, 1961, Soviet astronaut Yuri A. Gagarin was carried in *Vostok I* on man's first space trip. From blastoff to landing the trip took one hour, forty-eight minutes—eighty-nine minutes of which Gagarin spent in orbiting the earth at a maximum altitude of 203 miles. The speed of Gagarin's spacecraft was about seventeen thousand miles per hour. (In March 1968 Gagarin was killed in the crash of a training aircraft.)

Explorer I, the first American satellite, 1958. (NASA)

America's first man in space was Alan B. Shepard, Jr. His spaceship, *Freedom* 7, traveled a distance of 302 miles, during which Shepard reached a high point of 161 miles above the earth on May 5, 1961. The suborbital flight began at Cape Canaveral, Florida. It came to a successful conclusion when Shepard splashed down in the Gulf of Mexico, from which he was lifted by helicopter shortly after landing.

Soviet astronaut Yuri A. Gagarin. (Sovfoto)

Alan B. Shepard, Jr., first American in space, as he is retrieved by a Marine helicopter from the Gulf of Mexico, May 5, 1961. (NASA)

The first American to orbit the earth was John H. Glenn, Jr., who accomplished this on February 20, 1962. (The Soviet Union's Gherman S. Titov had already orbited the earth seventeen times in August 1961.) Glenn's spacecraft, *Friendship* 7, was put into orbit via a Mercury-Atlas system. The launch vehicle was an Atlas 109-D, an Air Force ICBM capable of great thrust (two booster engines of one hundred fifty thousand pounds each, a single sustainer engine of sixty thousand pounds of thrust, and two smaller vernier engines—all totaled more than three hundred sixty thousand pounds of thrust). This vehicle lifted the Mercury spacecraft into orbit, where Glenn took control. This was part of the Project Mercury, the first step in the National Aeronautics and Space Administration's manned space-flight program. Glenn guided the spaceship three times around the earth before returning after nearly five hours in space.

The Mercury space flights were followed by another series, called Gemini. The initial phase, which placed a single man in orbit to study man's capabilities of operating a spacecraft and to perform efficiently in the environment of space, tested American launch and space vehicles and methods of recovery of astronauts after they had splashed down in the ocean. Gemini was planned to employ two men (thus the name, for the Twins) and to extend orbital missions, develop techniques of orbital maneuvering, rendezvous, and docking of two vehicles in space. Several Gemini flights took place during 1965–66, beginning in March, when Virgil I. Grissom and John W. Young *(Gemini 3)* took a spacecraft through the first manned orbital maneuvers. One of the most fascinating missions was that of James A. McDivitt and Edward H. White II, who, on June 3, 1965, took off on the *Gemini 4* flight.

Mercury-Atlas, carrying John Glenn, Jr., lifts off the launching pad, Cape Canaveral, February 20, 1962. The Atlas portion carried the Mercury section, Friendship 7, into orbit. The two separated, leaving the capsule to circle the earth. (U. S. Air Force)

John Glenn, Jr., in spacesuit, and the *Friendship* 7. (NASA)

Practice for *Gemini 4*, planned as the longest (in duration) manned space flight up to that time. Edward H. White II is nearest camera; behind him, command pilot James A. McDivitt. (NASA)

The highlight of *Gemini 4* was Edward White's twenty-one-minute space walk. (Actually this was man's second such feat. The first space walk had been accomplished by Soviet Alexei A. Leonov in March 1965. Leonov remained outside the craft for ten minutes.) White was secured to the module by a twenty-three-foot tether line and a twenty-five-foot umbilical line (which supplied oxygen), both wrapped with gold tape to form a single cord. Wearing a special suit to protect him from space radiation, White also carried a hand-held self-maneuvering unit with which he could move himself about in the airless, weightless environment. Edward H. White II was the first American to walk in space. (He died tragically, along with astronauts Virgil I. Grissom and Roger B. Chaffee, on January 27, 1967, during a simulated countdown of an Apollo mission when the craft burst into flame.)

Gemini 4 begins liftoff from the Launch Complex, Cape Kennedy, Florida, June 3, 1965. Once in orbit the spacecraft was scheduled to circle the earth sixty-two times in four days. (NASA)

Edward H. White II engaged in "extravehicular activity" outside the *Gemini 4* spacecraft—the first American to accomplish this feat. During the third orbit of the craft, White left it and remained dangling in space for twenty-one minutes. (NASA)

A test of space endurance and space rendezvous was made in December 1965 in the *Gemini 6* and *Gemini 7* flights. *Gemini 7* took off first (December 4), with astronauts Frank Borman and James A. Lovell, Jr., aboard. Their objective was to remain in space for two weeks, rendezvous with *Gemini 6*, and continue with the flight until they had made 206 revolutions around the earth. *Gemini 6* was launched on December 15 with Walter M. Schirra, Jr., and Tom P. Stafford aboard. Their objective was to rendezvous with Borman and Lovell— which they did on December 16. The two craft were about 160 miles over the earth.

The Mercury and Gemini manned space flights were, of course, aimed toward one main objective: a flight to the moon. Each new step in these initial phases brought this goal a bit nearer realization. While men and machines—and delicate instru-

ments—were being tested, probes were being shot toward the moon to investigate its environment. The Soviets had photographed the dark side of the moon as early as 1959, but they rarely proved eager to share their discoveries with the world. However, in 1966 the United States launched the Lunar Orbiter, built by Boeing, equipped with powerfully lensed cameras and transmitters for sending photographs back to earth. On August 23, 1966, *Orbiter I* sent back strips of film which, when carefully spliced together, furnished the world with the first photograph of the earth from the moon. From a position about 730 miles from the moon, the Lunar Orbiter sent back a striking photograph (rather crude by more recent standards). The earth was 232,000 miles away. On November 23, 1966, the Lunar Orbiter photographed and sent back to the Deep-space network station at Gold-

Gemini 7 spacecraft as seen through the hatch window of the *Gemini 6* during rendezvous, December 16, 1965. (NASA)

Lunar Orbiter, which flew five moon scouting and photographing missions in preparation for Apollo astronauts. (The Boeing Company)

Man's first closeup of the moon as sent back to earth by the Lunar Orbiter. Copernicus crater from about twenty-eight miles above the moon. The highest mountains are about a thousand feet high. Distance from the foreground to the mountains on the horizon is about 150 miles. (Mark Nevils/The Boeing Company)

stone, California, the first closeup of the moon's crater Copernicus.

Before reviewing the various spacecraft that eventually led to a landing on the surface of the moon, mention should be made, if only in passing, of an interesting vehicle that had been projected for use in the space age. A strange anomaly for its time—a veritable return to the glider or even the kite—was the Ryan Flex Wing test vehicle, planned as the prototype of a new class of aircraft. The wings were constructed of a flexible aluminum alloy and covered with Dacron. The fuselage was attached to the wing at the wing's center. The metal leading edges of the wing formed a V; the trailing edge was fabric only. One of the features of the Fleep, as the vehicle was called, was that it could be mastered easily by practically anyone. It carried six people in addition to the pilot, and was adaptable to space missions for low-speed re-entry into the earth's atmosphere and for various recovery missions. It was little used, however, and was abandoned for other types of vehicles.

The first step toward an actual landing on the moon was made by the *Apollo* 7 launch on October 11, 1968. The objective of *Apollo* 7 was to test the reliability of the spacecraft for a journey to the moon. The commander of *Apollo* 7 was Walter M. Schirra, Jr. His crew consisted of Donn F. Eisele

Ryan Flex Wing Test vehicle. Originally intended for use in the space program ca. 1961, it was eventually abandoned. (Ryan Photo)

The Saturn IB space vehicle, which carried the *Apollo* 7 spacecraft (perched atop the 224-foot vehicle) on its eleven-day earth-orbit mission. (NASA)

Reaching for the moon: *Apollo* 7 commander Walter M. Schirra, Jr., approaches a transfer van that will take him and crew to Cape Kennedy's Launch Complex 34 and their waiting spacecraft. The mission tested the Apollo spacecraft system for future moon launchings and was the first three-man space flight. (NASA)

and Walter Cunningham. During the 163-orbit, 11-day voyage the three astronauts maneuvered their craft and tested various systems that would be essential to a successful moon launch.

On October 22, 1968, the *Apollo* 7 mission came to a successful conclusion when the spacecraft splashed down into the Atlantic 200 miles southwest of Bermuda and the three astronauts were recovered by helicopters.

The *Apollo* 7 crew boarded the aircraft carrier *Essex* after eleven days—and 4.5 million miles—in space. Although small problems occurred during the highly successful flight (one of them: Schirra's cold), the three men had proved that a flight to the moon and back was feasible.

Apollo 7 having proved successful, the time came for the next step—a moon orbit. This was *Apollo* 8, which was launched by a new and mighty space

End of the *Apollo* 7 mission. Commander Schirra is being lifted away from the command module after its splashdown in the Atlantic, October 11, 1968. (NASA)

Apollo 7 astronauts Walter M. Schirra, Jr., Donn F. Eisele, and Walter Cunningham safely aboard the *Essex*. (NASA)

vehicle, the Saturn V. Complete with its Apollo payload (that is, the man-carrying spacecraft), the Saturn V was 363 feet high and subdivided into three stages. The first, the 138-foot lower section, took the vehicle up to an altitude of 36 miles in 2½ minutes, achieving a speed of about six thousand miles per hour. During this phase of the operation it burned some fifteen tons of propellents per second. The second stage (81½ feet long) was operational for 6½ minutes and lifted the vehicle to a height of 108 miles. At this point the astronauts were moving at about 17,400 miles per hour. The third stage (fifty-eight feet long) took the vehicle into orbit around the earth. For a time the astronauts remained in the "earth parking orbit" checking instruments until ready to reignite the third stage in order to break away from the earth's gravity and head for the moon—this required a speed of about 24,900 miles per hour. When this had been achieved, the third stage was dropped and the astronauts began coasting toward the moon. *Apollo 8* marked the first use of the Saturn V launch vehicle.

Apollo 8 got under way on December 21, 1968, with astronauts Frank Borman, James Lovell, and William Anders. Their mission was planned to take them to the moon, around which they would orbit ten times and return in a journey of 147 hours. Modern technology made it possible for millions to experience much of the *Apollo 8* voyage to the moon. Television pictures of the interior of the spacecraft and views outside its windows were remarkably sharp. At that moment their craft was 120,653 miles away from earth, traveling at a speed of 3,207 miles per hour.

The photographs of the moon taken by the crew of *Apollo 8* were the best up to that time. After two days of traveling, the craft went into lunar orbit early in the morning of Christmas Eve. Their elliptical orbit ranged from 69 to 195 miles away from the moon; later a circular orbit at seventy miles was made. A total of 10 orbits were completed in a matter of twenty hours. During the flight it was Lovell who said, "The vast loneliness up here is awe-inspiring, and it makes you realize

Saturn V spacecraft being prepared for *Apollo 8*. Destination: moon orbit. (NASA)

just what you have back there on earth. The earth from here is a grand oasis in the big vastness of space." Borman commented that the moon's surface was a "vast, lonely, and forbidding sight . . . not a very inviting place to live or work." And Anders: "The color of the moon looks like a very whitish gray, like dirty beach sand with a lot of footprints in it."

After observing the moon's desolate landscape, the astronauts were grateful for a glimpse of home: the earth from 240,000 miles away. When a voice from Houston's Manned Space Center commented "A beautiful moon out there tonight," Borman replied: "Now, we were just saying that there's a beautiful earth out there."

Their mission completed, the *Apollo 8* crew broke out of moon orbit at a speed of 5,500 miles per hour. Back into the influence of the earth's gravity, they began falling toward the earth at a rapidly increasing velocity. The speed eventually reached nearly twenty-five thousand miles per hour, and the mission at this point reached a critical phase. Should the angle of entry into the earth's atmosphere at this speed be too steep, the spacecraft would burn to a cinder; if the angle were too shallow, it would bounce the craft back into space again. The craft had to enter at a point about eighty miles above the earth; this was a kind of doorway from outer to inner space, four hundred miles long by twenty-six miles wide. In terms of the space and mileage logged by *Apollo 8*, this represented little more than the eye of a needle.

To break the fall of the spacecraft, parachutes were used to slow the speed of the craft. At an altitude of 24,000 feet three drogue chutes automatically deployed to bring the speed of ascent down to about three hundred miles per hour. At ten thousand feet, when the speed has lessened to around 140 miles per hour, the main chutes began to blossom. These were eighty-three feet in diameter with orange and white gores; they more or less gently dropped the spacecraft into the water.

Apollo 8 liftoff, December 21, 1968. A Florida egret flies through the foreground. (NASA)

James Lovell (foreground) wishing his mother a happy birthday on the second day of the mission. Mission commander Frank Borman is in background. (NASA)

Planet earth rising above the moon. *Apollo 8* is 240,000 miles from home. (NASA)

Apollo 8 photographs of the moon. (NASA)

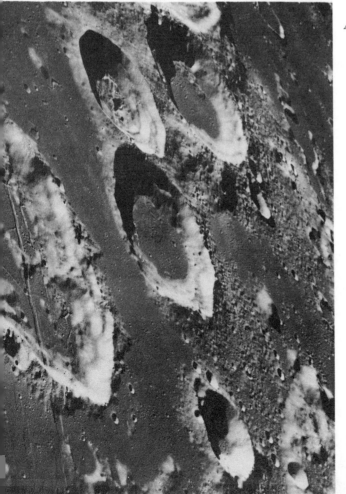

Apollo 8 astronauts, after recovery, safely aboard the *Yorktown*. To right of ship's officer they are William Anders, Frank Borman, and James Lovell. (NASA)

On the morning of December 27, 1968, astronauts Anders, Borman, and Lovell stood smiling on the deck of the recovery ship, the carrier *Yorktown*. They had brought their spaceship down into the Pacific, about a thousand miles south of Hawaii. In the summer of 1969 Borman became the first American astronaut to visit the Soviet Union, where he was warmly received, treated like a celebrity (complete with requests for autographs), and greatly contributed to a feeling of good will.

Apollo 8 was soon followed by *Apollo 9*, a test mission in which astronauts James A. McDivitt, David R. Scott, and Russell L. Schweikart tested the various components to be employed in an actual lunar landing, including the Lunar Module, the vehicle designed to leave the main spacecraft for the journey from orbit to the surface of the moon. This extremely complex mission was completed (after 10 days in space) on March 13, 1969.

Apollo 10, launched on May 17, 1969, combined the highlights of both *Apollo 8* and *Apollo 9*, in the penultimate rehearsal before the first landing on the moon by man. Not only would this mission orbit the moon, as had *Apollo 8*, it would also make one final test of the Lunar Module, which the astronauts had nicknamed *Snoopy*. This would be the first trying of the spidery LM in the actual vicinity of the moon. Mission commander Thomas P. Stafford and pilot Eugene A. Cernan left the command ship—its name was *Charlie Brown*—with senior pilot John W. Young aboard and skimmed the surface of the moon. *Snoopy* came within nine miles of the crater-pocked landscape, the closest man had yet come to it. This phase of the mission, besides gathering the most spectacular moon pictures yet taken, was to seek out a possible landing site for *Apollo 11* and to test the effects of the moon's weak and irregular gravitational field upon the LM and upon the crew's ability to maneuver it. Not the least of their chores was the rendezvous, and linkup, of *Charlie Brown* and *Snoopy* about seventy miles above the moon—and some 230,000 miles from home.

During the scouting voyage Stafford and Cernan saw the moon as no men had up to that moment. If it was a moment for grand phrases or even poetry, the technicians or explorers, though impressed with the view, were at a loss for words. There was

too much to do and see to get fancy. As *Snoopy* approached the unlovely surface of the moon, the word came back to Houston: "We is down among them, Charlie." And when the LM came so close that it appeared to be in reach of the moon, "Hey, I tell you we are low. We are close, Babe." And when they witnessed (and photographed) an earth-rise, it was described as "magnificent." The next step was to maneuver *Snoopy* back to the Command Module, and then rendezvous and dock. The Lunar Module was guided by radar into docking position. Once *Snoopy* had docked, Stafford and Cernan rejoined Young in the Command Module for the return to earth. *Snoopy* was then jettisoned and the Command Module's engines fired to break away from moon orbit and begin its fall to earth.

Splashdown of the command module, *Apollo 9;* impact of fall into the water was broken by parachutes. (NASA)

Lunar Module *Snoopy,* carrying mission commander Thomas P. Stafford and Eugene Cernan, ascends from near the moon's surface to rendezvous and link up with the command module flown by John Young. (NASA)

Apollo 10 photographs of the rising earth, approximately a hundred thousand miles (or more) away. (NASA)

The entire *Apollo 10* mission, from start to finish, was as near to perfection as man and machine could make it. *Charlie Brown* splashed down into the Pacific within three miles of the carrier *Princeton*. Thirty-nine minutes later the three astronauts, Stafford, Cernan, and Young, were safe aboard the ship. The stage was set for the next step, *Apollo 11*—man's first flight to the surface of the moon.

With the far side of the moon as a background, *Snoopy* begins docking procedures with the command module, *Charlie Brown*. Circular object in the lower left is the rendezvous radar dish; nozzlelike device (one of four) is the thruster, which controls the attitude of the spacecraft. (NASA)

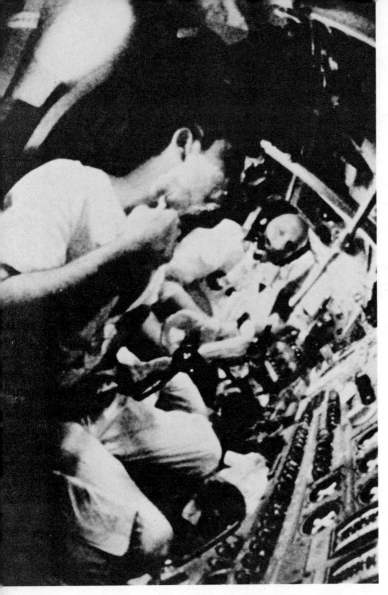

Prepare for landing: As astronaut John Young shaves, Commander Thomas Stafford observes. (NASA)

It is unlikely that any event in the history of the world was as thoroughly witnessed as the flight of *Apollo 11*. With the aid of modern technology—and especially the television camera—it was, during the summer of July 1969, quite literally "the greatest show on earth." As an estimated 600 million people (one fifth of the world's population) watched (and countless millions listened via radio) three astronauts lifted off from Cape Kennedy, Florida, at 9:32 A.M., Eastern Daylight Time, on July 16, 1969. These men were Neil Armstrong, the mission commander; Michael Collins, Command Module pilot; and Edwin Aldrin, Lunar Module pilot. Their vehicle was Apollo/Saturn V, which would free them of earth's gravity, take them to the moon—and, if all proceeded as planned, back.

The vehicle designed to take Armstrong and Aldrin to the surface of the moon was the Lunar Module, the spiderlike contraption that looks unlike any other flying machine. Within the cramped quarters of its cockpit Armstrong and Aldrin would have to man the complex controls and peer from the small triangular windows (inscribed with calibrations to gauge approach distances) as they lowered the "LEM" to the moon. Four days after liftoff, on Saturday, July 19, Armstrong and Aldrin climbed into the LEM, named *Eagle*, separated from the Command Module *Columbia*, and in a topsy-turvy attitude, began the final leg in the journey to the moon. As the two vehicles parted during the thirteenth moon orbit, Mission Control from Manned Space Center at Houston asked, "How does it look?" Armstrong, with characteristic terseness, replied, "*Eagle* has wings." Collins, observing from the Command Module, said, "It looks like you've got a fine-looking flying machine there, *Eagle*, despite the fact you're upside down." Armstrong's reply was laconically wry: "*Somebody's* upside down." In the gravity-free environment of their spaceships and away from the earth's up and down, it was anybody's guess.

Eagle approached the moon, leaving the Command Module in orbit some 69 miles over the lunar surface, and moved down to an altitude of fifty thousand feet to begin powered descent. The objective was a landing spot in the Sea of Tranquillity and would be accomplished by computer. Within twelve minutes *Eagle* was practically touching the surface of the moon. However, just before the landing Armstrong spotted a boulder-filled crater at the touch-down point. Taking over control manually, he guided *Eagle* downward. At 4:17 P.M. (EDT) the spindly spacecraft settled down to a perfect "soft" landing. Armstrong's voice crackled through the miles of space, "Houston: Tranquillity Base here. The *Eagle* has landed." Houston replied, "Roger, Tranquillity, we copy you on the

Moonmen: Neil A. Armstrong, Michael Collins, and Edwin R. Aldrin—the men selected for the *Appollo 11* mission to the moon (this photo was taken after the completion of the mission). (NASA)

ground. You've got a bunch of guys about to turn blue. We're breathing again. Thanks a lot." Six hours later, ahead of schedule because the astronauts found it difficult to wait because of the excitement, the permission for Armstrong to leave *Eagle* for the moon's surface was given. All the various checks had been made during the time *Eagle* rested in Tranquillity Base. Then before the eyes of millions of their fellow earthmen, Armstrong emerged from the LEM and gingerly stepped down the ladder that had been projected from *Eagle*. As his toe touched the moon's surface Armstrong said, "That's one small step for a man, one giant leap for mankind." On July 20, 1969, at 10:56 P.M. (EDT), the first man from earth stepped onto the surface of the moon.

Within twenty minutes Aldrin left *Eagle* to join

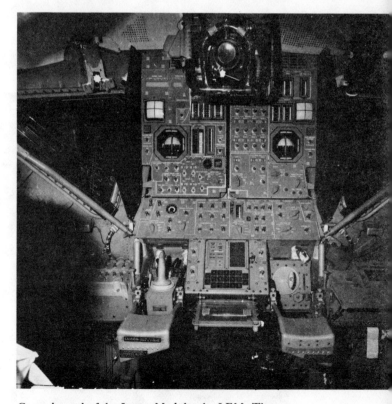

Control panel of the Lunar Module, the LEM. The manual controls are the blocklike projections at center bottom. Operation of the LEM was computerized and mechanical, but could be manually controlled when necessary—and was when close to the moon's surface. (NASA)

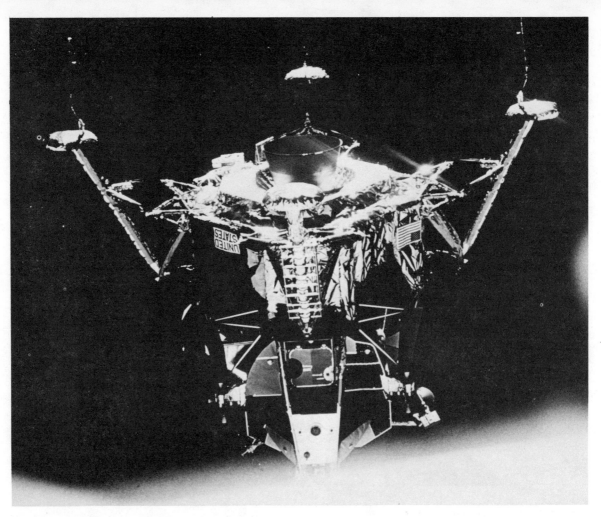

The Lunar Module separating from the command module. Armstrong and Aldrin are in the LEM; pilot of the command module, Michael Collins, snapped the photo. (NASA)

" . . . one small step for a man . . . " Armstrong, at the moment before stepping onto the moon as he was seen virtually around the world via television. (NBC News)

Armstrong. For a little over two hours the two astronauts went about the work that had brought them to the moon: the setting out of various pieces of scientific equipment (after planting the American flag, specially wired to remain unfurled in the airless moon atmosphere)—one of them being a sheet of aluminum foil to trap gases from the sun for study on earth. They also left a seismometer to record the impact of meteorites and lunar volcanic disturbances; they set up a lasar reflector pointed toward the earth for measurement (within inches, it was hoped) of the distances between the earth and the moon. And like all typical American tourists, they snapped photographs that revealed what Aldrin called the "magnificent desolation" of the moon. And finally they gathered up about fifty pounds of moon rocks and samples of lunar surface for the trip back to earth and study by scientists throughout the world.

The next steps were delicate ones: liftoff from the moon and linkup with Collins in *Columbia*. Had anything gone wrong, there would have been nothing for Collins to do but abandon the mission and return to earth alone. However, *Eagle* took off without a hitch on July 21 and docked with *Columbia* less than four hours later. The return flight was uneventful and, after eight days in space (which included a lunar visit of twenty-one hours, thirty-seven minutes), *Columbia* splashed down in the Pacific at 12:50 P.M. (EDT), July 24, 1969.

The successful conclusion of *Apollo 11* was but a beginning; it had proved the feasibility of travel from earth to another celestial body in the universe. It opened the Age of Interplanetary flight. Little known at the time was that it had been a close thing: An overworked computer nearly led to an abort of the mission during the final minutes of the descent to the moon. The problem was quickly solved—two hundred thousand miles away, at Houston's Mission Control—and *Apollo 11* was

Aldrin leaves the Lunar Module to join Armstrong on the surface of the moon to begin gathering materials for study on earth. (NASA)

Aldrin puts the solar-wind composition study device in place. (NASA)

Men on the moon. Aldrin poses for Armstrong, who can
be seen reflected in Aldrin's pressure helmet visor.
(NASA)

concluded to become one of the epochal flights in the history of mankind.

Between November 1969 and December 1972, six additional Apollo missions were launched, all but one—*Apollo 13*—successfully. The five landings refined, expanded, and enriched the promise of *Apollo 11*. All were distinctive for specific results (even the aborted *Apollo 13*, which was cut short when an oxygen tank exploded in the command module), and demonstrated the remarkable teamwork and technology that could be used to handle an emergency in space. (All three members of the *Apollo 13* flight team—James A. Lovell, Jr., Fred W. Haise, Jr., and John L. Swigert, Jr., who had calmly announced the emergency with the words, "Hey, we've got a problem here"—safely splashed into the Pacific.)

Apollo 12 (Alan L. Bean, Richard Gordon, and Charles Conrad) not only succeeded in making a pinpoint landing on the moon but also deployed scientific instruments on its surface and returned with samples of moon rocks. *Apollo 14* (Alan B. Shepard, Jr., Edgar D. Mitchell, and Stuart A. Roosa) did more of same besides making the first manned landing on the moon, explored some of the lunar highlands while pulling a small two-wheeled cart and, again, returned with more samples of moon rocks. *Apollo 15* (David R. Scott, James B. Irwin, and Alfred M. Worden) carried its own lunar roving vehicle, which enabled the astronauts to cover even more of the moon's surface and to return with more samples of moon rocks for study by scientists on earth. *Apollo 16* (John W. Young, Charles M. Duke, Jr., and Thomas K. Mattingly) blended engineering with science in carrying one astronaut who carried out experiments from the Command Module while it orbited the moon. A possible malfunction almost canceled the mission but, as with the ill-fated *Apollo 13*, the problem was solved by complex NASA teamwork.

The final mission of the series, *Apollo 17* (Eugene A. Cernan, Ronald E. Evans, and Harrison H. Schmitt), transported a trained geologist—Schmitt—to the moon's surface. Evans, who piloted the Command Module, was also trained in

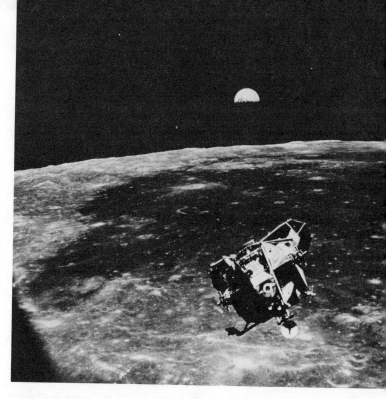

After completing the first walk on the moon, Armstrong and Aldrin, in *Eagle*, approach *Columbia* for docking. The earth is just above the moon's horizon. (NASA)

A moon buggy devised for easier transportation on the surface of the moon and used on later Apollo spaceflights—this one was for *Apollo 15* and was made in August 1971. (NASA, courtesy Robert A. and Michael Allen)

geology—although he studied the moon from a distance, while Cernan (who had only come close to the moon on the *Apollo 10* trip) and Schmitt walked the surface and gathered lunar samples. One of the larger boulders brought back by *Apollo 17* proved to be more than four billion years old.

At the time of *Apollo 17* (December 1972), closing the manned flights to the moon, there were both pro and con appraisals of the Apollo program, which had run for eleven years at a cost of $25 billion. The late Wernher von Braun, onetime director of NASA's Marshall Space Flight Center in Alabama and a pioneer in rocketry, wrote in the New York *Times* that the new discipline "lunar science" would "improve our understanding of earth's geologic structure and history, and so have a practical importance. Understanding the nature of our world and what causes certain events is a factor in human survival, and has been so since man appeared. Being able to compare earth with other planetary histories and materials vastly increases this vital comprehension."

Dr. Amitai Etzioni, professor of sociology at Columbia University, was happy to see Apollo end, but for other reasons. He saw *Apollo 17* as the "last gasp of a technologically addicted, public-relations-minded society, the last escapade engineered by an industrial-military coalition seeking conquests in outer space, while avoiding swelling needs on earth."

After the mission NASA continued its work more quietly, if less spectacularly, with various satellites that provide weather data, and the natural-resources satellite Landsat-1, which has, indeed, been studying some of the "swelling needs of earth." Landsat contributes to agriculture, to the unmasking of polluters of air and water, to urban studies, and to ecology, among others. Communications satellites (Intelsats) make instant communication throughout the world a common thing—and one now taken for granted.

Skylab, an experimental space station, was launched with some of the old fanfare in 1973 and, before the mission was concluded in February 1974, vast funds of knowledge about the earth and

Skylab experimental space station orbiting the earth. The 100-ton unmanned complex was lifted into orbit by Saturn V vehicle. A crew of three joined it later via a Saturn IB vehicle in a command and service module (CSM) to carry out the various studies for which Skylab was devised. (NASA)

the sun had been gathered. *Skylab 4* (Gerald P. Carr, Edward G. Gibson, and William R. Pogue) was the longest manned space mission to date and one of the most productive. The crew spent eighty-four days in space, working in and out of the station without ill effect, making studies of cosmic space, their craft, and themselves.

Unfortunately because of sunspot related ultraviolet radiation and upper atmosphere interference, the orbit of *Skylab* began serious deterioration in June 1978; attempts to correct it in July proved to be unsuccessful, partly owing to a power failure. Since it would be impossible to launch a manned mission to correct the situation (by attaching remotely controlled rockets to the exterior of *Skylab*), NASA officials expected the space station to fall from space in 1979, about four years short of its expected orbiting without assistance from earth.

Other NASA studies reached farther into space: Mariner spacecraft circled Mars, Venus, and Mercury. Pioneer sent back information on Jupiter and its inner moons and, in time for the American Bicentenniel, Viking landers had arrived on Mars and began sending information back to earth about that mysterious planet.

The Soviets, although they had been first to place the Sputnik and a man, Yuri Gagarin, in space, were outdistanced in the "space race" by American technology. Plagued at times by misfortune, which resulted in the death of four cosmonauts, the Soviet exploration of space has lagged a bit behind that of the United States.

Although they lost the race to the moon, the Soviets did place an unmanned lunar lander on the moon in July 1969; Soviet satellites and space stations share the outer skies with American "hardware." The Soviets have done good work in the study of space medicine, and have shared their findings with NASA.

Skylab 4, photographed from the CSM, with the earth in the background. A solar shield has been placed on the Skylab (to replace one that had been lost during launch); this shield protects the Orbital Workshop (OWS) from the sun's rays in space. Photo taken in February 1974. (NASA)

Mariner 9 portrait of Mars. This is a mosaic made from more than fifteen hundred computer-corrected television pictures taken in 1971 and 1972. The Martian polar cap is at the top of the photo; the giant volcano Nix Olympica (measuring 373 miles across) is at lower center. (NASA)

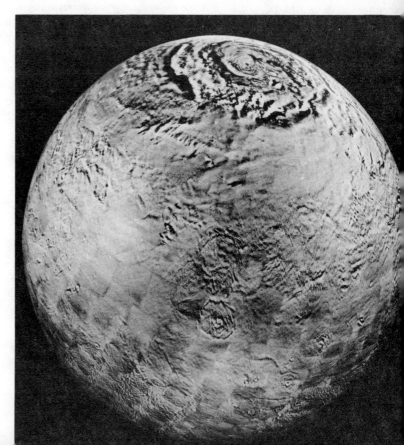

Venus from 450,000 miles (720,000 kilometers) as televised from *Mariner 10*. (NASA)

Mariner 10 mosaic of the South Pole region of Mercury revealing a heavily cratered area. The photographs were transmitted as the unmanned spacecraft flew past the planet on September 31, 1974. (NASA)

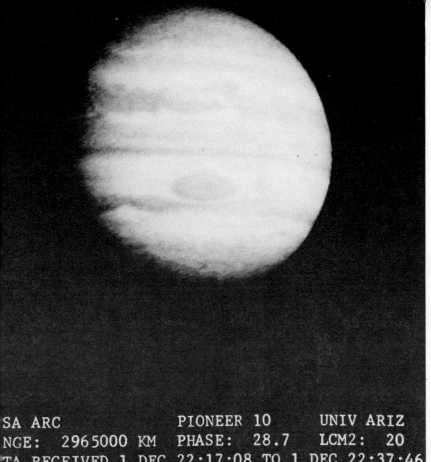

SA ARC   PIONEER 10   UNIV ARIZ
NGE: 2965000 KM   PHASE: 28.7   LCM2:   20
TA RECEIVED 1 DEC 22:17:08 TO 1 DEC 22:37:46
8 COLOR SECTOR 154 - 441   B   06/11/74

Jupiter from more than a million miles away photographed from the *Pioneer 10* spacecraft, December 1973. The Great Red Spot is readily visible; it measures twenty-five thousand miles across. (NASA)

Return to Mars for a closer look: mosaic by *Viking Orbiter I* on its 360th orbit, June 13, 1977. Most prominent feature is volcanic crater at the summit of Olympus Mons, Mars' tallest mountain (ninety thousand feet). (NASA)

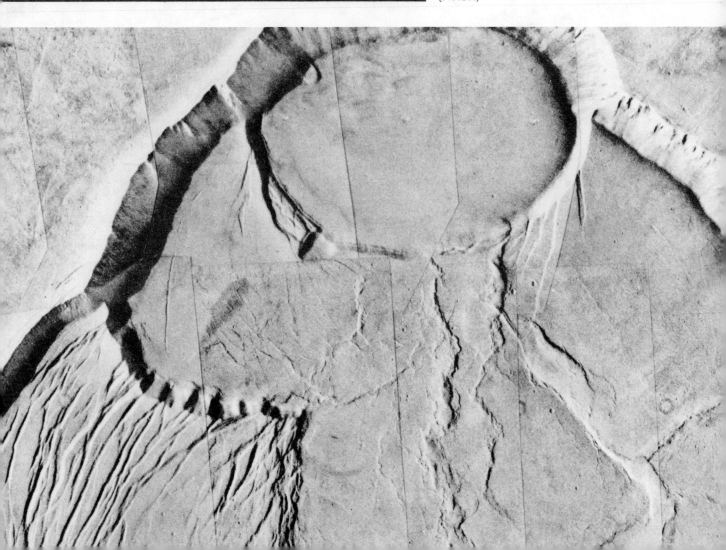

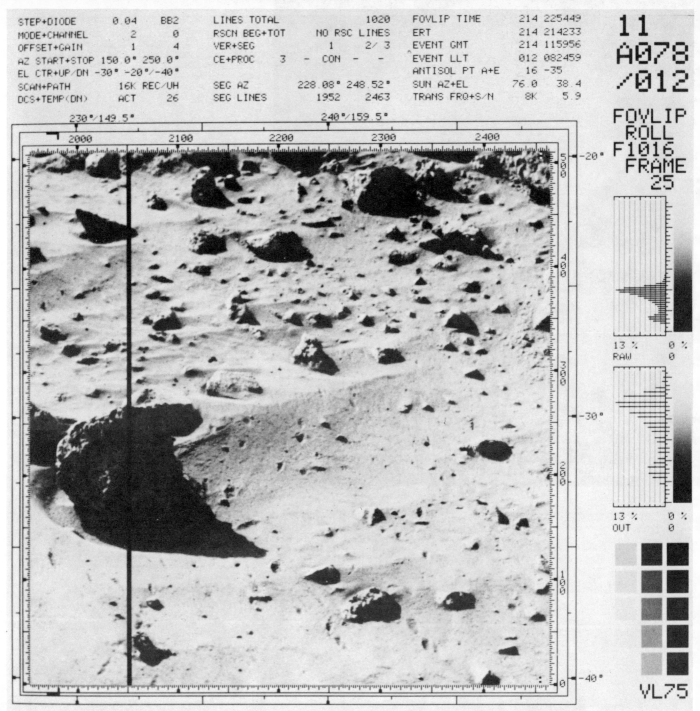

STEP+DIODE   0.04   BB2   LINES TOTAL   1020   FOVLIP TIME   214 225449   11
MODE+CHANNEL   2   0   RSCN BEG+TOT   NO RSC LINES   ERT   214 214233   A078
OFFSET+GAIN   1   4   VER+SEG   1   2/ 3   EVENT GMT   214 115956   /012
AZ START+STOP 150.0° 250.0°   CE+PROC   3 - CON -   -   EVENT LLT   012 082459
EL CTR+UP/DN -30° -20°/-40°   ANTISOL PT A+E   16 -35   FOVLIP
SCAN+PATH   16K REC/UH   SEG AZ   228.08° 248.52°   SUN AZ+EL   76.0   38.4   ROLL
DCS+TEMP(DN)   ACT   26   SEG LINES   1952   2463   TRANS FRQ+S/N   8K   5.9   F1016
                                                                                                            FRAME
                                                                                                             25

Viking I photo from the surface of Mars. Two spacecraft were dispatched to land on Mars in 1976. Landing successfully, they transmitted the first close-up photographs of the once unknown planet. (NASA)

Viking II photo of a Martian plain (four thousand miles northeast from the landing site of Viking I), revealing the nature of rocks in the area. There was no evidence of fictional Martians. (NASA)

American participants in the 1975 *Apollo-Soyuz* flight, the Soviet-American mission planned to test the feasibility of co-operative space ventures with American and Soviet equipment. The crew of the Apollo: Donald Slayton, docking module pilot; Vance D. Brand, command module pilot, and Thomas P. Stafford, command pilot. (NASA)

International experimental space team: Slayton, Stafford, Brand, and the Soviet members, Aleksey A. Leonov (standing), commander of the Soviet crew, and Valeriy N. Kubasov, engineer. In the foreground: a model of the joined spaceships. (NASA)

Postmission tourism. The crews of the *Apollo-Soyuz* in Red Square, Moscow, October 1975: Brand, Stafford, Leonov, Slayton, and Kubasov. (NASA)

A most spectacular example of U.S.—U.S.S.R. co-operation was the *Apollo-Soyuz* mission, which began on July 15, 1975, with the launching of the *Soyuz* at Baykonur, Kazakhstan, and the *Apollo* at Kennedy Space Center, Florida. Two days later the two spacecraft met at a pinpoint in limitless space and joined in a complex docking procedure. The implications of the mission were succinctly put by science-writer Walter Froehlich in his booklet *Apollo-Soyuz*.

"For two days in mid-1975 the crews of a combined U.S. and U.S.S.R. spacecraft orbiting the earth at an altitude of 225 kilometers (140 miles) vividly demonstrated that men of divergent national and cultural backgrounds and loyalties can work together for common advantage. Their purpose was to flight-test a mechanism for joining together two orbiting spacecraft.

"Millions of viewers in many parts of the world watched live telecasts as three astronauts in a U.S. *Apollo* and two cosmonauts in a U.S.S.R. *Soyuz* merged their two spacecraft into a single vehicle." This historic meeting was symbolically accomplished over the Elbe River, where in 1945 the Soviets and the Americans met at the end of the Second World War. Froelich described what followed: "The TV audiences also saw the crews share meals, exchange gifts, and conduct scientific experiments, some of which produced remarkable and highly significant astronomical findings."

Among the objects taken along on the mission were copies of two publications, *A Method of Reaching Extreme Altitudes* and *Liquid-propellant Rocket Development*, by pioneer Robert Goddard. All five participants in *Apollo-Soyuz* signed the pamphlets, which were then placed in the Smithsonian's National Air and Space Museum. The spaceships separated on July 19 and the *Soyuz* landed two days later; the *Apollo* splashed down on July 24—both crews landed safely. The two crew commanders made statements expressing their thoughts on the mission.

"When we opened this hatch in space," Brigadier General Thomas P. Stafford, a veteran of *Apollo 10*, said, "we were opening, back on earth, a new era in the history of man."

Colonel Aleksey A. Leonov said, "Together we have begun an irreversible thing. The machine of *Apollo-Soyuz* is operating now and no one can stop it."

The Soviets proceeded with their manned space program after *Apollo-Soyuz* to conduct experiments in space from orbiting space stations. In 1976 Boris Yolynov and Vitaly Zhobonov docked their *Soyuz 21* to space station *Salyut 5* and remained for fifty days of experimentation. *Soyuz 24* (Viktor Garbatko, Yuri Glazkov) took a short, comparatively, trip to *Salyut 5* in February 1977. The outstanding record-breaking flight was carried out by Georgi Grechko and Yuri Romanenko in the *Soyuz 26* mission which began on December 10, 1977, and ended on March 3, 1978—after ninety-six days in space, setting a new space endurance record. During this period, docked to *Salyut 6*, Grechko and Romanenko conducted numerous experiments and gathered much valuable information on the effects of long periods of space flight. As a sequel, *Soyuz 27* (Vladimir Dzhanibekov, Oleg Markarov) set out on January 10, 1978, to join their comrades orbiting in *Salyut 6* for a six-day visit.

The *Apollo-Soyuz* test project marked the final use of a manned disposable spacecraft by the United States. Even as the mission ended, NASA was working on a new space concept, a reusable spacecraft, comparatively economical, simpler in operation, capable of routine access to space. This is the Space Shuttle, which is expected to begin space operations in the late seventies or the early 1980s. The Shuttle, the main element of which is the winger Orbiter, can be lifted into orbit by solid-fuel rockets and its own liquid-fueled engine. The one expendable unit is the external tank carrying the liquid fuel. Once in orbit, the external tank can be ejected and the two solid-fuel rockets detached and parachuted for recovery and reuse. The Orbiter can then orbit the earth for as long as a month with an impressive payload—crew and a Spacelab for inumerable studies of the earth. The Spacelab will be the co-operative product of the European Space Agency, with contributions from Belgium, Denmark, France, West Germany, Italy, the Netherlands, Spain, Switzerland, the United

Rollout of the space shuttle *Orbiter 101* early in 1977 at Palmdale, California. (Rockwell International)

Flight test crews of the space shuttle glider (all NASA astronauts): Gordon Fullerton (pilot), Fred Haise (commander), Joe Engle (commander), and Dick Truly, pilot. The space shuttle underwent several taxi and flight tests before taking off on a demonstration of the first release flight. (Rockwell International)

Space shuttle *Enterprise* is carried aloft perched atop the modified Boeing 747 carrier craft. The crew on this flight: Haise and Fullerton. The Boeing crew: Fitzhugh L. Fulton, Jr. (pilot) and Thomas C. McMurtry. (Rockwell International)

Separation of the *Enterprise* from the carrier—at an altitude of 24,100 feet. Haise reported "a definite lurch upward," but no rolling motion or other instabilities. (Rockwell International)

With a Northrop T-38 "chase plane" accompanying, the *Enterprise* glides down to a high speed—two hundred miles per hour—landing in the Mojave Desert, Edwards Air Force Base, California. (Rockwell International)

Kingdom, and Austria, which is not a member of the Agency.

The Orbiter will be able to function not only as a laboratory in the fields of geology, hydrology, energy, and other disciplines, but also as a way station for launching, retrieving, and repairing orbiting satellites. Upon completion of its mission, the Space Shuttle would return to earth with crew, scientists, engineers, and all their data, "deorbiting," entering the earth's atmosphere, and landing like that simple craft it somewhat resembles—a glider. Twenty years after Sputnik man had gone back to wings.

The romance of primitive flight has not been totally dissipated by the coming of the Space Age. To accomplish something no one else has done, no matter how useless, is a human trait that has often led to great (maybe accidental) discoveries, harrowing adventures and, all too often, the death of the adventurer. Not many weeks after the first important Space Shuttle test (in August 1977), two (shall we say) intrepid (to revive the hoary cliché that applies) balloonists set out from Bar Harbor, Maine, to float across the Atlantic; they were re-

trieved from the drink a couple of days later, the fifteenth failure in a long series of fruitless attempts to cross the Atlantic by balloon. The first was tried by American balloon pioneer John Wise, who in July 1859 set out from St. Louis in a giant balloon appropriately named the *Atlantic*. Wise actually did make history with this attempt, the longest flight—809 miles—by balloon of his time; but, blown by storms and driven to the ground where the *Atlantic* was pierced by a tree, Wise never reached the Atlantic, let alone crossed it. Until 1978 the only Atlantic balloon crossing was the product of the lively, and rather strange, imagination of Edgar Allan Poe, who succeeded in planting his hoax in the New York *Sun* (April 13, 1844), setting off a flurry of excitement.

Real international excitement ensued in the summer of 1978 when three indomitable New Mexicans, Ben Abruzzo, forty-eight, Maxie Anderson, forty-four, and Larry Newman, thirty-one, actually succeeded in crossing the Atlantic by balloon. Setting out in their specially designed *Double Eagle II* (which cost $150,000) from Presque Isle, Maine, on August 11, 1978, the three men landed six days later in a wheatfield, just fifty-five miles short of their goal, Le Bourget, the airfield where Lindbergh had landed in 1927. The townspeople of Miserey greeted them with cries of "Vive les Américaines!" and in their excitement proceeded to trample their neighbor's wheat crop. (The owner was indifferent, his property having become a historical focal point; even so, the American balloonists insisted on reimbursing the farm owner.)

The celebrated voyage was no easy accomplishment, as temperature fluctuations and wind switches afflicted them (the day before they reached the Irish coast *Double Eagle II* dropped from an altitude of twenty-four thousand feet to four thousand.) Wearing oxygen masks proved uncomfortable, and there were periods of extreme cold—not to mention an occasional short temper. But good humor, determination, and courage led to success in a Normandy wheatfield on August 17, 1978. Abruzzo, Anderson, and Newman of Albuquerque, New Mexico, U.S.A., became the first

The silver and black *Double Eagle II* over France, near the end of an epic transatlantic crossing which began at Presque Isle, Maine. (Wide World Photos)

Crew of *Double Eagle II*. Larry Newman (with T-shirt), Maxie Anderson and Ben Abruzzo, near Evreux, France. (Wide World Photos)

men in history to cross the Atlantic Ocean by balloon. It was a magnificent leap backward.

Imagination, ingenuity, technology, and just plain youthful strength and stamina solved one of aviation's oldest problems in the summer of 1977, an even older one than that posed by the balloon. This was a puzzle whose solution eluded even the master Leonardo da Vinci, and generations of tower jumpers: man-powered flight. A team of California aero-enthusiasts, led by designer Paul MacCready and design assistant Peter Lissaman (using sophisticated computers), produced an aircraft built by Vern Oldershaw and flown and powered by pilot Bryan Allen. While the challenge was age-old, there was further incentive: a prize of eighty-five thousand dollars offered by British businessman Henry Kremer for the first man-powered flight.

Eighteen years later this was accomplished when Allen pedaled the one-manpower Gossamer Condor over a distance of a mile, at minimal altitude around two pylons, at a speed of about seven miles per hour. The aircraft weighed less than seventy pounds and had a wingspan of ninety-seven feet. The Royal Aeronautical Society of Britain certified the flight, making it official.

The MacCready-Allen team followed this feat with an even greater triumph. On June 12, 1979, twenty-six-year-old Allen took off from the dock at Folkestone, near Dover, England, and pedaled himself across the English Channel to a landing at Cape Gris-Nez, France, in a more advanced design of the *Condor* named the *Gossamer Albatross*. This craft, with a ninety-six-foot wing span, weighed in at sixty pounds. (Allen, at six feet, weighed 137 pounds.) Working up one-third horsepower, he covered the twenty-two miles in two hours fifty-five minutes at an "altitude" ranging from six to thirty feet.

Man had finally sprouted his own wings.

Man with wings: Bryan Allen, pilot and pedaler, mans
his wings at Shafter, California, August 23, 1977—the
first man in recorded history to achieve man-powered
flight. The plane is named the *Gossamer Condor*. (Photo
by Judy MacCready, Aerovironment, Inc.)

Acknowledgments

This book is, of course, a group effort and was compiled with much help from many. When the project began some years ago, the greater number of illustrations were provided by the Magazine and Book Division, Directorate of Defense Information of the Assistant Secretary of Defense, Washington, D.C. Commander Joseph W. Marshall, USN, and Lieutenant Colonel Harvey M. Ladd, USA, afforded me every access to the vast collection of photographs under their care; I might add that these included shots of civil and commercial as well as military aircraft. Ms. Bettie Sprigg and Mr. Robert P. Higdon attended to the logistics of gathering and mailing, and from time to time, sought out some forgotten or newly discovered individual or aircraft.

As usual, too, I received the accustomed gracious aid from the U. S. Air Force and particularly from a good friend, Mrs. Virginia Fincik. Her interest in the project made the search much simpler, and most pleasant, for an author and his assistant.

A word about my "assistant." Our son David, an aviation enthusiast, historian, short-story writer, author, editor, and paleontologist, was remarkably helpful when this work originally began (he was then about fifteen; he is now working on his doctorate); it was he who spotted the most striking illustrations. He has a keen sense of history and perspective. His interest, and mine presumably, affected his sisters, Emily and Carla, both of whom during their grade-school days presented quite sophisticated reports on aviation to their classes. Their reports are filed among my History of Aviation papers. My wife, Edith, has been her usual solid self throughout this long project.

Our superb National Air and Space Museum in Washington, D.C., has one of the most extensive collections of aviation photographs in the country. I have drawn heavily upon its staff for aid in compiling this book. I am especially indebted to Ms. Claudia Oakes and Mr. Robert B. Wood for their personal attention to my needs.

Another excellent source of photos pertaining to the history of aviation (and practically everything else) is our National Archives, Washington, D.C. I continue to be impressed with the uncanny skill that Mr. Paul L. White exhibits when he searches out photo requests.

Other more or less official sources include:

Musée de l'Air, Paris

Imperial War Museum, London—with special thanks to Ed Hine

Science Museum, London; Ms. Florence Vaughan

National Aeronautics and Space Administration (NASA), Washington, D.C., and New York; Mr. Stephen Rabb

Air Force Museum, Wright-Patterson Air Force Base, Ohio—with special gratitude to Royal D. Frey

Library of Congress, Washington, D.C.; Ms. Virginia Daiker

Port Authority of New York and New Jersey, John F. Kennedy International Airport; Mr. Milton A. Caine

Aircraft manufacturers and airlines have also been most helpful:

Air France, New York; Ms. Claire E. Devener

Airline Pilots Association, New York; Ms. Diane Ciaccia

American Airlines, New York; Ms. A. Vitaliano

Avions Marcel Dassault, Paris: Mr. A. Segura

The Boeing Company, New York; special thanks to Mark Nevils

British Aircraft Corporation, London; Ms. Dagmar Heller

British Airways, New York; Mr. Norman C. Lornie, Ms. J. Maiorano, and Mr. Arnold Turkheimer

Brown & Root-Northrop, Houston, Texas; Mr. Elmer "Butch" Goodwin

Douglas Aircraft Company, Santa Monica, California; Mr. Crosby Maynard

Fairchild Hiller, Republic Aviation Division, Farmingdale, New York; Mr. Roy E. Wendell

General Dynamics, New York; Mr. F. R. Kniffin

General Dynamics, Convair Division, San Diego, California; Mr. J. H. Mason and Mr. Gordon M. Jackson

Grumman Aircraft Engineering Company, Bethpage, New York; Mr. Kurt Kiska

Handley Page Limited, St. Albans, Hertfordshire, England; Mr. S. A. H. Scuffham

Hawker Siddeley Aviation Limited, Kingston-upon-Thames, England; Mr. G. Anderson

KLM, Royal Dutch Airlines, New York; Mr. James V. Reed

Ling-Temco-Vought, Inc., Dallas, Texas; Mr. Arthur L. Schoeni

Lockheed Aircraft Corporation, New York; Mr. Ray "Pappy" Houseman

Lockheed-California Company, Burbank, California; Mr. Erik Miller, Ms. Jan Boebel

Lufthansa—German Airlines, New York; Mrs. Gisela Ellison

North American Aviation, El Segundo, California; Mr. Charles F. Burlingame

Northrop Corporation, Beverly Hills, California

Pan American World Airways, New York; Ms. Althea Lister

Pratt & Whitney Aircraft Division of United Aircraft, East Hartford, Connecticut; Mr. John A. Cox

Rockwell International, Downey, California; Ms. Sue Cometo

Ryan Aeronautical Company, San Diego, California; Mrs. Frances L. Kohl

Sikorsky Aircraft, Stratford, Connecticut; Mr. Dan DeVito

Trans World Airlines, New York; Ms. Katherine Blanck

United Airlines, New York; Ms. Sally McElwreath

Special contributions were made by:

Jean and John Bartel, Bay City, Michigan

Alan Dashiell, Trenton, New Jersey (for rare airship photos).

Mr. Harry Gann, Jr. (American Aviation Historical Society), Huntington Beach, California

Mr. William Kavanagh, USM, Ret., for care and attention beyond the call of duty

Mr. Howard Van der Meulen, NBC News, New York

My special gratitude goes to copyeditor William Drennan, who, considering the state of the original manuscript, must have had himself one hell of a time.

And last though not least, Harold Kuebler, patient editor and even a more patient friend, without whom, etc., etc., etc.

Bibliography

GENERAL HISTORIES:

Angelucci, Enzo. *Aeroplanes*. New York: McGraw-Hill Book Co., 1973.

Becker, Beril. *Dreams and Realities of the Conquest of the Air*. New York: Atheneum, 1967.

Brewer, R. W. A. *The Art of Aviation*. London: Crosby Lockwood and Son, 1910.

Christy, Joe, and Shamburger, Page. *Summon the Stars*, Cranbury, N.J.: A. S. Barnes & Co., 1970.

Davies, R. E. G. *A History of the World's Airlines*. New York: Oxford University Press, 1964.

Emde, Heiner. *Conquerors of the Air*. New York: The Viking Press, 1968.

Gibbs-Smith, Charles H. *A History of Flying*. New York: Frederick A. Praeger, 1954.

———. *The Invention of the Aeroplane*. New York: Taplinger Publishing Co., Inc., 1965.

———. *Aviation: An Historical Survey*. London: Her Majesty's Stationery Office, 1970.

———. *Flight Through the Ages*. New York: Thomas Y. Crowell Co., 1974.

Guggenheim, Harry F. *The Seven Skies*. New York: G. P. Putnam's Sons, 1930.

Haining, Peter. *The Dream Machines*. New York: World Publishing Co., 1973.

Howard, Frank, and Gunston, Bill. *The Conquest of the Air*. New York: Random House, 1972.

Jobé, J., ed. *The Romance of Ballooning*, New York: The Viking Press, 1971.

Josephy, Alvin M., Jr., ed. *The American Heritage History of Flight*. New York: American Heritage Publishing Co., 1962.

Payne, L. G. S. *Air Dates*. London: Heinemann, 1957.

Rolt, L. T. C. *The Aeronauts*. New York: Walker & Co., 1966.

Shamburger, Page, and Christy, Joe. *Command the Horizon*. Cranbury, N.J.: A. S. Barnes & Co., 1968.

Stewart, Oliver. *Of Flight and Flyers*. London: Newnes, 1964.

———. *Aviation: The Creative Ideas*, London: Faber & Faber, 1966.

Taylor, John W., ed. *The Lore of Flight*. New York: Time-Life Books, 1970.

Taylor, John W., and Munson, Kenneth. *History of Aviation*. New York: Crown Publishers, Inc., 1972.

Ward, Baldwin H., et al. *Flight*. Los Angeles: Year, Inc., 1953.

SPECIALIZED HISTORIES, BIOGRAPHIES, AND MISCELLANEOUS:

Abbott, Patrick. *Airship (the R-34)*, New York: Charles Scribner's Sons, 1973.

Allen, Richard Sanders. *Revolution in the Sky*. Brattleboro, Vt: The Stephen Greene Press, 1964.

Brooks, Peter W. *The Modern Airliner*. London: G. P. Putnam's, Sons, 1961.

Cochran, Jacqueline. *The Stars at Noon*. Boston: Little, Brown & Co., 1954.

Collier, Basil. *The Airship*. New York: G. P. Putnam's Sons, 1974.

Delear, Frank J. *Igor Sikorsky*. New York: Dodd, Mead & Co., 1969.

Earhart, Amelia. *The Fun of It*. New York: Brewer, Warren and Putnam, 1932.

———. *Last Flight*. New York: Harcourt, Brace & Co., 1937.

Fokker, Anthony H. G., and Gould, Bruce. *Flying Dutchman*. New York: Henry Holt & Co., 1931.

Green, William, and Pollinger, Gerald. *The Aircraft of the World*. London: MacDonald & Co., 1965.

Harris, Sherwood. *The First to Fly*. New York: Simon & Schuster, 1970.

Irving, David. *The Rise and Fall of the Luftwaffe*. Boston: Little, Brown & Co., 1973.

Jablonski, Edward. *The Knighted Skies*. New York: G. P. Putnam's Sons, 1964.

———. *Ladybirds: Women in Aviation*. New York: Hawthorn Books, Inc., 1968.

———. *Seawings*. Garden City, N.Y.: Doubleday & Co., Inc., 1972.

———. *Atlantic Fever*. New York: The Macmillan Co., 1972.

———. *Airwar* (one-volume edition). Garden City, N.Y.: Doubleday & Co., Inc., 1979.

Kelly, Fred W. *The Wright Brothers*. New York: Harcourt, Brace & Co., 1943.

———. *Miracle at Kitty Hawk*, New York: Farrar, Straus & Young, 1951.

Ley, Willy. *Rockets, Missiles and Men in Space*. New York: The Viking Press, 1968.

Lieberg, Owen S. *The First Air Race*. Garden City, N.Y.: Doubleday & Co., Inc., 1974.

Lindbergh, Charles. *The Spirit of St. Louis*. New York: Charles Scribner's Sons, 1953.

———. *Autobiography of Values*. New York: Harcourt Brace Jovanovich, 1977.

Loening, Grover. *Our Wings Grow Faster*. Garden City, N.Y.: Doubleday, Doran & Co., 1935.

———. *Amphibian*. Greenwich, Conn.: New York Graphic Society, 1973.

Mansfield, Harold. *Vision, a Saga of the Sky*. New York: Duell, Sloan & Pearce, 1956.

Mason, Francis K. *Battle Over Britain*. Garden City, N.Y.: Doubleday & Co., Inc., 1969.

Maxim, Hiram. *Artificial and Natural Flight*. London: Whittaker and Co., 1908.

Montague, Richard. *Oceans, Poles and Airmen*. New York: Random House, 1971.

Morris, Lloyd, and Smith, Kendall. *Ceiling Unlimited*. New York: The Macmillan Co., 1953.

Norman, Aaron. *The Great Air War*. New York: The Macmillan Co., 1968.

Oakes, Claudia M. *United States Women in Aviation through World War I* (a monograph). Washington, D.C.: Smithsonian Institution Press, 1978.

Robinson, Douglas. *The Zeppelin in Combat*. London: G. T. Foulis & Co., Ltd., 1962.

Rolfe, Douglas, and Dawydoff, Alexis. *Airplanes of the World*. New York: Simon & Schuster, 1969.

Roseberry, C. R. *The Challenging Skies*. Garden City, N.Y.: Doubleday & Co., Inc., 1966.

———. *Glenn Curtiss: Pioneer of Flight*. Garden City, N.Y.: Doubleday & Co., Inc., 1972.

Rubenstein, Murray, and Goldman, Richard M. *To Join with the Eagles*. Garden City, N.Y.: Doubleday & Co., Inc., 1974.

Sikorsky, Igor I. *The Story of the Winged-S*. New York: Dodd, Mead & Co., 1938.

Simonson, G. R., ed. *The History of the American Aviation Industry*. Cambridge, Mass.: The M.I.T. Press, 1968.

Taylor, John W. *Combat Aircraft of the World*. New York: G. P. Putnam's Sons, 1969.

Thomas, Lowell, and Jablonski, Edward. *Doolittle, a Biography*, Garden City, N.Y.: Doubleday & Co., Inc., 1976.

Villard, Henry Serrano. *Contact! The Story of the Early Birds*. New York: Thomas Y. Crowell Co., Inc., 1968.

Vorderman, Don. *The Great Air Races*. Garden City, N.Y.: Doubleday & Co., Inc., 1969.

Wagner, Ray. *American Combat Planes*. Garden City, N.Y.: Doubleday & Co., Inc., 1968.

Wagner, William. *Ryan, the Aviator*. New York: McGraw-Hill Book Co., 1971.

Wilfred, John Noble. *We Reach the Moon*. New York: Bantam Books, 1969.

Wykeham, Peter. *Santos-Dumont: A Study in Obsession*. New York: Harcourt, Brace & World, 1962.

Also: Various publications and bulletins issued by the National Aeronautics and Space Administration, newspapers too numerous to mention.

Index

DATE DUE

SEP 21 83		
NOV 19 83		
FEB 28 84		
MAY 26		
30 505 JOSTEN'S